Routledge Library Editions

THE ECONOMICS
OF PHYSIOCRACY

ECONOMICS

Routledge Library Editions – Economics

HISTORY OF ECONOMIC THOUGHT
In 23 Volumes

THE ECONOMICS
OF PHYSIOCRACY

Essays and Translations

RONALD L MEEK

Routledge
Taylor & Francis Group

LONDON AND NEW YORK

First published in 1962
by Routledge

2 Park Square, Milton Park, Abingdon, Oxon OX14 4RN
605 Third Avenue, New York, NY 10017

Routledge is an imprint of the Taylor & Francis Group, an informa business

The publishers have made every effort to contact authors/copyright holders
of the works reprinted in *Routledge Library Editions – Economics*. This has
not been possible in every case, however, and we would welcome
correspondence from those individuals/companies we have been unable to
trace.

These reprints are taken from original copies of each book. In many cases
the condition of these originals is not perfect. The publisher has gone to
great lengths to ensure the quality of these reprints, but wishes to point
out that certain characteristics of the original copies will, of necessity, be
apparent in reprints thereof.

British Library Cataloguing in Publication Data
A CIP catalogue record for this book
is available from the British Library

The Economics of Physiocracy

ISBN13: 978-0-415-31332-2 (hbk)
ISBN13: 978-0-415-48884-6 (pbk)

Miniset: History of Economic Thought

Series: Routledge Library Editions – Economics

THE ECONOMICS

OF

PHYSIOCRACY

Essays and Translations

BY

RONALD L. MEEK

Senior Lecturer in Political Economy
at the University of Glasgow

Ruskin House

GEORGE ALLEN & UNWIN LTD

MUSEUM STREET LONDON

PRINTED IN GREAT BRITAIN
in 10 point Times Roman type
BY BILLING AND SONS LTD
GUILDFORD AND LONDON

To the Memory of
Georges Weulersse

PREFACE

The French Physiocrats are at once the most exciting and the most contemporary group of economists in the whole history of economic thought. The most exciting, because the birth of Physiocracy was in fact the birth of the science of economics in the broad general form in which it has come down to us today. The most contemporary, because the Physiocrats' major pre-occupations, in both the theoretical and the practical fields, were strikingly similar to those of present-day economists.

It is rather surprising, therefore, that the Physiocrats, whose honoured place in the history of economic thought is dutifully recognized in every text-book on that subject, should have received so little detailed attention from economists in the English-speaking world. There are only two books in English on the general subject of Physiocracy, and of these the only really useful one is now over sixty years old. And since the time of Adam Smith no more than a few pages from the vast economic writings of the Physiocrats have been translated into English.

The present volume is intended to fill part of this remarkable gap. It does not set out to be a full treatise on the history and doctrines of Physiocracy: the reader looking for such a treatise will find it, if he can read French, in the magistral works of the late Georges Weulersse. The volume begins with a relatively short and deliberately non-specialist introduction, which has been designed more with the aim of rousing the reader's interest than with that of displaying the results of any very profound research. Then follows a rather more solid section devoted to translations of Physiocratic writings: here the aim has been to present the main elements of the basic economic doctrines of the Physiocrats in their own words, and, where necessary, to assist in the understanding of these doctrines by means of notes.

The final section consists of five fairly lengthy and specialized essays, dealing with certain aspects of the Physiocratic doctrine, its history, and its influence. The first four of these essays are amended versions of articles published in academic journals during the period of preparation of this volume; the fifth is substantially new. Each of the essays is more or less complete in itself, and can be read in isolation from the others. They are linked with one another, however, not only by the cross-references which I have provided in order to avoid undue repetition, but also by a common method of approach to the problems dealt with.

My interest in the Physiocrats extends back to the years 1946-8, when I was reading for a post-graduate degree at Cambridge, and in a sense this volume has been in preparation ever since that time. The number of obligations which I have incurred to my colleagues and students is therefore very great indeed, and I cannot hope to list them all here. I must, however, mention my special debt to Dr André Classe, Professor H. D. Dickinson, Mr M. H. Dobb, Mme Jacqueline Hecht, Professor A. L. Macfie, and Dr Gerald Royce, who have been generous with their assistance and advice.

I am also grateful to the officials of the *Archives Nationales* and the *Bibliothèque Nationale* at Paris for their help, and in particular for their readiness to permit me to photograph and reproduce a number of documents; to the editors of the *Economic Journal* and *Economica* for allowing me to reproduce articles published in these periodicals; to the editors of *Economica* for the loan of blocks; and to the Carnegie Trust for the Universities of Scotland, and the University of Glasgow, for the generous financial assistance they have given me.

R. L. M.

University of Glasgow,
February 24, 1962.

CONTENTS

12 CONTENTS

ILLUSTRATIONS

(between pp. 112 *and* 113 *of the text)*

INTRODUCTION TO PHYSIOCRACY

1. THE INTERVIEW

Towards the end of July 1757, in an *entresol* at the Palace of Versailles, there took place a celebrated interview, which the Physiocrats were later to regard as marking the birth of their school. A master, looking for disciples, had discovered a possible convert: at this interview the potential disciple was won over, and from that date to his death played the role of Engels to his master's Marx.

At first sight, one could hardly imagine two less likely founders of a new school of political economy than the men who faced one another at this interview. François Quesnay, then doctor to Madame de Pompadour and first doctor-in-ordinary to the king, had at this time (he was then 63 years of age) published nothing directly pertaining to economics except one largely-unnoticed article on *Farmers* in the Encyclopedia: most of his writing had been in the field of medicine, and he was known chiefly for his efforts in championing the physicians in their struggle for status as against the doctors. The Marquis de Mirabeau, then 42 years of age, had achieved some recognition through a book on *The Utility of the Provincial Estates* (1750), and very considerable popular renown through his *Friend of Mankind*, which appeared shortly before the famous interview; but he himself was quite prepared to admit later that when he wrote the *Friend of Mankind* he was 'no more an economist than his cat'.[1]

Quesnay, however, having grown up in a rural environment,[2] had always retained a lively interest in agricultural problems, in spite of his medical preoccupations. Madame de Pompadour's chambermaid, Madame du Hausset, to whom we owe a number of illuminating anecdotes about Quesnay (including one or two charmingly improper ones), tells us that 'he loved to chat with me about the countryside; I had been brought up there, and he used to get me to talk about the

---

[1] '*Je n'étais pas plus économiste que mon chat, quand la force du tempérament, comme disait le vénérable Quesnay, me fit écrire "L'Ami des Hommes".*' From a letter to Longo, dated June 11, 1778, cited by Louis de Lomenie, *Les Mirabeau*, Vol. II, p. 135. Mirabeau was no doubt here using the word '*économiste*' in its contemporary sense as a synonym of 'Physiocrat' rather than in the broad generic sense in which we use the word 'economist' today.

[2] The most up-to-date biography of Quesnay is that by Jacqueline Hecht in Vol. I of *François Quesnay et la Physiocratie*, published by the *Institut National d'Etudes Démographiques*, Paris, 1958. This very useful work will hereafter be cited as 'I.N.E.D.'

meadows of Normandy and Poitou, the wealth of the farmers, and
the method of cultivation. . . . He was much more concerned at
Court with the best method of cultivating the land than with anything
which went on there.'[1] And Quesnay's medical writings had often
had important philosophical overtones, which began to assume
greater significance in his thought when the leisure afforded by his
post at Court enabled him to start serious contemplation of the
burning economic problems of the *ancien regime*. It is evident from
a reading of his Encyclopedia article on *Farmers*, and still more
evident from the articles on *Corn*, *Men*, and *Taxation* which were
written round about this time, that by the year of the interview his
new theoretical system, although not yet fully formed, was beginning
to take fairly definite shape in his mind. Mirabeau, too, was in the
year of the interview a rather better economist than a cursory reading
of the more flamboyant passages of the *Friend of Mankind* would
suggest. This book had originally been planned as an extended commentary on Cantillon's *Essay on the Nature of Commerce in General*,
the manuscript of which had come into Mirabeau's hands many
years before by what he tantalizingly describes as 'a kind of theft'.
When Cantillon's *Essay* was unexpectedly published in 1755,
Mirabeau had to change his plan; and the *Friend of Mankind*, when
it finally appeared, was an essentially original work.[2] Despite the
'populationist' thesis of the book, which Mirabeau had borrowed
from Cantillon, Quesnay recognized in its author a kindred spirit,
whose conclusions regarding the pre-eminence of agriculture con-
formed roughly with his own. Was Mirabeau, then, to be the chosen
vessel? Certainly it must at any rate have occurred to Quesnay that
it would be extremely useful if Mirabeau, who had achieved such
fame through his book that people paid as much as 12 sous for a seat
to watch him going to Mass,[3] could be converted to the new doctrine.

Here, then, are the two founders of Physiocracy, meeting together
in Quesnay's room at Versailles to discuss the *Friend of Mankind*. Let
us leave the description of the interview to Mirabeau himself, as he
gave it in an intriguing letter to Rousseau ten years afterwards. He is
explaining to Rousseau how he drew his first ideas on the subject of
population from Cantillon:

'I had, like him and so many others, concluded, according to the
superficial appearance of things, that, since when I put my hand in

[1] Auguste Oncken, *Oeuvres Economiques et Philosophiques de F. Quesnay*
(hereafter 'Oncken'), 1888, p. 125.

[2] The evidence relating to the connection between Cantillon's *Essay* and
Mirabeau's *Friend of Mankind* is surveyed in a note by Louis Salleron in the
edition of the *Essay* published in 1952 by the *Institut National d'Etudes Démographiques*.

[3] Georges Weulersse, *Le Mouvement Physiocratique en France* (hereafter
'Weulersse'), 1910, Vol. I, p. 53.

front of my eyes it hides the sun from me, my hand is bigger than the sun. I had, I say, reasoned in this way: Wealth is the fruit which comes from the land for the use of men; the labour of man alone possesses the capacity to increase wealth. Thus the more men there are, the more labour will there be; the more labour there is, the more wealth there will be. The way to achieve prosperity is therefore: (1) To increase men; (2) through these men, to increase productive labour; (3) through this labour, to increase wealth. In this position I felt myself invulnerable, and I gaudily decorated my political edifice with marriages, sumptuary laws, and the rest, just as I wanted to. Never did Goliath go into battle with as much confidence as I did when I sought out a man who, I had been informed, had written on the margin of my book these insolent words: *The child has been suckled on bad milk; the force of his temperament often puts him right so far as results are concerned, but he understands nothing as to principles.* My critic did not beat about the bush with me, and told me quite plainly that I had put the cart before the horse, and that Cantillon, as a teacher of the public, was nothing but a fool. This blasphemy made me regard as a fool the one who uttered it, but, reflecting that in every dispute the exchange of opinions usually proceeds by way of retaliation, I restrained myself, broke off the conversation, and, fortunately for me, returned in the evening to ask questions after thinking things over. It was then that Goliath's head was cloven asunder. My man asked me to do the same honour to men as is done to sheep, since anyone who wants to increase his flock begins by increasing his grazing-land. I replied to him that sheep were a secondary cause in abundance, whereas man was the primary cause in the creation of fruits. He started to laugh, and asked me to explain myself better and to tell him if man, when he arrived on the earth, had brought bread in his pocket to enable him to live until the time when the land, having been prepared, sown, covered with ripe crops, reaped, threshed, etc., could feed him. I was caught: one had either to imagine that man had licked his paws for 18 months, as the bear does during the winter in his lair, or to maintain that this creator of fruits had found some when he arrived which he had never sown. He then asked me to have the kindness to allow all the subsequent population to share the same benefit, because otherwise they too could not exist. In the case of a fool, the exposure of presumptuousness causes confusion and hatred; in the case of an honest soul, it brings about understanding and humility. This was my case. I begged my master to explain himself and to teach me, for I was a poor young fellow of 42, and he had not yet constructed his *Tableau Economique.* This was also fortunate for me, for, perceiving its utility and necessity as *Genesis* tells us that God saw the beauty of his work, he would have referred me to it, which would have discouraged me, since my nature finds the mechanical application which calculations require very distasteful. It was therefore necessary that he should give me an explanation of his system, or rather of that of nature; how the first men, whether shepherds or huntsmen, etc., had lived on the spontaneous products of nature; how the population of nations which have never engaged in cultivation always remains the same without any increase, and how they lead a nomadic existence in order to plunder the successive products; how the business of cultivation has caused nations to become settled; how the increase in products can proceed only from their quality as wealth; their quality as wealth only from their exchange value; and their exchange value only from the consumption of these products; how it is therefore the consumption of current products which is the source of greater products in the future, the necessary basis of an addition to the population.'[1]

Mirabeau evidently liked the idea of being converted, and no doubt in later years exaggerated the extent to which this interview changed his fundamental views. Certainly nothing is more amusing than to see the way in which Quesnay, in his marginal notes on the voluminous manuscripts which Mirabeau now began to submit to him, endeavoured with great tact to wean the Marquis away from certain political and religious ideas which Quesnay obviously regarded as reactionary. Nevertheless it is true that after the interview Mirabeau was never quite the same again: the disciple very soon rose to the status of joint master, and the increasing popularity of Physiocracy in the years that followed owed a great deal to the flood of works which flowed from his pen.

2. THE DOCTRINE

'We must not lose heart', wrote Quesnay in a letter to Mirabeau enclosing the first version of the *Tableau Economique*, 'for the appalling crisis will come, and it will be necessary to have recourse to medical knowledge.'[2] To cure a patient suffering from an illness requires a knowledge of the principles of physiology; similarly, to cure a society suffering from grave maladies requires a knowledge of the physiology of the social order. Since for Quesnay the basis of the social order lay in the economic order, an understanding of the laws and regularities governing economic life appeared to be of primary necessity if the sickness of society was to be cured.

---

[1] *Correspondance Générale de J.-J. Rousseau*, ed. T. Dufour, Vol. XVII (1932), pp. 176–8.
[2] Below, p. 108.

It is difficult to give a short summary of the basic doctrine of Physiocracy without distorting it, and without involving oneself in certain difficult problems of interpretation which I have reserved for discussion in the last part of the present volume. Let me, then, state here more or less dogmatically what I believe to have been the essence of the doctrine, setting aside for the time being all refinements and elaborations, and leaving it to the reader, if he wishes, to study the defence of my interpretation which he will find at the end of the book.

The Physiocrats assumed that the system of market exchange which it was their main purpose to analyse was subject to certain objective economic laws, which operated independently of the will of man and which were discoverable by the light of reason. These laws governed the shape and movement of the economic order, and therefore (on the Physiocrats' basically materialist hypothesis) the shape and movement of the social order as a whole. Now the relationships between the different variables in a system of market exchange are very intricate—so much so, indeed, that in a certain sense everything can be said to be dependent upon everything else. If the laws governing the particular type of exchange economy with which the Physiocrats concerned themselves were to be ascertained, therefore, it was necessary to put these variables into manageable form—in other words, to construct what we would call today an abstract theoretical model of the economy.

In the construction of this theoretical model, the Physiocrats' main aim was to illuminate the operation of the basic causes which determined the general level of economic activity. For this purpose, they believed that it was useful to conceive economic activity as taking the form of a sort of 'circle', or circular flow as we would call it today. In this circle of economic activity, production and consumption appeared as mutually interdependent variables, whose action and interaction in any economic period, proceeding according to certain socially-determined laws, laid the basis for a repetition of the process in the same general form in the next economic period.[1] Within this circle, the Physiocrats then endeavoured to discover some key variable, movements in which could be regarded as the basic factor causing an expansion or contraction in the 'dimensions' of the circle, i.e. in the general level of economic activity. The variable which they hit upon was the capacity of agriculture to yield a 'net product', i.e. a disposable surplus over necessary cost. Anything which increased this net product would cause an expansion in economic activity, and anything which reduced it would cause a contraction in economic activity. 'The discovery of the *net product*', wrote Mirabeau, 'which we owe to the venerable Confucius of

---

[1] Cf. Schumpeter, *Economic Doctrine and Method*, p. 43.

Europe, will one day change the face of the world. . . . The whole moral and physical advantage of societies is . . . summed up in one point, *an increase in the net product*; all damage done to society is determined by this fact, *a reduction in the net product*. It is on the two scales of this balance that you can place and weigh laws, manners, customs, vices, and virtues.'[1]

The leading assumption of the Physiocrats' theoretical system was that this net product was yielded by agriculture, and by agriculture alone. Agriculture was the supreme occupation, not only because it was morally and politically superior to others, not only because its produce was primary in the scale of wants and always in demand, but also—and mainly—because it alone yielded a disposable surplus over necessary cost. It was upon this latter aspect of agriculture that the Physiocrats concentrated in their theoretical system, and in particular in their definition of the word 'productive'. 'Productive' to them meant, essentially, productive of a net product. Manufacture and commerce, they contended, were by contrast 'unproductive' or 'sterile'. Not only were these occupations more precarious than agriculture, not only were they 'secondary' in the sense that they were dependent upon the supply of food and raw materials, but they were also incapable, at any rate in the absence of monopoly, of yielding a disposable surplus over necessary cost. 'Sterile' to the Physiocrats meant, essentially, incapable of yielding a net product.

The classification of basic social groups in the Physiocratic model was made with primary reference to the relation in which each group stood to the net product. The main distinction which they emphasized was that between the 'productive class' (i.e. those engaged in agricultural production) and the 'sterile class' (i.e. those engaged in non-agricultural activities). In the no-man's-land between these two classes, partaking to some extent of the character of each but belonging definitely to neither, lay the 'class of proprietors'. This class consisted of the landowners, the king, and the clergy, who were assumed to receive, in the form of rent, taxes, and tithes respectively, the value of the net product which agriculture annually yielded.

The circle of economic activity proceeds by means of the transactions which the three basic social classes enter into with one another in the course of a year. Let us for the sake of simplicity follow Quesnay's precedent in the early versions of the *Tableau* and leave the king and the clergy out of the picture, so that the net product can be assumed to take the form of land rent alone. The circle then begins with the expenditure by the landowners of their rent, which the productive class has paid to them out of the proceeds of last year's harvest. The rent is spent by the landowners partly on

---

[1] *Correspondance Générale de J.-J.Rousseau*, Vol. XVII, pp. 171–2.

the products of the productive class, and partly on those of the sterile class. In addition, there is an exchange of agricultural produce and manufactured goods, through the medium of money, between the productive class and the sterile class. Production determines consumption, and consumption in its turn determines production in the following year. If the aggregate receipts which accrue to the productive and sterile classes as a result of all these transactions are just sufficient to cover the paid-out costs of production, and to enable the productive class to pay its rent, the level of economic activity in the following year will remain the same as it is in the present year. If the aggregate receipts are more than sufficient to do this, the dimensions of the circle will be increased in the following year; and if they are insufficient to do it, the dimensions of the circle will be reduced.

Now the general level of economic activity, according to the Physiocrats, is largely determined by the level of agricultural output, and the latter is determined in its turn by the magnitude of the net product. If the net product is increasing from year to year, the level of agricultural output, and therefore the general level of economic activity, will rise. An increasing net product means, in the first place, that the landowners will spend more on agricultural produce; they will also spend more on manufactured goods, and the makers of these goods, whose incomes are thus increased, will in their turn spend more on agricultural produce; thus the aggregate demand for agricultural produce will increase, output will be stimulated, the net product will increase further, and the general level of economic activity will rise progressively from year to year. An increasing net product means, in the second place, that more will be available for investment. The landowners will have more to spare for investment in improving their land; the agricultural entrepreneurs, in so far as they happen at the time to be sharing in the net product,[1] will have more to spare for maintaining and expanding their fixed and working capital; thus aggregate investment in agriculture will increase, and once again output will be stimulated, the net product will increase further, and the general level of economic activity will rise progressively from year to year. The eventual result of this process will be the attainment of the maximum level of output consistent with the state of the country's resources and the existing techniques. If the net product is decreasing from year to year, on the other hand, a cumula-

---

[1] This begs a whole host of complex problems, which are dealt with fairly fully in the essays in the last part of the book. In the meantime, it is sufficient to note that the Physiocrats recognized that agricultural entrepreneurs might under certain rather special circumstances receive a share of the net product in the form of profit. They usually insisted, however, that this profit would sooner or later crystallize out into rents for the landowners.

tive downward trend in the level of economic activity will take place, leading either to complete ruin or to the achievement of a sort of sub-optimum equilibrium at a very low level.

The strategic variable, then, is the magnitude of the net product, and it is to the problem of increasing the net product that the government's policy should be primarily directed. Since the magnitude of the net product depends largely upon the aggregate *output* of corn and upon the *price* of corn, it follows that the government must take all possible measures to increase the first while at the same time increasing or at least maintaining the second. The encouragement of investment in agriculture and the stimulation of demand for agricultural produce must therefore be the main aims of government policy. Most of the specific policy measures advocated by the Physiocrats will be found upon investigation to fit into this simple pattern.

The Physiocrats' attempt to deal with the problem of long-term trends in income and economic activity in terms of variations in consumption and investment has a surprisingly 'modern' ring about it. What makes their system appear strange to contemporary economists is, first, the fact that they often clothed their propositions in the now unfamiliar language of 'natural law' doctrines, and, second, the fact that they insisted so strongly, and apparently so perversely, on the crucial economic significance of the distinction between agriculture and manufacture. How far is it in fact proper, when describing the work of the Physiocrats, to dismiss the 'ideal' and 'divine' elements in their system as of secondary importance, as as I have done in this brief summary, and to fit them out in modern dress? Was the doctrine of the exclusive productivity of agriculture a mere mental aberration, as it is often represented to have been, or was it in some sense the 'right' doctrine *for the times*? Let us withdraw temporarily from this sphere of doubt and danger, and proceed to an examination of the specific policy proposals of the Physiocrats.

3. THE ENVIRONMENT AND THE POLICY

In introducing the basic doctrine of the Physiocrats in the previous section, I have, as it were, abstracted it from the environment in which it was put forward; and I have also spoken as if the policy measures advocated by the Physiocrats were merely a sort of logical derivative from their doctrine. But the Physiocratic doctrine did not spring fully armed from the head of Jove: it was in fact related, in a very complex and subtle way, to the environment in which the Physiocrats lived and worked. And the policy measures which they advocated can in fact be said to have been 'derived' from the doctrine only in a very broad and general sense. Given the doctrine, it followed that the government should take positive action to encourage investment in agriculture and to stimulate the demand for agricultural produce. But what, precisely, should it do in order to secure these ends? What were the specific obstacles likely to stand in its way, and how should they be removed? The answers which the Physiocrats gave to these all-important questions dictated the actual content, as distinct from the general pattern and emphasis, of their policy proposals; and it is clear that the answers were largely determined by certain specific features of the contemporary French economy. Let us concentrate here on this relationship between policy and environment, taking the basic doctrine as given, and leave aside for treatment in the last part of the book the more controversial problem of the relationship between doctrine and environment.

Since France was overwhelmingly an agricultural country in Physiocratic times, it seems proper to begin by considering the general pattern of land-ownership and the forms of organization of agricultural production under the *ancien régime*. The main feature which distinguished French agriculture from that of England at this time was the relative lack of enclosures and the consequent survival of very large numbers of small peasant proprietors, who, although they were normally subject to fairly heavy seigneurial dues, had the right to transfer their property or pass it on to their heirs. A small minority of these peasants, mainly those who possessed relatively large pieces of land, were able to live reasonably comfortably from the cultivation of their property. The great majority, however, possessing very small pieces of land and cultivating them with the aid of primitive methods, lived a wretched existence, and were often obliged to make ends meet by hiring themselves out as daily labourers, engaging in one form or another of rural industry, and so on.

The privileged classes, i.e. the nobility and the clergy, besides possessing rights over peasant property which entitled them to receive their seigneurial dues and tithes, also owned directly a considerable proportion of the land. The proportion so owned varied greatly from district to district, but seems to have been rarely less than 20 per cent and quite often more than 40 per cent.[1] On the average, the proportion owned by the nobility was much greater than that owned by the clergy, whose main income was drawn from its tithes and its urban properties. The privileged classes did not very often, it seems, act as 'improving landlords'; absenteeism was rife, and in the majority of cases the land was cultivated by share-croppers (*métayers*), to whom the proprietor normally advanced seed and

---

[1] Cf. Henri Sée, *La France Economique et Sociale au XVIIIᵉ Siècle* (Armand Colin edn. of 1939), pp. 10–11.

live-stock and from whom he usually received one-half of the harvest.[1] The majority of the *métayers*, who had little incentive to spur them on and little or no capital, generally used methods of cultivation which were scarcely better than those of the poor peasant proprietors. Some land belonging to the privileged classes, however, particularly in certain northern provinces, was let out on lease to *fermiers*, i.e. farmers who to a greater or lesser extent exercised entrepreneurial functions. These *fermiers* often possessed considerable capital, and their methods of cultivation were frequently superior to those of the *métayers* and poor peasants. Finally, a moderately significant (and growing) proportion of the land, particularly in the neighbourhood of the big cities, was owned by the bourgeoisie, but generally speaking the methods of cultivation employed in the case of this land were much the same as in the case of the land owned by the privileged classes.[2]

The general picture we get, then, is one of a poverty-stricken agriculture, in which the great proprietors care little about the proper management of their estates, and in which the small peasant proprietors are discouraged by the burden of seigneurial dues and the *métayers* lack capital and initiative. There are few large-scale agricultural enterprises, except in the northern provinces, and methods of cultivation over by far the greater part of the country are scarcely superior to those employed in the Middle Ages. The rehabilitation and further development of agriculture, the Physiocrats believed, was the main precondition of general economic advance. How, then, was this to be achieved? One of the chief hindrances to further development, the Physiocrats recognized, was the prevalence of small-scale, capital-starved, subsistence farming. What was required in the countryside above all, they argued, was not *men*, but *wealth*, i.e. capital. Various factors, some of which will be considered shortly, were obstructing the flow of capital into agriculture; and the main policy measures advocated by the Physiocrats were aimed at the removal of these obstructions. Here they pinned their hopes quite largely on the new class of *fermiers*, the men of substance whose entrepreneurial activities were already beginning to make certain of the northern provinces relatively prosperous. Agricultural entrepreneurs were the main agents of agricultural reform, and government policy should be aimed in particular at stimulating and encouraging them.

Here the second salient feature of the *ancien régime* comes into the picture—the tremendous burden of taxation, which fell in an arbitrary and unpredictable manner on those who could least afford

[1] One of the best contemporary descriptions and criticisms of the system of *métayage* is that given by Arthur Young in his *Travels in France*.
[2] See below, pp. 393–4.

it. Not only was agriculture subject to the substantial and vexatious seigneurial dues and tithes, but it was also burdened, to an ever-increasing extent, by the multitude of taxes imposed by the fiscal policy of the Crown.[1] A series of disastrous wars, coupled with the extravagance of the Court, kept the Treasury on the verge of bankruptcy, and it was forced to adopt more and more new expedients for obtaining finance—expedients which, as the Physiocrats correctly observed, more often than not had the ultimate effect of increasing the deficit instead of reducing it. The direct taxes, notably the *taille*, from which the privileged classes were exempt, were usually very inequitable in their incidence, and were collected, like most of the taxes, with extreme harshness. The indirect taxes, such as the *gabelle* (salt-tax), the *aides* (taxes on beverages), and the *traites* (customs duties), were equally arbitrary and inequitable. Most of the taxes were farmed out to companies, which greatly increased both the vexatious character of the taxes and the costs of collection. During the eighteenth century, as the financial embarrassment of the Exchequer increased, resort was increasingly had to large loans from the tax-farmers and bankers; certain new taxes (notably the *vingtième*) were imposed which in theory should have been levied on all revenue but from which in practice many members of the privileged classes were more or less exempted; and the *corvée* (forced labour on roads, etc.) was extended to the whole country.

The problem here, as the Physiocrats saw it, was to enable the needs of the Exchequer to be adequately met while at the same time doing away with the obstacles to agricultural development imposed by the existing irrational system of assessment. They were especially concerned, of course, with the disincentive effects of taxation on cultivators in general and on agricultural entrepreneurs in particular —effects which in their opinion were magnified by (*inter alia*) the hoarding of the immense monetary fortunes gained through transactions in government securities. Their bold policy of an *impôt unique*, or single tax on land rent, was designed not only to solve the state's financial problems, but also, and primarily, to assist in the rehabilitation of agriculture.[2] Any immediate financial disadvantage to the proprietors, they claimed, would ultimately be much more than balanced by consequential increases in agricultural investment and productivity and therefore in the magnitude of future net products.

The general situation of French agriculture at this time was further worsened by a third feature of the economy, closely related to the two which have already been discussed—the continued survival of a whole host of policies and institutions of a Mercantilist character.

---

[1] For details, see Henri Sée, *Histoire Economique de la France: Le Moyen Age et l'Ancien Régime*, 1939, Part IV, chapters 1 and 4.
[2] Cf. Rogin, *The Meaning and Validity of Economic Theory*, pp. 37–8.

Notable among these were the important restrictions on internal and external trade in agricultural produce, which according to the Physiocrats exercised an unfavourable influence on agricultural investment and the magnitude of the net product by making the price of corn unnecessarily low and variable. Notable also were the 'exclusive privileges' of various kinds afforded to certain manufacturing establishments, particularly in the luxury industries. These monopolistic privileges, in the opinion of the Physiocrats, resulted in the artificial diversion of investment from agriculture to manufacture; the subsidies granted to the manufacturers concerned were in effect direct payments out of the net product; and the perversion of tastes which they permitted and encouraged lowered the internal demand for agricultural produce and therefore its price. And there were also certain related features of the economy, connected in particular with the fact that 'French mercantilism was to a large extent a financial mercantilism',[1] which according to the Physiocrats exercised an equally unfavourable influence on agriculture. Especially important here was the fact that the fortunes accumulated by the moneyed interest from their commercial activities, their operations in the sphere of tax-farming, and their speculative transactions in the public debt, were very often hoarded, and therefore (in the Physiocrats' terminology) 'abstracted from circulation', thus reducing even further the demand for agricultural produce.

These features of the French economy, then, as I have said above, dictated the specific content, as distinct from the general pattern and emphasis, of the Physiocrats' policy proposals. The main aim was to increase the magnitude of the net product by stimulating both the output of corn and the price of corn. On the output side, the chief means adopted must be the encouragement through all possible means of investment in agriculture, partly by the proprietors themselves, but more particularly by the agricultural entrepreneurs, whose activities would eventually result in the substitution of large-scale farming by up-to-date methods for small-scale farming by primitive methods. Thus all hindrances to the profitable exploitation of the land by agricultural entrepreneurs, notably those existing in the sphere of taxation, must be swept away; all policies and institutions which resulted in the unnatural diversion of capital from agriculture to commerce, industry, and speculation must cease to be favoured; and, in general, all restrictions on the freedom and immunity of the cultivator must be lifted. On the price side, the main means must be the removal of all physical and legal restraints on internal and external trade in corn; and the stimulation of the internal demand for corn by such measures as the abolition of the 'exclusive privileges' of manufacture, the condemnation of excessive

[1] Rogin, op. cit., p. 28.

expenditure on luxury goods, the cessation of all encouragement to the formation of monetary fortunes, and the raising of the general standard of living of the common people. A number of these policy proposals, we may note in conclusion, were subsumed by the Physiocrats under the heading of a general demand for *laissez faire*; but it should be emphasized both that this demand was severely qualified (particularly so far as the moneyed interest was concerned), and that it was made not so much because it was believed to be good or right in itself as because it was believed to be an essential precondition of the rehabilitation of French agriculture.

4. THE BEGINNINGS OF THE SCHOOL

With the Physiocrats, for the first time in the history of economic thought, we come face to face with that curious sociological phenomenon which we call a 'school' if we sympathize with it and a 'sect' if we do not. In many ways, the Physiocratic school was oddly similar to the Marxist school. Quesnay, like Marx, attempted to analyse the inner physiology of the society in which he lived, and to weld his economics, his philosophy, and his sociology into one all-embracing theoretical system; and the resultant doctrine, with its basically 'materialist' outlook, its concentration on the problem of the social surplus, and its 'reproduction schemes', bore certain important resemblances to the Marxist doctrine. Just as Marx had his Engels, so Quesnay, after the famous interview, had his Mirabeau to work alongside him and to take over the leadership of the school after his death. And owing their allegiance to Quesnay and Mirabeau were a number of eminent and faithful disciples, notably Mercier de la Rivière, Le Trosne, Baudeau, and Du Pont de Nemours. These disciples, as Schumpeter has said, accepted their masters' teachings with a fidelity of which there are only two analogues in the whole history of economics—'the fidelity of the orthodox Marxists to the message of Marx and the fidelity of the orthodox Keynesians to the message of Keynes'.[1] The Physiocrats eventually acquired a journal of their own, the *Ephémérides*; and they could boast that they numbered among their fellow-travellers thinkers of the calibre of the great Turgot.

A school requires a doctrine; and the doctrine requires systematization. Soon after the date of the interview with Mirabeau, Quesnay appears to have hit upon the idea that the 'circle' of economic activity with which his doctrine was mainly concerned could be represented schematically in a diagram; and the result was the first

[1] Schumpeter, *History of Economic Analysis*, p. 223.

version of the *Tableau Economique*, which was probably printed at Versailles towards the end of 1758. Many romantic legends later grew up around the episode of the printing of the 'first edition' of the *Tableau*, and in particular about the role which Louis XV allegedly played in it. The truth, so far as we can make an educated guess at it from the available evidence, is interesting enough, if not exactly romantic. Quesnay, on the pretext of amusing the king, had a luxurious printing press installed at the Palace. He presented his draft *Tableau* to the king as a manuscript whose printing would involve certain compositorial difficulties, and which would enable the king to show his typographical virtuosity.[1] There is little reliable evidence to suggest that the king took any interest other than a typographical one in the content of the manuscript. The subsequent history of the Physiocratic doctrine, in a sense, was the history of the gradual popularization, clarification, and elaboration of the *Tableau*. Quesnay seems to have brought out three successive 'editions' of the *Tableau* in 1758–59; Mirabeau published a lengthy 'Explanation' of the *Tableau* in the Sixth Part of his *Friend of Mankind* in 1760; in the *Rural Philosophy* (1763), an important joint product of the efforts of Mirabeau and Quesnay, the form of the *Tableau* was altered and still more varied uses found for it; and Quesnay, towards the end of his career as an economist, elaborated the *Tableau* further and employed it as a tool for the analysis of certain specific economic problems in three important articles.[2]

The presentation of the new doctrine to the public was continued in 1760 with the publication of Mirabeau's *Theory of Taxation*, written with astonishing rapidity under the direct inspiration of Quesnay. The boldness of Mirabeau's language startled the public and helped to make the book a great popular success; but it also drew down the wrath of the authorities upon Mirabeau's head, and he was put under arrest. The inestimable Madame du Hausset has left us the following remarkable account of a scene which took place at the Palace shortly after the news of Mirabeau's arrest reached Quesnay: it tells us a great deal, not only about this particular incident and Quesnay's reaction to it, but also about the general political atmosphere in which the new school was obliged to work. The account reads as follows:

'One day I found Quesnay in despair. "Mirabeau," he said to me, "has been put in Vincennes for his work on taxation. It is the farmers-

---

[1] See Weulersse, I, pp. 65–6, and I.N.E.D., I, p, 260.

[2] The three 'editions' of the *Tableau*, an extract from the *Rural Philosophy*, and Quesnay's three articles on the *Tableau* are all translated below; and the *Tableau* itself, in its various forms, is extensively commented upon in the essay on pp. 265 ff.

general[1] who have denounced it and had him arrested; his wife must go today and throw herself at the feet of Madame de Pompadour." A few moments afterwards I went in to Madame to attend to her toilet, and the doctor came in. Madame said to him: "You must be distressed by the disgrace of your friend Mirabeau, and I am sorry about it too, because I like his brother." Quesnay replied: "Madame, I am very far from believing him to have any evil intent; he loves the king and the people." "Yes," she said, "his *Friend of Mankind* did him great honour." At that moment the lieutenant of police came in, and Madame asked him: "Have you read M. Mirabeau's book?" "Yes, Madame," he replied, "but it was not I who denounced it." "What do you think of it?" Madame asked him. "I think," he replied, "that he could have put a large part of what he has said in more discreet terms. Among others there are two phrases at the beginning: *Your Majesty has 20 million men more or less; you can obtain their services only by paying them money; and there is no money at all to pay for their services.*" "What, doctor," asked Madame, "is that so?" "It is true," replied Quesnay, "that those are the first lines, and I agree that they are imprudent; but if you read the book you will see that what he is complaining about is the fact that patriotism is dying away in people's hearts, and that what he wants to do is to revive it." The king came in, we went out, and I sat at Quesnay's table and wrote down what I had just heard. Later I went back to go on with Madame's toilet, and she said to me: "The king is very angry with Mirabeau, but I have tried to mollify him, and the lieutenant of police has done so too. This is going to intensify Quesnay's fears. Do you know what he said to me one day? The king was talking to him in my apartment, and the doctor wore a very uneasy expression. After the king had gone out, I said to him: 'You have a worried expression in front of the king, and yet he is so good.' 'Madame,' he replied, 'it is forty years since I left my village, and I have very little experience of the world, to which I find it difficult to get accustomed. When I am in a room with the king, I say to myself: There is a man who can have my head cut off; and this idea makes me uneasy.' 'But should not the justice and goodness of the king reassure you?' I asked. 'That is fine so far as reason is concerned,' he replied, 'but feeling comes more quickly, and it fills me with fear before I have time to tell myself everything that is necessary in order to dispel it.'" I wrote this down so as not to forget it, and made myself repeat the words.'[2]

The tax-farmers, whom Mirabeau had attacked very bitterly, were unwilling to let the matter pass, and Mirabeau was imprisoned in the château at Vincennes. The subject of taxation was indeed a touchy one, as certain important predecessors of the Physiocrats like

---

[1] I.e. the tax-farmers.   [2] Oncken, pp. 130–2.

Boisguillebert and Vauban had also found to their cost. But thanks
to the efforts of his friends (notably, no doubt, those of Madame de
Pompadour herself), Mirabeau's imprisonment lasted only eight
days, and was followed by a brief exile at his estate at Bignon. The
martyrdom was obviously a very valuable one, at any rate potentially:
crowds thronged the windows in the towns through which he passed
en route from Bignon to Vincennes, and Mirabeau's popular
reputation as a true 'friend of mankind' was spectacularly con-
firmed.

The moral which the Physiocrats drew from this incident, however,
was not that the iron should be struck while it was hot, but rather
that counsels of caution should prevail. The year 1761, Du Pont
wrote later, 'passed away in silence. This did not mean, however,
that the zeal of the citizen-philosophers who were applying themselves to the study of the science of political economy had diminished;
but after the misfortune which fell upon the author of the *Theory
of Taxation*, their respect for the government made them believe that
this silence accorded with its attitude, whose meaning and motives
it was not for them to pass judgment upon.'[1] Possibly the temporary
pause in the advance of the school was also due partly to the death
of Gournay in 1759, which had dashed the hope of the Physiocrats
that his influence in high places might have assisted in the adoption
at least of those *laissez faire* principles which were later to be held
in common by the Physiocratic school and the 'school of Gournay',
if not of the whole range of Physiocratic policies. In the 'silence' of
1761, however, and in that of 1762 which followed, Quesnay and
Mirabeau worked together to produce the *Rural Philosophy*, which
was designed as a sort of basic text-book of Physiocratic doctrine
and policy, and which eventually appeared (after a brief period of
suppression) in 1763. In the meantime the government had begun to
make a few nods in the Physiocratic direction, most notably in the
shape of the Declaration of May 25, 1763, which authorized the
free transport of corn from one province to another inside the
kingdom. The government had also shown itself a little more tolerant
towards dangerous thoughts, even on matters of taxation policy,
than it had been in the case of Mirabeau's book on that subject.

The *Rural Philosophy* was received fairly quietly, as befitted its
relatively cautious, sober, and scientific tone. But from then on the
Physiocratic school—which up to now had consisted virtually of a
master and one disciple—began to gain new adherents. In particular,
Du Pont de Nemours, the young author of a book entitled *Reflections
on the Wealth of the State*, was roped in by Mirabeau and enrolled in
the ranks; and the adhesion of Abeille followed shortly afterwards.
By 1763 the doctrine had been formulated and the school had been

[1] Oncken, p. 158.

founded: it remained now to propagandize the doctrine and to work for the adoption of the policy.

5. THE RISE AND DECLINE OF THE SCHOOL

By the middle of the 1760s the Physiocratic school had become a real intellectual power in the land; by the end of the 1760s its influence was already beginning to wane. 'After 1770,' writes Weulersse, 'there were still Physiocrats, but they were soon to become isolated; there was still a Physiocratic doctrine, but it was tending towards dissolution. There was at any rate no Physiocratic *movement*.'[1] The story of the swift rise and decline of the school is fascinating enough, but I can do no more here than give a brief sketch of it. For details, the reader is referred to the very complete —in fact almost day-to-day—account given by Weulersse in his remarkable volumes.[2]

After 1763, the school began to conduct its propaganda with great zeal and energy. Regular gatherings seem to have been held in Quesnay's *entresol*, at which the Physiocrats talked with people of different schools of thought, and at which considerable freedom of expression seems to have prevailed. An intriguing scrap of conversation at one of these meetings has been preserved for us by our friend Madame du Hausset. M. de Marigni, she tells us, was with Quesnay when Mirabeau and Mercier de la Rivière came in. 'This kingdom,' said Mirabeau, 'is in a very bad way; there are neither powerful sentiments, nor money to take their place.' 'It can only be regenerated,' said Mercier de la Rivière, 'by a conquest as in the case of China, or by some great internal shake-up;[3] but woe to those who are there when it happens: the French people do not do things by halves.' 'These words,' writes Madame du Hausset, 'made me tremble, and I hastened to withdraw. M. de Marigni did the same, but without the appearance of having been affected by what had been said. "Well," he said to me, "you have heard; but don't be afraid—nothing of what is said at the doctor's is repeated. They are decent people, although a bit given to fancies; they don't know when to stop, but I think that they are nevertheless on the right track. The trouble is

---

[1] Weulersse, I, p. vi.

[2] Weulersse's *magnum opus* is that already cited—*Le Mouvement Physiocratique en France* (1910). A shortened version of this work, under the title of *Les Physiocrates*, was published in 1931 by G. Doin, Paris. Reference should also be made to two posthumous volumes, *La Physiocratie sous les Ministères de Turgot et de Necker* (Paris, 1950), and *La Physiocratie à la Fin du Règne de Louis XV* (Paris, 1959).

[3] *Bouleversement.*

that they go too far." I wrote this down when I got back.'[1] These gatherings were the prototype of Mirabeau's famous 'Tuesdays', at which views were exchanged, Physiocratic papers read, and converts made. The converts flowed thick and fast, the most notable being Le Trosne, Saint-Péravy, Mercier de la Rivière, and Baudeau, who all joined the ranks between 1764 and 1766.

The adhesion of Baudeau was particularly important because it enabled the Physiocrats to acquire a journal of their own. Baudeau had founded, in 1765, a literary and political journal entitled *Ephémérides du Citoyen*, after the model of Addison's *Spectator*: and following upon his spectacular conversion in 1766 he put this journal at the disposal of the Physiocrats, so that from the beginning of 1767 the *Ephémérides* became the official organ of the school. Prior to this, the Physiocrats had for a short period been in virtual control of the *Journal de l'Agriculture, du Commerce et des Finances*, of which Du Pont had been appointed editor in September 1765. The proprietors of this journal, however, had dismissed Du Pont in October 1766—largely, in all probability, because of his somewhat excessive zeal in publicizing the doctrines of the new school in what was supposed to be a more or less neutral publication. Thus the conversion of Baudeau, and the resultant handing-over of the *Ephémérides* to the Physiocrats, came at precisely the right moment. From then on, until the final demise of the *Ephémérides* in 1772, the school had an independent organ of its own in which it was free to publish what it wished.

The disciples proceeded diligently to popularize the basic doctrine. The publication of Mirabeau's abridgement of the *Rural Philosophy* (*Elements of Rural Philosophy*) early in 1767 was followed by the appearance later in the same year of a collection of Quesnay's writings edited by Du Pont under the title of *Physiocracy*, and by Du Pont's *Origin and Progress of a New Science*. In the same year, Baudeau published in the *Ephémérides* a new explanatory commentary on the *Tableau Economique*. In the same year, too, certain important steps were taken in the direction of the integration of Physiocratic economic theory with politics and philosophy. The doctrine of 'legal despotism', adumbrated by Quesnay in a piece on *Despotism in China* published in the *Ephémérides*, was worked out in detail by Mercier de la Rivière in his *Natural and Essential Order of Political Societies*, the most important work which the school had produced since the *Rural Philosophy*. Quesnay's article on *Natural Right*, first published in the *Journal de l'Agriculture* in 1765, was placed at the head of the collection of his writings in *Physiocracy*; and Du Pont, in his introduction to the latter work, laid a new emphasis on the abstract and philosophical character of the system.

[1] Oncken, pp. 136–7.

These attempts at a synthesis of economics, politics, and philosophy were accompanied by the invention of the name 'Physiocracy'—a name which dates only from 1767—to embrace all the elements of the wider doctrine.

These were indeed days of fame and hope. Relations with the members of the 'school of Gournay', most notably Turgot, became increasingly cordial as the Physiocrats began to lay rather more emphasis on the principle of freedom of competition. Relations with the Encyclopedists were also reasonably good, in spite of Mirabeau's strong reservations about their religious position: Diderot was full of praise for Mercier de la Rivière's book. The influence of the Physiocrats was slowly making itself felt on certain Societies of Agriculture, and on certain Parliaments. In the sphere of government policy, too, it seemed as if Physiocratic propaganda was beginning to have some effect: certain rather cautious and hesitant moves were being made in the direction of the encouragement of agriculture and the removal of the remaining obstacles to free trade. All in all, in spite of a number of reverses and a growing body of opposition to the doctrine, there seemed to be some warrant for the optimism which Mirabeau expressed in a letter to his brother in June 1769: 'If you saw our Tuesdays, the students whom we have produced, the young men of note going to them with such pleasure, the works which are coming out of them, and *évidence*[1]—so destructive of preconceived opinion, the eternal hangman of humanity—being diffused among young minds, these adepts succeeding to offices, and the revolution in the policy of nations visibly brewing; if you saw this, you would perhaps consider that *the fly on the coach wheel* has done well to stick to the helm.'[2]

It was not only a revolution in the policy of nations which was 'visibly brewing' at this time, however, but also strong and organized opposition to Physiocratic doctrine. The trouble about Physiocracy was that there was something in it for everybody to object to. The tax-farmers and other 'men of finance' could take exception to the direct attacks made against them; the 'school of Gournay' to the relatively subordinate emphasis given to free trade; the Encyclopedists to the doctrine of 'legal despotism'; the manufacturers and merchants to the description of their callings as 'sterile' and the agitation for the ending of their 'exclusive privileges'; the guilds to the cries for their abolition; the landowners to the advocacy of the single tax on land rent; and the common people to the doctrine of the 'proper price' which would make (and in fact appeared to be making) their bread dearer. In addition, the deliberately para-doxical terminology and turn of argument often employed by the

---

[1] On the meaning of this term, see below, p. 40.
[2] Cited in Loménie, op. cit., Vol. II, p. 276.

Physiocrats laid them wide open to the weapons of sarcasm and ridicule, so effectively wielded by men like Voltaire and Linguet.

The tide began to turn; but Physiocracy ended not with a bang but a whimper. The *Ephémérides* began to decline in circulation and influence, and it closed down in 1772, ostensibly as a result of government persecution. 'The book-trade was becoming exasperated,' wrote Mirabeau in a letter to Longo, 'the subscribers were becoming disgusted; and the journal was getting into debt, when we profited by the hail of blows on the journalists to bring it to an end at the fourth volume of 1772 with the *decorum* of persecution.'[1] Quesnay himself had by this time withdrawn from economics into the field of abstract mathematical speculation; he died in December 1774, shortly after Turgot's accession to power. It was no doubt the rise of Turgot which accounted for the strong optimistic note in Mira-beau's funeral oration, in which he called upon the assembled Physiocrats to carry on the propagation of the science which, as he put it, 'must one day render societies peaceful and prosperous and men reasonable and virtuous.'[2] But the fall of Turgot in 1776, and the reversal of his Physiocratic reforms, were blows from which the Physiocratic school as such was unable to recover; and the publica-tion of Adam Smith's *Wealth of Nations* in the same year slowly but surely destroyed such remnants of its doctrinal authority as remained. It was not until the days of the Revolution that the few Physiocrats who survived were able to see some of their most cherished reforms finally put into effect. Their influence remained alive for some time in the controversies attendant upon the diffusion of the new Smithian doctrine; but it was not until the second half of the nineteenth century that interest in their work really began to be revived—and even then the interest was more antiquarian than anything else. It is only in our own time, with a renewal of interest in certain of the basic theoretical and practical questions upon which the Physiocrats concentrated, that their full stature as economists is gradually being revealed.

[1] Cited in Loménie, op. cit., Vol. II, p. 253.   [2] Oncken, p. 14.

PART ONE

TRANSLATIONS

PREFACE TO THE TRANSLATIONS

The first and possibly the most difficult task facing a translator of Physiocratic writing is of course that of selection. The Physiocrats were extraordinarily prolific writers. Even Eugène Daire, whose famous collection of Physiocratic texts included work by Quesnay, Du Pont, Mercier de la Rivière, Baudeau, and Le Trosne, and who had a thousand large pages at his disposal, was unable to find room for any of the voluminous works of Mirabeau, the first and in some ways the most able of Quesnay's disciples. And a translator with very much less than Daire's space available to him must obviously be far more rigorous in his policy of exclusion.

I have thought it advisable, in my selection of passages for translation, to concentrate almost entirely on the work of Quesnay, and to make no attempt to include representative extracts from the work of any of his disciples.[1] It is not true to say, as Adam Smith did, that

[1] This is a convenient place to say something about the authorship of the several extracts from the *Philosophie Rurale* which I have included among the translations. The *Philosophie Rurale*, although it was and still is generally attributed to Mirabeau, was in fact, as I have mentioned above (p. 30), the product of an intimate collaboration between Mirabeau and Quesnay. Three manuscript drafts of the work exist in the *Archives Nationales* (M. 779). The first draft is all in Mirabeau's handwriting, with the exception of a portion of chapter 7 which is in the hand of an amanuensis. (On the question of the authorship of chapter 7, see below, f. 278 note (2).) The second and third drafts are in the handwriting of an amanuensis, but contain very many copious notes and additions in Quesnay's handwriting, together with a relatively small number in Mirabeau's handwriting. A comparison between these three drafts leads to the following conclusions concerning the authorship of the extracts translated below:

Section I, Extract 'B' (pp. 57 ff.): The version of this extract appearing in the first draft, in Mirabeau's handwriting, is very close to the version as finally published; and Quesnay's notes to it in the second and third drafts are relatively few and unimportant. We may therefore take it that it was in fact written by Mirabeau. The leading ideas expressed in it, however, were probably derived by Mirabeau from Quesnay: cf. p. 18 above and p. 65 below.

Section I, 3 (i) of Extracts 'C' (pp. 69–70.): There is a preliminary sketch of this passage in the first draft, in Mirabeau's handwriting, but the central section containing the hit at 'moralists and politicians' was added by Quesnay in notes to the second and third drafts. This passage, then, seems to have been a true joint product.

Section I, 3 (ii) of Extracts 'C' (p. 70): This appears in all three drafts in the form in which it was finally published, with no comments by Quesnay, and can therefore be taken to have been written by Mirabeau.

Section I, 3 (iii) of Extracts 'C' (p. 70–1): This appears in the first draft, in Mirabeau's handwriting, in something very close to its final form. Quesnay's notes and alterations in the second and third drafts are not very important, and

the works of the disciples 'all follow implicitly, and without any sensible variation, the doctrine of Mr. Quesnai'.[1] Such a view ignores the important fact that the Physiocratic system, like all such systems, did not remain static but was deliberately developed to meet changing conditions by certain 'revisionists' like Baudeau and Turgot. But it is certainly true that the *essence* of the system, and the basic postulates which men like Baudeau and Turgot developed and re-applied, were very largely contained in Quesnay's work, and that a great deal of the work of the disciples did consist of little more than popularization (sometimes vulgarization) and elaboration. An understanding of the foundations of Physiocratic political economy can indeed be obtained from a study of Quesnay's writings alone. To include representative extracts from the works of the other prominent Physiocrats would have been to run the risk of the translations degenerating into mere snippets, giving the reader little idea of the doctrine as a whole. Those who are interested in the ways in which Physiocracy was developed by Quesnay's successors will find ample references to the views of the latter in the last part of this book.

Which of Quesnay's writings, then, should be included? It seemed important, in the first place, that Quesnay's philosophical and sociological opinions, with which his economic doctrines were closely connected, should receive illustration. His sociological views, in particular, which have so far remained largely unnoticed by English-speaking commentators, seemed to me to require special attention, if only because of their striking resemblance to the doctrines of the Scottish Historical School of the eighteenth century, whose work is only today being rediscovered. Second, I felt that the translations should, to some extent at any rate, illustrate the way in which the Physiocratic system developed in Quesnay's own mind. The true significance of a doctrine can often best be found by considering its evolution in the mind of its progenitor; and for this reason if for no other it seemed proper to include in the translations not only such well-known end-products as the *General Maxims*,

---

the passage can be taken to have been written by Mirabeau. Once again, however, the basic idea probably came from Quesnay: cf. p. 66 below.

Section III, Extract 'F' (pp. 138 ff.): I can find no trace of this remarkable 'Memoir' in any of the three drafts of the *Philosophie Rurale* in M. 779, and no draft of it, or reference to it, in any of the other Mirabeau documents in the *Archives*. It seems probable that its interpolation after chapter 9 of the *Philosophie Rurale* was something of an afterthought, and we cannot be absolutely certain as to its authorship. Mirabeau, however, as he himself stated (p. 18 above), and as the evidence of the three extant drafts of the *Philosophie Rurale* abundantly confirms, found 'the mechanical application which calculations require very distasteful', and it seems extremely unlikely that he was the author of so complex a 'calculation' as this one. All the evidence, stylistic and otherwise, points to Quesnay as its author.

[1] *Wealth of Nations* (Cannan edn.), Vol. II, p. 177.

but also extracts from Quesnay's Encyclopedia articles, which were written at a time when his system was still struggling for coherent formulation. Third, I felt that so far as possible emphasis should be placed on those parts of Quesnay's work which were likely to be of special interest to present-day economists. This consideration to some extent determined the particular sections of the Encyclopedia articles which I decided to reproduce; the inclusion of the *Dialogue on the Work of Artisans* rather than the *Dialogue on Trade*; and the relatively large amount of space devoted to the *Tableau Economique*. One has to be careful here, of course: it is all very well to try to make the Physiocrats interesting to present-day economists, but one must not at the same time give a distorted impression of the doctrine as it appeared to the Physiocrats themselves and their contemporaries. Fortunately this danger is not as great today as it would have been had this book been published ten or twenty years ago: after all, our present-day concern with general equilibrium analysis, the development of under-developed countries, the economics of control, and input-output analysis, has in a certain sense made Physiocrats of us all. The list of items translated here, it may be interesting to note, does not differ very greatly from the list of Quesnay's works which Du Pont thought fit to include in his *Physiocracy*.

Quesnay's style is often extremely irritating, with its frequent repetitions, its incredibly long strings of wearisome relative clauses, and its occasional obscurity and lack of consistency in the use of technical terms. Up to a point I have tried to clean it up in the interest of readability, but only up to a point. I have not consciously tried, for example, to disguise the somewhat antique flavour of much of the language, or to impose my own personal interpretation of ambiguous passages on the translation itself. The reader of translations such as these does not, I think, have a right to be preserved from too much of the irritation which must have been felt by Quesnay's eighteenth-century readers. To assist readability I have therefore relied rather more on footnotes than on extensive stylistic amendments. In a number of cases, in order to help in the understanding of a particular word or phrase, I have reproduced the original French in a footnote; in the case of certain passages I have given cross-references to other parts of this book where the meaning of relevant terms or concepts is discussed; and in the case of the *Tableau Economique* I have taken special care to correct Quesnay's arithmetical errors and to fill in missing links in his argument. In this latter connection, I hope I have not laid myself open to the charge of fussiness: but it seemed better to risk this than to let the reader loose in what may appear at first sight as a wilderness of faulty and unexplained arithmetic without some attempt at guidance. After all, the *Tableau* does constitute, from all points of view, Quesnay's most significant contribution to economics; and I was not prepared to accept the advice of a recent French editor of Quesnay's works to the effect that we should not try too hard to understand Quesnay's 'hieroglyphics'.[1]

In order to economize on footnotes, I append here some comments on my translation of certain words and phrases which are frequently met with in the texts:

1. *Evidence, évidemment*, etc. Quesnay uses the word *évidence* in a special sense, defined as follows in his Encyclopedia article under that title: 'The term *évidence* means a certitude which is so clear and manifest in itself that the mind cannot deny it.'[2] I have used words like 'self-evident' and 'self-evidently', at the cost of some awkwardness in phraseology, to translate what Quesnay seems to have in mind here.

2. Two words of some importance, *droit* and *dépense*, have a double meaning in French which is difficult to reproduce in any English equivalent. *Droit* means both 'right' and 'law': I have usually translated it as 'right', which in most contexts is not unduly misleading. *Dépense*, which means both 'expenditure' and 'expense', and which Quesnay also sometimes uses to mean 'consumption' or even 'capital', is rather more difficult to deal with: I have usually translated it as 'expenditure', but the reader should bear in mind that the *dépenses* of the productive and sterile classes also constitute their 'expenses', or paid-out costs. In some places where the double meaning of *dépense* is particularly important, notably the latter part of the *Dialogue on the Work of Artisans*, I have changed the translation of the word according to the context.

3. *Fermier, laboureur, colon, paysan, cultivateur*. I have usually translated *fermier* as 'farmer', *laboureur* and *colon* as 'husbandman', *paysan* as 'peasant', and *cultivateur* as 'cultivator'. In most contexts, *fermier* means a capitalist entrepreneur who carries on large-scale cultivation (*la grande culture*) with the aid of the latest methods, as distinct from other poorer *cultivateurs* who usually carry on small-scale cultivation (*la petite culture*) with the aid of more primitive methods. *Laboureur* in contemporary writing often means a *paysan* who is more comfortably-off than the majority of his fellows, although not necessarily an entrepreneur. It should be noted, however, that Quesnay is by no means consistent in the meaning he gives to these terms.

4. *Productif, stérile, renaître, reproduction*, etc. Fairly literal translations which preserved so far as possible the important biological analogy seemed in order here. 'Productive class' and 'sterile class' have received the sanction of long usage. (In the early versions of the

[1] I.N.E.D., II, p. 687, footnote. Cf. ibid., p. 463, footnote.
Ibid., II, p. 397.

Tableau, however, Quesnay often uses the terms *classe des dépenses productives* and *classe des dépenses stériles*, which I have had to translate as 'productive expenditure class' and 'sterile expenditure class'.) *Naître* and *renaître* I have usually translated as 'generate' and 'regenerate', and *renaissant* simply as 'renascent'. 'Reproduction' seemed all right for *reproduction*, but the reader should bear in mind that the latter word means not only the process of reproduction but also the total amount reproduced. *Produit net* has been translated as 'net product', and *reprises* as 'returns'.

5. *Bon prix.* With some misgivings, and at the cost of a certain amount of awkwardness, I have translated this key term as 'proper price'. 'Good price' seemed weak, and 'high price' would have put undue emphasis on the level of the price—the point being that *bon prix* for the Physiocrats meant a price which was not only higher but also steadier than the current price.

6. *Avances annuelles, avances primitives.* These I have translated as 'annual advances' and 'original advances'. There is of course a strong temptation to translate them as 'working capital' and 'fixed capital', which are perhaps the nearest modern equivalents, but the parallel is not quite as exact as such a translation would imply.[1]

7. *Valeur vénale, valeur fondamentale.* 'Market value' is not too misleading for *valeur vénale*, provided that it is borne in mind that the *valeur* concerned is usually taken to be that which is received by the seller at first hand. *Valeur fondamentale* I have translated simply as 'fundamental value': 'cost price', I felt, although it expresses the meaning of the term fairly accurately, would not have been proper in view of the fact that the concept of cost was undergoing important changes of content in Quesnay's time.

8. *Profit, salaire.* These have usually, but not always, been translated literally as 'profit' and 'wages'. Here a special word of caution is necessary, however, in view of the fact that for Quesnay these words did not have quite the same significance as they usually have for economists today. The point is that in Quesnay's work *profit* does not necessarily (or indeed usually) refer to a general category of income bearing a more or less regular relation to capital employed; and *salaire* does not necessarily refer to the remuneration paid to a hired worker by a capitalist employer. Both words are often used simply with the significance of 'gain' or 'reward'.

9. *Bourgeois.* Town-dweller, man of the middle classes, or simply 'bourgeois'? Quesnay usually employs the word in a distinctly pejorative sense, and I have therefore ventured to use 'bourgeois'.

10. *Luxe de décoration, luxe de subsistence.* These I have usually translated as 'luxury in the way of ornamentation' and 'luxury in the way of subsistence'. The terms are difficult ones, and the reader

[1] See below, p. 274. R.L.M.

is referred to the general discussion below[1] on the concepts of *luxe* and *faste*.

11. *Impôt direct, impôt indirect.* I have translated these as 'direct tax' and 'indirect tax', but it should be carefully noted that Quesnay's use of these terms is quite different from their present-day use. For Quesnay, an *impôt direct* was a tax levied on the net product of the land, and an *impôt indirect* was any tax not so levied.

12. *Revenu.* This has usually been translated as 'revenue', but it should be noted that the word normally refers only to the 'revenue' payable to the class of proprietors out of the net product yielded by agriculture.

13. In the case of a few words like *taille, corvée, métayer, livre, écu, arpent, setier,* etc., I have retained the original French. This has also been necessary in the case of *Tableau Economique,* which I confess has beaten me. 'Table', the term usually employed, is clearly inappropriate, and I cannot find an adequate single-term substitute.

My own footnotes to the texts bear my initials; all others are those of the author whose work is being translated.

R.L.M.

[1] Pp. 316 ff.

Part One

TRANSLATIONS

I. PHILOSOPHY AND SOCIOLOGY

A.

'NATURAL RIGHT'[1]

CHAPTER I: WHAT THE NATURAL RIGHT OF MAN IS

The natural right of man can be loosely defined as *the right which man has to things suitable for his use.*

Before considering the natural right of man, we must consider man himself in his different states of bodily and mental capacity, and in his different states relative to other men. If we do not make this investigation before we attempt to explain the natural right of each man, we shall find it impossible even to discover what this right is.[2]

It is because philosophers have failed to go back to these primary questions that the ideas about the natural right of man which they have worked out have been so different and even so contradictory. Some of them, with a certain amount of reason, have been unwilling to acknowledge its existence; others, with more reason, have acknowledged it; and the truth lies with both sides. But one truth excludes another in the case of one and the same being when he undergoes a change of state, just as one form is the effective exclusion of another form in the case of one and the same body.

---

[1] This article was first published in the *Journal de l'Agriculture, du Commerce et des Finances* in September 1765, under the title 'Observations sur le Droit Naturel des Hommes Réunis en Société'. A separate edition, under the title *Le Droit Naturel,* was published in the same year, and the article also appeared in a slightly altered form in Du Pont's *Physiocratie*. The text translated here is that of *Physiocratie,* as reproduced in I.N.E.D., II, pp. 729–42. R.L.M.

[2] Some of the discussions on natural right have been similar to the philosophical disputes over liberty, and the just and the unjust: people have tried to conceive these relative attributes as if they were absolute entities. But we can obtain no complete and exact idea about them unless we reunite them with the correlatives upon which they necessarily depend, and without which they are only ideal and ineffectual abstractions.

Those who have said that the natural right of man is non-existent are correct.[1]

Those who have said that the natural right of man is the right which nature teaches to all animals are correct.[2]

Those who have said that the natural right of man is the right which his strength and intelligence assure to him are correct.[3]

Those who have said that natural right is confined to the individual interest of each man are correct.[4]

Those who have said that natural right is a general and paramount law which rules the rights of all men are correct.[5]

Those who have said that the natural right of man is the unlimited right of everybody to everything are correct.[6]

Those who have said that the natural right of man is a right limited by an implicit or explicit agreement are correct.[7]

Those who have said that natural right assumes neither just nor unjust are correct.[8]

Those who have said that natural right is a just, conclusive, and fundamental right are correct.[9]

But no one has been correct relatively to all the cases.

Thus the philosophers have not got beyond paralogisms, or incomplete arguments, in their enquiries into this important matter, which is the natural principle of all the duties of man which are ruled by reason.

A child, destitute of strength and intelligence, unquestionably has a natural right to subsistence, founded on the duty which nature makes known to the father and mother. This right is all the more firmly assured to him by the fact that the duty of the father and mother is accompanied by a natural inclination which operates much more powerfully on the father and mother than does the idea of natural order which establishes the duty. Nevertheless one cannot be unaware of the fact that this duty, inculcated and assured by feeling,

---

[1] See the example at the end of this chapter.

[2] This is Justinian's definition. Like the others, there is a sense in which it is true.

[3] See the example in chapter III, and chapter V, note.

[4] See the example in chapter II, note.

[5] See the example in chapter IV. This proposition, developed a little further, would be that which I adopt.

[6] This is the system of the sophist Thrasymachus in Plato, since revived by Hobbes, and after Hobbes by the author of the book entitled *Principles of Natural Right and Politics*. It is described and refuted in chapter II.

[7] See the example in chapter IV.

[8] This is the case of a man alone on a desert island, whose natural right to the products of his island admits of neither just nor unjust, since justice and injustice are relative attributes which cannot exist when there is no one over whom to exercise them. See the beginning of the fourth chapter.

[9] See the end of this chapter and the beginning of the fourth.

is in the order of justice; for the father and mother are doing no more than rendering to their children what they themselves received from their own fathers and mothers. And a precept which corresponds to a just right binds every rational being.

If I am asked what justice is, I reply that *it is a natural and paramount rule, recognized through the light of reason, which self-evidently determines what belongs to oneself or to another.*

If the child's father and mother die, and the child, without any other resource, is left to become the inevitable victim of its incapacity, it is deprived of the enjoyment of its natural right, and this right becomes non-existent. For a relative attribute cannot exist when its correlative is lacking. The enjoyment of eyesight is non-existent in a place which is inaccessible to the light.

CHAPTER II: THE EXTENT OF THE NATURAL RIGHT OF MAN

The natural right of man differs from his *legal* right, or the right conferred by human laws, in that it is self-evidently recognized through the light of reason, and through this self-evident character alone is binding independently of any coercion; whereas *legal* right, defined by a positive law, is binding because of the penalty attached to transgression by the sanction of this law, even though we have knowledge of it only through the simple indication expressed in the law.

These different conditions enable us to see in its entirety the extent of natural right, and the features which distinguish it from *legal* right.

Legal right often restricts natural right, because the laws of man are not as perfect as the laws of the Author of nature, and because human laws are sometimes imbued with unconscious motives[1] whose justice is not always recognized by enlightened reason, so that it becomes obligatory for the wise legislator to repeal the laws which he himself has made. The host of contradictory and absurd laws which nations have successively adopted proves clearly that positive laws are often apt to deviate from the immutable rules of justice and of the natural order which is most advantageous to society.

Some philosophers, engrossed with the abstract idea of the natural right of man which allows *to everybody a right to everything*, have limited the natural right of man to the state in which men are abso-

---

[1] *Les lois humaines sont quelquefois surprises par des motifs,* etc. This is a somewhat unusual use of *surprendre,* but I think my translation conveys Quesnay's real meaning. R.L.M.

lutely independent of one another, and to the state of war between them which provides the means for everybody to secure his unlimited right. Thus, these philosophers claim, when a man is deprived by contract, or by a legal authority, of some part of the natural right which he has to all things suitable for his use, his general right is destroyed; and this man finds himself subordinate to others through his agreement or through a coercive authority. He is no longer in the simple state of nature or of complete independence; he is no longer himself the sole judge of his right; he is brought into subjection to the judgment of others; thus, they maintain, he is no longer in the state of pure nature, and consequently no longer within the sphere of natural right.

But if we look carefully at the futility of this abstract idea of *the natural right of everybody to everything,* we see that in order to conform to the natural order itself we would have to reduce this natural right of man to *a right to the things whose use he can obtain,* and this so-called general right would then in actual fact be an extremely limited right.

From this point of view, it will be seen that the arguments just described are nothing but frivolous sophistry, or an intellectual game which is quite out of place in the examination of such an important matter; and we will be fully convinced that the natural right of each man is in reality reduced to a right to the share which he can procure for himself through his labour. For *his right to everything* is similar to the right of each swallow to all the midges which fly about in the air—a right which in reality is confined to those which it can catch through its labour or through the endeavours dictated by its needs.

In the state of pure nature, the things suitable for man's use are reduced to those which nature produces spontaneously and over which each man can exercise his indeterminate natural right only by procuring for himself a certain share through his labour, i.e. through his endeavours. Whence it follows: (1) that his right to everything is only ideal; (2) that the share of things which he enjoys in the state of pure nature is obtained through labour; (3) that his right to the things suitable for his use ought to be considered in the order of nature and in the order of justice; for in the order of nature it is indeterminate in so far as it is not assured by actual possession; and in the order of justice it is determinate because of an effective possession of natural right, acquired through labour, without encroaching upon other people's right of possession; (4) that in the state of pure nature men who require urgently to satisfy their needs, each through his own endeavours, will not waste their time by uselessly engaging in a mutual war which would only set up an obstacle to their engaging in the occupations necessary to provide their subsistence;[1] (5) that natural right, included in the order of nature and in the order of justice, extends to all the situations in which men may find themselves relatively to one another.

CHAPTER III: THE INEQUALITY OF THE NATURAL RIGHT OF MAN

We have seen that even in the state of pure nature or of complete independence men enjoy their natural right to the things they need only through labour, i.e. through the endeavours necessary to obtain them. Thus the right of *everybody to everything* is reduced to the share which each of them can procure for himself, whether they live by hunting, or by fishing, or on the natural produce of the earth. But in order to carry on these endeavours, and to succeed in them, they must possess those bodily and mental faculties, together with those means and instruments, which are necessary to enable them to act and to succeed in satisfying their needs. The enjoyment of their natural right must be extremely limited in this state of pure nature and independence, in which we are assuming that there is as yet no co-operation for purposes of mutual aid among them, and in which the strong are able to use violence unjustly against the weak. When they enter into society, and come to agreements among themselves for their mutual advantage, they thereby increase the enjoyment of their natural right; and they also assure for themselves the full extent of this enjoyment, if the constitution of the society conforms to the order which is self-evidently the most advantageous to men, with respect to the fundamental laws of their natural right.

But when we consider the bodily and intellectual faculties, and the other resources, of each man separately, we shall find that there is still great inequality among them with respect to the enjoyment of the natural right of man. In its first principles this inequality admits of neither just nor unjust; it results from the arrangement of the laws of nature; and man cannot fathom the purposes of the Supreme Being in the making of the universe, or grasp the intention of the immutable rules which he has instituted for the development and protection of his work. However, if we examine these rules carefully we shall at least see that the *physical* causes of *physical* evil are themselves the causes of *physical* good; that the rain which incon-

---

[1] This is the case of the proverb which can be applied to everyone living in the state of pure nature: 'If you want it, go and seek it; no one will stop you'. This rule also applies to animals: those of the same species who are in the same situation never make war on one another, for this would prevent all of them from obtaining their food through their endeavours.

veniences the traveller renders the land fertile; and if we reason in an unbiased way we shall see that these causes produce infinitely more good than evil, and that they are instituted only for the sake of good; that the evil which they incidentally cause is the unavoidable result of the very essence of the properties by means of which they bring about good. That is why, in the natural order relating to man, these laws are binding only for the sake of good: they impose upon us the duty of avoiding, so far as possible, the evil which we have to foresee by the use of our prudence.

We must thus be very careful not to attribute to physical laws the evils which represent the just and inevitable punishment for the violation of the very order of physical laws, instituted for the sake of bringing about good. If a government deviated from the natural laws which assure the success of agriculture, would we dare lay the blame on agriculture itself for the fact that we lacked bread, and for the fact that we saw at the same time both the number of men diminishing and the number of the poor and wretched increasing?

Transgressions of natural laws are the most widespread and usual causes of the physical evils that afflict men; even the wealthy, who have greater means of avoiding them, bring upon themselves through their ambition, their passions, and even their pleasures, many evils for which they can blame only their own irregular acts. This leads us naturally to another cause of physical and moral evil, a cause different in kind from physical laws—the improper use by man of his freedom. Freedom, that inherent attribute of man which he would like to extend beyond its limits, appears to man never to be wrong. If he injures himself, if he destroys his health, if he dissipates his wealth and ruins his family by the improper use of his freedom, he complains about the Author of his freedom when he tries to be still more free,[1] not perceiving that he is contradicting himself. Let him,

---

[1] What do the words 'more free' mean? Do they mean more arbitrary, i.e. more independent of the motives which operate on the will? No, for such independence, if it were complete, would reduce the will to the state of indifference, in which freedom would be non-existent. Thus one cannot use the words 'more free' in this sense. Still less can these words relate to the state in which the will is overcome by insuperable motives. These two extremes constitute the boundaries which limit the extent of the natural use of freedom.

FREEDOM is a faculty relative to effective and superable motives, counter-balancing and damping down one another, and presenting contradictory interests and attractions which are examined and weighed up by a more or less enlightened and more or less attentive reason. This state of deliberation consists in a number of acts in which freedom is exercised, backed up to a greater or less extent by introspection. But in order to obtain an even more accurate idea of freedom, we must not confuse the state of mental deliberation with the final act of will, which is a simple, definitive, and more or less precipitate act which puts an end to any exercise of freedom. It is not at all an act of freedom, but simply an absolute decision of the will, the latter having been more or less made ready for the act of choice through the exercise of freedom.

then, recognize his excesses; let him learn to use properly this freedom which is so dear to him; let him do away with ignorance and irregular acts, the sources of the evils he brings upon himself through the use of his freedom. He is by nature a free and intelligent being, although sometimes he may be neither the one nor the other. Through the blind and imprudent use of his freedom he may make bad choices; through his intelligence he may arrive at better choices, and conduct himself wisely, to the extent that he is permitted to do so by the order of physical laws which constitutes the universe.[1]

The origin of physical good and physical evil, and of moral good

---

Following on from these observations, which are familiar to anyone who has paid a little attention to the way he uses his mind, we may ask those who deny the existence of freedom *whether they are quite certain they have never deliberated.* If they admit that they have deliberated, we will then ask them *why they have deliberated.* And if they admit that they have done so *in order to choose,* they will have recognized that between the motives and the decision an intellectual faculty is exercised. Then both sides will be in agreement on the question of the actual existence of this faculty, and it will become useless to quarrel over its name.

But under this name we must not bring together contradictory conditions, such as the condition of being able equally to yield to all the existing motives and the condition of being able equally to yield to none—conditions which exclude all reason from preference, choice, and decision. For then all exercise, all use, in a word all the essential properties, of the very faculty which we would call freedom would be non-existent; that name would signify only an inconceivable abstraction, like that of a stick without two ends. If you strip man's will of all determinative causes, in order to make him free, you annul the will; for every act of will consists in willing something, and that something itself causes the will to will. Destroy motives and you destroy freedom itself, i.e. the intellectual faculty which examines and weighs up objects in accordance with the disposition of the mind. . . .

Without dwelling any longer on this absurdity, let me conclude by observing that it is only the wise man who concerns himself with improving his freedom. The others always believe that they are sufficiently free when they satisfy their desires; and in addition they are mindful only of procuring for themselves the means of increasing their range of choice, which cannot extend their freedom but only the imprudent use of their freedom. The man who has only one kind of food for his supper has only the choice between eating it and leaving it, and between eating more or less of it; but the man who has twenty kinds of food has the power of extending the exercise of his freedom over all the different kinds, to choose those which he finds the most attractive, and to eat more or less of those which he chooses. It is in this sense that uncultured men concern themselves only with extending further and further the use of their freedom, and with satisfying their passions with as little discernment as moderation. This has compelled men who live in society to establish for themselves penal laws in order to restrain the unbridled use of their freedom. Thus they extend their freedom through motives affecting them which counterbalance one another and stimulate introspection, which is so to speak the *active organ* of freedom or of deliberation. Thus freedom or deliberation can be extended through the very motives which limit the precipitate and imprudent use of freedom.

[1] There are many kinds and degrees of madness; but any man who is mad owing to the faulty structure of his brain is in the power of a *physical law* which *does not allow him to make the best choice or to conduct himself wisely.*

and moral evil, thus clearly lies in natural laws. Everything has its immutable essence, and the properties inseparable from its essence. Other laws would have other essential properties, very probably less in conformity with the perfection to which the Author of nature has brought his work. The laws which he has instituted are just and perfect within the design as a whole, where they are in conformity with the order and the ends which he has intended. For he himself is the Author of laws and rules, and therefore is superior to laws and rules. But their aim is to bring about good, and everyone is subject to those he has instituted. The man endowed with intelligence has the special privilege of being able to contemplate and understand them, so as to draw from them the greatest possible benefit, avoiding any rebellion against these supreme laws and rules.

It follows from this that each man has the natural right to avail himself thankfully of all the faculties allotted to him by nature, in the circumstances in which she has placed him, subject to the condition that he causes injury neither to himself nor to others—a condition without which no one would be assured of maintaining the use of his faculties or the enjoyment of his natural right. This leads us to the next chapter.

CHAPTER IV: THE NATURAL RIGHT OF MEN CONSIDERED
RELATIVELY TO ONE ANOTHER

Man can be considered in the solitary state and in the populous state.[1]

If we envisage men to be scattered to such an extent that no communication is possible between them, we see that they must be wholly in the state of pure nature and complete independence, without any relation of just and unjust between them. But this state can continue to exist only during the period of the life of each individual; or else it would be necessary to assume at least that each of these men had a wife living with him in his retreat. And this would completely alter the hypothesis of their solitary state, for this association with a wife and the children who would come into being would bring in an order of dependence, justice, duty, security, and mutual aid.

Every man is charged with his self-preservation under penalty of suffering, and he suffers only when he fails to fulfil this duty towards himself. This obliges him first to fulfil it towards everyone else. But all those with whom he is associated are charged with the fulfilment of the same duty towards themselves under the same penalty. It is

[1] *Dans l'état de solitude et dans l'état de multitude.* R.L.M.

part of the natural order that the strongest should be the head of the family, but it is not part of the order of justice that he should encroach upon the natural right of those who live in a community of interest with him. There is thus an order of compensation[1] in the enjoyment of the natural right of each person which must be to the advantage of all the individuals in the family, and which must be regulated by the head, according to the order of distributive justice itself, in conformity with the duties prescribed by nature and with the system of co-operation in which each person contributes to the welfare of the society according to his ability. Everybody makes his contribution to it in a different way, but the services performed by one lessen the services which have to be performed by another; as a result of this distribution of services, each person can perform his own more thoroughly; and as a result of this mutual supplementation each person contributes almost equally to the welfare of the society. Thus each person in it ought to enjoy his natural right to its full extent, in conformity with the benefit which accrues from the co-operative work of the society; and those who are not in a position to contribute to it ought to share in it in proportion to the degree of comfort which this particular society can procure for itself. These rules, which make themselves known of their own accord, guide the conduct of the head of the family in order that the natural order and the order of justice may be brought together in the society. He is also prompted by feelings of satisfaction, tenderness, pity, etc., which are also evidence of the aims of the Author of nature concerning the observance of the rules which he prescribes to men for the purpose of obliging them by way of duty to help one another.

If we consider men in the populous state, where communication between them is inevitable, but where there are nevertheless not yet any positive laws which unite them in society under the authority of a sovereign power and subject them to a form of government, we must envisage them to be like the savage tribes in sparsely populated regions, living on the natural products of the area, or by necessity exposing themselves to the dangers involved in banditry if they can make raids on nations where there is wealth to plunder. For in this state they could not procure wealth for themselves by means of agriculture, or by means of the pasturage of flocks and herds, because there would not be any tutelary power to assure their property in them. But it would at least be necessary that there should be implicit or explicit agreement between them regarding their personal security, for in this state of independence men have a fear of one another which causes mutual anxiety, but concerning which the minds of all can easily be set at rest, since nothing interests them more than to release themselves mutually from this fear. The people

---

[1] *Ordre de compensation.* R.L.M.

of each district see one another more frequently; they become accustomed to seeing one another, confidence is established between them, they assist one another, they ally themselves to one another through marriage, and to some extent they form individual nations in which all are banded together for their common defence, but in which each nevertheless remains in the state of full liberty and independence in relation to the others, conditional upon their personal security as between themselves and upon their ownership of the dwelling and the few effects or implements which each one has in his individual possession and keeping.

If their wealth in property were greater and more scattered, or more exposed to robbery, the constitution of these nations would not suffice to assure them in their ownership of it. They would then find it necessary to introduce positive laws, written or conventional, and a sovereign authority to enforce their observance; for their wealth, easy to carry off and at the mercy of public honesty, would excite in their less virtuous fellow-countrymen desires which would lead them to violate the rights of others.

Thus the form of societies depends on the greater or lesser quantity of property which each possesses, or may possess, and in respect of which it wants to assure for itself protection and ownership.

Thus men who put themselves under the dependence or rather under the protection of positive laws and a tutelary authority greatly increase their ability to be owners of property, and consequently greatly increase the use of their natural right, instead of restricting it.

CHAPTER V: THE NATURAL RIGHT OF MEN JOINED TOGETHER IN SOCIETY UNDER A SOVEREIGN AUTHORITY

There are some societies which are governed by a monarchical authority, others by an aristocratic authority, others by a democratic authority, etc. But it is not these different forms of authority which determine the essence of the natural right of men joined together in society, for laws vary greatly under each of these forms. The laws of governments, which determine the rights of subjects, almost always reduce themselves to laws which are positive or instituted by men. Now these laws do not constitute the essential and immutable foundation of natural right, and they vary to such an extent that it would be impossible to examine the state of the natural right of man under these laws. It is even useless to try to begin such an examination, for in those cases where the laws and the tutelary power fail to assure property and freedom there is neither government nor society in any beneficial sense; there is only domination and anarchy under the semblance of government; positive laws and domination protect and assure the depradations of the strong and destroy the property and freedom of the weak. Indeed, the state of pure nature is more advantageous than this violent state of society, which passes through all the vicissitudes of disorganization and changes in forms, authorities, and sovereigns. This state of affairs would appear to be so very inevitable that the men who devote themselves to the study of all these changes are thoroughly convinced that it is part of the inevitable order of things that governments should have their beginnings, their progress, their peaks of power, and their declines and falls. But they ought also to have seen that this order is extremely irregular, that the transitions are more or less rapid, more or less uniform, more or less unequal, more or less complicated by unforeseen events of a favourable or calamitous character, more or less planned or fortuitous, more or less attributable to prudence or error, to enlightenment or ignorance, to the wisdom or unbridled passions of those who govern. Thus they should have felt obliged to conclude from this at any rate that the inevitability of bad governments is not a consequence of the natural and immutable order, the *archetype* of governments.

In order to understand the order of time and space, and to control navigation and safeguard trade, it has been necessary to observe and calculate precisely the laws of the movement of celestial bodies. Similarly, in order to understand the extent of the natural right of men joined together in society, it is necessary to settle upon the natural laws which form the basis of the best government possible. This government to which men ought to be subject consists in the natural order and the positive order most advantageous to men joined together in society.

Thus men joined together in society ought to be subject to natural laws and positive laws.

Natural laws are either physical or moral.

I am here taking physical law to mean *the regular course of all physical events in the natural order which is self-evidently the most advantageous to the human race.*[1]

I am here taking moral law to mean *the rule of all human action in the moral order conforming to the physical order which is self-evidently the most advantageous to the human race.*[2]

These laws taken together constitute what is called *natural law*. All men and all earthly powers ought to be subject to these sovereign laws instituted by the Supreme Being. They are immutable and in-

[1] *Le cours réglé de tout événement physique de l'ordre naturel évidemment le plus avantageux au genre humain.* R.L.M.
[2] *La règle de toute action humaine de l'ordre moral conforme à l'ordre physique évidemment le plus avantageux au genre humain.* R.L.M.

disputable and the best laws possible;[1] thus they are the foundation of the most perfect government, and the fundamental rule for all positive laws. For positive laws are nothing but laws of administration relative to the natural order which is self-evidently the most advantageous to the human race.

Positive laws are *authentic rules established by a sovereign authority for the purpose of settling the order of the administration of government, securing the defence of society, ensuring the regular observance of natural laws, amending or maintaining the customs and usages introduced in the nation, regulating the personal rights of subjects relatively to their different situations; determining the positive order in doubtful cases reduced to probabilities of opinion or convenience; and deciding on questions of distributive justice.* But the primary positive law, the law which is fundamental to all other positive laws, is *the institution of private and public instruction in the laws of the natural order,* which is the sovereign rule of all man-made legislation and of all civil, political, economic, and social conduct. Without this fundamental institution, governments and the conduct of men can be characterized only by obscurity, aberration, confusion, and disorder. For without an understanding of the natural laws which ought to serve as the foundation of man-made legislation and as sovereign rules for the conduct of men, there is no self-evident knowledge[2] of just and unjust, natural right, and physical and moral order; there is no self-evident knowledge of the essential distinction between general and individual interests, and of the real nature of the causes of the prosperity and decline of nations; and there is no self-evident knowledge of the essence of moral good and evil, and of the sacred rights of those who command and the duties of those to whom the social order prescribes obedience.

Positive legislation consists, then, in the enunciation of the natural laws constituting the order which is self-evidently the most advantageous possible to men joined together in society—or we could say quite simply the most advantageous possible to the sovereign, for what is really the most advantageous to the sovereign is the most advantageous to his subjects. It is only the understanding of these supreme laws which can ensure the continuing peace and prosperity of an empire; and the more a nation applies itself to this science, the greater will be the sway of the natural order in it, and the more correct will its positive order be. In such a nation an unwise law

---

[1] The natural order which is most advantageous to men is perhaps not the most advantageous to the other animals; but included in man's unlimited right is that of making his lot the best possible. This superiority appertains to his intelligence; it is part of natural right, since man inherits it from the Author of nature, who has determined it in this way through the laws which he has instituted in the order of the formation of the universe.

[2] *Il n'y a nulle évidence.* R.L.M.

would not be put forward, for the government and the people would immediately perceive its absurdity.

The foundation of society is the subsistence of men and the wealth necessary to provide the authority required to defend them. Thus it could only be ignorance which would, for example, approve of the introduction of positive laws which militated against the order of the reproduction and the regular annual circulation of the wealth of a kingdom's territory. If the torch of reason illuminates the government, all positive laws harmful to society and to the sovereign will disappear.

What we are concerned with here is reason which is exercised, extended, and perfected by means of the study of natural laws. For reason alone does not raise man above the beasts; it is in its essence only a faculty or aptitude by means of which man can acquire the knowledge which is necessary for him, and by means of which he is able, with the aid of this knowledge, to procure for himself the physical and moral benefits essential to the nature of his being. Reason is to the soul what the eyes are to the body: without his eyes a man cannot enjoy the light, and without light he can see nothing.

Thus reason alone cannot tell man how to conduct himself; he must acquire through his reason the knowledge which is necessary for him, and through his reason he must make use of this knowledge to conduct himself worthily and procure for himself the goods which he needs. Ignorance is the original attribute of man in his uncultured and isolated state; in society it is man's most disastrous infirmity. In society it is even a crime, since men, being endowed with intelligence, ought to raise themselves to an order superior to the state of the beasts. In society it is a monstrous crime because of the nature of the offence which it entails, for ignorance is the most common cause of the ills which beset the human race and of its unworthiness in the face of the Author of nature, in the face of the eternal light, the supreme reason and the first cause of all good.

But reason which is enlightened, guided, and brought to the point of understanding as self-evident the working of natural laws, becomes the rule necessary for the attainment of the best possible government, under which the observance of these sovereign laws would abundantly increase the wealth necessary for men's subsistence and for the maintenance of the tutelary authority, whose protection guarantees to men joined together in society the ownership of their wealth and the security of their persons.

It is therefore self-evident that *the natural right of each man is extended in proportion to the degree to which he strives to observe the best possible laws, which constitute the order most advantageous to men joined together in society.*

These laws do not at all restrict man's freedom, which forms part of his natural right; for the advantages of these supreme laws are manifestly the object of the best choice of freedom. Man cannot reasonably refuse the obedience which he owes to these laws; otherwise his freedom would be only a freedom harmful to himself and to others. It would be nothing but the freedom of a madman, who, under a good government, must be checked and cured through the authority of the positive laws of society.

B.

EXTRACT FROM 'RURAL PHILOSOPHY'[1]

In order to understand as a statesman the true and simple principles of politics, which is the art of making men useful, and in order to become endowed with a share of that beneficial creative power which produces worthy founders of society or those who add permanent lustre to it, we must consider the common weal in terms of its essence, and humanity as a whole in terms of its root, *subsistence*. All the moral and physical parts of which society is constituted derive from this and are subordinate to it. It is upon subsistence, upon the means of subsistence, that all the branches of the political order depend. Religion, in a sense, is purely and simply spiritual, but natural law inspires us and also tells us about duties relative to our needs; the civil laws, which originally are nothing more than rules for the allocation of subsistence; virtues and vices, which are only obedience to or revolt against natural or civil law; government, the sciences, the liberal and mechanical arts, agriculture, trade, industry —all are subordinate to the means of subsistence. This is the fundamental force to which is due everything which men cultivate, navigate and build: *quae homines arant, navigant, aedificant, omnia virtuti parent*. If societies endowed with totally different products are seen to be to some extent on a par with one another so far as these aspects of their civil life are concerned, it is solely trade which must be thanked or blamed for this. Trade, which makes products common to all by means of exchange, transplants with the seed the other fruits of society. But imagine yourself suddenly faced with isolated nations, such as the Lapps and Samoyeds in their snowy abodes, or as the inhabitants of the island of Newfoundland were, confined to fishing for their subsistence; and ask yourself what laws relating to the division of the land, what methods of maintaining the population,

---

[1] The *Philosophie Rurale* first appeared in 1763, with the sub-title *Economie Générale et Politique de l'Agriculture, Réduite à l'Ordre Immuable des Loix Physiques & Morales, Qui Assurent la Prospérité des Empires*. The extract here translated occurs in the eighth chapter of the work, *Rapports des Dépenses avec la Population*. The text from which my translation has been made is that of the edition stated to be published in 1764, *A Amsterdam, Chez les Libraires Associés*, Vol. II, pp. 8–23. On several occasions when the wording of this edition appeared to be dubious, reference was made to the one-volume edition of 1763, and to the manuscript drafts of the *Philosophie Rurale* in the *Archives Nationales*, M. 779. On the question of the authorship of this extract, see above, p. 37, note. R.L.M.

what systems of taxation, and what kinds of arts you could get these peoples to accept.

Modern legislators who, without investigating what roots of this kind might exist in the different provinces of a great state, want to try to destroy all differences in manners and morals, in laws and customs, and in weights and measures, are self-evidently building on the basis of an illusion. The princes and ministers of former times who sought to enslave nations, either by violence or by corruption, were as foolish as they were barbarous. It is natural that when a society is formed it should want to govern itself: it possesses few types of goods and needs few laws. This is the situation in which all new-born societies find themselves. The whole body of the nation constitutes the magistracy, and the law has no need of assistance: what we have is a republic. This new-born state, which is preoccupied with supplying its needs, is also afraid of very little: it is not yet worth while invading. In order to increase the different kinds of goods it has to increase the number of laws and provide security. Desires are awakened, each person seeks to acquire gain for himself, and relinquishes his share of the public magistracy. The law requires assistance, and a controlling tutelary power is necessary to guarantee the industrious and prosperous society against invasion. What we have is a legitimate monarchy—though it is often neither very legitimate nor very long-lasting.

The government which wants to secure its authority and preserve it from opposition, then, far from blackening itself by adopting the atrocious and dangerous policies associated with tyranny, or lowering itself to degrade its people, should seek to make the latter a participant in all the different kinds of goods and all the refinements of products. Thenceforth it should anticipate the dangers of the anarchical authority which is urged upon it by individual interests: I say anarchical, because authority which disrupts the ties binding society together destroys power, and the annihilation of power destroys authority. In the case of everything in this world, abuse is a close neighbour of order. We have just shown the possibilities of the latter. I repeat, change or displace one figure and the whole calculation is thrown into disorder. Introduce one wrong note into the harmony of society, and the whole political mechanism feels the effect and falls apart, and concord is then as difficult to re-establish as it would be for the world to take shape as a result of the accidental concourse of atoms of Epicurus.

Thus in dealing here with population, a leading and especially important branch of the speculations of political economy,[1] we must look for its principle at the true fountain-head, and set out from the ideas which are really basic in this connection.

[1] *La politique économique.* R.L.M.

Man in this world has only three original needs: (1) that of his subsistence; (2) that of his preservation; and (3) that of the perpetuation of his species. These three needs are accorded to him, just as they are to all created species, with a degree of urgency depending upon the structure of his organs and the extent of his faculties. Of these three, the first is the only one which is imperative, indispensable, and individual. Numbers of men are unwilling or unable either to defend themselves or reproduce themselves; but no person can live through another. To give up consumption is to give up life. It is to this original need that we should relate the continuance of humanity, and it is to the means of providing for this need that we should relate the increase of humanity which we call *population*. Subsistence, or consumption,[1] is therefore at the heart of the matter which we are now discussing, and is the essence of population. Let us seek in the ways of nature and in the lessons of experience for the best methods of enabling the human race to subsist and increase.

It is commonly believed that need is the principle of the impulse which we call *desire*. But to argue thus is to confuse men with beasts. The only desire of the beast is to satisfy its present appetites; but man has more far-reaching views about happiness, and his desire to satisfy his appetites is only, as it were, a diversion from his dominant propensity, which is to desire the enjoyment of full and continual happiness, even if he does not make a perfectly clear distinction between the object of his desire and the aim of his enjoyment. This is the distinctive and superior characteristic of the human species. Those who seek to satisfy this desire through refinements in the satisfaction of their appetites lower themselves deliberately and to no purpose to the level of the farmyard. The others set themselves aims which are appropriate to their characters, their prepossessions and their faculties, and which are more or less satisfying according to the extent that they are free from the fetters of bestiality.[2] From this source have arisen the various idols of our moral passions—freedom, greed, ambition, fame, sensibility, etc.

It is from this point of view that politics ought to introduce man into its speculations. Man is compelled to obtain subsistence and induced to obtain enjoyment; and it follows from this that the subsistence which it is least troublesome to obtain is naturally that which suits him best. Thus politics, which is the art of making men useful, and the first of whose cares must be to procure subsistence for them, takes no account of the main motive force of its object if it sets in motion, in order to attain it, nothing but need, and either through ignorance or false principles neglects the most pressing and flexible spring of action—*desire*. It would be capable of governing only savages and beasts. The conjunction of these two motive forces,

[1] *Dépense.* R.L.M. [2] *Fers de la brutalité.* R.L.M.

need and *desire*, is the principle and the effect of society. The closer they are brought together, the more their driving power is directed towards the same object, and the more tightly-knit and consolidated does society become. The more the ties which bind them together are allowed to be loosened, on the other hand, the more do they part company, and the nearer therefore does society tend towards dissolution.

Such is the point from which we must start if we are to consider, in the light of the true principles of politics,[1] the different forms of society to be found in ancient and modern times, in order to come to a proper decision about the means of enabling them to increase in goods, strength, and population—three things which are indissolubly bound up together in the natural order, the necessary foundation of the political order. Man is compelled by need to seek his food, and induced by desire to obtain it for himself, and to secure it with the least possible toil and trouble. Such are the contrasting factors which perpetually bring human beings closer to one another, and which perpetually tend to separate them. Such is the source of that monstrous state of affairs in which, when order is subverted, men are almost always at war and engaged in slaughtering one another. This is the light which should guide us from now on in our examination of the principles of different societies.

In the beginning, man found himself faced with uninhabited spaces which, in relation to the small number of the first human beings, abounded in goods suitable for subsistence. At first they were able to consume the spontaneous gifts of nature without making any effort, and to enjoy freedom and idleness, the first objects of desire in uncultured and ignorant men. But the fruits of the earth last only for a short time, and do not come back until the following year, whereas man eats every day. He saw population increase, and the means of subsistence become proportionately more troublesome to acquire. Thus it was necessary for him to seek for new things on which to subsist. He had to cultivate the land, whence arose agricultural nations. He had to herd together and rear domestic animals, which was the origin of herdsmen. And he had to hunt wild animals and set traps for them, and do the same also for fish, which was the origin of hunters and fishermen.

Of these three modes of life, derived from three different kinds of subsistence, the first gives rise to settled laws, weights, measures, and everything which is concerned with determining and guaranteeing possessions. It was necessary, before putting one's toil and sweat into the regular cultivation of a piece of land, to be assured of the possession of the harvest and the enjoyment of its fruits. The second kept innocence and hospitality alive for a longer time, and devoted

[1] *En vrai politique.* R.L.M.

itself to the sciences, to astronomy, and to speculation. A life which was busy but without strain, abundant but without excess, constrained but without fetters, must have made human nature appear in its best light. Very few laws were needed by men whom nothing tempted to escape from the laws of nature. The third, finally, although the most contemptible and founded on the least secure basis, was in general better adapted to natural licentiousness, to the brutish man. The only laws it could accept were those relating to the formation of aggressive forces, the laws of invasion; for the laws of stability are based on the physical extent of the means of subsistence, which in this case were all fortuitous, uncertain and scattered. By virtue of these same principles, the first of these three kinds of society was settled, the second nomadic, and the third vagrant, piratical and marauding—always in accordance with the nature and kind of their means of subsistence.

Of these three forms of society, the first could very soon become populous in areas which had to rely on the fertility of the soil to increase the means of subsistence. The second only admitted of a small number of men entrusted with the care of flocks and herds— a small number, that is, in relation to the wide expanse of land required for pasturage. The third could be populous only in proportion to what was provided in the way of booty; and as it took no care at all to maintain and renew what was provided in this way, it must very quickly have been forced to rush headlong into marauding and to act aggressively against its neighbours, who had formed themselves into industrious or peaceful societies. The most ancient, reliable, and authentic annals of humanity (abstracting from all other ways of looking at them) corroborate the conjectures we have made on the basis of the nature of things. Cain, the first leader of husbandmen, we are told in the scriptures, invented weights and measures. Abraham and Lot, the sons of fellow-herdsmen, virtuous and bound together in friendship, were nevertheless forced to separate from one another, because together they were unable to subsist, increase, and multiply.[1] Nimrod, the first known leader of hunters, was also the first conqueror—a characteristic which can only be a consequence of marauding.

Time and the multiplication of the human species were naturally bound to lead to these different societies intermingling and uniting with one another: to the herdsmen settling down and becoming husbandmen, like the race of Abraham, or scattering out over distant regions, like the Arabs, the Tartars, the primitive nations of the north, and the nomadic peoples of America.

[1] *Genesis*, chapter 13. Cf. John Millar, *The Origin of the Distinction of Ranks* (1806 edn.), pp. 154–5, for an equally unembarrassed but rather more sophisticated use of this passage. R.L.M.

Of these nations, those which sooner or later adopted and practised the primitive art of agriculture have sooner or later come to enjoy the benefits of society, of union, of population, of good and equitable laws, and of the appropriate arts and skills. The others have grown old in a state of barbarism, and have to some extent declined every day in numbers, in skill, and in faculties of all kinds.

I say that these different kinds of society have intermingled and united with one another, because it was in fact necessary, in order to make a society complete, that it should adopt and take into its midst the seeds and characteristics of each of these original kinds. Agriculture constituted its foundation, but the rearing and feeding of live-stock became necessary in order to link the plains with the mountains, the pastures with the crops, and the grass-lands[1] with cultivation. The art of war, which it became necessary for it to take up in order to ensure the security of its territory, was soon bound to dominate it, both by the weight of its armies and by the direction and employment of the time it devoted to matters of public concern, while each individual attended to his own affairs. This predomination, necessarily constrained by equitable rules without which it would have led to invasions and the destruction and dispersal of society, constituted the basis of the sovereign authority created by the laws. The art of politics, maintained by force, has need of a leader; and government, having become capable of some extension, was naturally bound to fall into the hands of one man. From this originates the tutelary monarchy.

From the interrelationships and drawing together of the different societies there is born a new kind of secondary and artificial society, less secure so far as its basis and duration are concerned, less capable of extension, and unable to form a great empire, but nevertheless free, wealthy, and powerful within its narrow boundaries. Such societies, however, are transitory and subject to change, owing to their excesses, to their carelessness, or to the enterprise of their neighbours, since the way in which they are constituted renders them too much exposed to competition. These are commercial societies.

We have said that the division of the land was necessarily the primary law of the formation of agricultural societies. The distinction between thine and mine was here established in relation to the land, which was done only in order to ensure that it should be firmly established in relation to the fruits of the land. The exchange of the surplus of these fruits for the surplus of a neighbour in whose products the society was deficient was a natural consequence of this state of affairs, so that the exchange of goods through trade became the primary tie binding society together. Mercantile and resale trade, although its basis was only secondary in character and dependent

[1] *Les engrais.* R.L.M.

upon cultivation, was nevertheless so necessary that it afforded an assured means of subsistence. Whenever we speak of means of subsistence we speak of gain, which here consists in the recompense due for the service of distributing goods among the nations. Thus alongside the agricultural societies there could be, and were bound to be, set up commercial societies, just as granaries are set up alongside crops. The republican form of government is appropriate to these societies.

The very mainstay and organizational structure of these societies would contain the seeds of freedom. In reality, the basis of their subsistence was their industry, their knowledge of routes and of the surpluses and needs of different areas, and the reputation which they acquired because people grew accustomed to finding them always successful and always scrupulous in fulfilling their obligations. All their possessions consisted of scattered and secret securities,[1] a few warehouses, and passive and active debts,[2] whose true owners are to some extent unknown, since no one knows which of them are paid and which of them are owing. No wealth which is immaterial or kept in people's pockets[3] can ever be got hold of by the sovereign power, and consequently will yield it nothing at all. This is a truth which should be constantly repeated to the governments of those agricultural nations which take such pains to school themselves to become merchants, i.e. to plunder themselves. The wealthy merchant, trader, banker, etc., will always be a member of a republic. In whatever place he may live, he will always enjoy the immunity which is inherent in the scattered and unknown character of his property, all one can see of which is the place where business in it is transacted.[4] It would be useless for the authorities to try to force him to fulfil the duties of a subject: they are obliged, in order to induce him to fit in with their plans, to treat him as a master, and to make it worth his while[5] to contribute voluntarily to the public revenue. Such is his essential character, and such indeed it is important that it should be.

Commercial societies, designated by the name of counting-houses[6] and thus constituted free by nature, but obliged to make for themselves laws relating to association, warehousing, and security, continue to have recourse to sovereign power, without which important cases would never be resolved and the situation of individuals and the public would never be secure. But this sovereign power is mixed in character, and changes with changes in the things from which profit is made, in the uncertain means of subsistence. This kind of sovereign power admits of only a small number of fundamental laws,

---

[1] *Obligations.* R.L.M.
[2] *Dettes passives & actives*, i.e. liabilities and assets. R.L.M.
[3] *Richesse de tête & de poche.* R.L.M.   [4] *Le lieu du comptoir.* R.L.M.
[5] *L'intéresser réellement.* R.L.M.   [6] *Comptoirs.* R.L.M.

because the basis of sovereignty is stability, and few things have a stable character when possessions are of this type. On the other hand, it includes a large number of regulations relating to selling and police, because everything in this state of affairs is based upon continual activity, which changes according to different circumstances, and it is necessary at every moment to make provision for the decision of cases and to deal in an orderly and methodical way with a multiplicity of events, which is the general object of all legislation. It follows from this that a sovereign power of such a type has no need of a leader, and indeed that it would not be possible for it to rest in the hands of one man. It is necessary that the members of the social body who share in its benefits should themselves have an eye to instructing and assisting the sovereign power: here we have a republic. Such a state, moreover, does not have a continual need for military forces. Helpful to its neighbours and engaged in serving them, it civilizes them in making them wealthy, or rather in conferring the attribute of wealth on their goods. It is rather from its own arrogance, the child of prosperity, that it has everything to fear. If it alters its character, and exalts itself to the height of its ambition, it will perish, either as a result of its success which will soon cause it to discover a leader in its midst, or as a result of the interruption or evasion of its trade, or as a result of reverses which reduce it to a province of some neighbouring state—which so reduce, that is, its small maritime territory, for so far as its trade is concerned it escapes and will always escape conquest and oppression, through the flight and transplantation of those men whose wealth is scattered over different countries. Thus the more energetic and parsimonious these precariously-placed nations are in their prosperity, the more useful and worthy of commendation will they be so far as the agricultural states which border upon them are concerned, and the more it will be in the interests of the latter, when well governed, to favour and support them.

Such is the origin, the basis, and the form of the different kinds of society.

C.

MISCELLANEOUS EXTRACTS

1. EXTRACTS FROM THE ECONOMIC MANUSCRIPTS[1]

(i) Different kinds of government depend principally upon the nature of states. The republican form is appropriate to commercial or trading nations, and the monarchical form to nations which live by their land or to brigand peoples who live by their incursions into the land of others. Despotism is a consequence of tyrannical monarchical government: the sovereign power, the prince, and the nation are then subjugated by a superior power to which the prince has turned in order to assure his tyrannical domination and which brings the prince and the nation under subjection. From this arise ecclesiastical despotism, feudal despotism, and the despotism of military forces. It is true that there are republican governments in nations which are not commercial, and despotic governments among commercial peoples. It is indeed almost inevitable that despotism, above all military despotism, should reduce a people to commerce, that feudal despotism should reduce it to slavery, and that ecclesiastical despotism should superabound in celibatarian and clerical institutions. But the republican form of government is the most advantageous for commercial nations, just as the monarchical form would be the most appropriate for those which live by their land if it did not degenerate

[1] All the six extracts in this section have been translated direct from marginal notes by Quesnay written on certain manuscripts by Mirabeau which are to be found in the *Archives Nationales*. Details of the sources are as follows:

Extract (i): From Quesnay's marginal notes written on p. 15 of one of the drafts of Mirabeau's introduction to an unpublished work which was to be entitled *Traité de la Monarchie* or *Essai sur la Monarchie* (M. 778, no. 1). The notes were probably written in 1758.

Extract (ii): From Quesnay's marginal notes written on p. 17 of ibid.

Extract (iii): From Quesnay's marginal notes written on pp. 5–6 of one of the drafts of section 2 (*Progrès de la Monarchie*) of the same work (M. 778, no. 1).

Extract (iv): From Quesnay's marginal notes written on p. 7 of ibid.

Extract (v): From Quesnay's marginal notes written on p. 23 of ibid.

Extract (vi): From Quesnay's marginal notes written on p. 55 of a draft of Mirabeau's *Mémoire sur l'Agriculture* (M. 783, no. 5). The notes were probably written in 1759.

The text of extract (vi) has been published in Weulersse, *Les Manuscrits Economiques de François Quesnay et du Marquis de Mirabeau aux Archives Nationales* (1910), pp. 36–7. The text of the other extracts, so far as I am aware, has not been published. R.L.M.

into arbitrary power which destroys sovereignty and oppresses the people.

(ii) The historians concern themselves only with military expeditions, with marvellous happenings, in order to entertain and interest their readers, just as times of war entertain newsmongers. These authors take no account of the composition, the behaviour, and the advantages and disadvantages of governments, the states of prosperity or decline of kingdoms, the changes in the customs of nations, and the other most fundamental matters of history, upon which depend the sensational events, the revolutions, all the exploits, and the happiness and unhappiness of peoples. They concern themselves only with the senseless, tumultuous, violent, and disordered actions of nations. They are neither observers, nor philosophers, nor politicians; they are for the most part nothing but tellers of stories of sensational events, without discernment, insight, or penetration. All histories of states are very much alike: they consist only of tales of sieges, battles, conquests, and cruelties, of descriptions of the sovereign, and never of histories of nations, of the state of their power, their laws, their wealth, their manners, and their expenditure, of the condition of the different kinds of subsistence, their military discipline, their policies, their customs, their industry, their trade, their agriculture, their population, and their administration, of the causes of their prosperity and their decay.

(iii) The whole of this account simply sets out the disordered state of affairs among nomadic and conquering nations, which live on the plunder from vanquished nations, and which can continue in this state of brigandage only so long as they can expand by conquest and pillage. These voracious nations are simply collections of men who have no ties binding them together other than the common purpose of providing for their subsistence by force. For subsistence is the primary object of all societies. This object must never be lost sight of in the constitution of governments: everything else is only modification.[1] Disorder, barbarity, cruelty, heroism, domination, order, politics, courtesy, patriotism, humanity, the sciences, the arts, economic government, legislation, the assured possession of property, and customs, are nothing but the means and the results of different forms of society employed in different ways in satisfying, more or less abundantly and with more or less ease or difficulty, their needs. Brigand nations, which sometimes enjoy abundance but which more often live in poverty, put their trust only in force, violence, and pillage. Agricultural nations, abundantly supplied as a result of the products which are annually regenerated from the land which they

---

[1] *Tout le reste n'est que modification.* R.L.M.

cultivate and the peaceful trade which they carry on with other nations, establish their security only through force and good order. Each of these agricultural nations, then, should be regarded as being divided into two classes of men, one military and the other tax-paying. Both are equally essential to the happiness and protection of the nation. The second has the duty of providing for the needs of the first, and the first has the duty of assuring the wealth which enables both to subsist. This is the fundamental object of the government of agricultural nations; but each nation is composed of a multitude of individuals, of families, and of different orders of citizens distributed among different employments, and each of these has the right to enjoy on his own account the same security as that which is established for the protection of the whole. From this arises the necessity for a public guard, for stable regulations of economic government, and for an absolute authority to create and maintain internal security; and upon this more or less perfect constitution depend order, manners, talents, sciences, activity or idleness,[1] politeness or rudeness, patriotic zeal or indifference, wealth, value or debasement of value, and the strength or weakness of the nation. The strength of an agricultural nation consists at root of its wealth and its population. The population of a state is always proportionate to its wealth, but wealth is not always proportionate to population; and when population exceeds wealth it creates these brigand hosts which set out to make war with neighbouring nations in order to carry off their wealth. Wealth can bring about either the destruction or the defence of the peoples who possess it. It will constitute their strength if it is employed to build up strong defences, and to maintain large armies which are well disciplined and well paid. It will constitute their ruin if it simply attracts the enemy to plunder it, if it plunges the wealthy nation into sensual pleasures, slackness, and false confidence, and if each inhabitant, as a bad citizen, concerns himself only with his individual fortune. The army of the wealthy Carthaginians perished in extreme poverty, while that of their greedy enemy was in a state of abundance. The moderate wealth of the Romans easily subjugated the opulence of Carthage.

(iv) *Mirabeau's text reads as follows:*

As to the native disposition[2] of peoples, I venture to say that it is something which is more real and perhaps more insurmountable than the influence of climate. The different families which in a short time populated the three parts of the world bore with them from the beginning, each on its own part, an absolutely different native dis-

---

[1] The manuscript becomes rather illegible at this point, and I have been obliged to omit about a dozen words. R.L.M.
[2] *Génie.* R.L.M.

position, doubtless derived from that of the chief of the tribe, and perhaps relative in the sight of Providence to the diversity of the courses which they were destined to take.

Quesnay strikes out all the words after 'derived' and substitutes the following:
... from the behaviour and the manner of life to which the different nations devoted themselves in order to procure their subsistence and to conform to the advantages and disadvantages of the places and circumstances to which they were subjected.

(v) Conquests are too often envisaged as revolutions of government, which is only true in the case of the wars of barbarous nations, and is rarely so in the case of the wars of civilized nations. For the government has already been formed in the conquering country and in the country which is defeated, so that the changes of government as a result of conquests do not affect the institutions as a whole, and indeed are often hardly noticeable.

(vi) The little discoveries, the curious little experiments of Academies of Science, the little pieces of research, the dubious little dissertations of antiquaries, seem only frivolities in comparison with the study of the essential objects of economic government, considered in their different relations and from the point of view of their different results. This is the key to the history of nations, so far as concerns their power, their successes, their prosperity, their glory, their poverty, their decline, and their decay. What then are our historians? People who tell stories of battles, sieges, political dealings, craft and guile, the different roles played by great men in politics, war, religion, and love-affairs. They have taken no account of the state of the foundation upon which the nations which have undergone the revolutions they have told about are based.

2. EXTRACT FROM 'MEN'[1]

Armies are the instrument for the defence of the state; but it is the state itself which defends itself, by means of its strength and its intelligence, i.e. its wealth and its political negotiations. A historian passes down to posterity the military exploits of his nation, and dazzles his readers with the marvels involved in operations of war. But if he takes no account of the resources of economic and political administration the book he writes will be more entertaining than

[1] Translated from the text as reproduced in I.N.E.D., II, p. 520. R.L.M.

instructive: it will be a history of wars, and not a history of peace treaties and the causes of victory in war.

It is a good thing that the soldier and the officer, whose functions are limited to making military expeditions, should believe that the nation's fate depends solely upon the success of sieges and battles; that they should think that a highly-populated state is very powerful because it can supply a greater number of fighting men; and that they should be aware of the fact that sturdy peasants make better soldiers than townspeople. But a government which has a more extended range of vision will not depopulate the countryside and destroy the source of the state's revenue in order to pursue a particular good which is so opposed to the general good.

3. EXTRACTS FROM 'RURAL PHILOSOPHY'[1]

(i) Morals are with good reason regarded as the shield of a nation; but it is cultivation, that cornucopia, which governs morals. When the political speculations of a nation throw it into disorder, they damage its basis; morals become trivial, and then need obliges men to have recourse to the most irregular expedients; for political irregularity causes men to act in a disorderly way. Poverty follows, and morals are engulfed by violence and robbery. Why? Because when everyone is in need but few are engaged in labour, you are bound to find thieves and, in a word, extreme poverty. Then everything is reduced to cunning, dissoluteness, injustice, wrangling, enmity, and partisanship. If the fruits of ownership and the recompense due to labour are restored and assured, men will of their own accord set themselves back again within the moral order. Here we find the true foundations of natural law and the civil order. If the moralists and politicians do not base their sciences on the economic order, on agriculture,[2] their speculations will be useless and illusory: they will be doctors who perceive only the symptoms and ignore the disease. Those who depict for us the morals of their age without going back to causes are only speculators and not philosophers. The reformers and critics who try to set themselves in opposition to a stream without changing its gradient lay themselves open to public ridicule. Morals are the natural effects of causes. Causes which

---

[1] These extracts are translated from the text of the 1764 edition of the *Philosophie Rurale*, Vol. I, pp. 114–15 and 117, and Vol. II, pp. 46–8. On several occasions when the wording of the 1764 edition appeared to be dubious, reference was made to the one-volume edition of 1763, and to the manuscript drafts of the *Philosophie Rurale* in the *Archives Nationales*, M. 779. On the question of the authorship of these extracts, see above, pp. 37–8, note. R.L.M.

[2] *La charrue*. R.L.M.

destroy the basis destroy morals, making them degenerate into ignorance and individual interests, which in their turn become the shield and support of irregularities and perversions. If we consider the state of nations with our eyes open, we will always find that moral disorders are in proportion to political irregularities, and follow the same progression.

(ii) The whole magic of well-ordered society is that each man works for others, while believing that he is working for himself. This magic, the general character and effects of which are revealed by the subject we are studying, shows us that the Supreme Being bestowed upon us as a father the principles of economic harmony, when he condescended to announce and prescribe them to us, as God, in the form of religious laws.

(iii) The writers who have handed down to us the history of the revolutions which states have experienced tell us only about the revolutions affecting thrones and disdain to describe those affecting the wealth of nations—upon which, notwithstanding, all thrones whatsoever are solely based. No doubt this important point has not appeared to them to be worthy of their attention, or suitable for the entertainment of their readers. They believe that the lot of the masses does not touch hearts given over to passions or move imaginations greedy for marvels. But it is not to such readers as this that history can be useful; and the historian-philosophers should not have confined themselves to working in so useless a way for posterity,[1] and to satisfying the tastes of trivial men. The ruin of Spain in the reign of Philip II, that revolution which was so long-lasting and which had such an influence on the events which have since occurred in Europe, has not been remarked upon so far as either its effects or its causes are concerned.[2] People have attempted to explain it simply as a consequence of the discovery of the mines of Peru, which carried off a part of Spain's population—at a time when these mines, disastrous for the inhabitants of the country, constituted the sole wealth of the conqueror, the sole support of his domination, and the sole resource of his unfortunate subjects, who expatriated themselves and withdrew everywhere. It is nevertheless to the gold of Peru that the depopulation of Spain has been attributed, whereas it was the gold of Peru itself which propped up the ruins of that monarchy. But this gold has

---

[1] *Prospérité* in the 1764 edition and the one-volume edition of 1763, but *postérité* in the three manuscript drafts. I have taken *postérité* as the correct reading. R.L.M.

[2] The 1764 edition has here '*n'a été remarquée ni dans ses effets*'. The one-volume edition of 1763 and the three manuscript drafts, however, have '*n'a ete remarquee ni dans ses causes ni dans ses effets*', which I have taken as the correct reading. R.L.M.

not been sufficient to re-establish it, and to restore to it the many milliards of which it has been stripped by its foolhardy and unjust wars and its fantastic and insatiable intrigues. The arbitrary prince, who was alike ambitious, greedy, vain, and presumptuous, removed all the revenue, all the wealth involved in the cultivation of the kingdom, and all the expenditure, out of his country and into the very nations which he sought to ruin. He presented them with troops with which to make war against him; and the final result of this madness was that his successors, inheriting a devastated state and a disastrous policy, were to see the complete degradation of Spain and its resources; and this deserted monarchy remained shut up inside an area which was circumscribed and protected by natural barriers.

As we have shown, in the order prescribed by the Author of nature the expenditure of wealth must necessarily precede the reproduction of wealth. A nation which has been stripped of its wealth can no longer cause wealth to be generated. In this situation, the more populous it is the more devouring do its needs become, and the more impossible it is for it to subsist and re-establish itself, if the desertion of the nation—its last resource—does not provide relief to its wretched people in another country. Thus it is not enough to have plenty of men, or, as it is said, plenty of hands, in order to have wealth and strength: on the contrary, it is through the medium of wealth that men and hands are obtained.

TRANSLATIONS

II. THE ENCYCLOPEDIA ARTICLES

A.

EXTRACT FROM 'CORN'[1]

In order to obtain a better understanding of the advantages of foreign trade in *corn*, it is necessary to make a few fundamental observations about trade in general, with particular reference to trade in manufactured commodities and trade in raw produce; for re-export trade,[2] which consists simply in buying in order to sell again, is conducted only by a few small states which have no means of livelihood other than to become merchants. And since this kind of foreign trade is not worth any attention in the case of a large kingdom, we shall confine ourselves to comparing the advantages of the two other branches of trade, in order to arrive at an understanding of what interests us most.

MAXIMS OF ECONOMIC GOVERNMENT

I. *Industrial work does not increase wealth.* Agricultural work compensates for the costs involved, pays for the manual labour employed in cultivation, provides gains for the husbandmen, and, in addition, produces the revenue of landed property. Those who buy industrial goods pay the costs, the manual labour, and the gain accruing to the merchants; but these goods do not produce any revenue over and above this.

[1] Translated from the text as reproduced in I.N.E.D., II, pp. 495–510. R.L.M.
[2] *Commerce de trafic.* R.L.M.

Thus all the expenses involved in making industrial goods are simply drawn from the revenue of landed property; for work which does not produce any revenue at all can continue in being only by reason of the wealth of those who pay for it.

If you compare the gains received by the workers who make industrial goods with those of the workers whom the husbandman employs in the cultivation of the land, you will find that the gains in both cases are confined to the subsistence of these workers; that these gains do not constitute an expansion of wealth; and that the value of the industrial goods is proportionate to the very value of the subsistence which the workers and merchants consume. Thus the artisan destroys in the form of subsistence as much as he produces by his labour.

Thus no increase of wealth occurs in the production of industrial goods, since the value of these goods increases only by the cost of the subsistence which the workers consume. The big fortunes of merchants should never be looked at in a different light: they arise from large commercial enterprises which gather together gains similar to those of small merchants, just as large industrial enterprises[1] create large fortunes by virtue of the small profits which are derived from the labour of a large number of workers. All these entrepreneurs make fortunes only because other people engage in expenditure. Thus there is no increase of wealth.

The principle of wealth lies in the source of men's subsistence. Industry prepares wealth for the use of men. The proprietors, in order to have the enjoyment of it, pay for industrial work, and by this means their revenue becomes common to all men.

Thus men increase in proportion to the revenue of landed property. One group of men causes this wealth to be generated by means of cultivation; another group prepares it for use; and those who have the enjoyment of it pay both of these groups.

If we are to have wealth and men, then, we must have landed property, men, and wealth. Thus a state which was peopled only with merchants and artisans could subsist only by means of the revenue of the landed property of foreign countries.

II. *Industrial work contributes to population and to the increase of wealth.* If a nation gains a million livres through its labour by selling abroad manufactured commodities which it makes at home, and if it also sells abroad a million livres' worth of its raw produce, both of these products equally represent an addition to its wealth and are equally advantageous to it, provided that it has more men than the revenue of the kingdom's land can support. For in that case a certain

[1] *Entreprises de grands travaux.* R.L.M.

number of these men can subsist only through the manufactured commodities which they sell abroad.

In this case a nation draws from its land and its men the maximum product which can be drawn from them; but it gains much more from the sale of a million livres' worth of its raw produce than it does from the sale of a million livres' worth of manufactured commodities, because in the case of the latter it gains only the value of the artisan's labour, whereas in the case of the former it gains the value of the labour of cultivation and also the value of the materials produced by the land. Thus, given that the sums received from the sale of these different commodities are equal, trade in raw produce is always proportionately much more advantageous.

III. *Industrial work which employs men to the detriment of the cultivation of landed property has a harmful effect on population and the increase of wealth.* If a nation which sells abroad a million livres' worth of manufactured commodities and a million livres' worth of raw produce has insufficient men employed in farming its landed property, it loses a great deal through the employment of the men engaged in making manufactured commodities for export, because in such a case men can give themselves over to this labour only to the detriment of the revenue of the land, and because the product of the labour of men who cultivate the land can be two or three times as great as that arising from the making of manufactured commodities.

IV. *It is the wealth of the cultivators which causes the wealth employed in cultivation to be generated.*[1] The product of the labour of cultivation may be worth nothing or almost nothing to the state when the cultivator cannot meet the costs necessary for proper cultivation. A poor man whose labour extracts from the land only produce of little value, such as potatoes, buckwheat, chestnuts, etc., who feeds himself on them, and who buys nothing and sells nothing, works simply for himself alone. He lives in extreme poverty; neither he nor the land he cultivates bring in anything for the state.

Such is the effect of destitution in those parts of the country where there are no husbandmen in a position to employ the peasants, and where these peasants are too poverty-stricken to be able to procure by their own efforts anything but poor food and poor clothing.

Thus the employment of men in cultivation may be useless in a kingdom which lacks the wealth necessary to prepare the land so that it will yield abundant harvests. But the revenue of landed property is always assured in a kingdom which is well furnished with wealthy husbandmen.

[1] *Les richesses des cultivateurs font naître les richesses de la culture.* R.L.M.

V. *Industrial work contributes to the increase of the revenue of landed property, and the revenue of landed property maintains industrial work.* A nation which, owing to the fertility of its soil and difficulties of transport, had every year a surplus of produce which it was unable to sell to its neighbours, but which was able to sell them manufactured commodities which were readily transportable, would have an interest in attracting into the country a large number of manufacturers and artisans, who would consume the produce of the country, sell their goods abroad, and increase the nation's wealth through their gains and their consumption.

But it is not easy to arrange matters in this way, because manufacturers and artisans gather together in a country only in proportion to the current revenue of the nation, i.e. in proportion to the existence of proprietors or merchants who are able to buy their goods at prices which are about as high as those for which they could sell them elsewhere, and who are able to provide a market for them as fast as they are made. And this is hardly possible in the case of a nation which itself lacks a market for its produce, and in which the value-lessness of this very produce means that sufficient revenue is not at present being yielded to enable manufacturing businesses[1] to be set up.

Such a scheme can only be put into effect very slowly. Several nations which have tried it have even found it impossible to succeed in it.

Nevertheless this is the only case in which the government of a fertile kingdom could usefully concern itself with the improvement of industry.

For, when trade in raw produce is unobstructed and free, manufacturing work is always bound to be assured by the revenue of landed property.

VI. *A nation having a large trade in raw produce can always maintain, at any rate on its own part, a large trade in manufactured commodities.* For it can always pay, in proportion to the revenue of its landed property, the workers who make the manufactured goods which it needs.

Thus trade in industrial goods appertains just as surely to such a nation as trade in raw produce.

VII. *A nation which has little trade in raw produce, and which is reduced to trade in industrial goods in order to subsist, is in a precarious and uncertain position.* For its trade can be taken away from it by other rival nations which devote themselves more successfully to the same trade.

[1] *Des manufactures et des travaux de main-d'oeuvre.* R.L.M.

Moreover, such a nation is always subject to and dependent upon those which sell it primary necessities. It is obliged to economize very rigorously, because it has no revenue at all to spend, and because it can extend and maintain its trade, industry, and navigation only by stinting itself. Those nations which possess landed property, on the other hand, increase their revenue by means of their consumption.

VIII. *A large internal trade in manufactured commodities can continue to exist only through the medium of the revenue of landed property.* It is necessary to investigate the proportion in which a kingdom's trade in industrial goods is divided between external and internal trade. For if the internal trade in manufactured commodities amounted, for example, to three million livres, and the external trade to one million, then three-quarters of the total trade in manufactured commodities would be paid for by the revenue of the nation's landed property, since foreign countries would pay only one-quarter of it.

In this case, the revenue of landed property would constitute the main wealth of the kingdom, and the main object of the government would be to keep a watch on the maintenance and increase of the revenue of landed property.

The means consist in freedom of trade and the preservation of the wealth of the cultivators. In the absence of these conditions, revenue, population, and the products of industry are wiped out.

Agriculture produces two kinds of wealth, namely the annually-produced revenue of the proprietors, and the restitution of the costs involved in cultivation.

The revenue ought to be spent in order that it may be circulated annually among the whole people and provide funds for the state.

The wealth employed in meeting the costs of cultivation ought to be set apart for the cultivators and exempted from all taxation; for if it is appropriated, agriculture is destroyed, the gains of the country people are wiped out, and the source of the state's revenue is blocked up.

IX. *A nation with a large territory which causes the price of its raw produce to fall in order to favour the making of manufactured goods completely destroys itself.* For if the cultivator is not compensated for the heavy costs entailed in cultivation, and if he makes no gain, agriculture is ruined; the nation loses the revenue of its landed property; manufacturing work diminishes, because this work can no longer be paid for by the proprietors of landed property; and the country is depopulated through poverty and through the desertion of manufacturers, artisans, labourers, and peasants, who can subsist only in proportion to the gains which are procured for them by the nation's revenue.

Then the kingdom's strength is destroyed, its wealth is wiped out, the people are overburdened with taxes, and the sovereign's revenue diminishes. Thus a policy based on such grave misconceptions would alone suffice to ruin a state.

X. *The advantages of external trade do not consist in the increase of monetary wealth.* The surplus of wealth procured by a nation's external trade may not take the form of a surplus of monetary wealth, because external trade with foreign countries may be conducted on the basis of an exchange[1] for other commodities which are consumed by the nation in question. But what this nation comes into possession of is none the less wealth, which it could by means of thrift convert into monetary wealth for other uses.

Raw produce, moreover, considered as a commodity, is at the same time both monetary wealth and real wealth. A husbandman who sells his corn to a merchant is paid in money. With this money he pays the proprietor, the *taille*, and his servants and workmen, and buys the commodities which he needs. The merchant who sells the corn to a foreign country, and buys another commodity from it, or who trades with it on a barter basis, resells on his return the commodity he has brought back and with the money he receives once again buys corn. Thus corn, considered as a commodity, represents monetary wealth for the sellers and real wealth for the buyers.

Thus saleable produce ought always to be regarded by a state equally as monetary wealth and as real wealth, which subjects may make use of as it suits them.

A nation's wealth is not regulated by the amount of monetary wealth. Monetary wealth can increase or diminish without anyone noticing it, for it is always available[2] in a state, by reason of its quantity or its velocity of circulation, in proportion to the abundance and the value of raw produce. Spain, which owns the treasure of Peru, is always impoverished by its needs. England maintains its opulence by means of its real wealth; the paper which represents money in that country has a value which is assured by trade and by the revenue of the nation's property.

Thus it is not the greater or lesser quantity of monetary wealth which determines the wealth of a state; and the prohibition of the export of money from a kingdom, to the detriment of profitable trade, can only be based on some harmful prejudice or other.

What is necessary for the maintenance of a state is true wealth, i.e. wealth which is always renascent, always sought after and always paid for, in order that it may have the enjoyment of it, procure itself conveniences, and satisfy the needs of life.

[1] *Echange.* Quesnay seems to have barter trade in mind here. R.L.M.
[2] *Effective.* R.L.M.

XI. *The state of the balance of trade between different nations does not enable us to ascertain the advantages of trade for each nation and the state of its wealth.* For some nations may be richer in men and in landed property than others; and the latter may have a smaller internal trade, a smaller consumption, and a greater external trade than the former.

Moreover, some nations may have a greater re-export trade than others. The trade which returns them the purchase price of the commodities which they resell constitutes a larger item in their balance, but this trade is not as advantageously based as that of other nations which have a smaller trade but which export their own products.

Trade in manufactured commodities is also deceptive because in the value of the product the value of the raw materials is confused with the value of the labour of manufacture, whereas it ought to be distinguished from it.

XII. *It is by the internal and external trade of a nation, and above all by the state of its internal trade, that its wealth may be judged.* For if it consumes a large quantity of its produce at high prices, its wealth will be proportionate to the abundance and price of the produce it consumes, because this produce in fact constitutes wealth in proportion to its abundance and expensiveness; and by reason of the fact that it can be sold, it can be put to any other use in case of special need. It is sufficient if there is a basis of real wealth.

XIII. *No nation which draws the best possible product from its land, its men, and its navigation ought ever to be envious of the trade of its neighbours.* For it could not with evil intent do anything to encroach upon its neighbours' trade without thereby disorganizing and injuring itself, particularly with respect to the mutual trade which it has established with them.

Thus trading nations which are rivals or even enemies ought to pay more attention to maintaining or if possible extending their own trade, than to trying to do direct damage to that of others. They ought even to favour it, because the mutual trade of nations is reciprocally maintained by the wealth of the buyers and the sellers.

XIV. *In mutual trade, the nations which sell the most necessary or most useful commodities have an advantage over those which sell luxury goods.* A nation whose landed property ensures for it a trade in raw produce, and also, as a consequence, an internal trade in manufactured commodities, is independent of other nations. It trades with the latter only for the purpose of maintaining, facilitating, and extending its external trade; and in order to preserve its independence and its advantage in mutual trade it ought as far as possible to obtain from other nations only luxury goods, and to sell to them commodities necessary to satisfy the needs of life.

The other nations will believe that because of the real value of these different commodities this mutual trade is more advantageous to them. But the advantage always lies with the nation which sells the most useful and necessary commodities.

For then its trade is based on the needs of the others; it sells to them only its surplus, and the burden of its purchases is borne only by its opulence. Their interest in selling to it is greater than its need to buy from them; and it is easier for it to cut down on luxuries than it is for the others to economize on necessities.

It should also be noted that states which devote themselves to the manufacture of luxury goods experience serious vicissitudes. For when times are bad, trade in luxury goods slackens, and the workers find themselves without bread and without work.

Given free trade, France could bring forth an abundance of produce of primary necessity, which would be sufficient both for a large consumption and a large external trade, and which could maintain in the kingdom a large trade in manufactured goods.

But the state of her population does not permit her to employ a large number of men in making luxury goods; and it would even be in her interests, for the sake of facilitating external trade in her raw produce, to maintain mutual trade with foreign countries on the basis of the purchase of luxury goods.

Moreover, she ought not to aspire to an all-embracing general trade. She ought to sacrifice certain of the less important branches of trade in favour of other branches which are more profitable to her and which would increase and assure the revenue of the kingdom's landed property.

Nevertheless all trade ought to be free, because it is in the interests of the merchants to devote themselves to those branches of external trade which are the safest and most profitable.

It is enough for the government to watch over the expansion of the revenue of the kingdom's property; not to put any obstacles in the way of industry; and to give the people the opportunity to spend as they choose;

To revive agriculture by means of vigorous trading activity in those provinces where produce has become valueless;

To do away with prohibitions and hindrances which are detrimental to internal trade and mutual external trade;

To abolish or reduce the excessive rights to charge river dues and tolls, which swallow up the revenues of those remote provinces in which produce can only be sold if it is transported over long distances; those to whom these rights belong will be adequately compensated by their share in the general increase in the revenue of the kingdom's property.

It is no less necessary to do away with the privileges which provinces, towns, and townships have contrived to secure for their own private advantage.

It is also important to facilitate everywhere communications and the transport of commodities, by putting roads and river navigation in order.[1]

It is also essential that trade in the produce of the provinces should not be subjected to temporary and arbitrary prohibitions and licences, which ruin the countryside under the delusive pretext of assuring abundance for the towns. The towns subsist through the expenditure of the proprietors who live in them; thus, by destroying the revenue of landed property, this practice brings no advantage to the towns and no good to the state.

The power to control the nation's revenue should not be left to the mercy of subordinate or private bodies.

The export of *corn* by individual provinces should never be restricted on the grounds that their supplies become exhausted before the other provinces are able to replenish them, so that the inhabitants may for several months be subjected to a scarcity of food which is correctly attributed to the exportation.

For when freedom of export is general, the amount of *corn* sent away is hardly noticeable, since the merchants draw on all parts of the kingdom and above all on the provinces where *corn* is at a low price.

Then there are no longer any provinces where produce may become valueless. Agriculture revives everywhere in proportion to sales.

The progress of trade goes hand in hand with that of agriculture;

---

[1] Country roads and roads communicating with the main highways, the towns, and the markets, are either lacking or in poor condition almost everywhere in the provinces, and this is a serious obstacle to trading operations. Yet it seems that this could be remedied in a few years. The proprietors are too interested in the sale of the produce which is grown on their land to be unwilling to contribute to the expense of repairing these roads. A small tax could therefore be levied on them, assessed at the rate of one sou per livre of the *taille* of their farmers, a tax from which farmers and peasants who had no property would be exempt. The roads to be repaired would be decided upon by the intendants of each district, after consultation with the inhabitants, who would then have the work carried out by entrepreneurs. The most impassable places would be repaired first, and the roads would be successively improved; the farmers and peasants would then be made responsible for their maintenance. Similar arrangements could be made with the provinces in respect of those rivers which could be made navigable. Some provinces have been so fully seized with the utility of such works that they have themselves asked for authority to spend money on them. But the needs of the state have sometimes deprived them of funds earmarked for this purpose; and this lack of success has nipped in the bud arrangements which would have been very conducive to the well-being of the state.

and exportation never takes away more than a surplus which would not come into existence in its absence, and which always maintains abundance and increases the kingdom's revenue.

This increase in revenue expands population and consumption, because expenditure increases and provides gains which attract men.

In this way a kingdom can in a short time progress to a high degree of power and prosperity. Thus by very simple means a sovereign can win victories within his own state which are much more advantageous than those which he could win over his neighbours. Progress is rapid; under Henry IV the impoverished kingdom, burdened with debts, soon became a country of abundance and wealth. See the article *Taxation*.

Remarks on the necessity for wealth in the cultivation of corn. We must never forget that this state of prosperity, to which we are quite capable of aspiring, would be much less the result of the husbandman's work than the product of the wealth which he would be able to employ in the cultivation of the land. It is manure which procures abundant harvests; it is live-stock which produces the manure; and it is money which supplies the live-stock and provides the men to take charge of them. We have seen from the detailed account given above[1] that the costs involved in the small-scale cultivation of 30 million *arpents* of land are only 285 million livres, and that those involved in the thorough large-scale cultivation of the same area would be 710 million livres. But in the first case the product is only 390 millions, whereas in the second it would be 1,378 millions. Higher costs would produce still higher profits. In the case of proper cultivation, the greater expenditure required for the purchase of live-stock and the greater number of men required to look after it, themselves yield a product which is hardly less considerable than that represented by the harvest.[2]

Poor cultivation, however, requires a great deal of labour; but since the cultivator is unable to undertake the necessary expenditure his work is in vain; he goes under, and the bourgeois idiots attribute his lack of success to laziness. They believe, no doubt, that all one needs to do is to run a plough over the land, to tumble it about, in order to compel it to yield good harvests. People are delighted when a poor man who is unemployed is told to *go and plough the land*. It is horses and oxen which ought to plough the land, not men, and it is

---

[1] Quesnay refers to his calculations, made towards the beginning of the article *Grains*, comparing the costs and product involved in small-scale cultivation with those involved in large-scale cultivation. See in particular I.N.E.D., II, pp. 470 and 476–7. R.L.M.

[2] See Quesnay's estimates of the profits from live-stock in the article *Fermiers*, especially in I.N.E.D., II, pp. 450–2. R.L.M.

flocks and herds which ought to fertilize it. Without this assistance it yields little return to the work of the cultivators. And is it not also clear that the land never makes any advances, that on the contrary it makes us wait a long time for the harvest? What then would be the fate of that poor man who is told to *go and plough the land*? Could he cultivate it on his own account? Would he obtain work from the farmers if they are poor? Farmers who find it impossible to meet the costs required for proper cultivation and to pay the wages of servants and workmen cannot employ the peasants. The land, lacking manure and all but uncultivated, can only leave all of them to languish in poverty.

It must also be noted that all the kingdom's inhabitants should profit from the advantages afforded by proper cultivation, if the latter is to be maintained and made capable of producing a large revenue for the sovereign. It is by increasing the revenue of the proprietors and the profit of the farmers that it procures gains for all the other classes and supports a consumption and expenditure by which it is in turn maintained. But if the sovereign imposes taxes on the cultivator himself, if they swallow up his profit, there is a decline in cultivation and a diminution in the proprietors' revenue, whence follows an inevitable retrenchment which affects hired people, merchants, workers, and servants. The general system of expenditure, work, gain, and consumption is thrown out of gear; the state grows weaker; and the tax comes to have a more and more destructive effect. Thus a kingdom can be prosperous and powerful only through the medium of products which are continually renewing themselves or being generated from the wealth of a numerous and energetic people, whose industry is supported and stimulated by the government.

It has been thought that the disturbance which the government can bring about in the fortunes of individuals is a matter of indifference to the state. This is so, it is said, because if some become rich at the expense of others, there is still the same amount of wealth in the kingdom. This idea is false and absurd; for the wealth of a state does not maintain itself on its own, but is maintained and increased only in so far as it is made to renew itself by planning its employment intelligently. If the cultivator is ruined by the financier, the revenue of the kingdom is wiped out; trade and industry languish; the worker is unemployed; the sovereign, the proprietors, and the clergy are deprived of revenue; expenditure and gains become non-existent; and wealth, locked up in the coffers of the financier, remains barren, or, if it is put out at interest, overburdens the state. Thus the government should take special care to maintain unimpaired, in the case of all the productive occupations, the wealth which they require for the production and expansion of the kingdom's wealth.

Remarks on the population maintained by the cultivation of corn.
Finally, it should be recognized that the products of the land do not
by any means constitute wealth in themselves. They constitute wealth
only in so far as they are necessary to man and in so far as they are
exchangeable. Thus they constitute wealth only in proportion to their
consumption and to the number of men who have need of them. No
man who lives in society provides for all his needs with his own labour;
he obtains what he lacks through the sale of the produce of his
labour. Thus everything becomes exchangeable, everything becomes
wealth through the medium of mutual trade between men.[1] If the
number of men in a state diminishes by one-third, its wealth must
diminish by two-thirds, because the expenditure and the product of
each man constitute wealth twice over in the society. A hundred
years ago there were about 24 million people in the kingdom. After
the almost continuous wars over a period of 40 years, and after
the revocation of the Edict of Nantes, it was found as a result of the
census of 1700 that there were still 19½ million. But the disastrous
war over the succession to the Spanish crown, the diminution in the
kingdom's revenue caused by restrictions on trade and arbitrary
taxes, the poverty of the countryside, the exodus of people from the
kingdom, the host of servants whom poverty and the militia force
to withdraw to the big towns where debauchery takes the place of
marriage, the excesses of luxury which are unfortunately paid for by
a cutting down of propagation—all these causes go only too far to
confirm the view of those who believe that the kingdom's population
today has been reduced to 16 million; and of these a large number
living in the countryside are reduced to obtaining their subsistence
by cultivating buckwheat or other kinds of *corn* whose price is very
low; thus they are as of little use to the state through their labour as
they are through their consumption. The peasant is useful in the
countryside only in so far as he engages in production and makes a
gain as a result of his labour, and in so far as his consumption of
decent food and clothing contributes to maintain the price of
produce and the revenue of property, to increase the number and
ensure the gains of the manufacturers and artisans, who can all pay
taxes to the king in proportion to their products and their gains.

Thus it should be clear that if poverty were to increase, or if the
kingdom were to lose another few million men, the wealth which it

---

[1] Cf. Adam Smith, *Wealth of Nations* (Cannan edn.), Vol. I, p. 24: 'When the
division of labour has been once thoroughly established, it is but a very small
part of a man's wants which the produce of his own labour can supply. He
supplies the far greater part of them by exchanging that surplus part of the
produce of his own labour, which is over and above his own consumption, for
such parts of the produce of other men's labour as he has occasion for. Every
man thus lives by exchanging, or becomes in some measure a merchant, and the
society itself grows to be what is properly a commercial society.' R.L.M.

possesses today would diminish very greatly, and other nations would derive a twofold advantage from this disaster. But if the population were to be reduced to a half of what it ought to be, i.e. to a half of what it was a hundred years ago, the kingdom would be laid waste; only a few commercial towns or provinces would be inhabited, and the rest of the kingdom would be left uncultivated; property would no longer produce revenue; and land would everywhere be super-abundant and at the mercy of whoever wanted to have the use of it without paying or even knowing the proprietor.

Land, I repeat, constitutes wealth only because of the fact that its products are necessary to satisfy men's needs, and because it is these needs themselves which lay the basis of wealth. Thus the more men there are in a kingdom with a very extensive and fertile territory the greater its wealth will be. It is cultivation, stimulated by men's needs, which is the most fertile source of wealth and the most important mainstay of population. It supplies the materials which are required to satisfy our needs, and procures revenue for the sovereign and the proprietors. Population increases much more through revenue and expenditure than it does through the propagation of the nation itself.

Remarks on the price of corn. Revenue increases expenditure, and expenditure attracts men who seek gain; foreigners leave their own countries in order to come and share in the prosperity of an opulent nation, and their influx further increases its wealth, by maintaining through consumption the proper price of agricultural produce, and by stimulating through the proper price a plentiful supply of this produce. For not only is the proper price favourable to the progress of agriculture, but it is also in the proper price itself that the wealth which agriculture procures consists. The value of a *setier* of corn, regarded as wealth, consists only in its price. Thus the dearer and more abundant are corn, wine, wool, and live-stock, the more wealth there will be in the state. *Valuelessness plus abundance does not at all equal wealth. Dearness plus dearth equals poverty. Abundance plus dearness equals opulence.*[1] By dearness and abundance I mean per-manent dearness and abundance, for a transitory dearness would not

---

[1] This is the first formulation of what was later to become a famous Physio-cratic maxim: see below, p. 235. The original French reads as follows: '*La non-valeur avec l'abondance n'est point richesse. La cherté avec pénurie est misère. L'abondance avec cherté est opulence.*' Considered in the light of modern value theory the maxim has a paradoxical air, but Quesnay's meaning is fairly clear. An abundance of corn, he is saying, is of little use if its value sinks to zero; and a high price of corn is equally of little use if it is the result of an extreme scarcity of corn. What is required is a state of affairs in which an abundant supply of corn (to satisfy the needs of the people fully) is associated with a high price of corn (to stimulate agricultural investment and general economic progress). R.L.M.

bring about a general circulation of wealth among the whole nation; it would increase neither the revenue of the proprietors nor the revenue of the king; and it would be advantageous only to a few individuals who happened at that time to have produce to sell at a high price.

Thus produce can constitute wealth for the whole nation only through abundance and through a proper price which is constantly maintained by means of proper cultivation, a large consumption, and external trade. It should also be recognized that, relatively to a nation as a whole, abundance together with a proper price which is current abroad represents great wealth for the nation concerned, especially if this wealth consists in agricultural produce; for then it possesses a form of wealth which is limited in each kingdom to the territory which can produce it: thus through its abundance and dearness it always affords an advantage to the nation which possesses the most of it and sells it to the others. For the more wealth in the form of money a kingdom can procure for itself, the more powerful it is, and the more do the opportunities of its individual citizens increase, because money is the only form of wealth which can lend itself to all types of use and determine the strength of nations relatively to one another.

Nations are poor whenever those products of the country which are most necessary for life are selling at low prices. These products are the most precious and most readily exchangeable of goods, and they can become valueless only through a lack of population and external trade. Under these conditions, the source of monetary wealth dries up in areas deprived of the advantages of trade; men are reduced to a bare subsistence, and cannot obtain for themselves the goods which are necessary to satisfy their other needs of life and to ensure the security of their country. Such is the position in our provinces where produce is selling at a very low price, where abundance goes hand in hand with poverty, and where even the hardest labour and the most extreme frugality do not suffice to bring money in. When produce is dear, and revenue and gains increase in proportion, it is possible, through dispositions of an economic character,[1] to diversify one's expenditure, pay one's debts, make acquisitions, set up one's children, etc. It is in the possibility of making such dispositions that the state of well-being resulting from a proper price of produce consists. That is why the towns and provinces of a kingdom in which produce is dear are more highly populated than those in which all the produce sells at too low a price, since this low price wipes out revenue, curtails expenditure, destroys trade, and does away with the gains of all other occupations and the work and wages of artisans and manufacturers. In addition

[1] *Par des arrangements économiques.* R.L.M.

it blots out of existence the revenue of the king, since the greater part of trade for purposes of consumption is carried on by a simple exchange of produce[1] and does not contribute at all to the circulation of money. This means that the king can obtain no dues at all in respect of the consumption of subsistence goods in these provinces, and only very small ones in respect of the revenue of property.

When trade is free, the dearness of produce has necessary limits which are determined by the prices of the produce of other nations which have extended their trade to all parts of the world. The same cannot be said of the valuelessness or dearness of produce caused by the absence of free trade. These follow one another in turn and irregularly. Both are extremely harmful, and are almost always due to unsound government policy.

The ordinary proper price of corn, which procures such a large revenue for the state, does no harm at all to the lower orders. A man's consumption of corn is three *setiers*;[2] if as a result of the establishment of the proper price he were to buy each *setier* at a price four livres higher, this price would at the most cause his expenditure to increase by one sou per day. His wages would also rise proportionately, and this rise in wages would be a matter of little concern to those who paid it, in comparison with the wealth which would result from the establishment of the proper price of corn. Thus the advantages of the proper price of corn are by no means nullified by the rise in the wages of the workers, for this rise is very far from being as great as the rise in the profit of the farmers, the revenue of the proprietors, the yield of the tithes, and the revenue of the king. It is also easy to see that these advantages would not be accompanied by a rise of a twentieth, or perhaps not even of a fortieth, in the prices of the products of the manufacturers, who have been responsible for the unwise prohibitions on the export of our corn and who have caused an immense loss to the state. Besides, it is very harmful to allow the people to get used to buying corn at too low a price. As a result they become less hard-working; they spend little on the bread they eat and become lazy and presumptuous; farmers have difficulty in finding workers and servants and are very badly served by them in years of plenty. It is important that the common people should earn more, and that they should be spurred on by the need to earn. In the last century, when bread was much dearer, the people were used to it, they earned in proportion, and as a result were more hard-working and better off.

Thus when we speak of *dearness* we do not have in mind a price which could ever be excessive, but merely a price which is common

[1] *Par échange de denrees.* R.L.M.
[2] The calculation which follows shows that Quesnay has the man's *annual* consumption in mind. R.L.M.

to our own country and to foreign countries. For on the assumption of freedom of external trade the price will always be regulated by the competition of neighbouring nations in the produce trade.

Those who do not follow the circulation of the wealth of a state to its full extent may object that dearness is advantageous only to the sellers, and that it impoverishes the buyers, so that it reduces the wealth of the latter by as much as it increases the wealth of the former. Dearness, according to this idea, can never under any conditions mean an increase in the state's wealth.

But do not dearness and abundance of agricultural produce increase the profits of the cultivators, and the revenues of the king, the proprietors, and the recipients of the tithes? Does not this wealth itself also cause an increase in expenditure and gains? Do not the labourers, artisans, manufacturers, etc., get paid for their time and their goods in proportion to the cost of their subsistence? The more revenue there is in a state, the more do trade, manufacture, the arts, the crafts, and the other occupations become necessary and remunerative.

But this prosperity can be maintained only through a proper price for our produce; for when the government prevents the sale of the produce of the land and brings down its price, it sets itself against abundance and causes the nation's wealth to diminish in proportion to the extent to which it causes the price of the produce which is converted into money to fall.

A state of affairs in which there was a proper price and abundance existed in the kingdom so long as our *corn* was an object of trade, so long as the cultivation of the land was protected, and so long as the population was large. But the restrictions on the corn trade, the method of imposing taxes, the improper employment of men and wealth in the manufacture of luxury goods, the continual wars and other causes of depopulation and poverty, have wiped out these advantages; and the state loses every year more than three-quarters of the product which the cultivation of *corn* used to yield a century ago, without taking any account of the other losses which inevitably result from this tremendous deterioration in agriculture and population.

B.

EXTRACTS FROM 'MEN'[1]

(i) It is men who constitute the power of states. It is their needs which increase wealth: the more that nations increase the products which they need, and the more of them they consume, the more wealthy they will be. Without use and consumption, the products would be goods lacking utility. It is consumption which makes them exchangeable and maintains their price; and it is the proper price and the abundance of products which determine the revenue or annual wealth of each nation. Thus men, by increasing and consuming products, are themselves the primary and essential cause of their wealth.

Thus it is upon the employment of men and the increase of population that the maintenance and expansion of the successively regenerated wealth of nations depend. The state of the population and of the employment of men is therefore the principal matter of concern in the economic government of states, for the fertility of the soil, the market value of products, and the proper employment of monetary wealth are the results of the labour and industry of men. These are the four sources of abundance, which co-operate in bringing about their own mutual expansion. But they can be maintained only through the proper management of the general administration *of men, goods, and products; a situation in which monetary wealth is valueless* is clear evidence of some unsoundness in government policy, of oppression, and of a nation's decline.

STATE OF THE POPULATION

The population of a state increases in the proportion that the nation's revenue increases, because the revenue procures well-being and gains by which men are maintained and attracted. But it is

Texts of the six extracts translated here will be found in I.N.E.D., II, pp. 511–13, 525–31, 547–9, 553–4, 559 and 560–3. It should be noted, however, that there is a large number of discrepancies, some of them quite serious, between the I.N.E.D. text and that of Quesnay's original manuscript in the *Bibliothèque Nationale* (*Acquisitions Nouvelles Françaises*, no. 1900). My translation therefore follows the original manuscript. I have drawn attention to some of the discrepancies in footnotes. R.L.M.

through the proper employment of men, in conformity with the particular advantages at the disposal of the country, that the nation can cause its revenue to expand.

France, because of its situation, the navigable rivers which run through it, its very extensive and fertile territory, and the fact that its neighbours suffer from a lack of some of the products in which it abounds, can employ a large number of men in agriculture and foreign trade, which constitute the source of the renascent wealth and revenue of nations.

. . . . . .

(ii) *The goods which are most sought after by men, which attract them to a country and cause them to settle there*, consist in exchangeable wealth, in the price, and in monetary wealth.

Exchangeable wealth is that which is exchanged with monetary wealth, in accordance with the price which constitutes its market value. Wealth is marketable or exchangeable only to the extent that its possessors are able to sell it and that it is sought after by purchasers. Thus not all goods constitute marketable wealth: the air which we breathe, the water which we fetch from the river, and all other goods or forms of wealth which are in very plentiful supply and available to everyone, are not exchangeable. They are goods, but not wealth.[1]

Goods whose ownership is stable, like landed property, are also seldom regarded as exchangeable wealth. In fact even the produce of landed property, which is exchangeable and which regulates and maintains the value of the property when it is sold, even that produce which is necessary for men's needs, is not, merely by virtue of its exchangeability, regarded as a profitable form of wealth if its market value does not exceed the value of the work and the other costs which its production demands. That is why we should not confuse all goods which are suitable for men's subsistence, use, and enjoyment, with those items of marketable wealth which are of benefit because of their value in trade.

Men, then, stand in need of the utilities provided by different items of wealth,[2] and those items which they possess over and above their own requirements should serve to enable them to procure those which they lack and desire. Thus men desire a large quantity of the forms of wealth which can be mutually exchanged, one item for another. Such are marketable or exchangeable wealth, and money or monetary wealth: for all kinds of exchangeable wealth can be exchanged through the medium of money, and money can be exchanged for all

[1] Cf. Ricardo, *Principles* (Sraffa edn., I), p. 11: 'Water and air are abundantly useful; they are indeed indispensable to existence, yet, under ordinary circumstances, nothing can be obtained in exchange for them.' R.L.M.

[2] *Différentes richesses usuelles*. R.L.M.

kinds of wealth. Thus through the intermediacy of money, men who possess an item of exchangeable wealth of any kind whatsoever can acquire with it any other kind of exchangeable wealth, in proportion to the relative prices of the items concerned.

The price represents the market value of exchangeable wealth. Thus we should not confuse the price of items of exchangeable wealth with their use value, for these two values rarely have any connection with one another. The use value is always the same, and is always a matter of greater or lesser concern to men according to the relation it bears to their needs and their desire to enjoy it. But the price on the contrary varies, and is dependent upon different causes which are as inconstant as they are independent of men's will. This means that the price is not regulated at all by men's needs, and is far from being an arbitrary value or a value which is established by agreement between the contracting parties.

A diamond, the least useful of items of exchangeable wealth, almost always has a market value which greatly exceeds the market value of wealth in the form of food. For except in the case of an unusually severe scarcity of wealth in the form of food, the market value of a diamond is always much higher than that of this kind of wealth.[1]

But in the case of an extreme scarcity of wealth in the form of food, its price rises without limit, and then it is its use value which determines, by chance, its market value. I say by chance because the dearth or scarcity which raises its price is dependent upon causes which have no connection with the use value of the items of wealth concerned. Thus the value of all items of wealth, regarded from the point of view of their exchangeability, consists only in their price. The fact that one item of wealth yields more gain than another, then, does not derive from their use values. A *setier* of corn and a piece of lace of the same value represent equal quantities of wealth both to those who sell them and to those who want to have the enjoyment of them. Exchangeable wealth therefore constitutes wealth only in proportion to its price. Thus it is by the abundance and constant dearness of its exchangeable produce that we should judge the opulence and prosperity of a nation.

---

[1] Cf. Adam Smith, *Wealth of Nations* (Cannan edn.), I, p. 30: 'The word VALUE, it is to be observed, has two different meanings, and sometimes expresses the utility of some particular object, and sometimes the power of purchasing other goods which the possession of that object conveys. The one may be called "value in use"; the other, "value in exchange". The things which have the greatest value in exchange have frequently little or no value in use. Nothing is more useful than water: but it will purchase scarce any thing; scarce any thing can be had in exchange for it. A diamond, on the contrary, has scarce any value in use; but a very great quantity of other goods may frequently be had in exchange for it.' R.L.M.

Although the value of exchangeable wealth is far from being an arbitrary value or a value which is established by agreement between the contracting parties, the government of a state, above all in a maritime and trading kingdom, can nevertheless cause very harmful disturbances in prices by adopting unsound regulations. For since the government's authority does not extend to the other trading nations, the only result of these special regulations can be a price out of harmony with the price which is general and common among the other nations which trade freely with one another, and this wipes out the revenue of the kingdom whose trade is restricted by the government. Yet the price which is general and common among the trading nations is always, as we shall show, the least variable, the least irregular, and the most advantageous to each of these nations.

The price of exchangeable wealth regulates the ratio of exchange between this wealth and money, or monetary wealth, which is everywhere accepted in exchange for all kinds of exchangeable wealth. Thus money is a special kind of wealth, representing an equivalent for the market value in the purchase of all kinds of exchangeable wealth.

Money, or gold and silver in its capacity as money, is a form of wealth which possesses no use value at all. For money, so to speak, is nothing more than a tool of exchange, which is indestructible, which never wears out, which does not deteriorate at all when it is used to make purchases, and which after it has been used to make ten, a thousand, or a hundred thousand purchases[1] is still in existence as it was before and is just as useful in exchange. Thus a very small quantity of money may be sufficient to enable successive trading transactions in exchangeable wealth to be continued in perpetuity. In most sales and purchases money is really nothing more than the denominator of the prices of the items of exchangeable wealth concerned, and plays only an ideal role in trade. The written securities which represent it are more convenient, and by reason of their transferability from one merchant to another are used for successive transactions, which are maintained through sales and purchases of exchangeable wealth without the intervention of the money equivalent of this wealth. Thus the opulence of a state does not consist in the quantity of money it possesses, but in the abundance and the proper price of its exchangeable wealth.

One can always find a substitute for money, but one cannot find a substitute for commodities and prices, which constitute the foundation and the market value of wealth. An individual in France who possesses 100 hogsheads of wine, the current price being 54 livres a hogshead, is just as wealthy as if he possessed 100 marks of silver;

---

[1] *Apres dix, après mille, et cent mille achats.* The I.N.E.D. text has *après dix ans, après mille, et cent mille achats.* R.L.M.

and if he wishes he can in fact obtain for himself this sum of money, equivalent to the market value of his wine. In actual fact there is always enough money in a trading state to effect the exchange of commodities in accordance with their prices; for the very prices of the commodities are a sure indication that a money demand for them, proportionate to their current prices, actually exists.

If a kingdom is poor, this is not, as is vulgarly claimed, because it lacks money, but because it lacks exchangeable wealth, or because the price of this wealth in the kingdom is too low. For an agricultural state can be wealthy only through the abundance of its annual products and the proper price—that is, through proper cultivation and a large external trade in raw produce, which not only enables it to find a market but also constantly maintains an advantageous and equal price, established as a result of the general trade of the trading nations. It is not at all through the quantity of money it possesses that a kingdom attains to a high degree of prosperity. For a kingdom which has no mines of its own can expand the total quantity of its monetary wealth only through the sale of its raw produce abroad. Thus it is always the abundance and proper price of this produce which is the source of money, but money itself would be only sterile wealth in the absence of trade. The amount of wealth in a nation can grow greater, then, only so far as it is turned to account by the purchase of exchangeable wealth from abroad. Thus money ought not to be hoarded up in a state, to the detriment of the increase in wealth which ought to be brought about by trade.

An abundance of money withheld inside a state, then, would never constitute a profitable form of wealth. Thus all nations reciprocally turn their money to account, one through the other, by means of trade. As a result of this, the general mass of coined money is circulated among the trading nations, in proportions which depend upon the views of extortioners who believe that nations inevitably tend in their mutual trade only to grab money from one another.[1] Merchants follow quite a different system: they always turn their money to account by purchasing commodities which they export and commodities which they import, with the aim of making a profit out of both, and out of their shipping services.

The cultivator and the manufacturer, who sell to the merchant, similarly turn to account the money they receive from the merchant by regenerating exchangeable products. The proprietor uses the

---

[1] Bauer, by whom the text of *Hommes* was first published in the first number (1908) of the *Revue d'Histoire des Doctrines Economiques et Sociales*, says in a footnote to this sentence (on p. 27) that there is undoubtedly a gap in the manuscript between 'proportions' and the words which follow it. However, there is certainly no *visible* gap in the manuscript at this point, and the sentence seems to me to make reasonably good sense as it stands. R.L.M.

money he receives from his farmer to purchase the foreign com-modities which the merchant has imported; and the merchant returns this money to the farmer who sells him the products yielded by his cultivation. The workers who are paid by the manufacturer, by the husbandman, and by all those who employ them, buy produce and commodities for their consumption; and the money is turned back into the cultivation of the land and the production of the manufactured goods which are reproduced.[1] Thus the distribution of money as between nations should be roughly in proportion to the quantity and price of their exchangeable wealth; but a greater or lesser quantity of money, counterbalanced by a greater or lesser quantity of exchange-able commodities, neither increases nor diminishes the foundation of their wealth.

The revenue of a kingdom is regulated by the price of its produce; and the price of produce is maintained and regulated by foreign trade. For in a state which has no external trade at all, either of export or of import, the price of produce cannot be subject to any rule or any order. It necessarily follows the variations of scarcity and abundance in the country, and the state has to put up with excessively low or excessively high prices,[2] both of which are equally disastrous and inevitable.

The fundamental price of commodities is determined by the expenses or costs which have to be incurred in their production or preparation. If they are sold for less than they have cost, their price sinks to a level at which a loss is made. If they are sold at a price which is high enough to yield a gain sufficient to encourage people to maintain or increase their production, they are at their proper price. If as a result of scarcity their price rises to a level which is burdensome to the people, then this price is excessively high.[3] If such a price, in spite of the fact that it greatly exceeded the fundamental price, were not in fact burdensome to the people, it would then simply be a high price, and a very advantageous one. Such would be, for example, a continually high price of corn in a state where this form of produce was always abundant, where plenty of it was sold abroad, and where this high price of corn resulted in the creation for the king and the proprietors of the land of a large revenue, and the procurement for the inhabitants of the country of wages or gains the benefit of which would outweigh the burden of their expenditure on

[1] The germ of the *Tableau Economique* is contained in this passage. R.L.M.

[2] *Des non-valeurs et des chertés.* Quesnay here and in the following paragraph uses *cherte* to mean an excessively high price, whereas in other contexts (e.g. pp. 86-7 above) he uses it to describe a state of affairs in which the *bon prix* has been established. The three levels of price between which Quesnay thought it important to distinguish are clearly described in the following paragraph. R.L.M.

[3] *Cherté.* See the preceding note. R.L.M.

corn. Thus it is possible, by means of external trade, for a kingdom to establish for its corn and all its other produce a high price which is not burdensome to the inhabitants and which is very advantageous to the state. One must look into all these circumstances in order to judge whether the price of our raw produce is high, whether it is being sold too dear, and whether it is proper that its price should be lowered.

A low price which constantly failed to exceed the fundamental price would be a different matter; for there is no case in which such a price would not be ruinous, and in which it would not necessitate the abandonment of the production of the produce whose price was constantly limited to such a low level. Thus the government of a state ought not to rely on the advantages which prejudice attributes to the price which is vulgarly called *cheap*,[1] for this price may be detrimental equally to the revenue of the king and the proprietors of landed property, the gains of the other inhabitants, the progress of population, and the expansion of the products of the country. The reality of these destructive consequences can be seen in our provinces where produce has become valueless. Men live cheaply there, but their wages are so low, they earn so little, that they cannot procure for themselves any degree of comfort through their labour; and, not being sufficiently stimulated by the lure of gain, they give themselves up to idleness and poverty. The proprietors of the land have so little revenue that they are unable to undertake the expenditure necessary to improve their property, and to provide adequate work and gains for the workers and artisans. The latter desert these provinces in order to live in the towns, where living is dearer and gains greater. That is why countries where produce is dear are more highly populated and the people more industrious and better off than in countries where the cost of living is too low. Men's wants are not confined simply to food; they must have clothing, utensils, and other conveniences if they are to live in any comfort. The French do not cross the seas and go to the islands of St Domingo, Martinique, etc., in order to look for bread; they are attracted there by the prospect of gains which will enable them to live in comfort.

Prices, as we have said, are never subject to big variations in a kingdom with an import and export trade with other nations which is mutual, unobstructed, and perfectly free: because prices in such a kingdom are equal to the common prices which are current in the other countries. For then the poor harvests and abundant harvests which this kingdom may experience do not normally bring about any change at all in prices, because in one and the same year there are abundant harvests in some countries and poor harvests in others, and by means of free and unobstructed trade between these different

---

[1] *Bon marché*. R.L.M.

countries those which in a particular year are suffering from a scarcity are supplied by those which have an abundance, while in another year the latter, who are now in their turn suffering from a scarcity, are supplied by the former. Thus, as a result of this general intercommunication and these successive and mutual alternations of abundance and scarcity, prices always remain at an intermediate level, determined by the average fundamental price in these countries which are joined together by trade.

The Dutch and the English, whose corn trade is free, do not experience in their countries those huge variations in the price of corn to which we in France are always exposed because we have prohibited the foreign export and import trade in corn. Our harvests, limited to the subsistence of the nation, are sometimes superabundant and sometimes far below what is necessary, and are subject to irregular prices which vary from the excessively high to the excessively low. Thus the price of produce cannot be subject to any order, to any fixed rule, in a kingdom which is deprived of the freedom or facility of external export and import trade. The cultivator suffers too great a loss in abundant years, and the lower orders perish from hunger and the epidemics which follow famines in years of scarcity. Thus large and frequent variations in prices are the deadly causes of poverty and depopulation.

. . . . . .

(iii) *The more wealth men produce over and above their consumption, the more profitable they are to the state; but the more men spend over and above their revenue,* or the more they consume over and above the gains which their work brings in, the more burdensome they are to the state.

With the aid of this general principle one can estimate the best way of employing men, and the size of the population which a state can maintain. Men, relatively to the products which are useful to men, must be reduced to two classes—one of which actually produces wealth, through its work; and the other of which contributes in an auxiliary way to the production or maintenance of wealth, through its services. A servant who prepares his master's dinner, and the things necessary for his subsistence and his other needs, saves his master the time which he would otherwise have spent himself in performing these functions and which he in fact spends in productive work. Thus the servant contributes in an auxiliary way to the product of his master's work.

Strictly speaking, it is only those men employed in work which generates the materials necessary for men's needs who produce wealth; for all the revenue of the proprietors and the sovereign, all the wages of the workers, all the salaries of the servants, and all the gains of those in remunerative occupations, are drawn from the value of these products. Those who make manufactured commodities do not produce wealth, because their labour increases the value of these commodities only by an amount equal to the wages which are paid to them and which are drawn from the product of landed property. The manufacturer who makes cloth, the tailor who makes clothes, and the cobbler who makes shoes, do not produce wealth any more than do the cook who makes his master's dinner, the worker who saws wood, or the musicians who give a concert. They are all paid out of one and the same fund, in proportion to the rate of reward fixed for their work, and they spend their receipts in order to obtain their subsistence. Thus they consume as much as they produce; the product of their labour is equal to the cost of their labour, and no surplus of wealth results from it. Thus it is only those who cause to be generated from landed property products whose value exceeds their costs who produce wealth, or annual revenue.

Thus all classes of citizens, with the exception of the workers who are engaged solely in the manufacture and exchange of goods which are sold abroad, draw their revenue or their gains from the products of landed property.

Landed property provides subsistence to those who are engaged in cultivating it, and procures revenue for the sovereign and proprietors and tithes for the clergy. The expenditure of this revenue creates the gains of the citizens who carry on remunerative occupations. Thus a kingdom's population increases or diminishes in the proportion that its revenue increases or diminishes. This diminution or increase does not depend on the people: it is always the result of the policy of the government of a state. Nevertheless the government attributes the decline of the state to the idleness of the people, and the existence of uncultivated land seems to justify it in doing so. But men always aim towards well-being and wealth, and are never idle when it is possible to achieve them. Their idleness consists only in their powerlessness, and their powerlessness is the result of government policy. It causes them to lose heart and abandon their occupations; the countryside is depopulated and the fields remain uncultivated; the towns collect the men whom the last resources of the state can maintain; and the population is as great as it is possible for it to be in this state of decline.

·   ·   ·   ·   ·   ·

(iv) Men engaged in fishing ought to be included in the class of those who produce. Although fishing is not comparable with agriculture, it ought to be regarded as a very profitable pursuit.

Mackerel and herring fishing in the Dieppe department alone is estimated *at more than 13 million:* from this one can judge how large the product of fishing in all our harbours taken together might be. But fishing in the open sea, i.e. for whales, cod, etc., is a matter of much greater importance, to which considerable attention should be paid. It is the first school in which men are trained for the navy; and it would make much greater progress in the absence of the exorbitant duties to which it is subject. If these duties were less burdensome, fishing would greatly increase; the increase in the quantity of fish produced would yield as much money as the duties do; and this occupation would employ a greater number of sailors and procure an increase in wealth for the nation. But private interests do not lend themselves to an insight into general welfare. Such advantages can be expected only as a result of the wisdom of the government.

One should also leave to the same wisdom the product of the work of the men who are engaged in extracting minerals and metals from the mines. This employment of men is also an abundant source of products and wealth, although they do not, it is true, consist of wealth in the form of food or primary necessities, which in the natural order are the most precious and the most necessary of goods. But in the order of trading societies one does not have to be guided by the natural order, for products are really exchangeable wealth only in proportion to their prices. Thus it does not matter what kind they are or what their utility is, provided that each product can be exchanged through the medium of money or by barter for any other kind of wealth whatsoever, in conformity with the price which it bears. It is up to each individual to have a preference for one product rather than another, relatively to their utility. But when they are regarded as exchangeable wealth one must evaluate them relatively to their prices, and in this case corn, iron, vitriol, and diamonds are equally wealth, whose value consists only in the price.[1] Thus whatever products a trading nation can procure for itself through its work, the most profitable to it will always be those which create the greatest wealth through their abundance, their prices, and their lower cost. It is up to each individual to direct his own work and expenditure with the aim of producing what is most profitable for him, according to his means, and according to the situation and quality of the land from which he wants to extract the most advantageous product. If he makes a mistake, his own interest will not allow him to remain in error for very long.

Merchants ought to be included in the class of men who produce, provided that they contribute to abundance through the proper price

---

[1] The I.N.E.D. text omits all the words in this sentence after 'relatively to their prices'. R.L.M.

D

which ought to be established as a result of foreign trade. But one sees in all their writings that they have other views about the advantages of their trade, and one sees that their profit makes them completely forgetful of the nation's interests. . . .

. . . . . .

(v) The proprietors may also be regarded as men who produce through the direction and improvement of their property: even the sovereign and his ministers contribute directly and generally to the increase of wealth through their economic government of the state. It is on this, indeed, that the prosperity of the nation depends: but the administration must never lose sight of the true source of the kingdom's revenue.

. . . . . .

(vi) The men who produce constitute the fundamental section of the population; the others consist only of appendages or accessories who are always proportionate to them. This auxiliary section saves the other section the time it would have to spend in performing other functions necessary to look after its needs, to defend itself, and to safeguard the product of its work and the landed property which is the source of the wealth which it causes to be generated every year.

Every man who shares in the wealth of the kingdom, but who does not contribute[1] to it in any way, is useless to the state. But, it will be asked, is not every man profitable to the state by virtue of his consumption? Yes, when he makes restitution of this consumption through his work, or through his utility in contributing directly or indirectly to the production of what he consumes or appropriates for himself; for if he does not return to the stock of wealth the value of what he takes out of it, the stock must necessarily diminish. But if he pays for what he consumes, does he not in fact make restitution of it through his expenditure? No, if he does not earn what he spends; for if he simply pays with the property which he owns, he at most refunds to the stock of wealth a portion of it which has fallen into his possession; but he does not himself make any contribution at all to the reproduction of what he consumes. Wealth is regenerated and perpetuated only through men's work; thus every man who does not contribute at all through his work to the renewal of the wealth which he appropriates or consumes, annihilates for good what he destroys through his consumption. It would indeed appear as if he made restitution of it to society by paying the latter for what he consumes; but it is always certain that the portion of wealth which he destroys through his consumption will not be included in the reproduction of

[1] *Contribue.* The I.N.E.D. text has *participe.* R.L.M.

wealth,[1] if it is in fact true that he himself makes no personal contribution at all, either directly or indirectly, to this reproduction. But, you may say, other men will reproduce the wealth without his aid. It is true that other men will produce all that their labour or their utility will yield; but they will not reproduce what the labour or utility of this man, who consumes but does not restore what he consumes at all, would have yielded. His consumption is thus useless, since it fails to be reproduced. But if he continues to consume without restoring what he consumes, must it not be the case that this portion of wealth is nevertheless in fact reproduced, since he continues to consume? Yes, but it is taken from other men's labour, and what he fails to produce directly or indirectly is always lacking; thus it would be just the same if this useless man himself were also lacking.[2] But, you may object, what about children, who produce nothing, who consume, and who are nevertheless not regarded as burdensome to the state? In actual fact, however, children ought not to be regarded as an expense to the state, because man should be considered in relation to the whole duration of his utility. Then it is seen that the years of his infancy and his old age are compensated by the period of his utility. One should not say, either, that the consumption of a foreigner who comes to spend his money in our country, simply for his own satisfaction, is not profitable to us; for it is clear that he pays us for his consumption with foreign wealth and not with our own. But is it not also advantageous, you will ask me, that an idle rentier should spend his revenue? Is not this rentier therefore useful to the state? But this conclusion does not follow, unless you confuse the man himself with the wealth which he ought to spend. It is perfectly true that wealthy men, who contribute nothing to the production of wealth, would be very harmful individuals if they did not spend their revenue. But although they are not harmful so long as they do that, it does not follow that they are useful. It would be advantageous if they also consumed their capital, which, by passing into the hands of industrious men, would be rendered still more useful, since wealth is badly distributed when it belongs to idle men who personally are of no use or utility. Happily such men are not very numerous, for there are few among the great who do not devote themselves to some essential employment, whether in high office, or in the clergy, in the military world, in the administration of the kingdom, in the judiciary, etc. Those whose inheritance is smaller take up occupations suitable to their means and their education; but in the case of men of wealth and

---

[1] *Sera de moins dans sa reproduction.* R.L.M.

[2] The basic idea in this rather difficult passage appears to be roughly the same as that expressed by Ricardo in his criticism of Malthus's doctrine of unproductive expenditure. See *Notes on Malthus* (Sraffa edn., II), pp. 421 ff. R.L.M.

money, and all those who are called men of affairs,[1] one may estimate their utility by comparing their gains with the value of the work they do for the prosperity of the state.

In considering the employment of men, the government ought to estimate their utility not only with reference to the work which they actually do, but also, and to a greater extent, with reference to the considerable utility which the kingdom could derive from them, according to the state of population, through other more advantageous work, or through economizing on the men who are employed in too great a number on work which could be carried out with less men and at less cost. The men who are unnecessarily employed in such work are stolen from other work in which they would be profitable to the state. The costs which they uselessly add to the price of commodities or produce cause a diminution in their sale and production. Those who pay more attention to the progress of the population than to the increase of wealth will even claim that these costs eventuate in profit for the state, since they maintain a larger population, a larger consumption, a larger market, and a larger production of produce.

But all these advantages are illusory; for costs which increase the price of produce without increasing its supply, and without increasing the revenue of the proprietors, cause sales, consumption, and production to diminish. Consumption is proportionate to the wealth of consumers, and this wealth is proportionate to the nation's revenue. These costs do not increase the revenue at all; on the contrary they diminish it, for they cause the price of produce to fall below its proper value by surcharging it with an addition to the price which makes it so dear that it cannot find a market unless the price is lowered as far as possible, to the detriment of the proper value of the produce. Thus it is obvious that the costs which one could avoid adding on to the price of produce, and which create gains for a number of men whose labour is not worth the rewards which are paid to them, reduce the revenue or the wealth of consumers, and also reduce the sales, the consumption, and the production of this produce.

A reduction of products means a reduction of wealth; and the population of a state is always proportionate to the annual product and revenue of the nation. Thus men who contribute only to increase the cost of produce or commodities are detrimental equally to the increase of wealth and the increase of population. Thus all machines which can contribute to reduce the cost of men's labour, and all canals or rivers which avoid the costs which are paid to carriers, bring about a price which is favourable to the proper value of produce or commodities; they encourage sales and production,

[1] *Gens à affaires.* R.L.M.

which increases wealth and consequently population,[1] for the increase in wealth produces an increase in expenditure, which yields an increase in the gains of all the remunerative occupations and which attracts to them a greater number of men. Thus it is not true that population can expand to the detriment of the annual production of wealth: a population which consumes more than it ought to produce does not become as great as it would be possible for it to become.

[1] At Lyons they have forbidden the introduction of a machine invented for the manufacture of taffeta, which would have saved the labour of a great number of the men employed and reduced the price of this commodity. People were worried about what would happen to the men employed in this work who had no other trade to earn their living by. But they would have done better to support these workers for the rest of their lives than to suppress the machine and keep them on. It would have cost them less to support the men, even when they were doing nothing, and to allow them to die out, than to exert themselves to give permanent employment to them in such expensive work. During the life of these men, the manufacturers would have exerted themselves, as they did before and as they do now, to take the cost of their support out of the price of the commodity, assuming—which appears improbable—that they could not be employed in other work. It is said that the project for a canal from the Saône to the Loire was rejected on the representations of the carriers. As for the latter, they could have become husbandmen, and this employment would have been very profitable.

A project was also put forward for piping water to all the houses in Paris, but this was not put into effect out of consideration for the water-carriers. But this project could have been put into effect slowly, and the number of water-carriers would have diminished little by little until they had died out. Thus it is always possible to obviate transitory difficulties in order to profit from such benefits.

C.

EXTRACTS FROM 'TAXATION'[1]

(i) The dues or taxes which the subjects pay to the sovereign for the expenses of government are laid on the annual wealth of a nation. This wealth can be divided into four categories:

(1) The revenue of landed property;

(2) The wealth which restores the costs or expenses incurred to generate the revenue;

(3) The wealth produced by industrial work;

(4) Income consisting of annuities, interest on money, the rent of houses and other buildings and chattels from which the proprietors draw revenue, and which produce no revenue at all for him who pays them, in contrast with the land which produces by itself the annual revenue which the farmers pay to the proprietors. These forms of revenue do not strictly speaking constitute true revenue, but are rather debts which are paid every year for the rent of money which has been borrowed and houses which have been let. This revenue, however, although it is drawn from another fund of wealth and does not itself constitute a separate part of the wealth produced in a state, may be regarded as true revenue relatively to the proprietors to whom it is paid (because for them it really does constitute revenue). It should not be any less subject to taxation than the other forms of revenue; unless it be income based on landed property, in which case it ought not to be differentiated from the revenue of this property, since it then consists of this revenue itself.

Monetary Wealth

I do not speak here of another category of wealth which may be very great and which can be regarded as a subtraction from the quantity of monetary wealth employed in the production of the annual wealth. This category of wealth, which is as it were stolen from the state and which is called *circulating finance*,[2] consists in monetary wealth accumulated in the capital, where it is used, through the medium of public issues, in an agio trade of money for money, and through the discount on negotiable bills yields large gains to those who have plenty of money laid by for this sort of trade.

[1] Translated from the text as reproduced in I.N.E.D., II, pp. 579–84 and 594–7. R.L.M.

[2] *Finance circulante.* R.L.M.

Great monetary fortunes, which seem to demonstrate the opulence of the state, are in fact only an indication of its decadence and ruin, since they are amassed to the detriment of agriculture, navigation, foreign trade, manufactured goods, and the revenue of the sovereign.

They destroy the stock of productive wealth and evade taxation: that is why I do not include them here in the categories of wealth which ought to contribute to the revenue of the sovereign. Nevertheless, if the form of taxation were to become less burdensome to the state, and if agriculture and freedom of trade in raw produce were restored, this monetary wealth would of itself become incorporated again in the general order, since it would be attracted into it by more certain and steady profits than those which can be obtained from an agio trade of money for money, which is carried on through the medium of negotiable bills which are almost all based on the state's debts.[1]

Renascent Wealth

Wealth which is regenerated and which restores the expenses which have been incurred in the production of the revenue ought not to be regarded as new wealth, since it returns only the costs or expenses advanced in order to generate every year, from landed property, the products which are continually required to satisfy men's needs. The wealth employed for the production of revenue ought to be regarded in the same way as the seed which produces the crop and which ought to be held back from the harvest in order to sow the land in the following year. This seed which is held back from the harvest forms no part of the profit which the harvest yields, since it is only a restitution of the seed which has been employed to produce the harvest, and since it ought to be returned to the earth each year to produce new crops.

It is the same with the expenses which the husbandman incurs in order to cultivate the land; these expenses, which are about equal to two-thirds of the product of the harvest, ought to be returned to the husbandman through the harvest itself in order to be expended anew in the cultivation of the land. Thus two-thirds of the harvest forms no part of the profit which is yielded by this harvest. This kind of wealth, therefore, which is used in the cultivation of the land, ought not to bear the burden of any taxes at all, for if any part of it is taken away from the cultivator the products of landed property will be correspondingly reduced.

Taxes which are imposed in such an improper way as this have a more and more destructive effect on the revenue of the nation and that of the sovereign; they radically weaken a state and bring about its ruin. The wealth of the husbandman which is destined to be used

[1] See the article *Interest on Money*.

in the cultivation of the land should not be burdened with taxes.

Net Product

The annual wealth which constitutes the nation's revenue consists of the products which, after all expenses have been deducted, form the profits which are drawn from landed property.

The proprietors ought not to hold back the net product

It is necessary that the proprietors of landed property, who receive this revenue, should spend it annually so that this kind of wealth is circulated among the whole nation. Without this circulation the state would be unable to subsist; if the proprietors held back this revenue, it would be very necessary to deprive them of it. Thus this sort of wealth belongs as much to the state as to the proprietors themselves; the latter have the enjoyment of it only in order that they should spend it.

The proprietors are useful to the state only through their consumption; their revenue exempts them from labour; they produce nothing; and if their revenue was not circulated among those in the remunerative occupations, the state would be depopulated through the greed of these unjust and treacherous proprietors. Laws would be passed against these men, who would be useless to society and withholders of the fatherland's wealth.

The profit or revenue which the proprietors draw from their landed property, then, constitutes the true wealth of the nation, the wealth of the sovereign, the wealth of his subjects, the wealth which provides for the state's needs, and consequently the wealth which pays the taxes levied to meet the expenditure which is necessary for the government and defence of the state.

Industrial Revenue

Industrial work produces goods necessary for the needs and conveniences of life. These goods represent wealth for those who make them only in so far as they are paid for by those who buy them; thus it is necessary that those who buy them should have wealth with which to pay for them. But this wealth can be derived only from the profit or revenue which is produced by landed property. It is only the products of landed property which constitute original, free, and ever-renascent wealth, with which men pay for all the things they buy.

Manufactured goods demand on the part of those who make them expenses and costs which are equal to the value of these goods. It is the same with these costs as it is with the costs of cultivation which maintain the workers in the country: those who earn them spend them to meet their needs; the husbandmen who pay them draw them from the products of cultivation. These costs represent at the same time both wealth and expenditure: wealth because they maintain those who earn them; expenditure because this wealth is taken from those who pay the costs and consumed by those who earn them. These costs cannot perpetuate themselves on their own; they are generated from landed property through men's labour; we must not confuse the source which produces them with men's labour itself, nor with the goods which men make. Thus one must consider industrial wealth in the same light as the wealth which constitutes the costs of agriculture, in order to ascertain the extent and the nature of this wealth. The former costs enable the tradesmen in the towns to get a living; the latter enable the workers in the country to get a living; and both are annually renewed through the products of landed property.

Up to here the comparison is valid, but the wealth which constitutes the costs of agriculture differs greatly, as regards its employment, from industrial wealth. It is the former which causes revenue to be generated, whereas the product of industrial wealth is confined to goods which are worth only the expenses which they entail. The worker who makes a piece of cloth purchases the raw material and incurs expenses for his needs while he is making it. The payment he receives when he sells it returns him the purchase price and his expenses; the gain which his labour procures for him is confined to the restitution of the expenses he has incurred, and it is through this restitution that he is able to continue getting a living by his labour. The competition of workers who are trying to procure for themselves a similar gain in order to get a living restricts the price of manufactured goods to the level of this gain itself. Thus this gain, or restitution of expenses, is not, like the revenue of landed property, an original form of wealth representing a pure profit. On the contrary, this gain, even when it exceeds the restitution of the expenses, can exist only through the original and ever-renascent wealth which pays for the work of manufacture. Wealth in the form of manufactured goods is procured only through wealth in the form of revenue from landed property, and these goods in themselves constitute only sterile wealth which can be renewed only through the revenue of landed property. A nation subsists only through perpetual consumption and reproduction; the wealth which maintains a nation in being consists only in perpetual reproduction; thus sterile wealth, being simply wealth which is confined to consumption, is destroyed by consumption itself, and is unable, unless it is reproduced through other wealth, to perpetuate the existence of men and the successive existence of their wealth.

.   .   .   .   .   .

(ii) The profits of the farmers and the gains of the men whom the farmers employ in cultivation ought to be distinguished from the revenue which this same cultivation brings in every year for the proprietors; for it is the costs and profits of the husbandmen which assure cultivation and the revenue.

It is the wealth of the farmers which renders the land fertile; the cultivation of the land entails considerable expenses, and the more these expenses are increased, the more fruitful the land is, and the greater are the gains for the country workers, the profits for the farmers, and the revenue for the proprietors which the land brings in.[1]

Thus it is not on the productive wealth of the husbandmen that taxes should be assessed, since this would mean the destruction of the means necessary to produce the annual wealth of the nation.

The richer the husbandman is, and the more he is spurred on by profit, the more will cultivation be assured. The countryside will be rich in flocks and herds, the land will be covered with abundant crops, the peasants will be employed and their gains will be assured, and the revenue will increase. Thus the wealth of the husbandman should not be envied, nor should it be diminished. It ought to be privileged, because it is the essential principle of the very wealth of the state.

The most important and inviolable rule of economic government is not to cause injury, through taxation, to the security and progress of cultivation. Then a protected and flourishing agriculture will procure for the state, and assign to it itself, wealth which it may tax in the way which is safest and least burdensome to the nation. It will be the revenue of landed property, and not the profit of the farmers who turn it to account, which the nation will advantageously subject to taxation. I say advantageously, because although the taxes fall back on the proprietors they are less detrimental to them than if they fell on cultivation, or if they were placed on the produce.

It is easy to prove that they are less detrimental to the proprietors than if they fell on cultivation, i.e. on the means of their farmers, because the revenue, as I have mentioned above, is destroyed in proportion to the extent that taxes wipe out the means of the cultivators. Taxes which are laid on the revenue, and which do not fall on cultivation, are not destructive at all, for cultivation will always amply compensate the proprietor, through the revenue which it brings in for him, for the burden of the tax placed on this revenue itself. This truth has been developed and demonstrated self-evidently in the article *Corn*.

It is also easy to understand why taxes laid on revenue are less burdensome to the proprietors than if they were distributed over produce and commodities; for the proprietors would then pay

[1] See the article *Corn*.

through their consumption and their expenditure not only the taxes, but also the enormous costs which the collection of these taxes would entail if they were distributed over produce and different commodities.

A *taille* proportionate to the revenue of the proprietors, imposed on the farmers in proportion to the rent as evidenced by the lease and in conformity with the rules set out in the article *Corn*, would be paid costlessly, and would not be detrimental to the farmer, because he would know about it when he rented the proprietor's property; the farmer, feeling himself secure on that account, would calmly and openly incur the expenses necessary for the live-stock and work which the most advantageous kind of cultivation demands. The land of the proprietor would always be maintained at the highest level of improvement, and he would always, at each renewal of the lease, draw a revenue in conformity with the good condition of his property. This revenue would be assured to him because cultivation itself would be assured. None of the farmer's profit at all would be taken out of the proprietor's funds, since it would be the fruit of the farmer's expenses. Competition among farmers at the renewal of the leases always brings the proprietor's revenue into proportion with the product of his property. A *taille* proportionate to the revenue of the property brings about no change at all in the situation of the proprietor, since it is always landed property which pays the *taille*; the farmer will simply be relieved of the abuses associated with arbitrary imposition.

TRANSLATIONS

III. THE *TABLEAU ECONOMIQUE*

A.

LETTER FROM QUESNAY TO MIRABEAU[1]

I have tried to construct a fundamental *Tableau* of the economic order for the purpose of displaying expenditure and products in a way which is easy to grasp, and for the purpose of forming a clear opinion about the organization and disorganization[2] which the government can bring about. You will see whether I have achieved my aim. You have seen other *tableaux* in these days—it is a way of meditating on the present and on the future. I am quite amazed that Parliament holds out no means of putting the state in order other than through economies. It is not as wise to things as a steward, whose lord has spent more revenue than he possesses and who urges him to find funds for him: the steward will not tell his lord to economize, but will point out to him that he should not use working horses for his coach or allow coach horses to remain in the stable, and that if everything were in its proper place he would be able to spend a still greater amount without ruining himself. It would seem, then, that our remonstrants are simply town-dwellers who are very poorly informed on the matters they talk about and are thus of very little help to the public. In your last letter you say truly that the efforts of individuals are very unfruitful; but we must not lose heart, for the appalling crisis will come, and it will be necessary to have recourse to medical knowledge. *Vale.*

---

[1] This letter, written apparently at the end of 1758 or the beginning of 1759, has been translated from the original in the *Archives Nationales* (M. 784, no. 70). It was reproduced in the original French in the appendix to an article by Bauer in the *Economic Journal* of March 1895. R.L.M.

[2] *Des arrangements et des dérangements.* R.L.M.

B.

THE 'FIRST EDITION' OF
THE *TABLEAU*

Note: For reasons set out in the essay on the *Tableau* in the last part of this book, the 'first edition' of the *Tableau* is generally assumed by modern commentators to have been substantially identical with a manuscript draft in Quesnay's handwriting which exists in the *Archives Nationales* (M. 784, no. 71). This draft, which takes up three pages in all and is written on a single sheet of paper folded in two, consists of (a) one page containing a *Tableau*, base 400, with explanatory comments, followed by (b) two pages of notes headed '*Remarques sur les variations de la distribution des revenus annuels d'une nation*'. A photographic reproduction of the page containing the actual *Tableau* will be found below, between pages 112 and 113 (Plate 2). A translation of the '*Remarques*' follows immediately after this note and a translation of the actual *Tableau* is given on pages 110-111. The translations have been made from the original document in the *Archives Nationales*. A photographic reproduction of the whole document will be found in I.N.E.D., II, between pages 672 and 673. R.L.M.

REMARKS ON THE VARIATIONS IN THE DISTRIBUTION OF THE ANNUAL REVENUE OF A NATION

From the preceding *Tableau*, it can be seen that in the order of the regular circulation of 400 millions of annual revenue, these 400 millions are obtained by means of 600 millions of advances, and are distributed annually to four million heads of families. There are one million proprietors, whose average expenditure is estimated at 400 livres each; and three million heads of families engaged in remunerative work or employment, each of whom draws on the average 200 livres for his expenditure. But in this distribution it is assumed: (1) That the whole of the 400 millions of revenue enters into the annual circulation, and runs through it to the full extent of its course; and that it is never formed into monetary fortunes, which check the flow of a part of this annual revenue of the nation and hold back the money stock or finance of the kingdom, to the detriment of the reproduction of the revenue and the well-being of the people; (2) That no part of the sum of revenue passes into the hands of foreign

TABLEAU

Provided by agriculture, grasslands, pastures, forests, etc. On corn, drink, meat, wood, live-stock, raw materials for manufactured commodities, etc. Mutual sales from one expenditure class to the other, which distribute the revenue of 400 livres to both sides, giving 200 livres to each, in addition to the advances which are maintained intact. The proprietor, who spends the revenue of 400 livres, draws his subsistence from it. The 200 livres distributed to each expenditure class can support one man in each; thus 400 livres of revenue can enable three heads of families to subsist. On this basis 400 millions of revenue can enable three million families to subsist, estimated at three persons above the age of infancy per family. The costs of the productive expenditure class which are also regenerated each year, and about half of which consists of wages for men's labour, add 200 millions, which can enable another one million heads of families to subsist at 200 livres each. Thus these 600 millions which are annually generated from landed property could enable 12 million persons to subsist, in conformity with this order of circulation and distribution of the annual revenue.

PRODUCTIVE EXPENDITURE Annual Advances	*EXPENDITURE* of the *REVENUE* which is divided thus:
400 produce net...	400
200 reproduce net...	200
100 reproduce net...	100
50 reproduce net...	50
25 reproduce net...	25
12.10 reproduce net...	12.10
6.5 reproduce net...	6.5
3.2.6 reproduce net...	3.2.6
1.11.3 reproduce net...	1.11.3
0.15.7 reproduce net...	0.15.7
0.8.0 reproduce net...	0.8.0
0.4.0 reproduce net...	0.4.0
0.2.0 reproduce net...	0.2.0
0.1.0 reproduce net...	0.1.0

Total revenue of 400 livres together with agricultural livres.

Note: For technical reasons, the zigzag lines lines sketched in by Quesnay in the original "first edition" *Tableau* have been omitted from the above translation. See the photographic reproduction of the original appearing between pp. 112 and 113 below (Plate 2). R.L.M.

OECONOMIQUE

STERILE EXPENDITURE

On manufactured commodities, house-room, taxes, interest on money, servants, commercial costs, of reignproduce, etc. Mutual sales from one expenditure class to the other, which distribute the revenue of 400 livres.

Annual Advances

200

200

100

50

25

12.10

6.5

3.2.6

1.11.3

0.15.7

0.8.0

0.4.0

0.2.0

0.1.0

The two classes spend in part on their own products and in part mutually on the products of one another.

The process of circulation sends 400 livres to this column, from which 200 livres have to be kept back for the annual advances. 200 livres remain for expenditure.

The taxes which are included in this expenditure class are provided by the revenue and by the reproductive expenditure class. They get lost in the latter class, except for those which are brought back to the reproductive class, where they are regenerated in the same way as the revenue which is distributed to this same class. But they are always levied to the detriment of the proprietors' revenue, or of the cultivators' advances, or of economy in consumption. In the two latter cases they are destructive, because they reduce reproduction in the same proportion. It is just the same with those which are transferred abroad without any return, or which are held back in the monetary fortunes of the tax-farmers who are responsible for their collection and expenditure.

reproduced
costs of 400

countries without return in money or commodities; (3) That the nation does not suffer any loss in its mutual trade with foreign countries, even if this trade is very profitable to the merchants through the gains they make out of their fellow-citizens on the sale of the commodities they import; for then the increase in the fortunes of these merchants represents a deduction from the circulation of the revenue, which is detrimental to distribution and reproduction; (4) That people are not taken in by a seeming advantage in mutual trade with foreign countries, through judging it simply with reference to the balance of the sums of money involved and not examining the greater or lesser profit which results from the particular commodities which are sold and purchased; for the loss often falls on the nation which receives a surplus in money, and this loss operates to the detriment of the distribution and reproduction of the revenue; (5) That the proprietors and those engaged in remunerative occupations do not, by means of sterile saving, deduct from circulation and distribution a part of their revenue and gains; (6) That the administration of finance, whether in the collection of taxes or in the expenditure of the government, never brings about the formation of monetary fortunes, which steal a portion of the revenue away from circulation, distribution, and reproduction; (7) That taxes are not destructive or disproportionate to the total of the nation's revenue; that their increase is in accordance with the increase in the nation's revenue; that they are laid directly on the revenue of the proprietors, and not on the produce, where they increase the costs of collection and operate to the detriment of trade; and, in addition, that they are not taken from the advances of the farmers of landed property, whose wealth ought to be very carefully safeguarded in order to meet the expenses of cultivation; (8) That the advances of the farmers are sufficient to enable the expenses of cultivation to reproduce at least 100 per cent; for if the advances are not sufficient, the expenses of cultivation are higher and produce little net revenue; in France they reproduce in the form of net profit only about 30 per cent; (9) That the children of farmers are settled in the countryside, so that there are always husbandmen there; for if they are harassed into abandoning the countryside and withdrawing to the towns, they take there their fathers' wealth which used to be employed in cultivation; (10) That the desertion of inhabitants who take their wealth out of the kingdom is avoided; (11) That no barriers at all are raised to external trade in raw produce; for as the market is, so is the reproduction; (12) That the prices of produce and commodities in the kingdom are never made to fall; for then mutual foreign trade would become disadvantageous to the nation; (13) That people do not believe that cheapness[1] of produce is profitable

---

[1] *Bon marché.* R.L.M.

D. FRANCISCUS QUESNAY.

1   François Quesnay: The engraving by Jean-Charles
François, after the portrait by Fredou

2 The 'First Edition' of the *Tableau Economique*
(in the *Archives Nationales*)

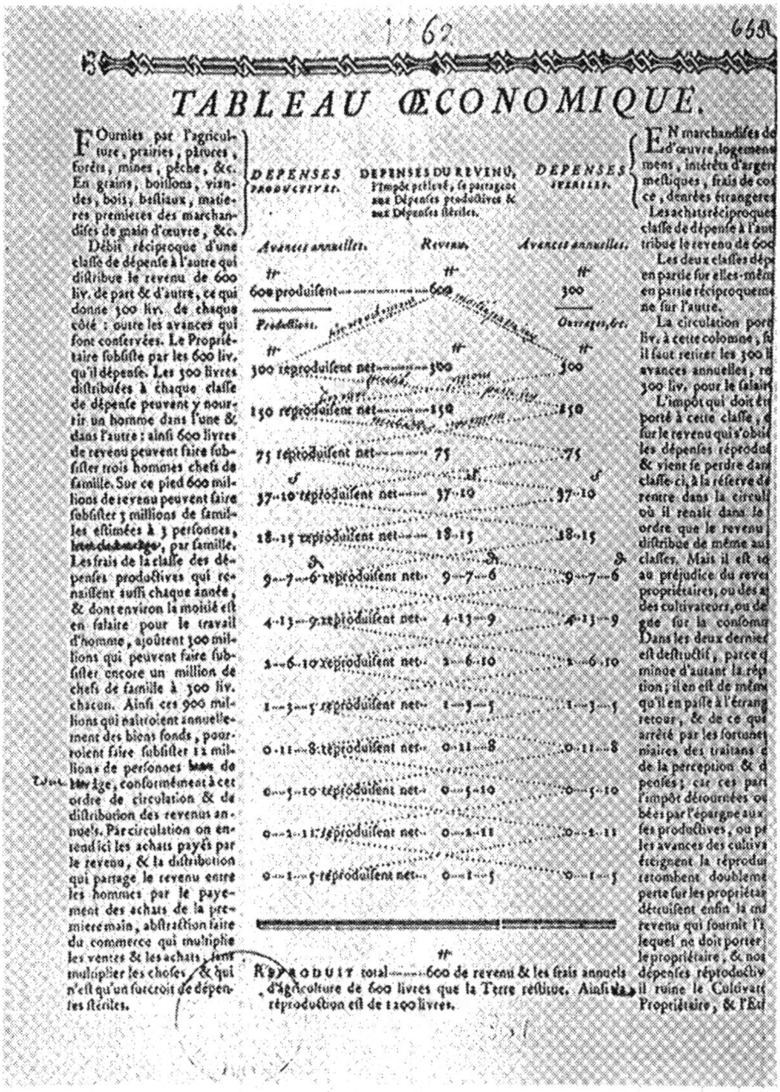

1762 — 665

TABLEAU ŒCONOMIQUE.

FOurnies par l'agriculture, prairies, pâtures, forêts, mines, pêche, &c. En grains, boissons, viandes, bois, bestiaux, matieres premieres des marchandises de main d'œuvre, &c.

Débit réciproque d'une classe de dépense à l'autre qui distribue le revenu de 600 liv. de part & d'autre, ce qui donne 300 liv. de chaque côté : outre les avances qui sont conservées. Le Propriétaire subsiste par les 600 liv. qu'il dépense. Les 300 livres distribuées à chaque classe de dépense peuvent y nourrir un homme dans l'une & dans l'autre : ainsi 600 livres de revenu peuvent faire subsister trois hommes chefs de famille. Sur ce pied 600 millions de revenu peuvent faire subsister 3 millions de familles estimées à 3 personnes, par famille. Les frais de la classe des dépenses productives qui renaissent aussi chaque année, & dont environ la moitié est en salaire pour le travail d'homme, ajoûtent 300 millions qui peuvent faire subsister encore un million de chefs de famille à 300 liv. chacun. Ainsi ces 900 millions qui naitroient annuellement des biens fonds, pourroient faire subsister 12 millions de personnes de âge, conformément à cet ordre de circulation & de distribution des revenus annuels. Par circulation on entend ici les achats payés par le revenu, & la distribution qui partage le revenu entre les hommes par le payement des achats de la premiere main, abstraction faite du commerce qui multiplie les ventes & les achats, sans multiplier les choses, & qui n'est qu'un surcroit de dépenses stériles.

DEPENSES PRODUCTIVES.	DEPENSES DU REVENU, l'Impôt prélevé, se partagent aux Dépenses productives & aux Dépenses stériles.	DEPENSES STERILES.
Avances annuelles.	Revenu.	Avances annuelles.
₶	₶	₶
600 produisent	600	300
Productions.		Ouvrages, &c.
₶	₶	₶
300 reproduisent net	300	300
150 reproduisent net	150	150
75 reproduisent net	75	75
37..10 reproduisent net	37..10	37..10
18..15 reproduisent net	18..15	18..15
9..7..6 reproduisent net	9..7..6	9..7..6
4..13..9 reproduisent net	4..13..9	4..13..9
2..6..10 reproduisent net	2..6..10	2..6..10
1..3..5 reproduisent net	1..3..5	1..3..5
0..11..8 reproduisent net	0..11..8	0..11..8
0..5..10 reproduisent net	0..5..10	0..5..10
0..2..11 reproduisent net	0..2..11	0..2..11
0..1..5 reproduisent net	0..1..5	0..1..5

REPRODUIT total ₶ 600 de revenu & les frais annuels d'agriculture de 600 livres que la Terre restitue. Ainsi la reproduction est de 1200 livres.

EN marchandises de main d'œuvre, logements, intérêts d'argent, domestiques, frais de commerce, denrées étrangeres ...

Les achats réciproques d'une classe de dépense à l'autre distribue le revenu de 600 ...

Les deux classes dépensent en partie sur elles-mêmes & en partie réciproquement l'une sur l'autre.

La circulation porte ... liv. à cette colonne, ... il faut retirer les 300 ... avances annuelles, ... 300 liv. pour le salaire ...

L'impôt qui doit être porté à cette classe, ... sur le revenu qui s'obtient ... les dépenses reproductives ... & vient se perdre dans ... classe-ci, à la réserve de ... rentre dans la circulation ... où il renait dans le ... ordre que le revenu ... distribue de même aux ... classes. Mais il est ... au préjudice du revenu ... propriétaires, ou des a... des cultivateurs, ou de ... gne sur la consomm... Dans les deux derniers ... est destructif, parce q... minue d'autant la rep... tion; il en est de même ... qu'il en passe à l'étrang... retour, & de ce qui ... arrêté par les fortunes ... naires des traitans ... de la perception & d... penses; car ces part... l'impôt détournées ou ... bées par l'épargne aux ... ses productives, ou p... les avances des cultiva... éteignent la reprodu... retombent doublement ... perte sur les propriétai... détruisent enfin la ma... revenu qui fournit l'I... lequel ne doit porter ... le propriétaire, & non ... dépenses reproductiv... il ruine le Cultivat... Propriétaire, & l'Et...

3 The 'Second Edition' of the *Tableau Economique* (in the *Bibliothèque Nationale*)

TABLEAU ÉCONOMIQUE.

[facsimile of Quesnay's Tableau Économique *— handwritten French text and the characteristic zig-zag diagram of* Dépenses Productives, Dépenses du Revenu, *and* Dépenses Stériles]*

4 The 'Third Edition' of the *Tableau Economique*
(in the *Archives Nationales*)

to the lower classes; for a low price of produce causes a fall in their wages, reduces their well-being, makes less work or remunerative occupations available for them, and reduces the nation's revenue; (14) That the well-being of the lower orders is not reduced; for then they would not be able to contribute sufficiently to the consumption of the produce which can be consumed only within the country, and the reproduction and revenue of the nation would be reduced; (15) That the increase of live-stock is encouraged; for it is live-stock which provides the land with the manure which procures abundant crops; (16) That no encouragement at all is given to luxury in the way of ornamentation; for this is maintained only to the detriment of luxury in the way of subsistence, which sustains the market for raw produce, its proper price, and the reproduction of the nation's revenue; (17) That the government's economic policy is concerned only with encouraging productive expenditure and external trade in raw produce, and that it refrains from interfering[1] with sterile expenditure; (18) That means to meet the extraordinary needs of the state are expected to be found only in the prosperity of the nation and not in the credit of financiers; for monetary fortunes are a clandestine form of wealth which knows neither king nor country; (19) That the state avoids contracting loans which result in the formation of rentier incomes[2] and which bring about an agio trade in finance through the medium of negotiable bills, the discount on which causes a greater and greater increase in sterile monetary fortunes; for these incomes and usurious gains are preferred to the revenue of agriculture, which is abandoned and deprived of the wealth necessary for the improvement of landed property and the cultivation of the land; (20) That a nation which has a large territory to cultivate, and the means of carrying on a large trade in raw produce, does not extend too far the employment of money and men in manufacturing and trading in luxury goods, to the detriment of the work and expenditure involved in agriculture; for more than anything else the kingdom ought to be well furnished with wealthy husbandmen; (21) That the government troubles itself less with economizing than with the operations necessary for the prosperity of the kingdom; for expenditure which is too high may cease to be excessive by virtue of the increase of wealth; (22) That less attention is paid to increasing the population than to increasing the revenue; for the well-being which a high revenue brings about is preferable to the pressure of subsistence needs which too great a population entails; and when the people are in a state of well-being there are more resources to meet the needs of the state.

There are no doubt kingdoms where none of these conditions are

---

[1] *Qu'il laisse aller d'elles-mêmes.* R.L.M.
[2] *Rentes financières.* R.L.M.

present, and it is said that all is well; this is true, for independently of these conditions a great state may be equal to a small one; and with these conditions a small state may be equal to a great one; whence springs that balance of power between nations which is sought after in the order of political policy.

C.

LETTER FROM QUESNAY
TO MIRABEAU[1]

Madame the Marquise de Pailli tells me that you are still bogged down in the zigzag. It is true that it relates to so many things that it is difficult to grasp the way they fit together, or rather to understand it self-evidently. One can see from this zigzag what takes place, without seeing its general applicability,[2] but that will not be enough for you.

It can be seen from it (1) that the employment of 400 livres of annual advances for the costs of agriculture produces 400 livres of revenue, and that 200 livres of advances employed in industry produce nothing over and above the wages which are paid to the workers; moreover, the wages are provided by the revenue which agriculture produces.

This revenue, as a result of the proprietor's expenditure, is divided almost equally. One-half returns to agriculture in payment for purchases of bread, wine, meat, wood, etc.; and the men who receive this half of the revenue, and who live on it, are employed in work on the land which causes the value of this same sum to be regenerated in the form of agricultural products; thus the same revenue is perpetuated. You will say, perhaps, that so far you have only seen one-half of it regenerated. But wait until you see the other distributions: the remainder will come back again. These husbandmen at the same time live on this same sum; but their labour, as a result of the earth's bounty, produces more than their expenses, and this net product is what we call revenue.

The other half of the revenue of the proprietor is employed by the latter in making purchases of manufactured goods in order to keep himself in clothing, furnishings, utensils, and all other things which are used up or destroyed without any renascent reproduction of these same things. Thus the product of the labour of the workmen who make them does not exceed their wages, which enable them to subsist and which restore their advances to them. Thus all there is here is expense incurred for the support of men who produce only to meet their own outgoings, which are paid to them through the

---

[1] This letter has been translated from the original in the *Archives Nationales* (M. 784, no. 70). It was reproduced in the original French in the appendix to Bauer's article in the *Economic Journal* of March 1895. R.L.M.

[2] *Le commun.* R.L.M.

115

revenue which agriculture produces. It is for this reason that I call it sterile expenditure.

Always bear in mind the axiom which says that when the costs of a commodity are not covered the trade has to be given up. This is true without exception. But if the costs of the commodity are at least covered, there is a distinction to be made: namely when the costs support men; for there are some expenses which support nobody and which are of interest to men only when there is a net product accruing to their profit. I want to have wood transported to Paris from a distance, and I look into the question of whether the costs of carriage will take away all the profit. These costs, which support horses but scarcely any men at all, are of a different kind from those which support men, and are not envisaged in my zigzag from the same point of view. For in the zigzag wealth is regarded in relation to men, and men relatively to wealth; and this relationship is one of the main subjects of the *Tableau*. A second subject is the process of the distribution of revenue, which ensures that the revenue is returned together with men's subsistence. From the *Tableau*, you can see first how the proprietor's expenditure is distributed to agriculture and industry; and then you can see how each sum, having reached one side or the other, is again mutually distributed from one side to the other right down to the last penny. The workers belonging to the industrial class spend half of the total amount of their wages within their own class, in order to keep themselves in the manufactured commodities they need; and the other half is returned to agriculture, in order to buy their subsistence goods. You can see the same thing happening on the side of agriculture: the husbandmen employ half of the sum which they receive to buy subsistence goods, and transfer the other half to industry in order to keep themselves in the manufactured commodities they require. Thus in the case of each class there is the same division of expenditure of the sums distributed to it as takes place in the case of the expenditure of the proprietor's revenue, except that each of these classes mutually receives sums from the other and sends sums back in the same way, and that the whole is reproduced in the agricultural class. You can also see that through the distribution of a revenue of 400 livres this sum amounts to 800 livres, which is divided up in the same way by the proprietor as it is in the agricultural and industrial classes, where it is everywhere employed in the purchase of things which provide support and enjoyment for men.

But another subject to be considered in our zigzag is the advances necessary for putting into motion the machine which is kept going by men, and the relation of these advances to the revenue *positis ponendis*. You can see that on the agricultural side the advances employed as costs are regenerated as well as the revenue, and that a portion of these advances is used as wages for the men who do the work of cultivation and who get their living from these wages. From this you can see at a glance how much wealth and how many men there are and how they are employed, their interrelationships and their influence on one another, and the whole essence of the economic government of agricultural states. Thus the zigzag, if properly understood, cuts out a whole number of details, and brings before your eyes certain closely interwoven ideas which the intellect alone would have a great deal of difficulty in grasping, unravelling, and reconciling by the use of the method of discourse. Moreover these ideas themselves would be very elusive if they were not fixed securely in the imagination by the *Tableau*. Neither in themselves nor in their interrelationship will it now be possible for them to escape us; or at any rate it will be very easy to picture them as a whole in their order and interconnection at a single survey, so that we can contemplate them at our ease without losing anything from sight and without the mind having to worry about putting them in order. I shall be sending you a second edition, enlarged and amended in the customary way. But have no fear—this Little Book of Household Accounts[1] will not become too bulky. I am having three copies printed so as to get a better idea of things, but I think that the proper place for it would be at the end of your dissertation for the prize offered by the Society of Berne, together with an introduction written by yourself if you thought it worthy of it. The dissertation itself is already a good introduction, but since you have run across certain difficulties in it you will for that reason be in a better position than I am to foresee possible obstacles, because you have come up against them yourself. In my second edition I talk in terms of a revenue of 600 livres in order to make everybody's share a little larger; for it was too far below the mark to start off with a revenue of 400 livres. It was too similar to the unhappy lot of our poor inhabitants of the Kingdom of Atrophy, or Marasmus, which to crown its misfortunes has fallen under the guidance of a doctor who does not stint bleedings and iron rations but who has forgotten all about restoratives. But I shall not say any more about this to you, most worthy citizen, for fear of awakening in you feelings which would be too painful. Rest at least in the quietness of your countryside. *Vale.*

[1] *Livret du Ménage.* R.L.M.

D.

THE 'SECOND EDITION' OF
THE *TABLEAU*

Note: Two printed copies of what is generally assumed to be the 'second edition' of the *Tableau* announced in the preceding letter from Quesnay to Mirabeau are extant—one in the *Bibliothèque Nationale* ($4° T^{18}$. 121 (ix, 62)), and the other in the *Archives Nationales* (M. 784, no. 71). This 'edition' consists of (a) one page containing a *Tableau*, base 600, with explanatory comments, followed by (b) four pages of notes headed '*Extrait des Oeconomies Royales de M. de Sully*'. The two folded sheets of which each copy consists are lightly sewn together, the *Archives Nationales* copy inside a third sheet which serves as a cover. The *Bibliothèque Nationale* copy contains a number of corrections in Quesnay's hand. Documents (a) and (b) were reproduced by the British Economic Association in 1894 as part of what was described as the 'second printed edition'.[1]

Document (a) does not differ very substantially from the 'first edition' of the *Tableau* itself translated on pp. 110-11 above. So far as this document is concerned, therefore, I have contented myself with giving above a photographic reproduction of the *Bibliothèque Nationale* copy of it (Plate 3, between pp. 112 and 113), and with giving in the present section a note listing the various changes which have been made in it as compared with the 'first edition' (pp. 119-20). So far as document (b) is concerned, however, although many of the maxims in it are identical or substantially identical with those in the '*Remarques*' of the 'first edition', there are a number of important amendments and additions: I have therefore given on pp. 120-5, at the cost of a certain amount of repetition, a complete translation of it, taken from the *Bibliothèque Nationale* copy. All the translations incorporate Quesnay's corrections.

A photographic reproduction of the *Bibliothèque Nationale* copy of (a) will also be found in I.N.E.D., II, facing p. 673; and the text of (b) is reproduced in ibid., pp. 669-73. R.L.M.

[1] On this edition, see below, pp. 270 ff. R.L.M.

CHANGES IN THE 'SECOND EDITION' OF THE *TABLEAU*[1]
(As compared with the 'first edition')

LEFT-HAND COLUMN

Line 2: The words 'mines, fishing' are inserted after 'forests'.

End of column: The following sentence is added: 'By circulation is here meant the purchases paid for by the revenue, and the distribution which shares out the revenue among men by means of the payment for purchases at first hand, abstracting from trade, which increases sales and purchases without increasing things, and which represents nothing but an addition to sterile expenditure.'

Throughout: Alterations are made throughout to bring the figures into conformity with the enlarged base of 600 livres. There are also a few minor amendments designed to improve the wording.

CENTRE COLUMNS

For the words 'which is divided thus' under the heading 'Expenditure of the Revenue' are substituted the words 'taxes having been deducted, is divided between productive expenditure and sterile expenditure'.

The figures are altered throughout in conformity with the enlarged base of 600 livres; and the first row of figures is divided from the following rows (see photographic reproduction).

For the words at the foot of the columns of figures the following words are substituted: 'Total *reproduced* . . . 600 livres of revenue and the annual costs of agriculture of 600 livres which the land restores. Thus the reproduction is 1200 livres.'

RIGHT-HAND COLUMN

Line 1: The word 'clothing' is inserted after 'house-room'.

Line 12: The word 'wages' is substituted for the word 'expenditure'.

Last paragraph: A number of additions and amendments are made so that the paragraph now reads as follows:

'The taxes which ought to be included in this class are taken out of the revenue which is obtained through reproductive expenditure, and gets lost in the latter class, except for those which come back into circulation, where they are regenerated in the same way as the revenue, and are distributed in the same way to the two classes. But they are always detrimental to the proprietor's revenue, or to the cultivator's advances, or to economy in consumption. In the two latter cases they are destructive, because they reduce reproduction in the same proportion. It is just the same with those which are transferred abroad without any return, or which are held back in the monetary fortunes of the tax-farmers who are responsible for their collection and expenditure; for these parts of the

[1] The line references are to the English translation of the 'first edition' on pp. 110-11 above. R.L.M.

taxes, diverted or stolen from productive expenditure through saving, or taken out of the cultivator's advances, extinguish reproduction, fall back on and cause a double loss to the proprietors, and in the end destroy the mass of revenue which provides the taxes, which ought to fall only on the proprietor, and not on reproductive expenditure, where they ruin the cultivator, the proprietor, and the state.'

Throughout: Alterations are made throughout to bring the figures into conformity with the enlarged base of 600 livres. There are also a few minor amendments designed to improve the wording.

EXTRACT FROM THE ROYAL ECONOMIC MAXIMS OF M. DE SULLY

From the preceding *Tableau*, it can be seen that in the order of the regular circulation of 600 millions of annual revenue, these 600 millions are obtained by means of 900 millions of annual advances,[1] and are distributed annually to four million heads of families. There are one million proprietors, whose average expenditure is estimated at 600 livres each;[2] and three million heads of families engaged in remunerative work or employment, each of whom draws on the average 300 livres for his expenditure. But in this distribution it is assumed:

1. That the whole of the 600 millions of revenue enters into the annual circulation, and runs through it to the full extent of its course; and that it is never formed into monetary fortunes, or at least that those which are formed are counterbalanced by those which come back into circulation; for otherwise these monetary fortunes would check the flow of a part of this annual revenue of the nation, and hold back the money stock or finance of the kingdom,

---

[1] If we added taxes to the 600 millions of revenue, and these taxes amounted to 200 millions, the annual advances would require to be at least 1,200 millions, without taking account of the original advances necessary in the beginning to set the husbandmen up in their enterprises; thus it should be noted that the most fertile land would be worthless without the wealth necessary to meet the expenses of cultivation, and that the deterioration of a kingdom's agriculture ought to be attributed not to men's idleness but to their poverty.

[2] The 600 millions of revenue may be divided among a smaller number of proprietors: in that case, the fewer proprietors there were the more would the expenditure of their revenue exceed the amount which each of them would personally be able to consume. But then they would indulge in liberality, or gather together other men to consume with them the things with which the expenditure of their revenue would supply them, so that this expenditure would turn out to be distributed in almost the same way as if there had been a greater number of proprietors limited to a smaller individual expenditure. Inequalities in the gains or profits of men in the other classes should be regarded in the same way.

to the detriment of the reproduction of the revenue and the well-being of the people.

2. That no part of the sum of revenue passes into the hands of foreign countries without return in money or commodities.

3. That the nation does not suffer any loss in its mutual trade with foreign countries, even if this trade is very profitable to the merchants through the gains they make out of their fellow-citizens on the sale of the commodities they import; for then the increase in the fortunes of these merchants represents a deduction from the circulation of the revenue, which is detrimental to distribution and reproduction.

4. That people are not taken in by a seeming advantage in mutual trade with foreign countries, through judging it simply with reference to the balance of the sums of money involved and not examining the greater or lesser profit which results from the particular commodities which are sold and purchased; for the loss often falls on the nation which receives a surplus in money, and this loss operates to the detriment of the distribution and reproduction of the revenue.

5. That the proprietors and those engaged in remunerative occupations are not led by any anxiety, unforeseen by the government, to give themselves over to sterile saving, which would deduct from circulation and distribution a portion of their revenue or gains.

6. That the administration of finance, whether in the collection of taxes or in the expenditure of the government, never brings about the formation of monetary fortunes, which steal a portion of the revenue away from circulation, distribution, and reproduction.

7. That taxes are not destructive or disproportionate to the total of the nation's revenue; that their increase is in accordance with the increase in the nation's revenue; that they are laid directly on the revenue of the proprietors, and not on the produce, where they increase the costs of collection and operate to the detriment of trade; and, in addition, that they are not taken from the advances of the farmers of landed property, whose wealth ought to be very carefully safeguarded in order to meet the expenses of cultivation and to avoid the loss of revenue.

8. That the advances of the farmers are sufficient to enable the expenses of cultivation to reproduce at least 100 per cent; for if the advances are not sufficient, the expenses of cultivation are proportionally higher and yield less net product.[1]

---

[1] In a kingdom of this kind the advances produced, on the average, apart from taxes, only about 20 per cent, which was distributed to the tithes, the proprietor, and to the farmer for his gain, the interest on his advances, and his risks. Thus there was a *deficit* of three-quarters in the net product.

The taxes were almost all laid on the farmers and on commodities, with the result that they fell upon the advances of expenses, which were burdened with about 500 millions for taxes, gains, administration costs, etc. And they yielded to the nation, judging from the tax of one-tenth, only about 400 millions of

9. That the children of farmers are settled in the countryside, so that there are always husbandmen there. For if they are harassed into abandoning the countryside and withdrawing to the towns, they take there their fathers' wealth which used to be employed in cultivation. It is not so much men as wealth which must be attracted to the countryside; and the more wealth is employed in the cultivation of corn, the less men it requires, the more it prospers, and the more net profit it yields. Such is the large-scale cultivation carried on by rich farmers, in comparison with the small-scale cultivation carried on by poor *métayers* who plough with the aid of oxen or cows.[1]

10. That the desertion of inhabitants who take their wealth out of the kingdom is avoided.

11. That no barriers at all are raised to external trade in raw produce; for as the market value is, so is the reproduction.

12. That the prices of produce and commodities in the kingdom are never made to fall; for then mutual foreign trade would become disadvantageous to the nation. *As the market value is, so is the revenue.*

13. That people do not believe that cheapness of produce is profitable to the lower classes; for a low price of produce causes a fall in their wages, reduces their well-being, makes less work or remunerative occupations available for them, and reduces the nation's revenue.

---

revenue. Productive expenditure was successively eaten away by taxation, to the detriment of reproduction. The additional burden of taxes on the natural price of produce added one-third to the price of the commodities upon which the revenue of 400 millions was spent, which meant that in real terms its value was reduced to 300 millions; and it did the same damage to foreign trade and to the employment of the taxes which came back into circulation.

Mutual trade with foreign countries brings in commodities which are paid for by the nation's revenue in money or in bartered goods. Thus we do not have to put this down as a separate item, since that would constitute double-counting. House-rent and income derived from interest on money must be regarded in the same way; for these constitute expenditure from the point of view of those who pay them, with the exception of income charged on land, where the liability is placed on a productive fund; but this income is included in the product of the revenue of the land.

[1] In large-scale cultivation, one man alone drives a plough drawn by horses, which does as much work as three ploughs drawn by oxen and driven by six men. In the case of small-scale cultivation, because of a lack of the advances necessary for the introduction of large-scale cultivation, the annual expenses are excessive and yield hardly any net product at all. It is said that there is a nation which is reduced to this small-scale cultivation over three-quarters of its territory, and in which, in addition, a third of the cultivable land is going to waste. But the government is engaged in stopping the course of this decline, and in providing the means for setting things right again. See the articles *Farmer*, *Farm*, and *Corn* in the Encyclopedia.

14. That the well-being of the lower orders is not reduced; for then they would not be able to contribute sufficiently to the consumption of the produce which can be consumed only within the country, and the reproduction and revenue of the nation would be reduced.

15. That the increase of live-stock is encouraged; for it is live-stock which provides the land with the manure which procures abundant crops.

16. That no encouragement at all is given to luxury in the way of ornamentation; for this is maintained only to the detriment of luxury in the way of subsistence, which sustains the market for raw produce, its proper price, and the reproduction of the nation's revenue.

17. That the government's economic policy is concerned only with encouraging productive expenditure and external trade in raw produce, and that it refrains from interfering with sterile expenditure.[1]

18. That means to meet the extraordinary needs of the state are expected to be found only in the prosperity of the nation and not in the credit of financiers; for monetary fortunes are a clandestine form of wealth which knows neither king nor country.

19. That the state avoids contracting loans which create rentier incomes, and which bring about a trade or traffic in finance, through

[1] The work involved in making manufactured and industrial commodities for the nation's use is simply something which costs money [*un objet dispendieux.* R.L.M.] and not a source of revenue. It cannot yield any net profit through sale abroad, except in countries where manufacturing labour is cheap because of the low price of the produce which serves for the subsistence of the workers; a condition which is very disadvantageous so far as the product of landed property is concerned. Also, such a condition should not be found in states with a free and unobstructed external trade which maintains the sales and prices of raw produce, and which happily does away with the small net product which could be obtained from an external trade in manufactured commodities, the gain from which would be based on the loss which would result from the low prices of the products of landed property. Here the net product or revenue accruing to the nation is not confused with the gains of the merchants and manufacturing entrepreneurs; these gains, from the point of view of the nation, ought to be ranked as costs. It would not be sufficient, for example, to have rich husbandmen, if the territory which they cultivated were to produce for them alone. There are kingdoms where the greater part of the manufactures can be kept going only by means of exclusive privileges, and by laying the nation under contribution through prohibitions forbidding it to use other manufactured commodities. This is not the case with agriculture and trade in the products of landed property, where the most energetic competition results in the expansion of the wealth of nations with large territories. I am not speaking here of re-export trade, to which small maritime states are fated; but a large state should not abandon the plough in order to become a carrier. It will never be forgotten that a minister of the last century, dazzled by the trade of the Dutch and the glitter of luxury manufactures, brought his country to such a state of frenzy that no one talked about anything but trade and money, without reflecting on the true employment of money or on a country's true trade.

the medium of negotiable bills, the discount on which causes a greater and greater increase in sterile monetary fortunes, which separate finance from agriculture, and which deprive the latter of the wealth necessary for the improvement of landed property and the cultivation of the land.

20. That a nation which has a large territory to cultivate, and the means of carrying on a large trade in raw produce, does not extend too far the employment of money and men in manufacturing and trading in luxury goods, to the detriment of the work and expenditure involved in agriculture; for more than anything else the kingdom ought to be well furnished with wealthy husbandmen.[1]

21. That each person is free to cultivate in his fields such products as his interests, his means, and the nature of the land suggest to him, in order that he may extract from them the greatest possible product; for monopoly in the cultivation of landed property should never be encouraged, because it is detrimental to the general revenue of the nation. The prejudice which leads to the encouragement of an abundance of produce of primary necessity, in preference to that of less necessary produce, to the detriment of the market value of one or the other, is inspired by short-sighted views which do not extend as far as the effects of mutual external trade, which makes provision for everything and determines the price of the produce which each nation can cultivate with the most profit. Thus it is revenue and taxes which are of primary necessity in order to defend subjects against scarcity and against the enemy, and to maintain the glory and power of the monarch.

22. That the government troubles itself less with economizing than with the operations necessary for the prosperity of the kingdom; for expenditure which is too high may cease to be excessive by virtue of the increase of wealth.

23. That less attention is paid to increasing the population than to increasing the revenue; for the greater well-being which a high revenue brings about is preferable to the greater pressure of subsistence needs which a population in excess of the revenue entails; and when the people are in a state of well-being there are more resources to meet the needs of the state, and more means to make agriculture prosper.[2]

---

[1] A nation ought to devote itself only to those manufactured commodities for which it possesses the raw materials and which it can make at less expense than in other countries; and it should purchase from abroad such manufactured commodities as can be bought at a price lower than the cost which would be involved if the nation made them itself. Through these purchases mutual trade is stimulated; for if nations tried to buy nothing and sell everything external trade and the advantages of the export of raw produce would be done away with.

[2] The predominant idea which nations have about war makes it thought that the strength of states consists in a large population; but the military part of a

Without these conditions, an agriculture producing 100 per cent, as we have assumed it to do in the *Tableau* and as it does in England, would be fictitious; but the principles displayed in the *Tableau* would be no less certain.

---

nation can subsist only through the tax-paying part. One would imagine that the great wealth of a state is obtained through an abundance of men; but men can obtain and perpetuate wealth only by means of wealth, and to the extent that there is a proper proportion between men and wealth. Nations always believe that they do not have enough men, and it is not understood that there are insufficient wages to support a greater population, and that men are plentiful in a country only to the extent that they find assured gains there to enable them to subsist.

E.

THE 'THIRD EDITION' OF
THE *TABLEAU*

Note: A copy of what has now become known as the 'third edition' of the *Tableau* was discovered by Schelle and described by him in an article in the *Revue d'Economie Politique* in 1905. The present whereabouts of Schelle's copy is not known, and so far as I am aware no other copy has since been found. Judging from Schelle's description, however, and from other evidence discussed in the essay on the *Tableau* in the last part of this book,[1] the 'third edition' probably consisted of three parts:

(a) An engraved *Tableau*, base 600, identical with or at least similar to a *Tableau* of which three copies exist in the *Archives Nationales*.[2] This *Tableau* was reproduced as part of the British Economic Association's edition of 1894.

(b) An *Explication du Tableau Economique*, a copy (probably proof copy) of which, with corrections in Quesnay's hand, is to be found in the *Archives Nationales* (M. 784, no. 71). This *Explication* was also reproduced as part of the British Economic Association's edition; and the text will be found in I.N.E.D., II, pp. 675–82.

(c) A set of 24 maxims, similar in form to those of the 'second edition' but considerably augmented and amended.

I give below a translation of the relevant parts of Schelle's general description of the 'third edition'; a translation of the comments at the head and foot of (a); a translation of (b) taken from the original document in the *Archives Nationales* and incorporating Quesnay's corrections; and finally some notes on (c). A photographic reproduction of (a) is given above (Plate 4, between pp. 112 and 113). R.L.M.

SCHELLE'S DESCRIPTION OF THE 'THIRD EDITION'

. . . A proof [of the *Tableau*] has been discovered in the *Archives*

---

[1] See below, pp. 268 ff. R.L.M.

[2] The first will be found in M. 784, no. 57, together with a manuscript of the 6th part of Mirabeau's *L'Ami des Hommes*; the second will be found in M. 784 no. 71 (document 2); and the third will also be found in M. 784, no. 71 (document 10). The second of these three *Tableaux* has been extensively altered in Quesnay's hand, apparently for the purpose of making it serviceable for the *Philosophie Rurale*. R.L.M.

Nationales, and has been reproduced recently;[1] the definitive edition of the *Tableau*, distributed by the author to his friends, has been regarded as lost.

Fortune, which always smiles upon the curious, has placed a copy of this edition in our hands. . . .[2]

The proof reproduced by the British Economic Association contains only 23 maxims, with notes which are much briefer than those in *Physiocracy*. Our copy contains the 24 maxims of the *Friend of Mankind*, and notes which are almost the same as those of *Physiocracy*.[3]

He [Quesnay] brought out a third edition, as he had brought out a second, and sent it not only to Mirabeau, but also to a small number of persons, as Forbonnais says.

This is the copy which we have before us; its appearance is less splendid than the copy of the second edition, but it is larger in size; the Little Book of Household Accounts has become more bulky.[4] The corrections made in ink on the second proof have been included in the text or put in a printed erratum.[5]

COMMENTS ON THE 'THIRD EDITION' OF THE *TABLEAU*

Comments at Head of Tableau:

Objects to be considered: (1) three kinds of expenditure; (2) their source; (3) their advances; (4) their distribution; (5) their effects; (6) their reproduction; (7) their relations with one another; (8) their relations with the population; (9) with agriculture; (10) with industry; (11) with trade; (12) with the total wealth of a nation.

Comments at Foot of Tableau:

Total reproduced . . . 600 livres of revenue; in addition, the annual costs of 600 livres and the interest on the original advances of the

[1] The reference is to the British Economic Association's edition of 1894. R.L.M.

[2] *Revue d'Economie Politique*, Vol. XIX, 1905, p. 490. R.L.M.

[3] Ibid., p. 501. R.L.M.

[4] Cf. above, p. 117. R.L.M.

[5] Schelle, op. cit., pp. 502–3. Schelle inserts the following note at this point: 'It is a booklet in 4to of xii pages for the explanation and 22 pages for the maxims and their notes; the engraved *Tableau* at the front has for its starting-point a revenue of 600 livres; the printed *Tableau* has disappeared. One maxim has been added; one other has been completed; the notes have been considerably expanded. The extract from the memoirs of Sully, which includes these notes, takes up 22 pages instead of six. The notes are not completely identical with those of *Physiocracy*; in this case too Du Pont has corrected his master in order to make his work clearer.'

husbandman amounting to 300 livres, which the land restores. Thus the reproduction is 1500 livres, including the revenue of 600 livres which forms the base of the calculation, abstraction being made of the taxes deducted, and of the advances which their annual reproduction entails, etc. See the Explanation on the following page.

EXPLANATION OF THE *TABLEAU ECONOMIQUE*

Productive expenditure is employed in agriculture, grass-lands, pastures, forests, mines, fishing, etc., in order to perpetuate wealth in the form of corn, drink, wood, live-stock, raw materials for manufactured goods, etc.

Sterile expenditure is on manufactured commodities, house-room, clothing, interest on money, servants, commercial costs, foreign produce, etc.

The sale of the net product which the cultivator has generated in the previous year, by means of the *annual advances* of 600 livres employed in cultivation by the farmer, results in the payment to the proprietor of a *revenue* of 600 livres.

The *annual advances* of the sterile expenditure class, amounting to 300 livres, are employed for the capital and costs of trade, for the purchase of raw materials for manufactured goods, and for the subsistence and other needs of the artisan until he has completed and sold his goods.

Of the *600 livres of revenue*, one-half is spent by the proprietor in purchasing bread, wine, meat, etc., from the productive expenditure class, and the other half in purchasing clothing, furnishings, utensils, etc., from the sterile expenditure class.

This expenditure may go more or less to one side or the other, according as the man who engages in it goes in more or less for luxury in the way of subsistence or for luxury in the way of ornamentation. We assume here a medium situation in which the reproductive expenditure renews the same revenue from year to year. But it is easy to estimate the changes which would take place in the annual reproduction of revenue, according as sterile expenditure or productive expenditure preponderated to a greater or lesser degree. It is easy to estimate them, I say, simply from the changes which would occur in the order of the *Tableau*. Suppose, for example, that luxury in the way of ornamentation increased by one-sixth in the case of the proprietor, by one-sixth in the case of the artisan, and by one-sixth in the case of the cultivator. Then the revenue reproduced, which is now 600 livres, would be reduced to 500 livres. Suppose, on the other hand, that an increase of the same degree took place in expenditure on the consumption or export of raw produce. Then the revenue reproduced would increase from 600 to 700 livres, and so on in progression. Thus it can be seen that an opulent nation which indulges in excessive luxury in the way of ornamentation can very quickly be overwhelmed by its sumptuousness.

The 300 livres of revenue which according to the order of the *Tableau* have passed into the hands of the class of productive expenditure, return to this class its *advances* in the form of money. These advances reproduce 300 livres net, which represents the reproduction of part of the proprietor's revenue; and it is by means of the remainder of the distribution of the sums of money which are returned to this same class that the total revenue is reproduced each year. These 300 livres, I say, which are returned at the beginning of the process to the productive expenditure class, by means of the sale of the products which the proprietor buys from it, are spent by the farmer, one-half in the consumption of products provided by this class itself, and the other half in keeping itself in clothing, utensils, implements, etc., for which it makes payment to the sterile expenditure class. And the 300 livres are regenerated with the net product.

The 300 livres of the proprietor's revenue which have passed into the hands of the sterile expenditure class are spent by the artisan, as to one-half, in the purchase of products for his subsistence, for raw materials for his goods, and for foreign trade, from the productive expenditure class; and the other half is distributed among the sterile expenditure class itself for its maintenance and for the restitution of its *advances*. This circulation and mutual distribution are continued in the same way by means of subdivisions down to the last penny of the sums of money which mutually pass from the hands of one expenditure class into those of the other.

Circulation brings 600 livres to the sterile expenditure class, from which 300 livres have to be kept back for the *annual advances*, which leaves 300 livres for wages. These wages are equal to the 300 livres which this class receives from the productive expenditure class, and the advances are equal to the 300 livres of revenue which pass into the hands of this same sterile expenditure class.

The products of the other class amount to 1200 livres, abstracting from taxes, tithes, and interest on the husbandman's advances, which will be considered separately in order not to complicate the order of expenditure too much. The 1200 livres' worth of product are disposed of as follows: The proprietor of the revenue buys 300 livres' worth of them. 300 livres' worth passes into the hands of the sterile expenditure class, of which one-half, amounting to 150 livres, is consumed for subsistence within this class, and the other half, amounting to 150 livres, is taken for external trade, which is included in this same class. Finally, 300 livres' worth are consumed within the productive expenditure class by the men who cause them to be generated; and 300 livres' worth are used for the feeding and maintenance of live-stock. Thus of the 1200 livres' worth of product, 600 are consumed by this class, and its *advances* of 600 livres are returned to it in the form of money through the sales which it makes to the proprietor and to the sterile expenditure class. One-eighth of the total of this product enters into external trade, either as exports or as raw materials and subsistence for the country's workers who sell their goods to other nations. The sales of the merchant counter-balance the purchases of the commodities and bullion which are obtained from abroad.

Such is the order of the distribution and consumption of raw produce as between the different classes of citizens; and such is the view which we ought to take of the use and extent of external trade in a flourishing agricultural nation.

Mutual sales from one expenditure class to the other distribute the revenue of 600 livres to both sides, giving 300 livres to each, in addition to the advances which are maintained intact. The proprietor subsists by means of the 600 livres which he spends. The 300 livres distributed to each expenditure class, together with the product of the taxes, the tithes, etc., which is added to them, can support one man in each: thus 600 livres of revenue together with the appurtenant sums can enable three heads of families to subsist. On this basis 600 millions of revenue can enable three million families to subsist, estimated at four persons of all ages per family.

The costs provided for by the *annual advances* of the productive expenditure class, which are also regenerated each year, and of which about one-half is spent on the feeding of live-stock and the other half in paying wages to the men engaged in the work carried on by this class, add 300 millions of expenditure to the total; and this, together with the share of the other products which are added to them, can enable another one million heads of families to subsist.

Thus these 900 millions, which, abstracting from taxes, tithes, and interest on the annual advances and original advances of the husbandman, would be annually regenerated from landed property, could enable 16 million people of all ages to subsist, according to this order of circulation and distribution of the annual revenue.

By circulation is here meant the purchases at first hand, paid for by the revenue which is shared out among all classes of men, abstracting from trade, which increases sales and purchases without multiplying things, and which represents nothing but an addition to sterile expenditure.

The *wealth of the productive expenditure class*, in a nation where the proprietors of land regularly receive a revenue of 600 millions, can be worked out as follows:

A revenue of 600 millions for the proprietors presupposes an extra 300 millions for taxes; and 150 millions for tithes on the annual product, all charges included, which are levied on the tithable branches of cultivation. This makes a total of 1050 millions, including the revenue. Add to these the reproduction of 1050 millions of annual advances, and 110 millions of interest on these advances at ten per cent, and the grand total becomes. . . .2,210,000,000 livres.

In a kingdom with many vineyards, forests, meadows, etc., only about two-thirds of these 2210 millions would be obtained by means of ploughing.

Assuming a satisfactory state of affairs in which large-scale cultivation was being carried on with the aid of horses, this portion would require the employment of 333,334 ploughs at 120 *arpents* of land per plough; 333,334 men to drive them; and 40 million *arpents* of land.[1]

With advances amounting to five or six milliards, it is possible for this type of cultivation to be extended in France to more than 60 million *arpents*.

We are not speaking here of small-scale cultivation carried on with the aid of oxen, in which more than a million ploughs and about two million men would be required to work 40 million *arpents* of land, and which would bring in only two-fifths of the product yielded by large-scale cultivation. This small-scale cultivation, to which cultivators are reduced owing to their lack of the wealth necessary to make the original advances, and in which the land is largely employed merely to cover the costs, is carried on at the expense of landed property itself, and involves an excessive annual expenditure for the subsistence of the great numbers of men engaged in this type of cultivation, which absorbs almost the whole of the product. This thankless type of cultivation, which reveals the poverty and ruin of those nations in which it predominates, has no connection with the order of the *Tableau*, which is worked out on the basis of half the employment of a plough of land,[2] where the annual advances are

---

[1] Quesnay assumes here, as he does in *Grains*, that the total area of cultivable land in France is 60 million *arpents*. R.L.M.

[2] *Qui est réglé sur l'état de la moitié de l'emploi d'une charrue.* Here and in the next paragraph Quesnay is apparently using '*charrue*' to mean a plough *of land* (a carucate or plough-land), being the amount of land which can be tilled with one plough in a year. In the present context, what he is saying in effect is that the amount of the total annual agricultural product depicted in the *Tableau* has been worked out by estimating the value of the harvest which each plough of land could produce under conditions of large-scale cultivation, multiplying this by the number of ploughs of land in cultivation, and dividing the total by two—the latter operation being necessary because each unit of land is assumed to lie fallow in alternate years. See Mirabeau's remarks in *L'Ami des Hommes* (1762 edn.), Vol. VI, pp. 174–5, and the comments at the foot of the *Tableaux* facing pp. 179 and 194 in ibid. R.L.M.

able, with the aid of the fund of original advances, to produce 100 per cent.

The full total of the original advances required for putting a plough of land[1] under large-scale cultivation, for the first fund of expenditure on live-stock, implements, seed, food, upkeep, wages, etc., in the course of two years' labour prior to the first harvest, is estimated at 10,000 livres. Thus the total for 333,334 ploughs is 3,333,340,000 livres. (*See the articles* Farm, Farmers, Corn *in the Encyclopedia*.)[2]

The interest on these advances ought to amount to ten per cent at least, since the products of agriculture are subject to disastrous accidents which, over a period of ten years, destroy at least the value of one year's harvest. Moreover, these advances require a great deal of upkeep and renewal. Thus the total of interest on the original advances required for setting up the husbandman is..............
.... 333,322,000 livres.[3]

Meadows, vineyards, ponds, forests, etc., do not require very great advances on the part of the farmers. The value of these advances, including in them the original expenditure on plantations and other work carried out at the expense of the proprietors, can be reduced to 1,000,000,000 livres.

But vineyards and gardens require large annual advances which, taken together with those of the other branches, may on the average be included in the total of annual advances set out above.

The total annual reproduction of net product,
of annual advances with the interest thereon,
and of interest on the original advances,
worked out in accordance with the order of the
Tableau, *is* ....2,543,322,000 livres.[4]

The territory of France, given advances and markets, could produce as much as this and even a great deal more.

Of this sum of 2,543,322,000 livres, 525 millions constitutes that half of the reproduction of the annual advances which is employed in feeding animals. There remains (if the whole of the taxes go back into circulation, and if they do not encroach upon the advances of the husbandmen) .... 2,018,322,000 livres.

That makes, FOR MEN'S EXPENDITURE, *504,580,500 livres on the average for each million heads of families, or 562 livres for each individual head of family, which accidents reduce to about 530*

---

[1] *Charrue*. See previous note. R.L.M.
[2] See, e.g. I.N.E.D., II, p. 428. R.L.M.
[3] This presumably should read 333,334,000. R.L.M.
[4] This represents the sum of 2,210,000,000 livres estimated (p. 131 above) for the total annual reproduction, plus the sum of 333,322,000 livres estimated for the annual interest on the original advances. R.L.M.

livres.[1] On this basis a state is wealthy, and its people live in easy circumstances.

The stock of land which annually produces for the benefit of men 2,543,322,000 livres, of which 1,050,000,000 take the form of net product, when evaluated at the rate of one in 30,[2] constitutes from this point of view wealth amounting to 33,455,000,000 livres, to which must be added the original advances of 4,333,340,000 livres,[3] making a total of 36,788,340,000. Adding to this the 2,210,500,000 livres[4] of annual product,

the total, costs included, of the wealth of the
productive expenditure class will be: ....40,331,660,000 livres.[5]

The value and the product of live-stock have not been separately calculated, since they have been included in the advances of the farmers and in the total of the annual product.

We include the land here because, relatively to its market value, it can be considered in something the same way as movable property, since its price is dependent upon changes in the other items of wealth required for cultivation. For land deteriorates, and the proprietors lose on the market value of their landed property, to the extent that the wealth of their farmers is wasted away.

The *wealth of the sterile expenditure class* consists of:
1. The total of the annual sterile advances...525,000,000 livres.[6]

---

[1] The figure of 504,580,500 livres apparently represents one-quarter of the sum of (a) the annual revenue, (b) interest on the productive class's original and annual advances, and (c) the half of the productive class's annual advances which is spent on wages. Obviously this falls considerably short of the *total income* distributed among the four million families concerned, so that the calculations 'for each individual head of family' which immediately follow cannot be taken as representing what we would today call income per head. Also the figures 562 and 530 are a little obscure. Probably 530 should read 505, since (a) the 'accidents' referred to can probably be taken to result in a reduction of 10 per cent in the sums involved; (b) 562 less 10 per cent is roughly 505; and (c) 505 is roughly one-millionth of 504,580,500. R.L.M.

[2] I.e. at a rate of 3⅓ per cent. Quesnay seems to have tried to work out the capital sum which would yield 1,050,000,000 livres per annum at this rate of interest. If so, the figure of 33,455,000,000 which follows is obviously incorrect. In the corresponding passage of the sixth part of *L'Ami des Hommes* the figure is given correctly as 31,500,000,000. R.L.M.

[3] The original advances should actually be 3,333,340,000. With this amendment the total of 36,788,340,000 is correct. R.L.M.

[4] The figure here should actually be 2,210,000,000 (see p. 131 above). R.L.M.

[5] Quesnay's procedure in arriving at this total is not quite clear. Probably he decided that he ought also to include in the total the figure of 333,322,000 livres given on p. 132 above for the interest on the original advances. 36,788,340,000 plus 2,210,000,000 plus 333,322,000 gives 39,331,662,000, which is near enough to the total actually arrived at to suggest that Quesnay, having adopted this procedure, simply made another arithmetical error. R.L.M.

[6] This is apparently made up of the sterile class's annual advances of 300 million, plus a proportionate share of the taxes and tithes. R.L.M.

2. The original advances of this class for setting up manufactures, for tools, machines, mills, forges, and other works, etc.[1].........
.... 2,000,000,000 livres.

3. The coined money or money stock of an opulent agricultural nation is about equal to the net product which it obtains annually from its landed property through the medium of trade...........
.... 1,000,000,000 livres.[2]

[1] *Usances.* This is probably a misprint for *usines*, which is the word used by Mirabeau in the corresponding passage in the sixth part of *L'Ami des Hommes.* R.L.M.

[2] Or about 18,600,000 marks of silver. It is to be noted that the money stock of England remains fixed at about this proportion, which in the present state of its wealth maintains it at approximately 26 millions sterling, or 11 million marks of silver. If this nation has found itself in urgent need through its wars, and has been obliged to contract excessive loans, this was not due to a lack of money, but to the fact that the state's expenditure exceeded its revenue. When money is provided for loans, the debts add no less of a burden to the revenue, and the nation is ruined, if the very source of the revenue is progressively wasted away, causing a reduction in the annual reproduction of wealth. It is from this point of view that the state of a nation should be considered; for the money stock is always renascent in a nation where wealth is being renewed continually and without abatement. For about a century, i.e. from 1450 to 1550, there was a great reduction in the quantity of money in Europe, as can be seen from the prices of commodities in those times. But this smaller quantity of money was a matter of indifference to the nations, because the market value of this form of wealth was the same everywhere, and because, in proportion to the money stock, their condition was the same relatively to their revenues, which were everywhere measured alike in terms of the uniform value of silver. In such a case it conduces more to men's convenience that it should be value which makes up for quantity rather than quantity which makes up for value. We are led to believe that it was the discovery of America which procured a greater abundance of gold and silver in Europe; yet the value of silver had fallen relatively to commodities, to the level at which it stands today, before the arrival of the American gold and silver in Europe. But all these general variations have no effect at all on the state of the money stock of each nation, which is always proportionate to the revenue from its landed property and to the gains from its external trade. In the last century, under Louis XIV, the mark of coined silver was worth 28 livres. Thus 18,600,000 marks were then worth about 500 million livres. This was roughly the size of the money stock in France in those times, when the kingdom was much wealthier than it was towards the end of the reign of this monarch.

In 1716, the general recoinage of specie did not amount to 400 millions; the mark of coined silver was at 43 livres 12 sous; thus the total amount of specie involved in this recoinage did not amount to nine million marks; and this was more than one-half less than the amounts involved in the general recoinages of 1683 and 1693. This total money stock can have been increased as a result of the annual production of specie only to the extent that the nation's revenue has been increased. However great the total of this annual production may have been since this recoinage, it will have served less to increase the total stock of coined money than to make up for what has been abstracted from it annually as a result of smuggling, the various branches of passive trade, and other methods of employing money in foreign countries; for over a period of 44 years the total of these annual transfers, if properly calculated, would be found to be very considerable. The rise in the money unit, which has been fixed for a long time

4. The capital value of four million houses or dwelling-places for four million families, each house being valued on the average at 1500 livres, comes to ....6,000,000,000 livres.

5. The value of the furnishings and utensils of four million houses, estimated on the average at about one year's revenue or gain of four million heads of families, comes to ....3,000,000,000 livres.[1]

6. The value of silver plate, jewellery, precious stones, mirrors, pictures, books, and other durable manufactured goods, which are purchased or inherited, may in a wealthy nation amount to......
.... 3,000,000,000 livres.

7. The value of merchant and military shipping, and their appurtenances, in the case of a maritime nation; in addition, the artillery, weapons, and other durable goods required for land warfare; the buildings, ornamental structures, and other durable public works: all these things taken together can be valued at...2,000,000,000 livres.

We do not take account here of the manufactured commodities which are exported and imported, and which are stored in the shops and warehouses of the merchants and destined for annual use or consumption, since they are included and taken account of in the figures of annual product and expenditure, in conformity with the order set out in the *Tableau*.

---

at 54 livres, does not prove that the quantity of the nation's money stock has greatly increased. These views are hardly consistent with the notions vulgarly held concerning the quantity of coined money in a nation. The people believe that it is in money that the wealth of a state consists. But money, like all other products, constitutes wealth only in proportion to its market value; and it is no harder to acquire, by paying over other kinds of wealth for it, than any other commodity. Its quantity in a state is limited by the uses to which it can be put; these are regulated by the sales and purchases which take place in its annual expenditure; and its annual expenditure is regulated by its revenue. Thus a nation's stock of coined money should be no more than proportionate to its revenue; a greater quantity would be of no use to it; it would exchange the surplus with other nations in order to obtain other items of wealth which would be of greater benefit to it or which would afford it more satisfaction; for those who possess money, even the most thrifty of them, are always concerned with getting some profit from it. If it is found that money is being lent at a high rate of interest in a country, this is proof that the quantity of money is at most only in the proportion we have described, since those who need it or want the use of it are paying such a high price for it. This has been the position regarding interest on money in France for a long time.

[1] Here, in contrast to the calculation on pp. 132-3 above, Quesnay appears to be thinking in terms of the *total income* of society. He is probably adding (a) the revenue of 1050 millions; (b) the incomes of 1050 generated by the circulation of this revenue among the productive and sterile classes; (c) the interest of 110 millions on the productive class's annual advances; (d) the interest of approximately 333 million on the productive class's original advances; and (e) the 525 millions of the productive class's annual advances which is spent on wages. The total comes to a little over 3,000,000,000. R.L.M.

TOTAL OF THE WEALTH OF THE
  STERILE EXPENDITURE CLASS....18,000,000,000 livres.
GRAND TOTAL ....59,000,000,000 livres.[1]
That is, assuming a possible error of one-
twentieth either way ....55 to 60,000,000,000 livres.

We are speaking here of an opulent nation with a territory and advances which yield annually and without any abatement a net product of 1050 millions. But all these items of wealth, which are successively maintained by this annual product, may be destroyed or lose their value if an agricultural nation falls into a state of decline, simply through the wasting away of the advances required for productive expenditure. This wasting away can make considerable headway in a short time for eight principal reasons:

1. A bad system of tax-assessment, which encroaches upon the cultivators' advances. *Noli me tangere*—that is the motto for these advances.

2. An extra burden of taxation due to the costs of collection.

3. An excess of luxury in the way of ornamentation.

4. Excessive expenditure on litigation.

5. A lack of external trade in the products of landed property.

6. A lack of freedom of internal trade in raw produce, and in cultivation.

7. The personal harassment of the inhabitants of the countryside.

8. Failure of the annual net product to return to the productive expenditure class.

THE MAXIMS OF THE 'THIRD EDITION' OF
THE *TABLEAU*

Schelle publishes the maxims of the 'third edition' in full in his article, but the notes to them only in part and in a rather haphazard way. I give below comparisons between the maxims as published by Schelle and the maxims of the 'second edition'; but where the maxims of the 'third edition' differ at all substantially from those of the 'second edition' I give a comparison with the maxims of *Physiocratie*, which are translated below (pp. 231ff.). In the case of maxims 4 and 21 I have translated in full some passages which appear neither in the 'second edition' nor in *Physiocratie*. R.L.M.

Maxims 1, 2, and 3:   Substantially identical with maxims 1,
                              2, and 3 of the 'second edition'.

---

[1] This is the sum of the wealth of the productive expenditure class (see above, p. 133) and the wealth of the sterile expenditure class. R.L.M.

Maxim 4:	Substantially identical with maxim 4 of the 'second edition', but the following sentence is added at the end: 'In the mutual trade of the raw produce which is purchased from abroad and the manufactured commodities which are sold abroad, the disadvantage usually lies on the side of the latter commodities, because much more profit is yielded by the sale of raw produce.'
Maxims 5 and 6:	Substantially identical with maxims 5 and 6 of the 'second edition'.
Maxim 7:	More similar to maxim 5 of *Physiocratie* than to maxim 7 of the 'second edition'.
Maxims 8, 9, 10, and 11:	Substantially identical with maxims 8, 9, 10, and 11 of the 'second edition'.
Maxim 12:	Substantially identical with maxim 18 of *Physiocratie*.
Maxims 13, 14, 15, 16, 17, and 18:	Substantially identical with maxims 13, 14, 15, 16, 17, and 18 of the 'second edition'.
Maxim 19:	Very similar to maxim 30 of *Physiocratie*.
Maxim 20:	Substantially identical with maxim 20 of the 'second edition'.
Maxim 21:	This is a new maxim not included in the 'second edition'. It is similar to maxim 15 of *Physiocratie*, but after the words 'than in small ones' the following is inserted: 'Because the latter employ uselessly, and at the expense of the revenue of the land, a greater number of the families of farmers, the extent of whose activities and means hardly puts them in a position to carry on wealthy cultivation. This multiplicity of farmers is less favourable to population than is the increase of revenue, because. . . .' The maxim then carries on, as in *Physiocratie*, with 'the population whose position is most assured. . . .', etc.
Maxim 22:	Very similar to maxim 21 of the 'second edition'.
Maxim 23:	Substantially identical with maxim 27 of *Physiocratie*.
Maxim 24:	Substantially identical with maxim 23 of the 'second edition'.

F.

EXTRACT FROM 'RURAL PHILOSOPHY'[1]

*PROGRESSION OF THE RESTORATION OF
AGRICULTURE, through the abolition of the causes of
its decline. MEMOIR sent to a Society of Agriculture*

*CURRENT PRODUCT yielded by the cultivation of
corn in a kingdom where agriculture is in a state of
decline:*[2]

Revenue	⎧ Tithes	50 millions
	⎨ Territorial taxes	38
	⎪ Revenue of the	
	⎩ proprietors . . .	76

Total	164 millions

The annual advances are about 450
Which generate 164 millions of net
   product; thus the net product is
   approximately 35 per cent of the
   annual advances.
The total product of the revenue
   and the annual advances is 614
The original advances are four times
   the annual advances, so that they
   amount to 1800

Total Annual Product	⎧ The total product above 614	
	The interest on the annual	
	and original advances is	
	not very great, because it is	
	obtained only in countries	
	with vigorous large-scale	
	agriculture, and one must	
	add to it the compensation	
	for the indirect taxes,	
	corvées, etc.; which, taken	
	together, may be estimated	
	at more than . . . . 646[3]	

Total	1260 millions

[1] Translated from *Philosophie Rurale* (1764 edn.), Vol. II, pp. 315–30. On the
question of the authorship of this extract, see above, p. 38, note. R.L.M.

[2] Encyclopedia, article on *Corn*.

[3] The greater part of this compensation drawn by the cultivators, to indemnify

Total wealth in the ⎰ Total annual product 1260
cultivation of corn ⎱ Original advances 1800

Total .... 3060 millions

If corn rose about 4 livres, as a result of freedom of trade, the total annual product of this increase would be about 360 millions, representing an addition of about one-quarter to the current total product of 1 milliard 260 millions. Thus this product would be 1 milliard 620 millions instead of 1 milliard 260 millions. Nevertheless the annual advances would be barely 526 millions. For the total expenses of the cultivator would not increase by more than one-sixth as a result of the increase of 4 livres. This calculation is worked out on the basis of 90 million *setiers* of corn at an average of about 14 livres per *setier*, or of other grains in proportion.[1] The addition of 4 livres per *setier* brings the price up to about 18 livres: at this price the 90 million *setiers* amount to 1 milliard 600 millions.[2] Corn would rise very little in the vicinity of the capital, but it would rise by much more than 4 livres in distant provinces, while rising overall to 18 livres, as a result of freedom in the export trade.

Advances .... 550 millions
The interest on the annual and original
    advances, which is obtained only in coun-
    tries with vigorous large-scale agriculture,
    would increase as a result of the rise in the
    price of corn; but there is in addition the
    compensation for the indirect taxes and
    corvées, etc., which, without increasing in
    strict proportion to the rise in the price of
    corn, may together with the interest increase
    to 676

them for the indirect taxes, may not exist, for it may be resolved into savings. And savings out of the expenses of cultivation mean the extinction of product, and a successive increase in the process of decline.

[1] The harvest of corn is much less great than that which is assumed here. For when agriculture is in a state of decline, small-scale cultivation carried on by oxen becomes dominant. And the annual advances of this kind of cultivation largely consist in the consumption of the produce of the grass-lands, the pastures reserved for the maintenance of the working oxen, which should be deducted from the returns of corn in the total product of 1 milliard 264 millions. Moreover there are other products dependent upon cultivation by the plough, such as hemp, flax, potatoes, mangolds, turnips, etc., so that in reality the harvest of corn enters into the total product of 1 milliard 264 millions only to the extent of about 60 million *setiers*; but this amounts to the same thing so far as the calculation is concerned. [Presumably '264 millions" in this note should read '260 millions'. R.L.M.]

[2] Presumably '600 millions' here should read '620 millions'. R.L.M.

The revenue, together with the tithes and
   territorial taxes 418

   Total .... 1644 millions[1]

The returns of the cultivator would
   be......................... 1260 mill. instead of 1096 mill.
The tithes would be .... 124 mill. instead of   50 mill.
The revenue of the proprietors
   would be.................... 172 mill. instead of   76 mill.
The territorial taxes would be.... 88 mill. instead of   38 mill.

   Total .... 1644 mill.[2]instead of 1260 mill.

If full freedom and security of internal and external trade in corn
were allowed, it could be completely restored and its effects fully felt
only by degrees in the course of at least five or six years.

If indirect taxes, _corvées_, etc., were abolished, everything would in
a few years return to the natural order of agricultural expenditure
and products.

The advances of the cultivators
would then be .... 965 ⎫ Returns of the cultivators
The interest on their original   ⎬ 1447
and annual advances would be.. 482 ⎭

The total revenue for the proprietors and the territorial tax
would be.................................... 786

---

[1] This figure for the total product, 1644 millions, is 24 millions more than one
would expect from the description of the data in the previous paragraph. The
reason is apparently that the figure for the annual advances given in the previous
paragraph, 526 millions, has been raised in the table to 550 millions, and the
figure for the total product has accordingly been raised by a similar amount. The
figure given for the revenue is of course simply the balance of the total product
remaining after the annual advances of 550 and the interest, etc., of 676 have
been deducted from it. R.L.M.

[2] Although this total is correct, the individual figures comprising it obviously
are not. What seems to have happened is this: Quesnay has calculated the
cultivator's returns wrongly, stating them as 1260 instead of the correct figure
1226. (The returns should equal the advances of 550 plus the interest, etc., of
676, i.e. 1226.) He has then subtracted 1260 from the total product of 1644,
and distributed the balance of 384 between tithes, proprietors' revenue, and
territorial taxes in roughly the same proportion as they were distributed in the
original table at the beginning of the memoir. The balance which should properly
have been so distributed is of course 418, as shown in the immediately preceding
table. R.L.M.

The tithes would be 179

Total .... 2412 millions[1]

Now two-thirds of the revenue, after tithes have been deducted, belong to the proprietor, and the other one-third to the sovereign. Thus the proprietors would have two-thirds of 786 millions, or 524 millions, instead of 172 millions. The territorial taxes going to the sovereign would be 264[2] instead of 88, leaving out of account the territorial part of other property, such as vineyards, meadows, etc., which would then yield, without any abatement, a direct tax which would greatly exceed the amount yielded to the sovereign by the present tax, which is today raised almost completely by indirect and destructive assessments, and which falls back again two-fold, three-fold, four-fold, etc., on the revenue of the land. It has also been shown that what the sovereign loses on his share of the falling-off in the revenue of landed property greatly exceeds what he receives from the indirect taxes, which ruin the proprietors of the land. But this increase in revenue—an increase of 672 millions over and above what it was originally, when it amounted to only 114 millions after deducting the tithes—would be returned in its entirety to the proprietors and the sovereign only by degrees in the course of nine years, during which all the leases of rented land would be successively renewed. For each farmer would profit, up to the termination of his lease, from the increase in the net product, and this gain would build up the wealth employed in cultivation proportionately. But in each

The way in which the figures in this table have been derived is not explained. The general idea, of course, is that when the indirect taxes, *corvées*, etc., are abolished, the 'compensation' for them formerly received by the cultivator will be added to his annual advances. To estimate the amount so added to the annual advances, one must first work out how much of the item of 676 in the previous table consists of this 'compensation'—i.e. one must deduct from this item the amount of the interest which it includes. Quesnay may have taken the annual advances as 526 (as stated in the paragraph preceding the table in question); assumed that the original advances were four times this, i.e. 2104; and worked out the interest at 10 per cent on the total of these annual and original advances. 10 per cent of (526+2104) is 263. Deducting 263 from the item of 676, representing interest plus 'compensation', we arrive at a figure of 413 for the interest. Adding 413 to the annual advances of 550 assumed in the table, we arrive at 963, which is near enough to the figure of 965 given by Quesnay in the present table. Having arrived at a figure of 965 for the new annual advances, the rest is easy: you simply proceed on the basis of the normal Physiocratic assumptions about the quantitative relations between annual advances, interest, and net revenue in the 'natural order'. The total net revenue (including taxes and tithes) is taken to be equal to the annual advances, and the interest is taken to be equal to one-half o the annual advances. R.L.M.

[2] Actually 262. R.L.M.

year there would be leases which terminated. Assuming that one-ninth of the leases were renewed each year, this would mean that in nine years one-half of the increase in the revenue would pass to the proprietors and the sovereign, and the farmers would benefit from the other half, some more and others less according to the different dates at which their leases expired.

The total of this increase of net product is 672 millions each year, being the balance when the original revenue of 114 millions including taxes is subtracted from the new revenue. This addition of 672 millions of revenue would over the nine years yield a total of 6 milliards 48 millions, of which the proprietors and the sovereign would receive 3 milliards 24 millions, and of which an equal amount would remain with the farmers. This would result in an increase of 3 milliards 24 millions in the wealth employed in cultivation. But there would also result, through the successive annual employment of this increase in the wealth used in cultivation, a new addition to the net product which would further increase the wealth of the cultivator and the revenue for the proprietors and the taxes. In order to visualize this gradual and cumulative increase in wealth, it is necessary to put it in the form of an arithmetical progression which starts from the sum of 672 millions representing the first increase in revenue, with the aim of making this progression tell us the amount of the total increase in the annual advances of the farmers, which are built up by accumulation during the nine years, when the farmers have annually increased the wealth employed in cultivation by the profit procured for them by the sum of 672 millions representing the first increase in gains. For when we know the result of the progressive increase in the annual advances of the cultivators, we can easily work out the actual amount of revenue which the annual advances reproduce each year. Thus the object of the following calculation is to arrive at the total of the cumulative increase in the annual advances over the period of nine years, during which the farmers make a greater and greater profit each year out of the sum of 672 millions representing the first increase in gains.

See the table showing the progression of the cultivator.[1] [p. 145.]

---

[1] This table, which bears an interesting resemblance in certain respects to modern growth models of the Harrod type, may require some explanation. It is assumed that in each of the years of the nine-year period which is under consideration the net product is 672 millions higher than it was in the years before the commencement of the nine-year period, and that this 'first increase' in the net product crystallizes out into rents only gradually, as the leases are renewed at the rate of one-ninth each year. The purpose of the table is to show how the investment of this 'first increase in gains' by the farmers will lead to a secondary increase in the net product, which will 'further increase the wealth of the cultivator and the revenue for the proprietors and the taxes'.

It is assumed that the postulated increase of 672 millions in the net product occurs for the first time in 1761, and that in that year it accrues in its entirety to the cultivators. The latter invest it by distributing it between their original advances and their annual advances in the ratio of 4 : 1. Their original advances thus increase by 537 and their annual advances by 135. These additional annual advances of 135 are assumed, when used in production, to 'reproduce 100 per cent' —i.e. they yield an extra addition to the net product of 135. One-seventh of this extra addition to the net product has to be paid out in tithes, but the balance of 115 is assumed to remain at the disposal of the cultivators and to be available for investment by them in 1762. (Minor discrepancies in the figures in the table are ignored here and elsewhere in this note.)

In 1762, the 'first increase' of 672 in the net product occurs again, but this time it does not accrue in its entirety to the cultivators as it was assumed to do in 1761. One-ninth of the leases are assumed to fall due for renewal in 1762, so that one-ninth of the 672 millions—i.e. 75—crystallizes out into rents, leaving only 598 in the hands of the cultivators. Thus the total amount available for investment by the cultivators in 1762 is this sum of 598 plus the sum of 115 referred to in the previous paragraph—i.e. 713. As before, this is distributed between original advances and annual advances in the ratio 4 : 1, so that original advances rise by a further 572 and annual advances by a further 143. The total increase in the annual advances employed, as compared with the years before 1761, is now 143+135, i.e. 278. These additional annual advances of 278, when used in production, once again 'reproduce 100 per cent'—i.e. they yield an additional net product of 278. As before, six-sevenths of this amount, i.e. 237, is assumed to remain at the disposal of the cultivators and to be available for investment by them in 1763.

Here an important inconsistency in the table becomes apparent. If, as we are assuming, one-ninth of the leases fall due for renewal in 1762, it is clear that the whole of this 237 would not in fact remain at the disposal of the cultivators in 1763. Some of it would crystallize out into rents. And, indeed, when we look at the last column of the table, showing the successive increases in rent in each year, we see that rents in 1762 are assumed to increase not only by the 75 considered in the previous paragraph, but also by an additional 135, equal to the amount by which the annual advances of the cultivators in 1761 exceed their annual advances in the years before 1761. In other words, in the last column Quesnay seems to be assuming that the successive secondary additions to the net product brought about by the successive additions to the annual advances crystallize out into rents with only one year's time-lag. And this appears to be inconsistent (a) with the assumption in the other part of the table that these secondary additions to the net product accrue in their entirety (or, rather, less one-seventh for tithes) to the cultivators and become available for investment by them in the following year; and (b) with the assumption that one-ninth of the leases fall due for renewal each year. Quesnay could conceivably be rescued from the charge of inconsistency with the first assumption if we interpreted the figures 135, 277, 429 . . . 1653 in the last column as meaning, not that the rent would actually be 135, 277, 429, etc., higher in 1762, 1763, 1764, etc., than it was in the years before 1761, but rather that at the end of 1769, after all the leases had fallen due for renewal, there would be an increase in rent from the secondary cause amounting o 1653. But this would be tantamount to assuming that no leases were renewed until the ninth year, and Quesnay would still be open to the charge of inconsistency with the second assumption. To rescue him completely, it is necessary to reconstruct the table on the assumption that the annual renewal of one-ninth of the leases results in the crystallization out into rents not only of one-ninth, two-ninths, three-ninths, etc., of the 'first increase' in the net product, but also of one-ninth, two-ninths, three-ninths, etc., of the secondary increases in the

Of this 1 milliard 481 millions remaining after tithes have been deducted, two-thirds, or 988 millions, would go to the owners of the land, and 493 millions of revenue would go to the sovereign, not including the other parts of the territory's revenue.[1]

But this addition, which works out at 1 milliard 481 millions, would in reality not be nearly as great as it is in the arithmetical progression we have just examined.

1. Because we have assumed that the annual advances yield 100 per

---

net product brought about by the successive increases in the annual advances. The results one then obtains are not *substantially* different from those shown in Quesnay's table. It is true that the figures in columns 1 and 2 now stop increasing and begin to decline after a certain point; but the additions to the annual advances shown in column 3 continue to increase, finally reaching a figure which is not as far below Quesnay's figure of 1653 as one might expect at first sight. In other words, the essence of the process illustrated by Quesnay's table is not affected by this necessary technical modification.

Let us proceed with our examination of the table, however, on the assumption that the secondary increases in the net product, as distinct from the 'first increase', do not crystallize out into rents until the end of the nine-year period. On this assumption, the amount available for investment by the cultivators in 1763 is 237 plus that part of the annually-recurring 'first increase' of 672 which does not crystallize out into rents in that year. Since another one-ninth of the leases fall due for renewal in 1763, only seven-ninths of this 672, or 524, will remain in the hands of the cultivators, so that the total amount available for investment by them will be 524+237, i.e. 761. Rents will increase by a further 75 as compared with 1762—in other words, rents in 1763 will be 75 higher than they were in 1762, and 150 higher than they were in the years before 1761. (On our assumption, we ignore the additional increase of rent of 277 noted by Quesnay opposite 1763.) The 761 available for investment will once again be distributed by the farmers between original advances and annual advances in the ratio 4 : 1, so that original advances rise by a further 608 and annual advances by a further 152. The total increase in the annual advances employed, as compared with the years before 1761, is now 152+278, i.e. 430.

The process then continues in the same way from year to year until, at the end of the nine-year period, all the leases have been renewed. By this time, the whole of the 'first increase' in the net product will have crystallized out into rents, the total increase in the annual rent from this cause (as compared with the years before 1761) being of course 672. On our assumption, the total of the secondary increases in the net product brought about by the successive increases in the annual advances will now also crystallize out into rents. Since by the end of the nine-year period the annual advances will have risen, according to the table, by 1653 (as compared with the years before 1761), this will add 1653 to the increase in the annual rent brought about by the first cause. Rents will thus be 672+1653, or 2325, higher than they were in the years before 1761. Quesnay, in the next sentence of the text, implies that the total increase in the annual rent (or, more strictly, in the annual net product) will be 1653+75, i.e. 1728. This is clearly wrong: the 1653 represents a difference between rent in 1769 and rent in the years before 1761, whereas the 75 represents a difference between rent in 1769 and rent in 1768. R.L.M.

[1] The '1 milliard 481 millions' is the sum of the two bracketed items at the foot of the last column of the table, less one-seventh for tithes. See the last paragraph of the preceding note. R.L.M.

YEARS	FIRST INCREASE IN GAINS, which rises each year by the successive addition of the increase in the net product.	ADDITION TO THE ORIGINAL ADVANCES, which each year consists of the annual increase in gains and its successive additions.	ADDITION TO THE ANNUAL ADVANCES, which increase each year by the addition of those of the preceding year.	ADDITION TO THE NET PRODUCT, of which 1/7 is taken for tithes and 6/7 remains for the farmers.	YEARS	ADDITION TO THE NET PRODUCT, which is successively added to the revenue of the proprietors, the sovereign, and the tithe-holders, and which is increased each year by the new addition to the annual advances and by 1/9 of the 672 millions of the first increase in gains.
1761	672	537	135			
1762	598 ⎱ 713 / 115	572	143 ⎱ 278 / 135	115	1762	75 ⎱ 210 / 135
1763	524 ⎱ 761 / 237	608	152 ⎱ 430 / 278	237	1763	75 ⎱ 352 / 277
1764	450 ⎱ 818 / 368	655	163 ⎱ 592 / 429	368	1764	75 ⎱ 504 / 429
1765	375 ⎱ 882 / 507	706	166 ⎱ 768 / 592	507	1765	75 ⎱ 667 / 592
1766	300 ⎱ 958 / 658	767	191 ⎱ 959 / 768	658	1766	75 ⎱ 843 / 768
1767	225 ⎱ 1047 / 822	838	209 ⎱ 1168 / 959	822	1767	75 ⎱ 1034 / 959
1768	150 ⎱ 1151 / 1001	921	230 ⎱ 1398 / 1168	1001	1768	75 ⎱ 1243 / 1168
1769	75 ⎱ 1264 / 1199	1019	255 ⎱ 1653 / 1398	1199	1769	75 ⎱ 1473 / 1398
1770		6 milliards, 123 millions		1417	1770	75 ⎱ 1653 / 1728, or 1481 when tithes have been deducted.

cent of net product every year during the course of the nine years, as would in fact happen in the case of land which had for a long time past been properly improved with the aid of sufficient manure; but here the land is at first in quite the contrary condition—in a condition of deterioration and impoverishment as a result of apathetic cultivation and the poverty of the cultivators. At the very basis of the above arithmetical progression lies the assumption that the land is from the very first in the best state of cultivation, which could only be the case after eight or nine years, i.e. towards the end of the assumed progression, when only a few leases remained to be renewed. Thus it is easy to see that this progression would not increase to the extent of one-half of the addition shown in the table.

2. This progression assumes that all indirect taxes have been abolished. But in order to make up the revenue of the sovereign in the first part of the period, until his share of the increase in the net product had at least reached a level sufficient to meet his requirements, there would be a need for a supplementary indirect tax, as simple, as uncomplicated, and as unburdened with costs as possible. Nevertheless, in spite of these favourable conditions, this tax would still reduce by more than one-quarter the addition to the net product resulting from our arithmetical progression.

3. Because the restoration of deteriorated land which is lying fallow requires, besides the original and annual advances, preliminary expenditure for clearing and for the repair of abandoned buildings, and the setting-up of new farms in districts where they have been destroyed. This inevitable expenditure would once again slow down by more than one-eighth the course of the progression of the addition to the net product.

4. The conditions which are essential to this progression, such as an increase in labouring animals and live-stock kept for profit, and an increase in population, could not fully keep in step with this progression, which must therefore once again be slowed down as a result of the deficiency of these indispensable conditions. Thus all the obstacles which we have just set out show us that the addition to the original and annual advances would not, in the nine years, reach more than one-tenth of that which appears to result from our arithmetical progression. This progression comes to a halt at the conclusion of the renewal of all the farmers' leases, for then the addition to the net product no longer contributes to increase the wealth which the farmers employ in cultivation. Thus the progressive increase in this addition to the net product, and to the wealth employed in cultivation, comes to its final conclusion when all the leases have been renewed.

Nevertheless, if the rapid advance of the simple arithmetical progression shown above is applied to vigorous colonies with a large territory, which can be cultivated with the labour of animals, assisted by large advances supplied by a wealthy metropolis, it can be seen that such colonies may be able to make very great progress in a short time. 1. Because new land when it has been cleared yields a large product. 2. Because in such places little or no taxes are paid. 3. Because the cultivators are themselves proprietors, so that all the profits from cultivation are all the time continually used to increase the wealth employed in cultivation: for it is clear, in fact, that if the leases of the farmers were for 18 years instead of the nine years which we have assumed here (which would be disadvantageous so far as the proprietors and the taxes were concerned), then, if the obstacles which we have just set out were to disappear completely in the first nine years, our arithmetical progression would in actual fact be realized during the course of the nine years following, and would even extend beyond the limits of the territory of a great kingdom. But we ought to base our calculation on the normal term of farmers' leases, and on the obstacles which during this term would retard the progress of our agriculture, in spite of the great benefits which we have seen that good administration can procure. Thus our arithmetical progression would be retarded, as we have just said, by at least nine-tenths. The addition to the annual advances, which appears in the calculation as 1 milliard 518 millions,[1] would therefore in actual fact be confined to 151 millions, which, when added to the 965 millions of annual advances which already existed before this latter addition, would form a total of 1 milliard 116 millions of advances. We are now going to see a *Tableau* setting

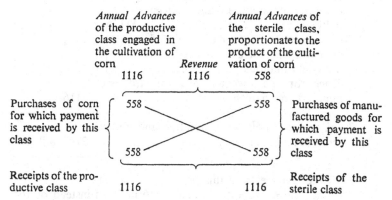

out the situation of agriculture in the tenth year, i.e. at the conclusion of the renewal of all the leases; but six years would first be

---

[1] Quesnay apparently arrives at this figure by deducting the addition of 135 to the annual advances in 1761 from the accumulated additions of 1653 shown for 1769. R.L.M.

required to achieve the complete restoration of free trade in corn and to feel its full effect, which makes a total of 16 years. But during this period of 16 years the enjoyment of the increasing wealth is not checked; for the farmers spend their annual advances every year; they also spend on their original advances; and the proprietors' revenue, which increases proportionately as the leases are renewed, also comes back again into the annual circulation of the nation's expenditure. The *Tableau* on p. 147 shows what the final state of expenditure would be (assuming that no unforeseen incidents occurred) at the end of the increase in annual wealth, when the renewal of all the leases had been concluded.

The total reproduction of corn is equal to the total of the sums annually returned to the cultivators of this product, viz:

The advances of the productive class.........	1116 millions
The receipts of this class	1116
The advances of the sterile class, used to purchase raw materials from the productive class	558
Total	2790 millions

Thus the total reproduction of corn is two milliards seven hundred and ninety millions, of which the cultivators take for their advances one milliard one hundred and sixteen millions...................... 1116⎤
For the interest on their original and annual advances, five hundred and fifty-eight millions............... 558⎦ 1674

Balance for the revenue, one milliard one hundred and sixteen millions.............. 1116

Total, two milliards seven hundred and ninety millions................................. 2790 millions

Thus the revenue from this part of the landed property is .... 1116 millions instead of 164
Of this revenue, arising solely from the cultivation of corn, two-sevenths would be taken for taxes, or .... 318 millions instead of 38
For the tithes, one-seventh, or.. 159 millions instead of 50

For the proprietors, four-sevenths, or	639 millions instead of	76
Total	1116 millions instead of	164

TOTAL QUANTITY OF WEALTH in the production of corn, included in the Tableau

The total product........................	2790 millions
The money for the revenue[1]	1116
The advances of the sterile class, maintained intact by the agents of this class..........	558
Total	4464 millions

Although in this fixed state of affairs, *in which the revenue of the current year is equal to the revenue of the preceding year,* the proprietors, the taxes, and the tithes swallow up the whole of the net product, there are nevertheless still means—although much more slowly-acting ones—of enabling agriculture to make further progress, if the qualities and extent of a kingdom's territory are capable of it.[2] 1. A reduction in luxury by way of ornamentation, which would result in a proportionate increase in the amount spent with the productive class. 2. The proper employment of the interest on the original and annual advances of the farmers, by which the latter can further improve their agricultural enterprises. 3. Progress in the improvement of land, which could in itself lead once again to a better state of affairs. 4. Profits from cultivation, which would attract new and wealthy agricultural entrepreneurs from the cities to the countryside. 5. Improvement and increase in the revenue of the other kinds of landed property, which would all mutually contribute to the general prosperity. 6. The proprietors, who as a result of the increase in their revenue could themselves contribute to the restoration and improvement of their properties. This account of the progression of the restoration of agriculture enables us easily to understand the rapid and successful advances made under the administration of M. de Sully.

[1] *L'argent du revenu.* Quesnay is no doubt here making the usual Physiocratic assumption that the country's money stock is equal to the revenue. R.L.M.

[2] The net product of the cultivation of corn in the kingdom of France, when the annual advances yielded 100 per cent, could hardly extend beyond 1200 millions, which implies a total annual product of about 3 milliards, including costs. Thus, given all the conditions, it is possible by calculation to get some notion of the time it would take to reach this situation.

G.

THE 'ANALYSIS'[1]

ANALYSIS OF THE ARITHMETICAL FORMULA OF THE *TABLEAU ECONOMIQUE* OF THE DISTRIBUTION OF ANNUAL EXPENDITURE IN AN AGRICULTURAL NATION

Εὖ μὲν γὰρ φερομένης τῆς γεωργίας ἔρρωνται καὶ αἱ ἄλλαι τέχναι ἄπασαι, ὅπου δ' ἂν ἀναγκασθῇ ἡ γῆ χερσεύειν, ἀποσβέννυνται καὶ αἱ ἄλλαι τέχναι σχεδόν τι καὶ κατὰ γῆν καὶ κατὰ θάλατταν.

ΣΩΚΡΑΤΗΣ παρὰ Ξενοφῶντι.

For when husbandry flourishes, all the other arts are in good fettle; but whenever the land is compelled to lie waste, the other arts of landsmen and mariners alike well-nigh perish.

SOCRATES, in *Xenophon*.[2]

The nation is reduced to three classes of citizens: the *productive class*, the *class of proprietors*, and the *sterile class*.

The *productive class* is that which brings about the regeneration of the nation's annual wealth through the cultivation of its territory, which advances the expenses which agricultural work entails, and which annually pays the revenue of the proprietors of the land. We include within this class all the work done and all the expenses incurred up to the sale of the products at first hand; it is through this sale that the value of the annual reproduction of the nation's wealth is ascertained.

The *class of proprietors* includes the sovereign, the owners of land, and the tithe-owners. This class subsists on the revenue or *net product* of cultivation, which is paid to it annually by the productive class, after the latter has first deducted, out of the reproduction which it causes to be annually regenerated, the wealth necessary for the reimbursement of its annual advances and for the maintenance of the wealth it employs in cultivation.

The *sterile class* is composed of all the citizens who are engaged in providing other services or doing other work than that of agriculture,

---

[1] The *Analyse* first appeared in the *Journal de l'Agriculture, du Commerce et des Finances* in June 1766. It was later republished, in an amended and enlarged form, in *Physiocratie*. The present translation is from the text of *Physiocratie*, as reproduced in I.N.E.D., II, pp. 793–812. R.L.M.

[2] Xenophon, *Oeconomicus* (Loeb Classical Library edn., 1923), p. 405. English translation by E. C. Marchant. R.L.M.

and whose expenses are paid by the productive class, and by the class of proprietors, which itself draws its revenue from the productive class.

In order to follow and calculate clearly the relations between these different classes, one must fix one's attention on a particular case of some sort, for a concrete calculation cannot be based on elementary abstractions.

Let us assume, then, a large kingdom whose territory, fully cultivated by the best possible methods,[1] yields every year a reproduction to the value of *five milliards*; and in which the permanent maintenance of this value is ensured by the constant prices which are current among trading nations, in a situation where there is unremitting free competition in trade and complete security of property in the wealth employed in agriculture.[2]

The *Tableau Economique* includes the three classes and their annual wealth, and describes the trade between them in the following way:

PRODUCTIVE CLASS	CLASS OF PROPRIETORS	STERILE CLASS
	Revenue	
Advances	A *revenue* of *two milliards* accrues to this	*Advances*
The *annual advances* of this *class* amount to *two milliards*.[3] They have produced *five milliards*, of which *two milliards* take the form of *net product* or *revenue*.	class. It spends *one milliard* in purchases from the *productive class* and the other milliard in purchases from the *sterile class*.	The *advances* of this *class* amount to *one milliard*, which is spent by the *sterile class* in purchases of raw materials from the *productive class*.

[1] *Porté à son plus haut degré d'agriculture*. This phrase clearly implies not only that the kingdom is fully cultivated, with no land going to waste, but also that large-scale agriculture, using the most productive methods available, has been widely introduced. R.L.M.

[2] The extent of the territory is about *130 million arpents* of land of different qualities; the total amount of wealth employed in cultivation which is necessary to keep this territory in good shape is about *12 milliards*; and the population consists of about *30 million* people, who can subsist comfortably, in accordance with their positions, on the annual product of *five milliards*.

But it should not be forgotten that wherever the population enjoys a peaceful life it normally increases beyond the product of the territory; moreover, the strength of a state and the number of citizens who compose it are always assured when they are based on a quantity of wealth employed in cultivation which is sufficient to maintain a wealthy agriculture. The maintenance of this fund of wealth employed in cultivation should be the main object of economic government; for the revenue of the sovereign and the nation depends entirely upon it, as will be demonstrated by the description of the regular order of the distribution of the expenses paid for and maintained by the annual reproduction.

[3] The annual advances consist of the expenses which are annually incurred for the work of cultivation; these advances should be distinguished from the original advances which constitute the fund for the establishment of cultivation, and which are valued at about five times the annual advances.

Thus the *productive class* sells *one milliard*'s worth of products to the *proprietors* of the *revenue,* and *one milliard*'s worth to the *sterile class*, which buys from it the raw materials necessary for its goods................   2 milliards

The *one milliard* which the *proprietors* of the *revenue* have spent in purchases from the *sterile class* is employed by this class to provide subsistence for the agents of whom it is composed, by means of purchases of products obtained from the *productive class* ....   1 milliard

Total of purchases made by the *proprietors* of the *revenue* and by the *sterile class* from the *productive class*   3 milliards

Of these *three milliards* received by the *productive class* for *three milliards*' worth of products which it has sold, it owes *two milliards* to the proprietors for the current year's revenue, and it spends *one milliard* in purchases of goods from the *sterile class*. This latter class retains this sum for the replacement of its advances, which have been spent with the *productive class* at the beginning of the process in purchases of the raw materials which it has used in making its goods. Thus these advances produce nothing; the sterile class spends them, they are returned to it, and they always keep on being laid by from year to year.

The raw materials and labour used in making the goods of the *sterile class* bring the sales of this class out at *two milliards*,[1] of which *one milliard* is spent for the subsistence of the agents who make up this class. It is seen that nothing is involved here but the consumption or destruction of products, with no reproduction at all; for this class subsists only through the successive payment of the recompense due for its labour, which is inseparable from expenditure employed in subsistence—i.e. *from expenditure on pure consumption, without regeneration of what is destroyed through this sterile expenditure, which is taken in its entirety out of the territory's annual reproduction.* The other *one milliard* is reserved for the replacement of its advances, which, in the following year, will be employed anew in purchasing from the *productive class* the raw materials for the goods which the *sterile class* makes.

Thus the *three milliards* which the *productive class* has received from the sales which it has made to the *proprietors* of the *revenue* and to the *sterile class* are employed by the *productive class* in paying the

---

[1] The sterile class uses one milliard's worth of raw materials, and consumes one milliard's worth of subsistence goods while it is working them up. This, on Quesnay's assumptions, brings the total market value of its products out at two milliards. R.L.M.

current year's revenue of *two milliards*, and in purchasing *one milliard*'s worth of products from the *sterile class*.

The course of this trade between the different classes, and its essential conditions, are by no means hypothetical. Anyone who wants to think about it will see that they are faithfully copied from nature; but the *data* which have been used, as the reader has been warned, are applicable only to the case which is here being dealt with.

The different states of prosperity or decline of an agricultural nation offer a host of other cases, and consequently other sets of *data*, each of which serves as the foundation of a special calculation which is in all strictness applicable to it.

The data with which we began, according to the most constant rule of the natural order, fix at *five milliards* the total reproduction which the *productive class*, working with *two milliards* of annual advances, causes to be annually regenerated in a territory such as that we have described. According to this hypothesis, the annual advances reproduce 250 per cent.[1] The proprietors' revenue can then be equal to the annual advances. But these data imply certain conditions *sine quabus non*. They assume that freedom of trade maintains sales of products at a proper price—a price of 18 livres per *setier* for corn, for example; moreover they assume that the cultivator does not have to pay, either directly or indirectly, any charges other than the revenue, of which one part, for example *two-sevenths*, should form the *revenue* of the sovereign. On the basis of these data, with a total revenue of two milliards the sovereign's share would be 572 millions;[2] that of the proprietors would be *four-sevenths*, or one milliard 144 millions; and that of the tithe-owners would be *one-seventh*, or 286 millions, taxes included.[3] There is no other way of laying taxes which are capable of supplying as large a public revenue as this without causing any decline in the annual reproduction of the nation's wealth.[4]

---

[1] Here the rate of reproduction is estimated by relating the annual advances to the total product reproduced. In most of the earlier versions of the *Tableau* it is estimated by relating the annual advances to the net product. R.L.M.

[2] Note that the taxes levied on tithes which have been rented out are not included in this estimate. Adding them to the calculated amount, it will be seen that the *two-sevenths* which constitutes the sovereign's share would yield without deterioration about 650 millions in taxes every year.

[3] In the earlier versions of the *Tableau*, the net product or revenue is usually reckoned exclusive of taxes and tithes. In the present context it is reckoned inclusive of them. R.L.M.

[4] If some landed property were exempt from contributing to the taxes, this could only be on account of certain benefits conducing to the welfare of the state, in which case these benefits should be counted as forming part of the public revenue. Moreover, such exemptions should be granted only on good cause shown.

It is very much in the interests of the proprietors, the sovereign, and the nation as a whole that all taxes should be directly laid on the revenue of the land; for any other form of imposition would be contrary to the natural order, since it would be detrimental to reproduction and to taxation, and the taxes would fall on the taxes themselves. Everything in this world is subject to the laws of nature: men are endowed with the intelligence required to understand and observe them; but the great number of factors involved demands that they should be grouped together in comprehensive patterns, which form the foundation of a very far-reaching and self-evident science,[1] whose study is indispensable if we are to avoid mistakes in policy.

Of the total reproduction of *five milliards*, the *proprietors* of the *revenue* and the *sterile class* have purchased *three milliards'* worth for their consumption; thus *two milliards'* worth of products still remain in the hands of the *productive class*. In addition, this class has purchased *one milliard's* worth of products from the *sterile class*. This adds up to an annual sum of *three milliards*, which is consumed by the various agents employed in the different types of work of this class, which are paid for by the annual advances of cultivation, and in the various types of day-to-day work involved in keeping the capital of the enterprise in proper repair, which are paid for by the interest shortly to be discussed.

Thus the annual expenditure of the productive class is *three milliards*, made up of *two milliards* of products which it retains for its consumption, and *one milliard* of goods which it has purchased from the sterile class.

These *three milliards* form what are called THE RETURNS of the *productive class*, *two milliards* of which constitute the annual advances which are consumed for the labour directly involved in the reproduction of the *five milliards* which this class causes to be annually regenerated, in order to restore and perpetuate the expenses which are destroyed by consumption. *The other one milliard* is taken by this same class out of the proceeds of its sales for the interest on the advances of its enterprises. We are now going to see why this interest is necessary.

(1) The fund of wealth employed in cultivation which constitutes the original advances is subject from day to day to a wearing-away which demands continual repairs, absolutely necessary if this important fund is to remain intact and not to move progressively towards complete annihilation, which would destroy cultivation, and consequently the reproduction, and consequently the wealth of the state, and consequently also the population.

---

[1] *Mais la multiplicité des objets exige de grandes combinaisons qui forment le fond d'une science évidente fort étendue.* R.L.M.

(2) Cultivation is inseparable from a number of serious accidents which sometimes almost completely destroy the harvest; such are frost, hail, blight, floods, mortality among live-stock, etc., etc. If the cultivators did not have any fund in reserve, it would follow that after such accidents they would be unable to pay the proprietors and the sovereign, or unable to meet the expenses of their cultivation in the following year. The latter event would always be that which in fact occurred, since the sovereign and the proprietors have the power to see that they get paid; and we know the fatal results of such a destruction of cultivation, which would soon fall, without any means of escape, on the proprietors, the sovereign, the tithe-owners, and the whole of the remainder of the nation.

The interest on the advances of the cultivators' enterprises ought therefore to be included in their *annual returns*. It enables them to face these serious accidents and the day-to-day maintenance of the wealth employed in cultivation, which requires to be constantly kept in repair.

It has been noted above (note (3), p. 151) that the *original advances* are about five times as great as the *annual advances*. According to our present hypothesis of *annual advances* amounting to *two milliards*, the *original advances* are therefore *ten milliards*, and the annual interest of *one milliard* represents a rate of only ten per cent. If we consider the amount of expenditure for which the interest must provide; if we think about the importance of its destination; if we reflect that without it the payment of rent and taxes would never be assured, that the regeneration of society's expenses would be destroyed, that the fund of wealth employed in cultivation and consequently cultivation itself would disappear, and that this devastation would destroy the greater part of the human race and force the remainder to live in the forests—we shall see that it is very far from being the case that a rate of ten per cent for the interest on the perishable[1] *advances* of cultivation is too high.

I am not saying that all cultivators draw annually, in addition to their *annual advances*, ten per cent for the *interest* on their original advances. But I do say that this is one of the main conditions of a state of prosperity; and that whenever it is not to be found in a nation, that nation is in a state of decline, and in a state of decline which progresses from year to year in such a way that when its course is known we can make a calculation enabling us to announce the moment of its complete destruction. I am also saying that a fund which is as advantageous to the nation as that of the advances of its cultivation ought in itself to bring in net to the farmers, who combine their work and the use of their intelligence with it, an annual interest at least as high as that which is paid to idle rentiers.

[1] *Périssables.* R.L.M.

The total amount of this interest is spent annually, because cultivators never allow it to remain inactive; for in the intervals when they are not obliged to use it for repairs, they do not fail to put it to profit in order to increase and improve their cultivation, without which they would be unable to provide for serious accidents. That is why interest is included in the total of annual expenditure.

SUMMARY

The total of *five milliards*, which is divided at the beginning of the process between the *productive class* and the *class of proprietors*, is annually spent in a regular order which perpetually assures the same annual reproduction. *One milliard* is spent by the *proprietors* in making purchases from the *productive class*, and *one milliard* in making purchases from the *sterile class*. The *productive class*, which sells *three milliards'* worth of products to the two other classes, returns *two milliards* of its receipts in payment of the revenue, and spends *one milliard* of them in making purchases from the sterile class. Thus the *sterile class* receives *two milliards*, which it employs in making purchases from the *productive class* for the subsistence of its agents and for the raw materials for its goods. The *productive class* spends annually *two milliards* on its own products, which completes the expenditure or total consumption of the *five milliards* of annual reproduction.

Such is the regular order of the distribution of the expenditure of the *five milliards* which the *productive class* causes to be annually regenerated through the expenditure of *two milliards* of annual advances, included in the total expenditure of the *five milliards* of annual reproduction.

We are now going to put before the reader the arithmetical formula of the distribution of this expenditure.

On the right,[1] at the top, is the sum of the advances of the *productive class*, which have been spent in the previous year in order to generate the present year's harvest. Below this sum is a line which separates it from the column showing the sums which this class receives.

On the left[2] are the sums which the *sterile class* receives.

In the middle, at the top, is the sum of the *revenue* which is divided out, to the right and left, between the two *classes* with whom it is spent.

The division of expenditure is indicated by dotted lines[3] which

---

[1] Should read 'on the left'. R.L.M.   [2] Should read 'on the right'. R.L.M.
[3] For technical reasons, the dotted lines have been replaced by ordinary lines in the reproduction of the *Tableau* on p. 158 below. R.L.M.

start from the sum of the revenue and go down slantwise to one class and the other. At the end of these lines on both sides is to be found the sum which the proprietors of the revenue spend in making purchases from each of these classes.

The mutual trade between the two classes is also indicated by dotted lines which go down slantwise from one class to the other from which the purchases are made. At the end of each line is the sum which one of the two classes receives in this way from the other by means of the mutual trade which they carry on among themselves for their expenditure.[1]

Finally, the calculation terminates on each side with the total sum of the receipts of each of the two classes. It is seen that in the given case, when the distribution of the expenditure follows the order which has been described and detailed above, the receipts of the productive class, including its advances, are equal to the total amount of the annual reproduction, and that cultivation, wealth, and population remain in the same state, without any increase or decline. A different case, as we have said above, would yield a different result.

If the proprietors were to spend more with the *productive class* than with the *sterile class*, in order to improve their land and increase their revenue, this addition to the expenditure employed on the work of the productive class should be regarded as an addition to the advances of this class.

The expenditure of the revenue is assumed here, in the state of prosperity, to be distributed equally between the productive class and the sterile class, whereas only one-third of the expenditure of the

---

[1] Each sum which the *productive class* and the *sterile class* receive implies a double value, because it involves a sale and a purchase, and consequently the value of what is sold and the value of the sum which is used to purchase it. But real consumption is involved only to the value of the *five milliards* which form the total receipts of the *productive class*[2]. The sums of money which pass into the hands of each class are distributed among them by means of the circulation of a total sum of money which every year starts the same circulation again. This total sum of money can be assumed to be more or less large, and its circulation more or less rapid; for the rapidity of the circulation of money can in large part make up for the total quantity of money. For example, in a year in which, without there being any reduction in reproduction, there was a big rise in the price of the products, whether by reason of facilities granted to trade or otherwise, it would not be necessary for there to be an increase in the stock of money in order to enable payment for these products to be made. Nevertheless, larger sums of money would pass into the hands of buyers and sellers, which would lead most people to believe that the total quantity of money in the kingdom had been greatly increased. Thus the vulgar, taking this appearance for the reality, find it very mysterious.

[2] Quesnay is clearly assuming here that the consumption of the two milliards' worth of manufactured goods is simply the consumption in another form of the one milliard's worth of subsistence goods and the one milliard's worth of raw materials which are as it were incorporated in the manufactured goods. R.L.M.

productive class goes to the sterile class, the reason being that the cultivator's expenditure is less freely disposable than that of the proprietor. But the more agriculture is in a state of stagnation, the more one should then devote a portion of the disposable expenditure to building it up again.

FORMULA OF THE *TABLEAU ECONOMIQUE*

Total Reproduction: Five milliards

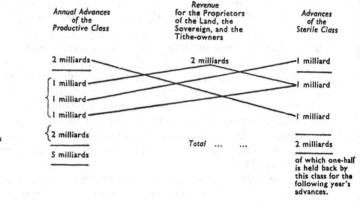

Annual Advances of the Productive Class	Revenue for the Proprietors of the Land, the Sovereign, and the Tithe-owners	Advances of the Sterile Class

	2 milliards	2 milliards	1 milliard
Sums which are used to pay the revenue and the interest on the original advances	{ 1 milliard		1 milliard
	{ 1 milliard		
	{ 1 milliard		1 milliard
Expenditure of the annual advances	{ 2 milliards		
		Total	2 milliards
Total	5 milliards		of which one-half is held back by this class for the following year's advances.

IMPORTANT COMMENTS

First Comment

The expenditure of the proprietors with the *sterile class*, which is used for the subsistence of this *class*, should not be confused with the proprietors' direct expenditure with the *productive class* for their own wants and those of their guests, and for the animals which they keep; for this expenditure of the proprietors with the *productive class* can be much more profitable to agriculture than their expenditure with the *sterile class*.

Among the proprietors of the revenue there are a great number who are very wealthy and who consume the most expensive products. Thus the volume of products which they consume is proportionately much less great than that of the least expensive products which the other classes consume. The men who spend the revenue and who buy at such high prices must then also be proportionately much less numerous relatively to the total value of their purchases. But their expenditure maintains the price of the best quality products, and thus maintains gradationally the proper price of the other products, to the advantage of the territory's revenue.

It is not the same with the large amount of money which the *proprietors* may spend with the *sterile class*; and this is what constitutes the difference between conspicuous consumption of primary produce and luxury in the way of ornamentation.[1] The effects of the first are not as much to be feared as those of the second.

The man who purchases a *litron* of green peas for 100 livres pays this sum to a cultivator who employs it in the expenses of cultivation, to the advantage of the annual reproduction. The man who purchases a piece of gold braid for 100 livres pays this sum to a worker who employs a part of it to re-purchase the raw material from abroad; it is only the other part, employed to purchase his subsistence, which is returned to the *productive class*. And this return, moreover, is not as advantageous as the direct expenditure of the proprietor with the *productive class* would have been, for the worker does not purchase expensive products for his subsistence, and therefore does not contribute, as the proprietor does, to the maintenance of the value and the revenue of the good land which has the capacity to produce this costly produce. So far as the part which has been sent abroad in payment for purchases is concerned, if this returns to the *productive class*, as does in fact happen at least in part in nations where there is a mutual trade in products,[2] it always does so burdened with commercial costs, which bring about a reduction in it and prevent its return from being complete.

Second Comment

The expenditure involved in simple consumption is expenditure which is itself destroyed without any return. It can be maintained only through the *productive class*, which in this respect can provide for itself. Thus this expenditure, when it is not employed in reproduction, ought to be regarded as *sterile* expenditure, and even as harmful, or as luxury expenditure, if it is superfluous and detrimental to agriculture.

The greater part of the expenditure of the *proprietors* is at least *sterile* expenditure; we can except only that which is undertaken for

---

[1] *Faste de subsistance et luxe de décoration.* The concepts involved in the Physiocratic distinction between *faste* and *luxe* are discussed below, pp. 316 ff. R.L.M.

[2] This is not normally the case in trade with the East Indies; except when it is carried on by foreign merchants who sell us what they have purchased, and who employ in our country, in purchasing products, the same money with which we have paid for their East Indian commodities. But it is not the same when this trade is carried on by our own native merchants, when it is restricted to exchanges between ourselves and the East Indians who want nothing but money.

the maintenance and improvement of their property and for the expansion of its cultivation. But as the proprietors are by natural law entrusted with the care of the administration of their patrimony, and with the expenses involved in keeping it in repair, they cannot be confused with that part of the population which forms the purely sterile class.

Third Comment

In the state of prosperity of a kingdom whose territory was fully cultivated by the best possible methods, where trade was as free and unobstructed as possible, and where consequently the revenue of the *proprietors* could not be further increased, the *proprietors* would be able to spend *one-half* of their revenue in making purchases from the *sterile class*. But if the territory were not completely cultivated and improved, if roads were lacking, if there were rivers to be made navigable and canals to be constructed for the transport of products, the proprietors ought to economize on their expenditure with the *sterile class*, in order to undertake the expenditure necessary to increase their revenue and their enjoyments to the maximum possible. Until they had reached this point, their superfluous expenditure with the *sterile class* would be luxury expenditure, detrimental to their opulence and to the nation's prosperity; for everything which is disadvantageous to agriculture is detrimental to the nation and the state, and everything which favours agriculture is profitable to the state and the nation. It is the necessity of the expenditure which the proprietors alone can make for the expansion of their wealth and for the general well-being of society, which makes security of landed property an essential condition of the natural order of the government of empires.

Under the feudal political system this landed property was formerly regarded as the basis of the military strength of the nobles, but it was only the ownership of the land which people thought about. That is why so many curious customs and laws relating to the inheritance of landed property still exist today in spite of the changes which have occurred in the monarchy, while at the same time so little attention has been paid to security of property in the movable wealth necessary for cultivation, which alone can turn landed property to advantage. It has not been sufficiently recognized that the true foundation of the military strength of a kingdom is the nation's prosperity itself.

Rome knew how to conquer and subjugate many nations, but she did not know how to *govern*. She despoiled the countries fallen under her domination of their agricultural wealth; thenceforth her military strength disappeared; the conquests which had enriched her were taken from her; and she found herself left alone and defenceless against the ravages and violence of the enemy.

Fourth Comment

In the regular order which we are following here, the total amount which the *proprietors* and the *sterile class* pay out every year for their purchases is returned every year to the *productive class*, so that it may pay the annual revenue of *two milliards* to the *proprietors*, and the interest on its original and annual advances to itself.

If anything were taken away from this distribution of expenditure to the detriment of agriculture, or if anything were taken away from the returns of the cultivator, by any exactions or impediments to trade, a decline in the annual reproduction of the nation's wealth and a reduction in the population would be bound to follow—a decline easy to demonstrate with the aid of calculation. Thus *it is with reference to the order of the distribution of expenditure, according to whether it is returned to or taken away from the* productive class, *according to whether it increases or diminishes the advances of this class, and according to whether it maintains the prices of products or causes them to fall, that we may calculate the effects of the good or bad leadership of a nation.*

The *sterile class* can spend for the subsistence of its agents only about one-half of the *two milliards* which it receives, because the other half is used in purchasing raw materials for its goods. Thus this class constitutes only about one-quarter of the nation.

We have seen that the returns of *three milliards* accruing to the *productive class* include *one milliard* for the interest on the original and annual advances of this class, which is continually employed in keeping these advances in good repair. Thus only about *two milliards* remain with this class for the expenditure of its own immediate agents, whose number is consequently about double that of the agents of the *sterile class*. But each of them, with the aid of labouring animals, can generate a reproduction which can support eight men, i.e. his own family, which may be assumed to consist of four persons, and one other family containing the same number of persons belonging to the *sterile class* or to the *class of proprietors*.[1]

---

[1] The population of the kingdom in the present case is assumed to be 30 million, as compared with 16 million in some earlier versions of the *Tableau*. But the proportions in which families are divided between the different classes, and the relative amounts of their consumption, are the same. As before, one-quarter of the families are assumed to belong to the sterile class, one-half to the productive class, and one-quarter to the class of proprietors. Consumption per head in the class of proprietors is twice as high as it is in the other two classes: thus the proprietors consume two value-units, the productive class two value-units, and the sterile class one value-unit. See below, pp. 227 and 282–3. R.L.M.

F

If it is desired to make a more detailed examination of the distribution of a nation's expenditure, it will be found in Chapter 7 of the *Rural Philosophy*. It will be seen there that in addition to the *five milliards* which are assumed here to make up the nation's portion, there are other expenses: such are commercial costs and the fodder for the labouring animals employed in cultivation. These expenses are not included in the distribution of expenditure represented in the *Tableau*, and when they are added to the latter they cause the total value of the annual reproduction to rise to *6,370,000,000*. But it should be noted in this connection that the commercial costs may increase, to the detriment of the nation, or diminish, to the benefit of the nation, according to whether this branch is or is not directed in contradiction to the natural order.

Fifth Comment

In the pattern of expenditure which has just been described, it has been assumed that the nation trades only with itself. But there is no kingdom whose territory produces all the kinds of wealth suitable for the enjoyment of its inhabitants: thus there must be external trade, by means of which a nation sells abroad a part of its products in order to buy from abroad those which it needs. Nevertheless, since it can buy from abroad only as much as it sells abroad, the state of its expenditure must always be in conformity with the reproduction which its territory annually regenerates. Thus the calculations regarding this expenditure can be regularly based on the quantity of this reproduction itself, abstracting completely from external trade, the details of which are indeterminate, incalculable, and useless to inquire into. It is enough to draw attention to the fact that in a situation where there is free competition in external trade there is simply an exchange of value for equal value, without loss or gain on either side.

So far as the costs of transport are concerned, the nation and the foreign country each pay for them in their sales or purchases; and they constitute for the merchants a fund separate from that of the nation, because in the external trade of agricultural nations every merchant is a foreigner relatively to the interests of these nations. Thus an agricultural kingdom which engages in trade unites in itself two nations which are distinct from one another: one, bound to the territory which provides the revenue, constitutes the essential part of the society; and the other is an extrinsic addition which forms part of the general republic of external trade, employed and paid by the agricultural nations. The costs of this trade, although necessary, should be regarded as a burdensome expense, taken out of the revenue of the proprietors of the land. Thus it ought to be freed from all forms of monopoly and from all surcharges which would fall in a ruinous way on the revenue of the sovereign and the other proprietors.

When there is free competition in external trade, the prices which are current among the trading nations ought to form the basis of the calculation of the wealth and annual expenditure of nations which have an immune and unobstructed trade.[1] External trade is more or less extensive according to the diversity of the consumption of the inhabitants, and according to whether the products of the country are more or less diverse. The more diverse are the products of a kingdom, the less will be its imports and exports, and the more will the nation be able to save on the costs of external trade. Nevertheless, external trade should always be quite free, cleared of all encumbrances and exempt from all impositions, because it is only by means of the communication between nations which it maintains that we can make sure of always having the best possible price for the territory's products in internal trade, and the highest possible revenue for the sovereign and the nation.

Sixth Comment

It can be seen that the same products pass several times through the hands of the merchants and artisans; but attention should be drawn to the fact that these repetitions of sales and purchases, which unproductively increase *circulation*, represent only the transposition of commodities, and an increase in costs, without any production of wealth. Thus the sum of the products is reckoned with reference to quantity and their prices when they are sold at first hand.

The more these prices are subject to the natural order, and the more they are constantly high, the more profitable they are in the exchanges made with foreign countries, the more they stimulate

---

[1] I.e. exempt from all fiscal, seigneurial, etc., contributions, all forms of monopoly, and all salaries of inspectors and other useless officials. Trade, like agriculture, should have no other government than the natural order. In every act of trade there is a buyer and a seller, who stipulate their interests freely and in contradiction with one another; and their interests, regulated in this way by those who are the sole competent judges of them, are in conformity with the public interest. Any intervention of officers invested with authority is foreign to it, and all the more dangerous because one has to expect in them ignorance and even more formidable motives. Monopoly in trade and agriculture has only too often found protectors: the planting of vines, the sale of spirits of cider, freedom of trade in corn, and the import of foreign manufactured commodities, have been prohibited; the manufactures of the kingdom have obtained exclusive privileges to the detriment of one another; manufacturing entrepreneurs have been compelled to employ foreign raw materials to the exclusion of those of the country, etc. Faint and false lights have glittered in the darkness, and the natural order has been turned upside down by individual interests, which always hide under the cloak of general welfare and make their requests in its name.

agriculture,[1] the more they maintain the value of the various products of the territory, the more they increase the revenue of the
sovereign and the proprietors, and the more also they increase the
nation's currency and the sum of the wages paid in return for the
labour or employment of those who are not original possessors of
products.

The employment of these wages, and their good or bad distribution,
contribute greatly to the prosperity or decline of a kingdom, to the
regularity or irregularity in the habits and customs of a nation, and
to the increase or decrease in the population. Men may be harassed in
the countryside and attracted to the capital by the pleasures of
luxury and sensuality, or alternatively they may be evenly distributed
throughout the provinces. In the latter case they can maintain
consumption close to the place of production, whereas in the other
case they cannot avoid high transport costs which make products fall
to a low price in sales at first hand and cause the territory's revenue
and the total of wages and population to diminish.

The extent of resale trade[2] depends upon the energy and means of
the merchants; but that of an agricultural nation is regulated by the
annual reproduction of its territory. The profits which provide a clear
gain for the merchants of a nation should never be confused with the
wealth of the nation itself, for the extent of the merchants' annual
trade cannot exceed the sales of the existing reproduction of the
territory, as determined by the current prices paid in sales at first
hand. The merchant tries to buy at the lowest possible price and to
sell at the highest possible price, so as to make his gain as high as
possible at the expense of the nation: his individual interest and that
of the nation are opposed. Nevertheless, taking a broad view of the
matter and considering all its ramifications, it is not the case that the
whole body of merchants, and even each member of this huge body,
does not have a very real interest in products being constantly sold
at first hand at the highest possible price. For the more they are sold
at high prices, the more net product cultivation yields; the more net
product cultivation yields, the more profitable it is; the more
profitable cultivation is, the more it expands on every hand; the more
production it regenerates, the more returns it provides for the
cultivators, the more revenue for the sovereign, the proprietors, and
the tithe-owners, and the more wages for all the other orders of

---

[1] The interest of the cultivator is the mainspring of all economic operations
and all agricultural progress: the more that products constantly sell at high
prices, the more assured are the annual returns of the farmers, the more cultivation is extended, and the more revenue the land brings in, as much through the
proper price of the products as through the increase in the annual reproduction.
And the more reproduction increases, the more the wealth of the nation is
expanded, and the more the power of the state is augmented.

[2] *Commerce de revendeur.* R.L.M.

citizens; the more does expenditure of every kind increase, the more does trade find objects and opportunities and the more energetic does it become; and consequently the more does the sum total of the gains of the merchants increase, precisely as a result of competition, which, in each individual case, prevents these gains from being excessive to the detriment of the prices of the products. But there are very few merchants who look thus far into the matter, and still fewer who are capable of sacrificing a present gain for the certainty of these considerable future benefits. Thus it is never the merchants, but rather the needs of consumers and the means which they have to satisfy them, which in the first instance ensure the prices of products in sales at first hand. The merchants never cause prices or the possibility of trade to come into being: it is the possibility of trade and the intercommunication of prices which causes merchants to come into being.[1]

Seventh Comment

We have said nothing about the stock of money which circulates in each nation's trade, and which is vulgarly regarded as the true wealth of the state, since, as it is said, 'with money one can buy everything one needs'. But people do not ask themselves with what one can procure money for oneself. Money does not give itself away for nothing, however: it costs as much as it is worth to the man who buys it. It is trade which supplies it to those nations which do not possess gold or silver mines; but these nations would have neither gold nor silver if they did not possess the wherewithal to pay for them; and they will always have as much of them as they want to buy, or as it suits them to buy, if they have products to give in exchange.[2]

I say as much as it suits them to buy, because money is not a form of wealth which men need for their enjoyment. What we have to obtain are the goods necessary for life and the annual reproduction of these goods themselves. To convert these products into money, by abstracting this money from expenditure which is beneficial to agriculture, would be to reduce correspondingly the annual reproduction of wealth. The stock of money in a nation can increase only so far as this reproduction itself increases; otherwise an increase in the

[1] It is the same with them as with a well-rope and the use to which it is put. These do not constitute the source of the water which is in the well: on the contrary, it is the water which is in the well, together with the knowledge and the need which we have of it, which is the cause of the use to which the rope is put. Enlightened men do not confuse causes with means.

[2] Cf. Hume's view that the stock of money will tend to be 'nearly proportionable to the art and industry of each nation' (*David Hume: Writings on Economics*, ed. E. Rotwein, p. 63). R.L.M.

stock of money could be brought about only to the detriment of the annual reproduction of wealth. And the decrease in this reproduction would necessarily, and quickly, bring in its train a decrease in the stock of money and the impoverishment of the nation. The stock of money in a nation can decrease, however, without there being any decrease in the wealth of that nation, because one can in numerous ways make up for a lack of money when one is wealthy and has a free and unobstructed trade; but nothing can make up for a lack of annual reproduction of the wealth suitable for men's enjoyment without involving a loss. We should even expect that the money stock of a poor nation would require to be proportionately greater than that of a wealthy nation; for there remains to both only the amount which they need for their sales and purchases. And in poor nations there is a much greater need for the intervention of money in trade: they have to pay for everything in cash, because there is scarcely anyone whose promise can be relied on. But in wealthy nations there are many people who are known to be wealthy, and whose written promise is regarded as quite safe and fully guaranteed by their wealth, so that all the major sales are made on credit, i.e. through the medium of sound bills which stand in the place of money and greatly facilitate trade. Thus it is not with reference to the greater or lesser quantity of money that one should judge a state's opulence; also it is estimated that a money stock equal to the revenue of the proprietors of the land is much more than sufficient for an agricultural nation in which circulation takes a regular course and trade is carried on with confidence and under conditions of complete freedom.[1]

So far as the universal trading republic spread over the different countries is concerned, and the small purely trading nations which are only parts of this huge republic and which can be regarded as capital cities or if you like as principal counting-houses, the total of their coined money is proportionate to the extent of their resale trade. They increase this total as much as they can by means of their profits and their savings, in order to expand the capital employed in their trade; money is their appropriate patrimony; and merchants employ it in their purchases only in order to get it back with a profit in their sales. Thus they can expand their money stock only at the expense of the nations with whom they trade. It is always kept in reserve in their hands; it goes out of their counting-houses and circulates only in order that it should come back again together with an additional amount; thus this money does not form part of the

---

[1] A long note is inserted by Quesnay at this point. Since most of it is substantially identical with the note translated on pp. 134–5 above, and the remainder contains material which is substantially duplicated in other items translated in this volume, it has been omitted. R.L.M.

wealth of agricultural nations, which are always limited to their reproduction, out of which they continually pay the gains of the merchants. The latter, in whatever country they may happen to reside, are bound to other nations by their trade; it is their trade, indeed, which is their fatherland and the store-house of their wealth; they buy and sell both where they live and where they do not live; and the area over which they carry on their occupation has no determinate boundaries at all and is not confined to any particular territory. Our merchants are also other nations' merchants; other nations' merchants are also our merchants; and all of them also carry on trade with one another. Thus their trading connections penetrate and extend everywhere, their final goal always being money, which trade itself supplies and distributes among the nations in conformity with the prices determined by the natural order which regulates from day to day the market value of the products. But agricultural nations look at things from another point of view, more useful for them and more far-reaching: they should seek only for the greatest reproduction possible in order to increase and perpetuate the forms of wealth suitable for men's enjoyment. Money for them is only a minor form of intermediary wealth which would disappear in a moment if there were no reproduction.

H.

THE 'FIRST ECONOMIC PROBLEM'[1]

QUESTION

Does the profit which a nation receives from an increase in the price of the products of its territory exceed the disadvantage caused by the increase in expenses which the rise in the price of the products brings about? For it might appear that an increase in prices which brought us a gain in our sales which we lost in our purchases would not leave us any profit.

ANSWER

This question may relate to a number of cases which differ from one another and are difficult to disentangle. Different data must produce different results; thus we have to begin by laying down the data and settling on a particular case.

We shall take a very complicated case, which will make clearer the application of the calculation and rules of the *Tableau Economique*, and throw light on a number of questions relative to the question which has been propounded.

EXAMPLE

If 1950 *millions* of annual advances of the productive class brought in only 400 *millions* of revenue, because of the existence of indirect taxes which fell to the extent of 450 *millions* on the productive class, and because agriculture had greatly degenerated owing to a deficiency in the original advances required to carry on proper cultivation, then the total annual reproduction, considered in its present state and without regard to the progressive development of the decline, would be only 3 *milliards* 100 *millions*.[2]

---

[1] This article first appeared in the *Journal de l'Agriculture, du Commerce et des Finances* in August 1766, under the title '*Problème Economique*'. It was later republished with certain additions and amendments in *Physiocratie*. The present translation is from the text of *Physiocratie*, as reproduced in I.N.E.D., II, pp. 859–77. R.L.M.

[2] This represents the sum of the following three items: (a) the revenue (assumed to be 400); (b) the annual advances of 1950 (representing 1500 for the actual

168

The 450 *millions* of indirect taxes would represent an imposition upon the annual expenditure devoted to the labour of cultivation, and would cause this expenditure to increase to 1950 *millions*. Thus to get a proper indication of what the annual expenditure on the labour of cultivation would really be, we must subtract from the sum of 1950 *millions* that of 450 *millions* of indirect taxes. Thus the 1950 *millions* would be reduced to 1500, which would represent the real amount of the productive class's annual advances.

The interest on the original and annual advances of this class, being equal to one-half of the annual advances, would amount to 750 *millions*.[1]

Suppose that full freedom and immunity of external trade in the sale of the territory's products was then permitted, and that as a result of this the prices of these products increased by one-sixth above their present level. What would be the effect of this rise in prices?

WORKING

In order to estimate this effect, a large number of matters have to be considered.

FIRST MATTER TO BE CONSIDERED

The rise in prices of which we are speaking would produce its effect

---

work of cultivation and 450 for the taxes); and (c) the interest of 750 on the annual advances (taken as being equal to one-half of the annual advances, reckoning the latter here net of taxes). See the two following paragraphs. R.L.M.

[1] The annual advances increase to the detriment of the product in proportion to the extent that the original advances diminish, because this diminution is made up for as much as possible by undertaking very costly work at the expense of the annual reproduction, which means that the costs of this work are due to the lack of original advances sufficient to enable cultivation of the most profitable kind to be carried on every year at minimum cost. The interest on these original advances diminishes in the proportion that these advances themselves decline. Normally, this decline itself occurs because the farmers are not receiving the interest necessary to maintain the advances. Thus, in such a case, we ought not to include the full amount of the interest in the calculation of the total annual reproduction. This consideration has not held us up, because it has not appeared to be essential to the solution of the problem, which always reduces to the state of the base of any reproduction whatsoever, and because it would have further complicated the calculation and greatly altered the order of the *Tableau*, which is not yet sufficiently familiar to enable the reader's mind to follow with understanding the considerable variations which the alteration would involve. But I felt that I should at least warn the reader to be on the watch when it is a question of the real total of the reproduction, which is examined here in abstraction from the consideration with which this note is concerned.

only on those products which enter into trade. Thus it is necessary to subtract from the calculation of the increase in prices that part of the total reproduction which does not enter into trade. Such is in fact one part of the annual advances of cultivation.

On the given hypothesis, the annual advances of the productive class, abstracting from the 450 *millions* of indirect taxes which they have to bear, amount to 1500 *millions*; and of these about one-half, or 750 *millions*, are consumed directly and *in natura* by the cultivators. Thus we should not apply to this one-half, which is not the subject of trade, either the rise in prices or the increase in expenses caused by the rise. Therefore it should not enter into the calculation of the price-change we are discussing here, since it does not enter into trade, and since the constant consumption of it by the cultivators does not increase or diminish the costs of cultivation when prices change.

Thus from the total reproduction of 3 *milliards* 100 *millions* we must take away 750 *millions*, representing the value of the products directly consumed by the productive class. There remain 2 *milliards* 350 *millions* for the value of the products which enter into trade, and whose price will according to our hypothesis be raised *by one-sixth*, or 470 *millions*.[1] The total reproduction, which was formerly worth only 3 *milliards* 100 *millions*, will now be worth 3 *milliards* 570 *millions* as a result of this first effect of the rise in prices.

In order to ascertain the increase in the revenue to be shared between the sovereign, the proprietors of the land, and the tithe-owners which will be associated with this increase in the value of the total reproduction, we have to subtract from the latter the returns of the cultivators.

As we have noted above, one part of these returns participates in the rise in prices and expenses, and the other does not participate in them.

The portion of these returns which participates in the rise includes (1) one-half of the annual advances of the productive class, the farmers being obliged to sell the products which form this half of their advances in order to provide for the wages which they give to their servants and the other workers engaged in cultivation; and (2) the interest on the advances of their enterprise which the entrepreneurs of cultivation spend annually, as has been seen in the analysis of the *Tableau Economique*.

The portion of the returns in respect of which the rise in prices does not bring about any change comprises (1) the one-half of the annual advances of the productive class which is consumed directly and *in natura* by the cultivators, as we have noted; and (2) the indirect taxes amounting to 450 *millions* which similarly remain *in*

[1] One-sixth of 2,350,000 is of course approximately 390 millions, not 470 millions. R.L.M.

statu quo, since they do not consist of products, and since it is a question of an increase in the prices of products brought about by the restoration of freedom of trade.

Thus the returns of the cultivators are composed of the following:

1. Their annual advances.

Namely { One-half consumed *in natura,* which has not risen in price, amounting to .... 750 / One-half which enters into trade and which has risen in price by one-sixth, making it........... 900[1] } 1650 *millions*

2. Their interest, which the rise in prices increases by one-sixth over and above its former level, making it .... 900[2]

3. The 450 *millions* of indirect taxes, which do not participate at all in the increase of prices, as the products which are traded do, and which consequently remain in the calculation of the returns of the cultivator at............................. 450

Grand Total of the returns of the cultivators ...... 3 *milliards*

When these returns are subtracted from the total reproduction of 3 *milliards* 570 *millions,* there remain 570 *millions* for the revenue which is shared among the proprietors of the land, the sovereign, and the tithe-owners, who before the rise in prices received a revenue of only 400 *millions.*

Thus, considering only this first matter, the increase in their revenue is already 170 *millions.*

SECOND MATTER TO BE CONSIDERED

It has been proved that freedom of external trade, at the same time as it raises the price of the country's products, assures for them a price which is much less variable than it would be in the absence of this freedom of trade.

It has been calculated that the establishment of this greater equality between the price of the product in its sale at first hand and its price in the last purchase, i.e. in the purchase made by the

---

[1] Figure apparently taken to the nearest 100. R.L.M.
[2] Figure apparently taken to the nearest 100. R.L.M.

consumer, yields to those who sell at first hand a profit of more than *one-tenth*,[1] without causing any damage to the purchaser-consumer.[2]

This *one-tenth* increase in profit for those who sell at first hand will only apply, for the reasons stated above, to the products which enter into trade, the market value of which before the rise in prices amounted to 2 *milliards* 350 *millions*. But an increase of *one-tenth* in these 2 *milliards* 350 *millions* means an increase of 235 *millions* in sales at first hand, which, coupled with the increase of 170 *millions* brought about as we have seen above by a *one-sixth* increase in the price of the 2 *milliards* 350 *millions* of products which are the subject of trade, means a total increase of 405 *millions* in the revenue; for we have already deducted the whole of the increase which must be taken into account in the cultivators' returns.

This addition to the revenue, added to the 400 *millions* of revenue which were received before the increase in prices brought about by restoration of the freedom and immunity of trade—this addition, I say, would cause the revenue to rise from 400 to 805 *millions*.

DISTRIBUTION OF THE INCREASE IN REVENUE

We are now going to represent in a *Tableau*[3] the order of the distribution between the productive class and the sterile class, and the results of this distribution. We shall disregard 5 *millions* of revenue in this *Tableau*, as much with the aim of preventing the reader from being worried with fractions as with the aim of keeping our figures below rather than above the true ones.

[1] What Quesnay means here is that the *receipts from sales* 'at first hand' will increase by 'more than one-tenth'. The addition may in the first instance bring about an increase in the *profit* of the farmer, but this will eventually crystallize out into rent. In the calculation in the following paragraph, the whole of the increase in receipts from sales is simply added to the revenue. R.L.M.

[2] See the article *Corn* in the Encyclopedia; the treatise on *The Improvement of Land* by Pattullo; the treatise on *The Export and Import of Corn* by Du Pont; and the *Ephémérides du Citoyen*, 1766, Vol. VI, pp. 33 ff.

[3] This *Tableau* (p. 173) is of course modelled on Quesnay's original '*Formule*' in his *Analysis* (see p. 158 above). The way in which the various figures are arrived at is easy enough to follow if one bears in mind the particular data of the problem Quesnay is now considering, and the principles according to which the '*Formule*' is constructed.

In the present problem, we are given a situation in which, after the rise in prices, the revenue is 800; the interest on the productive class's original advances is 900; the productive class's annual advances are 2100 (the 'true' annual advances of 1650 plus the taxes of 450); and the total annual reproduction is therefore 3800, the sum of these three amounts.

Before the rise in prices, the 'true' annual advances of the productive class

TABLEAU SHOWING THE DISTRIBUTION

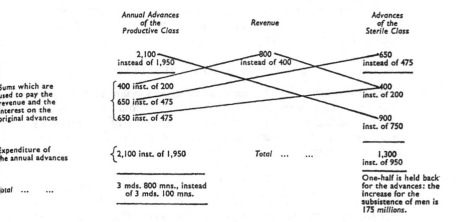

	Annual Advances of the Productive Class	Revenue	Advances of the Sterile Class
	2,100 instead of 1,950	800 instead of 400	650 instead of 475
Sums which are used to pay the revenue and the interest on the original advances	400 inst. of 200		400 inst. of 200
	650 inst. of 475		
	650 inst. of 475		900 inst. of 750
Expenditure of the annual advances	2,100 inst. of 1,950	Total	1,300 inst. of 950
Total	3 mds. 800 mns., instead of 3 mds. 100 mns.		One-half is held back for the advances: the increase for the subsistence of men is 175 *millions*.

were 1500. One-half of the product representing the refund of these advances was consumed *in natura* by the productive class; and the other half 'entered into trade', the receipts from its sale being used by the productive class to buy manufactured goods from the sterile class. In the present case, this second 'half' has risen in value to 900, thus raising the total value of the 'true' annual advances from 1500 to 1650, and raising the value of the productive class's purchases of manufactured goods from the sterile class from 750 to 900. The proprietors' purchases of manufactured goods from the sterile class amount to one-half of the amount of the revenue—i.e. in this case, 400, so that the total value of the sterile class's annual product is 1300. Of this 1300, in accordance with Quesnay's usual assumptions, one-half consists of the value of raw materials purchased from the productive class, and the other half consists of the value of food purchased from the productive class. The annual advances of the sterile class, as usual, are taken to be equal to one-half of the total value of its annual product, i.e. 650. The items on the sterile side of the *Tableau* are thus fully accounted for.

The sterile class, then, purchases 650 raw materials and 650 food from the productive class. Of the resultant product of 1300, 900 is sold to the productive class and 400 to the proprietors.

The productive class sells 400 food to the proprietors; 650 raw materials to the sterile class; and 650 food to the sterile class. The receipts from these sales, amounting *in toto* to 1700, are shown in the first three (bracketed) items on the productive side. Of these receipts of 1700, 800 is in effect reserved for the payment of the revenue; and the remaining 900, equal in value to the interest on the productive class's original advances, is employed to purchase manufactured goods from the sterile class.

The remainder of the total reproduction (exclusive of the taxes of 450) consists in real terms of (a) food to the value of 750 which is consumed *in natura* by the productive class; and (b) agricultural produce to the value of 900 which is exchanged within the productive class and used for the 'repair' of the productive class's original advances. R.L.M.

The distribution which has just been depicted[1] is still only that of the sums which have been increased by the rise in prices, and is not sufficient to enable us to understand the effects of the rise in the expenses of the purchaser-consumers, which is inseparable from the increase in the prices of products. It simply points to the paths which lead to this understanding.

LAST QUESTION TO BE RESOLVED

It remains to determine what the increase in gain would be, in the given case, upon the expenditure of an additional 400 millions of revenue, brought into existence by the increase in the prices of the territory's products, due to the restoration of the regular order of trade, its freedom, and its immunity.

EXACT SOLUTION

or calculation of the *actual effects of the rise in prices in the given case.*

Before the increase in prices, the market value of the total annual reproduction was 3 *milliard* 100 *million livres.* Thus the total amount of this reproduction could then be assumed to be 3 *milliard* 100 *million measures,* each *measure* being valued at *one livre.*

These 3 *milliard* 100 *million measures* were divided among the

---

[1] We have not shown in this *Tableau* the order of the distribution of the expenditure of the 450 *millions* of indirect taxes. This part of the distribution would have required the inclusion of particular details and amplifications which I have not thought it expedient to deal with, in order that readers who are not well-informed about these matters should not have their attention distracted by too great a number of items. Emphasis has been laid on the result, which is that the sum of 450 *millions* returns to the productive class to which it should remain attached, to the detriment of the revenue; also this sum is expended in almost the same way as the revenue.

Thus one can easily get an idea of the circulation of this expenditure between the sterile class and the productive class by putting it together with the revenue, instead of keeping it attached to the annual advances of the productive class. On this supposition, it would cause the total of revenue to rise to 1250 *millions,* the distribution of the expenditure of which would be carried out in the manner depicted in the *Tableau*—i.e. one-half to the productive class, and one-half to the sterile class which would spend it again in making purchases of products from the productive class. This would complete the sum which the productive class would have to pay in revenue. The extra amount paid would be equal to the amount it pays in indirect taxes, which increase its expenses and returns by 450 *millions.*

The only difference which would then be found as between the two classes would be an additional expenditure of 225 *millions* with the sterile class, which would not bring about any change in the total of the successive annual reproduction. Thus it is easy to get a complete idea of the whole circulation of expenditure in the case in question, and also to keep in mind the idea of the actual state of affairs, in which the 450 *millions* of indirect taxes should in reality remain attached to the annual advances of the productive class, which itself makes the advances of these indirect taxes.

different classes of consumers in proportion to the share of each in the 3 *milliard* 100 *million livres*. The question we now have to determine is how many *measures* each class will be able to procure for itself after the increase in price of *one-sixth* which has caused the value of each *measure* which enters into trade to rise to 1 *livre* 4 *sous*.[1]

In our examination of this distribution of *measures* relative to the *livres* which have to be paid for them, we shall group together the sales which the productive class makes and those which the sterile class makes. For the purchases which are made from the sterile class are of products converted into finished goods or into expenses by this class itself, so that everything which is purchased from the sterile class ought to be regarded as a purchase of products from the productive class, or if you like as a resale of these same products by the sterile class which enables it to be reimbursed for its raw materials and to incur the expenditure which it employs in purchasing products for its subsistence from the productive class.

Thus the productive class purchases, or is assumed to purchase, for its returns, from itself and from the sterile class, 2250 *million measures*,

$$\text{Namely} \begin{cases} \text{From the productive class, } 1500 \ million \\ \text{From the sterile class, } \quad\;\; 750 \ million \end{cases} \begin{array}{c} 2250 \ million \\ measures^2 \end{array}$$

which cost only 2550 *million livres*, since there are only 1500 *million measures* which participate in the rise in prices and are valued at 1 *livre* 4 *sous* each, or 1800 *millions* in all, and since there are 750 *million measures* which do not enter into trade at all. The latter are consumed by the productive class out of its own product, so that one cannot suppose that there is any increase in their price and must assume that they remain as before at 1 *livre per measure*, and are valued at only 750 *million livres*.[3]

---

[1] A rise of 4 sous in one livre is one-fifth, not one-sixth. Cf. the footnote on p. 170 above. R.L.M.

[2] Quesnay here returns to the data given at the beginning of the article, representing the situation prior to the rise in prices. The 'true' annual advances of the productive class are 1500. According to Quesnay's usual assumptions, the purchases of manufactured goods by the productive class from the sterile class amount to one-half of this sum, i.e. 750. In real terms, the productive class in this situation finishes up with the following products available for its consumption: (a) 750 food which is consumed *in natura*; (b) 750 agricultural produce, representing the interest on the original advances, which is exchanged within the productive class and used for the 'repair' of these advances; and (c) 750 manufactured goods. The calculation of the cost of this total of 2250 'measures' which follows is based on the assumption that only items (b) and (c) participate in the rise in prices. R.L.M.

[3] The expenditure of the productive class with the sterile class is always estimated at one-third of the productive class's returns; whereas one-half of the revenue is assumed to be devoted to expenditure with the sterile class. The reason is that the proprietors indulge much more in conspicuous consumption in the way of ornamentation than the cultivators do.

	Millions of measures	Millions of livres

The productive class purchases, then, as we
have just said, for its returns, from itself
and from the sterile class,
2250 *million measures* for
2550 *million livres*   2250   2550

The Exchequer purchases, with the 450
millions of indirect taxes which it spends,
375 *million measures*,[1,2] namely:

From the productive class, 188 *million*⎫
From the sterile class,   187 *million*⎭   375   450

Foreign trade can be estimated at about
one-tenth of the total product, or 300
million measures, which before the rise
in prices foreign countries paid for on the
average with 300 *million measures* of
their own products, and which after the
rise in prices they will only be able to pay
for with 360 *million of their measures*,[3,4]
because in accordance with our hypothesis foreign products have not become
dearer through the increase in the price of
the home products, the latter having increased by *one-sixth* in price only because
they were previously deprived by com-

---

[1] Quesnay apparently arrives at the figure of 375, somewhat illogically, by reducing the figure of 450 millions by one-sixth. R.L.M.

[2] It is necessary to include in the expenditure of the Exchequer the payment of interest on the loans which it has contracted and which remain, like the indirect taxes, in the same state, since none of this consists of products, and therefore none of it participates at all in the change in the price of products. Thus on this side the Exchequer does not lose any of its enjoyments, and on the other side it gains a great deal through the doubling of its direct revenue, as has been seen above.

[3] 360 should evidently read 350. R.L.M.

[4] It is a question here of the measure of products which the nation could obtain for 20 *sous* from foreign countries, or from itself prior to the rise in the price of its products.

It is not that the same measure of the same products was worth 24 *sous* in foreign countries during the period when it was worth only 20 *sous* in the nation deprived of its freedom of trade, so that if one product of the same kind had then been exchanged for another the foreign countries would have supplied measures one-sixth smaller than those of the nation. Trade is not carried on in this way. It is products of different kinds which are exchanged, and then it is not the equality of the measure but the equality of the value with which one is con-cerned. Thus we have thought it proper to fix upon this equality of value, which, in the case of similar products, supposes measures one-sixth smaller in foreign countries than in the nation.

mercial prohibitions, constraints, and surcharges of the natural price which freedom and immunity in this branch assure to them.

Thus foreign countries continue to purchase 300 *million measures* of the country's products, namely:

From the productive class, 150........⎫
From the sterile class,   150........⎬ 300
and they pay for them at the current price with 360 *million measures* of foreign products.   ——

    Total of purchases................ 2925

    Total of expenditure 3000

Thus in order to complete the sale of the total reproduction, there remain to be sold only 175 *million measures* of the country's products, which are worth 1 *livre* 4 *sous* each, or 210 *million livres* in all. But 800 *millions* of revenue, which are in the hands of the sovereign, the proprietors of the land, and the tithe-owners, remain to be employed.

These proprietors of the revenue purchase the 175 *million measures* of the country's products from the other two classes, as follows:

From the productive class, 88.... ⎫ 175 *million measures*, which
                      ⎨ cost 210 *million livres*, on the
From the sterile class,   87.... ⎬ basis of 1 *livre* 4 *sous* per
                      ⎩ *measure*;

and the proprietors still have 590 *millions* of revenue available for employment in foreign countries, with which they will purchase 590 *million measures*, one-half in produce and the other half in manufactured goods; since, as we have seen, the *measures* of foreign products have not participated in the rise in prices of the country's products, and have remained at the same price as before; whence it follows that this rise in prices avoids loss, or procures gain, in external trade.

The proprietors of the revenue will thus have, in *measures* of the country's products............................. 175 *million*

In *measures* of foreign products .... 590 *million*

    Total .... 765 *million*
measures, for 800 *millions* of revenue.

Before the rise in prices they had only 400 *millions* of revenue, with which they were able to procure for themselves only 400 *million measures*.

Thus since the rise in prices their enjoyments have increased by 365 *million measures*, and it is only by 35 *millions*, or a little less than *one-eleventh*, that the 400 *millions* of additional revenue fall short of representing an absolute gain for the sovereign, the proprietors, and the tithe-owners.[1]

Of the sum of 590 *millions* available for employment in foreign countries, the foreign countries themselves have furnished 360 which they have given in payment for the 300 *million measures* of the country's products which they have purchased; the gain from the equality of prices gives the other 230.[2, 3]

The 230 or 235 *millions* of gain from the constant equality of prices represent a true increase of wealth for the nation, because this gain does not cause it to suffer any rise in its expenses. The nation employs it in making purchases from abroad, without reducing its money stock; it represents for the nation an annual increase of wealth which pays for the purchases it makes from abroad;[4] and when purchases from abroad increase on one side, mutual trade is extended almost immediately on both sides, for the merchants know just as well as other men that money ought not to remain idle in their hands.

The increase of 365 *million measures* in the enjoyments of the proprietors of the revenue is provided:

By the gain of 230 *millions* from the equality of prices, which does not cause the purchaser-consumers of the country to suffer any rise in their expenses;

[1] If these calculations were restricted to the increase of *one-sixth* in the price of corn alone, the value of which constitutes only about *two-fifths* of the total value of the annual reproduction of the territory, the results would be proportionately reduced. The revenue would be increased by only 160 *millions* instead of the 400 by which it increases in the case where the increase of prices by *one-sixth* extends over the totality of products. Of these 160 *millions* of gain on the price of corn, there would be only 68 which would be the result of export, assuming that 3 or 4 *million setiers* of all kinds of corn were exported. The balance would be the result of the restoration of the constant equality of prices, set once again at the level of those which are current among trading nations, and which vary little, above all so far as corn is concerned, in the case of full freedom of trade and competition.

[2] It actually gives 235, but we are continuing to disregard the 5 *millions* which we have already disregarded in the *Tableau* of the distribution, which was calculated on the basis of only 800 *millions* of revenue instead of 805 which was the true figure.

[3] This is the 'increase of 235 *millions* in sales at first hand' discussed by Quesnay above, p. 172. R.L.M.

[4] This increase in wealth, it is true, is only a subtraction of the loss which, when freedom and immunity of trade are lacking, is caused by the successive inequality of the prices in sales at first hand, these prices in a normal year being reduced to a level lower by more than *one-tenth* than the expense to the purchaser-consumers. Freedom and immunity of trade do away with this inequality of the prices in sales at first hand, and set them back again almost at the level of the purchases of the purchaser-consumers. It is in this sense that this subtraction of the loss to the seller at first hand represents for him an increase in wealth.

By the gain of 75 *millions* on the sale of products which is made in order to pay the 450 *millions* of indirect taxes;[1]

By the gain of 60 *millions* on the 360 *million measures* which foreign countries give in return for the 300 *million measures* sold to them.[2]

All the profits which come in from different sides as a result of the increase in the price of the territory's products are included in the revenue; because, in whatever manner the effects of this increase are shared among the different classes through trade, the whole gain, after subtracting the profits of the merchants and full compensation to everybody for the rise in prices, comes to be united together with the revenue, inasmuch as competition between the farmers of landed property, and between the agents of the sterile class, compels all of them to subtract from their gains the profit which ought to belong to the revenue.

But perhaps it will be said that *an increase in wealth accruing solely to the proprietors should not be regarded as an increase in wealth for the nation in general.*

We reply: (1) That the only wealth of which cognizance is taken in a state is disposable wealth;[3] it is this which lies at the basis of the

---

[1] See above, p. 176. R.L.M.   [2] See above, p. 176. R.L.M.

[3] All the other kinds of annual wealth are called *costs*; and although these latter support men, they are regarded in some way as burdensome, and in general they would not be kept up if they were not under the protection of nature, which cuts down the disposable wealth of those who are imprudent enough to cut down on the wealth employed in cultivation. But in spite of this strict and inevitable punishment, there are few countries which are sufficiently enlightened to safeguard properly the ownership of wealth employed in cultivation. Even in England, where its importance has been recognized, where the intention has been that it should be immune, and where it is not answerable for any territorial taxes, it is ceaselessly attacked by a host of new indirect impositions which are always springing up again, and by a crowd of prohibitions on trade which are perpetually being altered, which act to the detriment of the farmers by changing from moment to moment the data of the calculation which they have to make in order to settle on the level of the rent of the land. This disorderliness exposes the cultivators to frequent diminutions in their productive advances, and to sacrifices of a part of the wealth which they employ in cultivation in order to meet the payments under the leases which they have entered into before the coming into existence of the unforeseen indirect taxes, which increase their expenses or reduce their receipts to no purpose. In all countries the farmers of the land should enter into leases only after having calculated the expenses of cultivation, the taxes on the land, and the average value of the harvests, by means of which a simple subtraction brings them within reach of knowing what sum they can annually pay to the proprietor; their agreements, made in accordance with these principles and on proper grounds, conform to reliable rules and are entrusted to the protection of the tutelary authority of the government, which guarantees them, and which undertakes to compel the contracting parties to fulfil their obligations. It is incredible, in the light of this, that while following policies which destroy the elements of the calculation according to which contracts of such importance, determining the territory's revenue, are drawn up, while following policies which increase the farmers' expenses and taxes or reduce their receipts, the

common weal, which maintains the tutelary authority, and which constitutes its power; it is this which enables the proprietors of the land who are not cultivators to subsist, and which diversifies their enjoyments *ad infinitum;* it is this alone with which the proprietors of the land, as well as their co-proprietors the sovereigns and the tithe-owners, are generally concerned.

(2) That in spite of the fact that the class of proprietors profits wholly from the increase in wealth due to the rise in prices which results from freedom and immunity of trade, it is not less true that this increase is also very advantageous to the two other classes.

First, the farmers of landed property profit up to the renewal of their leases from the constant increase in the prices of products which occurs during the terms of these leases. And this gain is most fruitful, most profitable, and most necessary in a nation whose agriculture is in need of extension and improvement. For farmers, if they are not oppressed, never leave their occupation; the profits which they make increase the wealth which they employ in cultivation, which is greatly to the advantage of agriculture. And these profits, which increase the number of wealthy farmers, promote at

---

governments of almost every country have nevertheless thought fit to compel these same farmers to fulfil the very contracts the basic and essential conditions of which have been destroyed so far as the farmers are concerned. This *violation of natural right and the sacred law of contracts in which the authority protecting contracts has involuntarily allowed itself to become involved*, this unhappy and very general imprudence which will some day become fatal *in England*, ought nowhere to be attributed to anything but a profound ignorance of the effects of this disorderliness, for there is no one who is more interested in preventing it than the sovereigns, since they are everywhere co-proprietors of the net product of the territory of the nation which they govern, and consequently one cannot do harm to the farmers of the land or destroy the wealth employed in cultivation without cutting off the unique source of the taxes or the sovereigns' revenue. It is also to ignorance that we should attribute the imprudent conduct of those proprietors who abuse the ascendancy given to them over their farmers by the difficulties and high costs involved in removal, and rent out their land above its value. In ruining their farmers, they ruin their land, deprive it of fertility, and strip it of straw. In whatever manner the masters of the territory act to increase their share for the time being, when they appropriate a portion of the wealth employed in cultivation which generates their wealth and which constitutes the sustenance of the most hard-working part of the population, their rapacity falls ruinously on their own heads through the diminution in the value of their *properties* and the sometimes irremediable extinction of their revenue and enjoyments.

This is not the case with the increase in the proprietors' revenue which results from the rise in prices. This is actually an increase in disposable wealth; but far from being a burden on the productive class it operates wholly to its advantage during the term of the existing leases, and at the end of the term is wholly placed by the productive class to the credit of the class of proprietors. Any alleged increase in disposable wealth to which these conditions did not apply would disappear in a flash, and would represent a loss instead of a profit.

the time of the renewal of the leases a greater degree of competition between them, which then assures to the proprietors and the sovereign the full return of the net product—not only that which results directly from the increase in prices, but also that additional amount which is generated by the more ample means of the farmers;[1,2] for we know that wealth is the great and principal implement of cultivation, and that a wealthy farmer can often profitably rent land at a rate one-third or one-half above that which a poor farmer could pay only with difficulty and at the risk of ruining himself.[3]

[1] For the opposite reason, a reduction in price is disastrous. The farmers, who are obliged during the term of their leases to pay constantly the same sums for rent, taxes, and other fixed charges, can no longer meet them out of the receipts from their sales. They are forced to make up for them by successively cutting down on the amount of wealth employed in cultivation, which necessarily results in a progressive reduction of the annual reproduction, ruinous to the sovereign and the nation. Thus rises and falls in prices are the principal causes of the prosperity or decline of empires. The effects of these causes are not confined to those which are discussed here; there are many others which merit no less attention. Thus the rises and falls in the prices of the territory's products are matters of great importance, which require very profound and strict examination in the decisions of economic government. But it will always be found, according to the different cases (apart from that of scarcity), that rises in prices cause a greater or lesser amount of gain, and falls in prices cause a greater or lesser amount of harm.

[2] This is of course the point which Quesnay has already discussed in the extract from the *Philosophie Rurale* translated above, pp. 138 ff. R.L.M.

[3] It does not follow from this that one never finds poor farmers who offer more for the land than wealthy ones; ignorance and the extreme longing to create something unfortunately make this only too common an occurrence. But to offer and to pay are two different things: these poor farmers who, because they have not made proper calculations, have taken on an enterprise beyond their means, end up by ruining themselves, sometimes go bankrupt half way through the lease, or, if they carry on to the end, give back the land in an exhausted state, without straw, without manure, and incapable of being put under proper cultivation again without unusually high expenses. In every kind of contract, if it is to be sound and successful, the two parties must mutually obtain an advantage from it.

It would be extremely desirable if the proprietors of the land were sufficiently well-informed to be able, with pen in hand, to calculate with their farmers the expenses involved in the cultivation of their land, to come to a clear, equitable, and friendly decision on the annual returns which these useful and respectable entrepreneurs of cultivation ought to receive, and consequently to estimate the net product which they can demand. This is an advantage which we may expect from the great number of inventories of cultivation published by citizens who possess the talent and the zeal necessary for this kind of work. It is still more essential that farmers should be assured that during the term of their leases they will not have to bear any increase in their direct or indirect taxes. It is clear that the government is much concerned with these matters. As to us, until our agriculture securely enjoys these two conditions which are vitally necessary for its existence, we shall not cease repeating that one cannot be too much afraid of *killing the goose that lays the golden eggs*, and that prudent people who have an interest in this matter should on the contrary provide the goose with a large ration of corn so that it will lay more.

So far as the sterile class is concerned, we have seen from the *Tableau* that as a result of the increase of *one-sixth* in the price of products its receipts have risen from 950 *million livres* to 1300 *million*. We know that it employs one-half of these receipts in purchasing raw materials for the goods it makes, and the other half in purchasing products for its subsistence.

Thus before the rise in prices it had 475 *million livres* to spend for its subsistence, which enabled it to buy 475 *million measures* of products, which could support 3 *million* 167 *thousand persons*, assuming the average consumption per head, taking one with another, to be 150 *measures*.

After the rise in prices, it has 650 *million livres* to spend for its subsistence, with which it will be able to buy 542 *million measures*[1] of the country's products. Thus the rise of *one-sixth* in the prices of products brought about by freedom and immunity of trade procures for the sterile class a profit of 67 *million measures*, which will enable it to increase its numbers by about *one-seventh*, or 446 *thousand persons*.[2]

This is quite opposed to the opinion held in the last century, when it was believed that it was a good thing to put barriers in the way of trade in products, with the aim of keeping them at a low price for the advantage and increase of the manufacturing class. It is now seen, on the contrary, that this class has a considerable interest in the rise in prices, and that it gains from it an increase in goods, well-being, and population, since it participates in the increase in the wealth and expenditure of the proprietors of the revenue.

---

[1] 542 = $\frac{5}{6}$ (650). The correct figure is $\frac{6}{7}$ (650), i.e. 557. R.L.M.

[2] It should also be noted that we have assumed here that the sterile class buys all its raw materials and its subsistence inside the country. But this class takes part a great deal in foreign trade, and in the consumption of foreign products which have not risen in price at all. Thus it would appear that as a result of the increase in its receipts it would have a greater number of measures and would be able to support a greater number of people than we estimate here. It should be remembered, however, that in order to simplify the *Tableau* and to avoid burdening readers who are still not very accustomed to its formula with too great a number of items, we thought fit not to depict in it the transfer of the expenditure of one-half of the receipts from indirect taxes to the sterile class and to take account of them only so far as their return to the advances of the productive class is concerned. Thus there appears to be included in the productive class a part of the population which actually subsists in the sterile class, before the rise in prices as after it, on the expenditure of one-half of the indirect taxes. Thus the calculation of this part of the population in one case and the other would reduce the extent of the increase of the sterile class a little. So we can stick to the total which is given here, abstracting from the profit which this class makes on its purchases from abroad, and which at least compensates for the voluntary omission of the details of this part of the population, which, strictly calculated, would make a difference in our calculation of only 25 *thousand persons*, or about 6 *thousand families*.

Here then is the summary of the solution to this problem. The proprietors would annually gain 365 *million measures* of products, and the sterile class 67 *million*, and the total population of the nation could increase by about *one-tenth*. These figures would become much greater if we took into account the successive increases which would result from the profit made by the farmers of landed property during the term of their leases.

Furthermore, we should warn the reader that if, in the case of a second rise in price, we made use of the results of the present solution, which is based on data or facts appropriate to a first rise in price, the application of these results would lead us much further away from the truth. Thus if a second rise in price were added to the first, another problem would be presented which would have its own special data; and it would be necessary to possess oneself of these data and subject them to a new and rigorous calculation, as a result of which one would find that a second increase in prices would not procure nearly such a great increase in revenue as that which arises from the first increase; unless in the case of the second increase in prices there were causes which could contribute anew to this increase, such as would be, for example, the construction of canals, and the invention of machines which made transport easier or saved manu-facturing labour, etc., etc.[1]

COMMENTS

The main object which we have had in mind in the solution of this problem has been to make it understood, through the development of the question itself, that it is of the greatest importance to a nation to achieve, by means of complete freedom of trade, the highest possible prices in the sale of its territory's products.

[1] Some people believe that the sciences to which calculation is applicable are not of the same nature as the other sciences, so far as research into truth is concerned. But calculations are neither causes nor effects; thus in the sciences they never constitute the objects of our researches. Now in all the sciences certainty consists in the fact that objects are made self-evident [*la certitude consiste dans l'évidence des objets*]. If we do not attain to these self-evident objects [*cette évidence*], which supply calculation with facts or data capable of being counted and measured, calculation will not rectify our errors. The sciences which admit of calculation thus have the same basis of certainty as the others. This certainty, it is true, can be extended by means of calculation to cover quantities which only calculation can compute, and in this case it is always essentially infallible, i.e. it always infallibly and consistently presents us with either errors or realities, according to whether we apply it to errors or realities. Whence it follows that in research into truth by means of calculation, the whole certainty lies in the self-evidence [*évidence*] of the data.

Our hypothesis has not been limited to freedom of export of corn alone; it includes all the products of the territory which are the subject of trade, because internal and external trade in products of all kinds may be hindered in a number of ways, direct or indirect, which make prices fall. This is a branch of government which demands a great deal of attention and discernment, and very little in the way of actions or *proceedings*.[1]

It has been assumed that the indirect taxes do not participate in the increase in prices, because they are not comprised in the order of products which are the subject of trade, and because this part of the gain from the increase in prices has been taken into account to the extent of 75 *millions* in the increase of the revenue. Without it the revenue of 400 *millions*, which has risen to 800 *millions*, would have risen to only 725 *millions*; and it would in fact be to this figure of 725 *millions*, all other things remaining the same, that the increase in the revenue would be reduced, if these indirect taxes did not exist.

But in that case the 450 *millions* which we have postulated under this head would be restored to the revenue, which instead of 850 *millions*[2] would be about 1200 *millions*,[3] of which the sovereign would from then on, independently of the successive increases in cultivation, have one-third or 400 *millions* as his share, without causing any decline in the successive order of the annual reproduction. In that case the revenue of the proprietors of landed property would be more than trebled,[4] and the part accruing to the tithe-holders would also be increased by one-sixth over the whole of the reproduction, assuming again that there are no new increases so far as the total quantity of the reproduction is concerned.

It should be noted, however, that such a change would at first have almost similar effects to those of a big change in the legal value of money, when the value of products, the value of manufactured commodities, and the level of wages would take some time, in the course of trade, to regain the level relative to this change. People are then not in a position to make exact detailed calculations in their sales and purchases, in conformity with such changes. The farmers, in the leases by which they bind themselves to pay the sum of the revenue, would thus be unable to ascertain exactly and in detail the great multitude of indirect taxes which would have fallen on them

---

[1] *Procédés*. R.L.M.

[2] 850 should probably read 800, or possibly 805. R.L.M.

[3] I.e. 725 millions+450 millions, taken to the nearest 100 millions. R.L.M.

[4] Quesnay inserts an explanatory note at this point, comparing the level of rent before the imposition of the taxes he is talking about with its present level. The note provides an interesting illustration of the care which Quesnay usually took to see that his data were realistic, but since it is extremely long and detailed, and adds little to our understanding of the *Tableau* or of the present problem, I have not thought it worth while to translate it. R.L.M.

and from which they would now be released, and of which they ought to take account in estimating the increase of revenue which they would have to pay to the profit of the sovereign and the proprietors. It is only time and experience which can teach them, in accordance with the receipts recovered from the products[1] and the total of the expenses. It would only be after they had found this out that competition between them would force them to bring the rent into conformity with its true rate. Then it would come about that the revenue imperceptibly settled down at the just level, in conformity with the products and the expenses involved in cultivation; and order would also be established in the same way between the taxes and the portion of the revenue which belongs to the proprietors of landed property. It is thus easy to see that before such a reform (which should come about naturally, as a consequence of the re-establishment of order), it would not be possible to make a cadastral survey do duty for it, so long as the territory's revenue was in a distorted state diverging from its natural one, because a cadastral survey could not then be based on any regular and fixed foundation. Nevertheless, it would be indispensable to prevent the revenue of the sovereign being exposed to diminution, in a reform which required time to come to completion and to put agriculture on the road which would lead it surely towards the expansion of which it would be capable: Thus it would be important to base this reform on a very regular and certain plan. This is a task which demands time, intellectual power, and a degree of enlightenment which is difficult to acquire and rather uncommon.

[1] *Le recouvrement des produits*. R.L.M.

I.

THE 'SECOND ECONOMIC PROBLEM'[1]

Προσῆκον δὴ τὸ μάθημα ἂν εἴη, νομοθετῆσαι καὶ πείθειν τοὺς μέλλοντας ἐν τῇ πόλει τῶν μεγίστων μεθέξειν ἐπὶ λογιστικὴν ἰέναι καὶ ἀνθάπτεσθαι αὐτῆς μὴ ἰδιωτικῶς.

ΣΩΚΡΑΤΗΣ παρὰ Πλάτωνι.

It is befitting, then, that this branch of learning should be prescribed by our law and that we should induce those who are to share the highest functions of state to enter upon that study of calculation and take hold of it, not as amateurs.

SOCRATES, in Plato.[2]

————

TO DETERMINE THE EFFECTS OF AN INDIRECT TAX

PRELIMINARY EXPLANATION

There are some indirect taxes which are simple and not very costly to collect. Such are those which may be laid on men in the form of a personal *taille*, a capitation-tax, *corvées*, taxes on house-rent, on rentier income, etc. There are others which are very complicated and involve high costs of collection. Such are those which may be laid on produce and commodities, when they are imported and exported, at toll-houses and customs-houses, or on shipping and transport in internal and external trade, or on the circulation of money in purchases and sales of all kinds; such also is the creation of offices and posts to which duties and taxes are attached in perpetuity or for a term, to the profit of those who are invested with them, the privileges of exclusive trade, etc.

The examination of the effects of each of these indirect taxes would form the subject of a special calculation, rigorously based on the data which would be presented by the greater or lesser degree of complexity of the tax concerned, the greater or lesser degree of restraint to which it would subject trade and other human activities, and the greater or lesser total of the costs of collecting it. But if these different indirect taxes, burdensome to a greater or lesser degree, are brought together to form a total which we may call in a general sense *the indirect taxes*, the costs of collection and other surcharges which

[1] This article was first published in *Physiocratie*. The present translation is from the text in I.N.E.D., II, pp. 977–92. R.L.M.

[2] Plato, *The Republic* (Loeb Classical Library edn., 1935), Vol. II, p. 163. English translation by Paul Shorey. R.L.M.

all these different taxes bring in their train may also be brought together to form another total which we may call in a general sense *the costs of the indirect taxes*, the total of which, considered relatively to the total sum which the sovereign receives from indirect taxes, gives us the average rate of costs of collection for taxes of this kind.

It is the indirect taxes, taken together in this way and reduced by an average rate of costs and surcharges of collection, which we are going to examine here. We shall consider them at the beginning of their establishment in a nation whose agriculture has until then been protected against all causes of deterioration, and in which the annual advances of cultivation produce on the average *three* for *one*, so that an expenditure of *one hundred* in annual advances brings about the regeneration of *one hundred and fifty* for the revenue and *one hundred and fifty* for the cultivators' returns.

Thus 2 *milliards* of annual advances made by the productive class would result in the generation, at the rate of 300 per cent, of a total reproduction of 6 *milliards*, which would provide the cultivators with 3 *milliards* for their returns, comprising their annual advances and interest on their original advances, and would yield in addition a revenue of 3 *milliards* for the landed proprietors and the sovereign.[1]

We have early records of a state of affairs in agricultural production in France which was at least comparable with this, and in which the relation between the annual advances and the total product was in the same proportion as that which we are assuming here.

It is the cultivator's annual advances, and their relation with the revenue which they generate, which form the data of the calculation of the arithmetical formula of the *Tableau Economique*.

Any action of the government which leads to an increase in these advances, or which on the contrary reduces them, increases or reduces the nation's wealth.

These effects, whether good or bad, can be easily and exactly demonstrated in their full extent by a calculation based on the formula of the *Tableau Economique*.

The annual advances are themselves reproduced each year together with the interest which should annually be received to complete the *cultivators' returns*. This interest is normally equal to one-half of the annual advances. Thus when the annual advances are, for

---

[1] Quesnay assumes here, as usual, that the interest on the original advances is one-half the amount of the annual advances, so that when the annual advances are 2 milliards, the 'returns' (i.e. annual advances + interest on original advances) will be 3 milliards. Since revenue = total reproduction—returns, the amount of the revenue will depend upon the value of the product generated by the given annual advances. Normally Quesnay assumes that 2 units of annual advances will generate 5 units of product (exclusive of fodder); here, however, he assumes that they will generate 6 units of product (exclusive of fodder), so that the revenue is 3 instead of the usual 2. R.L.M.

example, 2 *milliards*, the returns of the cultivators amount to 3 *milliards*.

When these *returns* are deducted from each year's total reproduction, the surplus is called the *net product*.

This *net product* forms the revenue which is shared between the sovereign, the tithe-owners, and the proprietors.

Thus if the total reproduction is 5 *milliards*, produced with the aid of annual advances of 2 *milliards*, there will remain, when the cultivators' returns of 3 *milliards* have been deducted, 2 *milliards* for the revenue. The ratio of this revenue to the advances will then be 100 per cent.

If the total reproduction is only 4 *milliards*, the cultivators' returns being 3 *milliards*, the revenue will be only 1 *milliard*. The ratio of this revenue to the advances will then be 50 per cent.

If the total reproduction were 6 *milliards*, the revenue would be equal to the 3 *milliards* of the cultivators' returns, and its ratio to the advances would be 150 per cent; and so on.

These different relations between the advances and the revenue, because of their diversification, may present different data at different times. In accordance with this data, we must calculate the expenditure of the three classes in order to ascertain the changes which occur in the annual production of a kingdom's wealth and in the basic relations between the cultivators' returns and the revenue, *which taken together form the sum total of the annual reproduction.*

Thus in order to get an exact idea of these relations in all cases, it is sufficient to discover the causes which may bring about changes in the order of the distribution of expenditure as represented in the *Tableau*, and to follow by calculation the course of this distribution, in conformity with the change whose effects one wishes to understand. The result of the calculation will give us the sum total of the reproduction increased or reduced as a result of the change which has occurred.

From this sum we must subtract the cultivators' returns, and the remainder will constitute the revenue, except in the case of changes which make the nation's expenditure exceed the annual reproduction of the kingdom's territory.

In that case the calculation includes this surplus of expenditure over reproduction in the receipts of the productive class.

But it is easy to detect this through the disproportion between these receipts and the productive class's annual advances, the present relation of which to the total product which they annually regenerate is known.

We then know the amount of the surplus expenditure which the country's product cannot supply and which therefore can be obtained only through purchases from abroad.

Those who are well-versed in the calculation of the arithmetical formula of the *Tableau Economique* can exactly ascertain and determine these variations, and the advantages or disadvantages which they bring to the economic order, through the increase or reduction which occurs in the advances, or in the revenue, or in the sterile class; for the latter class always loses in proportion to the decline which occurs in the revenue; and the revenue always loses in proportion to the decline which occurs in the cultivators' advances. All these parts are so intimately bound together that they should all be included in the arithmetical formula, with the aid of which we can bring calculation to bear upon them.

For example, in the case which we now have before us for calculation, where the annual advances of cultivation are 2 *milliards*, the reproduction 6 *milliards*, the cultivators' returns 3 *milliards*, and the revenue consequently 3 *milliards*, the annual distribution of expenditure and trade between the three classes will be that represented in the following *Tableau:*[1]

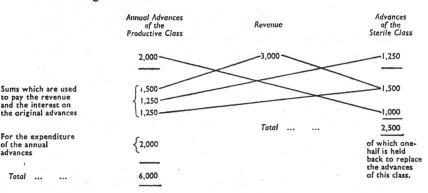

	Annual Advances of the Productive Class	Revenue	Advances of the Sterile Class
	2,000	3,000	1,250
Sums which are used to pay the revenue and the interest on the original advances	1,500 1,250 1,250		1,500 1,000
		Total	2,500
For the expenditure of the annual advances	2,000		of which one-half is held back to replace the advances of this class.
Total	6,000		

[1] The differences between this *Tableau* and the original formula on p. 158 above arise, of course, from the fact that the revenue is now assumed to be 3 milliards instead of 2 milliards. The productive class continues to buy 1 milliard's worth of manufactured goods from the sterile class, but the proprietors now buy 1½ milliards' worth, making the total product of the sterile class 2½ milliards and its annual advances consequently 1¼ milliards. The productive class now receives an extra ½ milliard from its sales of food to the proprietors, an extra ¼ milliard from its sales of raw materials to the sterile class, and an extra ¼ milliard from its sales of food to the sterile class. The productive class therefore receives in all an extra 1 milliard from these sales, thus enabling it to pay the extra 1 milliard of revenue to the proprietors. In real terms, the annual reproduction of 6 is made up and disposed of as follows: (a) 1½ food sold to the proprietors; (b) 1¼ raw materials sold to the sterile class; (c) 1¼ food sold to the sterile class; (d) 1 food consumed *in natura* by the productive class; and (e) 1 'interest goods' consumed by the productive class for the 'repair' of its original advances. On the assumption that the average level of consumption of families in the productive class and in the sterile class is the same, it is evident that the number of people in the sterile class must be 25 per cent greater than in the situation depicted in the original formula. R.L.M.

Assuming such a state of affairs in production, if the sovereign's share were *two-sevenths* of the revenue, this share would constitute a public revenue of about 800 *millions;* and this large direct revenue, which would be sufficient on its own to maintain in the highest degree the magnificence and power of the sovereign authority and the expenditure necessary for the security and prosperity of the nation, would not bring about any decline in the annual reproduction. This can be seen from the following *Tableau,* which represents the expenditure of the taxes and that of the revenue of the landed proprietors separately:[1]

It can be seen that the imposition of the taxes, taken in this way directly from the net product, causes no change at all in the order of expenditure and distribution; that the cultivators as before receive the sums necessary to pay the revenue and to ensure their returns; and that consequently the reproduction is necessarily the same.

But this public revenue of 800 *millions,* directly comprising *two-sevenths* of the territory's net product, would seem excessive to the landed proprietors. Their ignorant greed has never allowed them to understand that taxes ought to be taken only from the revenue of the land. They have always thought that taxes ought to be laid on men, or on men's consumption, since all men share in the protection of the sovereign power. They have never dreamed that men, whose physical constitution presents nothing but needs, can by themselves pay nothing, and that all taxes laid upon men, or on their consumption, will necessarily be taken from the wealth which enables men to subsist and which only the land produces. They are convinced that if they give directly *one-tenth* of the revenue of their land they are paying their share of public contributions in full. The nobility and the clergy have demanded limitless exemptions and immunities, which they have claimed are bound up with their property and their

---

[1] There is no essential difference between this *Tableau* (p. 191) and the one just discussed. The expenditure of the Exchequer is assumed to be divided equally between the sterile class and the productive class, just as the proprietors' expenditure is, and is put side by side with the latter. Of the first five (bracketed) items on the productive side, the first two, representing receipts from sales of food to the Exchequer and the proprietors respectively, and totalling 1500, correspond to the first item in the previous *Tableau.* The third item of 1250, representing receipts from sales of raw materials to the sterile class, is identical with the second item in the previous *Tableau.* The fourth and fifth items, representing receipts from sales of food to the sterile class, and totalling 1250, correspond to the third item in the previous *Tableau.* On the sterile side, the first two items, representing receipts from sales of manufactured goods to the proprietors and the Exchequer respectively, and totalling 1500, correspond to the first item in the previous *Tableau.* The third item of 1000, representing receipts from sales of manufactured goods to the productive class, is identical with the second item in the previous *Tableau.* R.L.M.

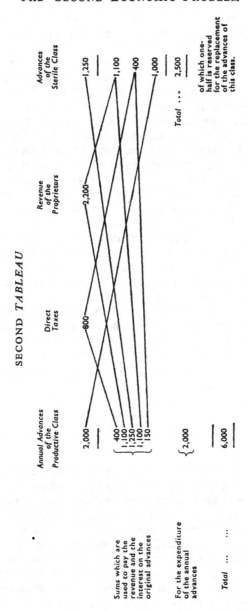

SECOND *TABLEAU*

estate. Sovereigns have also thought it appropriate to grant complete exemptions to their officers, and to all those who are invested with posts or employments in all the different branches of government administration. As a result of this state of affairs the revenue of the Exchequer has been reduced to such a low level, and the proprietors have put forward so much opposition to its direct increase, that sovereigns have had recourse to indirect taxes of various kinds, which have extended further and further in the proportion that the nation's revenue has diminished as a result of the deterioration which is the inevitable consequence of these taxes themselves. The landed proprietors, who did not foresee these consequences, and who during the time that they were destroying their revenue did not understand, did not even perceive the cause of the reduction in their wealth, gave their approval to these indirect taxes, by means of which they believed they could evade taxation, which ought to have been laid directly and immediately on the revenue of their property, where it would have caused no decline in the annual reproduction and would not have required to be successively increased; whereas in fact, as a result of the progressive increase and disastrous effects of the indirect taxes, successive increases in both indirect and direct taxes alike become necessary in order to meet the state's needs. In addition, the landed proprietors have not only got out of the payment of the *two-sevenths* of the revenue which belongs to the sovereign, but have also brought upon themselves indirect taxes, causing a progressive and inevitable deterioration which destroys their own revenue, that of the sovereign, and the wealth of the nation.

This is the effect which it is here a question of demonstrating. We shall do this through the solution of the problem whose data we are now going to lay down in accordance with the hypothesis which we have just put forward.

DATA

We assume, then, that instead of the single and direct tax which could be established at the rate of *two-sevenths*, which on a revenue of 3 *milliards* would yield a total of 800 *millions*, the proprietors of the land prefer a tax which falls directly and immediately on the revenue of land only to the extent of *one-tenth*, or 300 *millions;* and that in order to meet public expenditure a contribution of 500 *millions* is laid on persons and consumption, one-half of which would be swallowed up by the costs of collection, by the profits of the tax-farmers and those associated with them, by the additional charges which are imposed on the nation by smugglers, who inevitably spring up in the wake of taxes on trade and whom no fiscal army has ever been able to hold in check, by the costs of litigation entailed by a complicated system of collection whose rules are subject to a great number of interpretations, by the secret settlements made by individuals who are afraid of going to law against the employees of the Exchequer, by arbitrary fines, by the annual gains of the incumbents of offices, posts, and alienated duties, and by the profits of the owners of exclusive privileges, etc., etc.

If we were to make use of the calculations of *M. le duc de Sully* this evaluation could be made much greater. But as we have said, we are taking an average rate in between the most costly and the least costly of the indirect taxes; and furthermore we prefer to keep to a figure which is below the true one rather than above it.

COMMENTS

First Comment

All expenditure is paid for by the renascent wealth which the land alone produces, as we have proved in the preceding dialogues.[1]

The first proprietors of this renascent wealth are therefore the first distributors of the expenditure; it is they who really incur all the expenditure, partly by themselves, and partly by getting themselves assisted by other men whose services they make use of, and whom in reward for these services they substitute for themselves in the expenditure and consumption of a portion of their wealth.

Thus all the expenditure of wage-earners[2] is paid for by those who pay their wages.

Thus taxes laid on wage-earners, or on their expenditure, are self-evidently paid for in their entirety by those who pay their wages.

It would be useless to object that the class of wage-earners could itself pay these taxes by increasing its labour in order to increase its remuneration. For (1) in order to increase its goods, the class of wage-earners would require a greater amount of advances than it possesses; and (2) when the class of wage-earners increased its goods, it would not thereby increase its remuneration, since the total value of the wages which it is in a position to obtain is limited by the means, by the wealth, of those who are in a position to pay its wages. Now it is self-evident that the establishment of a tax on persons, on labour, on commodities, and on consumption, does not increase the wealth of nations, and that far from increasing the opportunities for trade it reduces them. How then could we suppose that the effect of a tax on the wage-earning class would be an increase of goods on the part of this class? Will a manufacturer make cloth which people are

---

[1] The reference is to the dialogues *Sur le Commerce* and *Sur les Travaux des Artisans*, the latter of which is translated in the next section of the present volume. R.L.M.

[2] *Salariés.* R.L.M.

G

unable to buy from him? Will a merchant send a thousand pieces of cloth to a place where people are able to pay for and consequently to consume only 500? Will or could a watchmaker go and sell watches to the peasants of Westphalia or Limousin?

It would also be useless to object that the wage-earners, by restricting their consumption and depriving themselves of enjoyments, could pay the taxes demanded of them, without their falling back again upon the first distributors of the expenditure. It will be seen below that without contributing to the payment of the indirect taxes the wage-earners suffer from the effect of these taxes, which destroy subsistence: a wiping-out, a distressing curtailment of wages, which reduces the wage-earners to poverty and necessarily diminishes their numbers. The level of wages, and consequently the enjoyments which the wage-earners can obtain for themselves, are fixed and reduced to a minimum by the extreme competition which exists between them. If a nation seeks through a tax to force these wage-earners doubly to restrict their enjoyments, they will emigrate in order to settle in other nations where their subsistence is more assured and their industry more protected. Then the small number of them who remain in the country, being less constrained by competition, will lay down the law to the first distributors of the expenditure, and force them to pay the normal wage, plus the tax and the costs of the land into the bargain. The result is that these first proprietors of renascent products, bound to the land through their possessions, will necessarily bear the whole burden of this destructive tax.

If the wage-earners, whose enjoyments it is sought to restrict by means of the tax, are unable to emigrate in order to get back to their former level, they will become beggars or thieves—a kind of arbitrary and walking indirect tax, which is very burdensome to the first distributors of the expenditure.

Thus, however things are arranged, the productive class, the proprietors of the land, and the taxes themselves, as first distributors of the expenditure, inevitably pay the whole of the indirect taxes which are laid on the men whose wages they provide, or on the produce and commodities which they consume; and they each contribute to them in proportion to the distribution of their expenditure.

Second Comment

It might appear that the expenditure of the productive class, which is incurred in the countryside, contributes to the indirect taxes proportionately less than the expenditure incurred in the towns by the proprietors who reside there and by the expenditure there of the taxes themselves. But one could hold this view only if one failed to consider that if the agents of the productive class suffer proportionately less, in their expenditure, from taxes on consumption, they suffer much more from personal and arbitrary *tailles*, and are exposed to many more and much more severe harassments than those whose expenditure is incurred in the towns. If proof of this were necessary, it would be found in the abandonment of the countryside by the children of husbandmen, whose fathers make them leave the countryside in order to send them to the towns to purchase offices or carry on mercenary occupations.

Third Comment

If we envisage the cultivator not only as one of the first distributors of the expenditure but also as a first seller, and observe the extent to which indirect taxes weigh upon the prices received in sales at first hand, we see that almost the entire burden of indirect taxes is borne by the productive class. For the means of purchasers are limited: if the indirect tax does not increase the prices of the products to the purchaser-consumers, it is self-evident that it must be paid at the expense of the prices received in sales at first hand; whereas if the indirect tax does increase the prices to the purchaser-consumers, the latter are forced to reduce their consumption, and thenceforth the lack of a market for the products forces their prices down; for the cultivator has either to sell at whatever the price happens to be or to give up cultivation for the market.[1] In reality both cases are intermingled and counterbalance one another. But whether they are intermingled or occur separately, the result can never be anything but ruinous and fatal so far as the prices of products are concerned.

These truths are still too little known to be readily accepted by those readers who are not very accustomed to these patterns of thought; that is why in the present calculation we limit the contribution to the indirect taxes made by the productive class to one which is proportionate to the expenditure of this class. It is enough for us to have given warning that this assumption is not strictly

[1] One might, it is true, think at first sight that the expenditure of the indirect taxes maintains the market for the territory's products. But this would be to ignore the fact that the market for products is limited, as we have shown in the preceding dialogues; that the expenditure of the indirect taxes never *returns* what they have taken away from the price of the products, but merely *resells* it; that the market would not become smaller, and would be constituted in a more advantageous way, if there were no indirect taxes at all, because this kind of tax and its expenditure are not favourable to provincial trade or to the sale of the products which are ordinarily used by consumers of an inferior order, and also because a large part of the receipts from these taxes is accumulated and forms individual fortunes which abstract it from the circulation, which ought all to be returned to the cultivators to enable them to pay the revenue of the proprietors.

accurate, and that of all those which it is possible to make it is the most advantageous to the indirect taxes.

Fourth Comment

Although the total reproduction is 6 *milliards*, only 5 *milliards* of products enter into trade, since the productive class keeps back 1 *milliard*'s worth which it consumes *in natura* within the class, as we have already noted above in the problem concerning a rise in prices.[1] But the total expenditure liable for indirect taxes is nevertheless, in the given case, 5 *milliards* 500 *millions*, made up as follows:[2]

1. 2 *milliards* which the productive class spends out of its returns of 3 *milliards*, of which it keeps back only 1 *milliard* for the direct consumption which is engaged in without the intervention of any trade	2000 *millions*
2. 300 *millions* of direct taxes	300 *millions*
3. 2 *milliards* 700 *millions* of revenue, which remains to the proprietors after the direct taxes on the net product have been deducted	2700 *millions*
4. 500 *millions* which the indirect taxes cause to be levied and spent.	500 *millions*
Total	5500 *millions*

It will be seen that the indirect taxes, which are levied on the expenditure and which themselves cause expenditure equal to the amount levied, are duplicated in the total of expenditure, which does not increase this total at all, but which alters the proportion of the expenditure subject to the indirect taxes, which themselves contribute to pay themselves.

DEDUCTIONS

The 500 *millions* of indirect taxes are assessed on the 5500 *millions* of expenditure which are subject to them, and each of the first distributors of this expenditure contributes to them, as we have noted, in proportion to the expenditure which he causes to be distributed.[3]

[1] This is of course the *Premier Problème Economique* translated above. R.L.M.
[2] See the 'Data' outlined on p. 192 above. R.L.M.
[3] This means, of course, that the expenditure of each of the 'first distributors' is simply divided by 11. R.L.M.

The productive class, which spends 2 *milliards*, contributes	182 *millions*
The direct taxes of 300 *millions* contribute	27 *millions*
The portion of the indirect taxes amounting to 250 *millions* which accrues to the sovereign[1] contributes	23 *millions*
The 250 *millions* of costs entailed by the indirect taxes contribute	23 *millions*
The proprietors of the land contribute	245 *millions*
Total	500 *millions*

Up to this point this state of affairs is very agreeable to the proprietors of the land. It seems to them that the total of 800 *millions* of direct and indirect taxes costs them only 545 *millions*, instead of the 800 which they would pay were this total taken directly from the revenue of their property. Poor calculators that they are, they do not have an inkling that by entering into this plausible arrangement they are providing the spade which will be used to dig their own graves.

The 282 *millions*[2] annually deducted from the advances of the productive class as a result of the indirect taxes of 500 *millions*, and diverted from their productive employment, would have produced *three for one*, i.e. 546 *millions*. This represents, therefore, a destruction of 546 *millions* of annual reproduction. This reproduction will therefore be reduced to 5 *milliards* 454 *millions*, instead of 6 *milliards*.

We assume that this reduction in the total reproduction will be thrown back in its entirety on to the revenue, for if this did not happen all the advances of the cultivators, original as well as annual, would be destroyed in a few years. Thus the revenue to be divided between the proprietors and the direct taxes will not be more than 2 *milliards* 454 *millions*, instead of 3 *milliards*. The 2 *milliards* of annual advances of the productive class will produce a revenue which is not more than 123 per cent of the advances, instead of 150 per cent.[3]

The direct taxes, which were one-tenth of the revenue of 3 *milliards*, will be reduced to one-tenth of 2 *milliards* 454 *millions*. Thus they will be not more than 244 *millions*, instead of 300 *millions*.

The 800 *millions* of direct and indirect taxes, burdened with costs of

[1] This is the total of the indirect taxes minus the one-half which is absorbed, according to Quesnay's assumption, in costs of collection, etc. R.L.M.

[2] This should read 182. R.L.M.

[3] We concentrate here on the uniform changes which take place in the existing relation of the advances to the revenue, without going into detail about the petty methods of economizing to which cultivators may resort in order to retard the development of the process of decline. For to economize is not to reproduce; and most of these methods, moreover, ineffective palliatives of the moment, become very disadvantageous later on.

250 *millions*, a *repompement*[1] of 73 *millions*, and a wastage[2] of 56 *millions*, would yield to the Exchequer only 421 *millions*. Thus, abstracting from the direct taxes of 300 *millions*, the indirect taxes of 500 *millions* actually bring in to the sovereign only 121 *millions*, which destroy about one-eleventh of the total reproduction of his territory and consequently of the population of his empire; whereas a direct tax, levied at the rate of *two-sevenths* on the 3 *milliards* of revenue, would bring him in 379 *millions* more without any wastage.

The revenue of 3 *milliards*, moreover, which is reduced to 2 *milliards* 454 *millions*, contributes 245 *millions* to these indirect taxes, all to no purpose; this reduces it in fact to 2 *milliards* 209 *millions*, upon which 244 *millions* of direct taxes are paid. Thus there remain to the proprietors of the land only 1 *milliard* 965 *millions*, instead of the 2 *milliards* 200 *millions* which they would have had if the 800 *millions* of taxes had been laid directly and immediately upon the revenue of 3 *milliards*; and the sovereign would then really have had 800 *millions*, whereas he now has only 421 *millions*. Thus the sovereign loses 379 *millions* and the proprietors 235 *millions*, which means a total loss of 614 *millions* for these co-proprietors of the territory's net product.

In order to get an exact idea of the other effects of the change which has occurred in the distribution of wealth as a result of the decline caused by the 500 *millions* of indirect taxes, we are now going to show the situation regarding the decline of the revenue in a *Tableau*. The revenue, instead of being 150 per cent of the advances of the productive class as it was before the levying of 500 *millions* of indirect taxes, is now, as a direct result of these taxes, not more than 123 per cent, which reduces it from 3 *milliards* to 2 *milliards* 454 *millions*. In this *Tableau* we shall abstract from the 500 *millions* of indirect taxes, in order to avoid the duplication of expenditure which these taxes involve.

---

[1] *Repompement* is an unusual word (with obvious biological connotations), which defies translation. It means, in general terms, a process whereby something which has been pumped or sucked in is pumped or sucked out again. In the present context, what Quesnay is saying in effect is that since the 'indirect' taxes are really assessed on the total national expenditure and therefore fall on the 'first distributors' of this expenditure, those who receive and spend the tax receipts will themselves contribute (in proportion to their expenditure) to the payment of the 'indirect' taxes. In other words, the government and the tax-farmers, when they spend the tax receipts on goods and services, will lose to the extent that these goods and services have risen in price as a result of the imposition of the 'indirect' taxes. In assessing the net yield of taxes to the Exchequer, therefore, one should properly deduct the amount which has been 'pumped out again' in this way. The total *repompement* of 73 millions is obtained by adding the second, third, and fourth items in the table on p. 197 above. R.L.M.

[2] *Dépérissement*. R.L.M.

THIRD *TABLEAU*

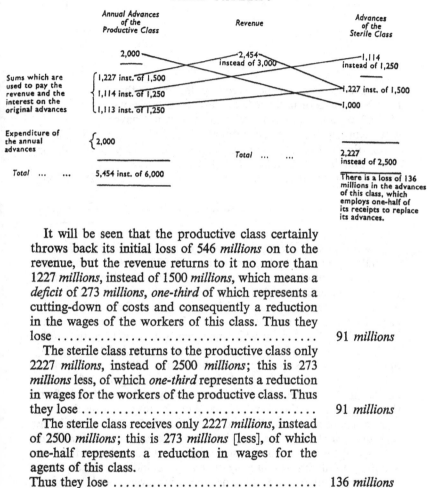

Annual Advances of the Productive Class	Revenue	Advances of the Sterile Class

2,000 — —2,454— —1,114
instead of 3,000 instead of 1,250

Sums which are used to pay the revenue and the interest on the original advances

1,227 inst. of 1,500
1,114 inst. of 1,250
1,113 inst. of 1,250

1,227 inst. of 1,500
1,000

Expenditure of the annual advances

2,000

Total   2,227
instead of 2,500

Total ... ...   5,454 inst. of 6,000

There is a loss of 136 millions in the advances of this class, which employs one-half of its receipts to replace its advances.

It will be seen that the productive class certainly throws back its initial loss of 546 *millions* on to the revenue, but the revenue returns to it no more than 1227 *millions*, instead of 1500 *millions*, which means a *deficit* of 273 *millions*, *one-third* of which represents a cutting-down of costs and consequently a reduction in the wages of the workers of this class. Thus they lose ....   91 *millions*

The sterile class returns to the productive class only 2227 *millions*, instead of 2500 *millions*; this is 273 *millions* less, of which *one-third* represents a reduction in wages for the workers of the productive class. Thus they lose ....   91 *millions*

The sterile class receives only 2227 *millions*, instead of 2500 *millions*; this is 273 *millions* [less], of which one-half represents a reduction in wages for the agents of this class.
Thus they lose ....   136 *millions*

Total ....   318 *millions*[1]

---

[1] Quesnay's enthusiasm to prove his point seems to be running away with his logic here. It is true enough that the real rewards of the sterile class will decline: it is now able to buy only 1114 food from the productive class, instead of 1250 as before, which does indeed represent a loss of 136. But it is difficult to see why the real rewards of the productive class should suffer. On Quesnay's assumption that the initial loss is thrown back on to the revenue, the total receipts of the productive class are reduced by no more than the amount by which the revenue is reduced. The productive class is still able to pay the (reduced) revenue; and

The *TOTAL* of the loss in wages is thus.......... 318 *millions*
And the loss in revenue is .... 546 *millions*

Total .... 864 *millions*

SOLUTION

It has been noted in the preceding deductions that
the 500 *millions* of indirect taxes cost the proprietors
of the land 235 *millions* more than they would have
cost them had the taxes been direct............... 235 *millions*
And that the sovereign loses .... 379 *millions*
We find in the calculation of the last *Tableau* a
reduction of wages amounting to .... 318 *millions*

Grand Total of the deterioration.............. 932 *millions*

As we have seen above, the sovereign receives only 121 *millions* of
the indirect taxes which cause a loss of 932 *millions*. Thus these
taxes cost about *eight times* more to the nation than the 121 *millions*
which the sovereign receives from them. And the sovereign, instead
of receiving the 500 *millions* which ought to have formed the greater
part of his revenue, receives only one-quarter of it. Thus out of *four*
he loses *three*, and for *one* which he receives it costs the nation *eight*.

The proprietors of the land, who at first appeared to be paying
only 545 *millions* as their share of the total of 800 *millions* of direct
and indirect taxes, and who believed that they gained from not
paying the total taxes of 800 *millions* directly and immediately from
the net product of their land, actually pay or lose, as a result of the
form of taxation we are discussing, 1 *milliard* 35 *millions*,[1] while the
total taxes of 800 *millions* bring in to the sovereign only 421 *millions*.

It would be useless for the sovereign to try to make up for such
a falling-off in his revenue by increases in indirect taxes. These
would serve only to increase the decline in his revenue and that of the
nation. Thus the more one increases indirect taxes, the more it is
necessary to increase direct taxes in order to make up for the decline
in the taxes themselves.

---

just as before it receives 1000 for its interest, 1000 manufactured goods, and
1000 food which it consumes *in natura*. Quesnay's first two figures make more
sense, however, if we assume that they represent the position *during the terms
of the existing leases*, before the productive class is able to throw the burden of
the taxes on to the proprietors. R.L.M.

[1] This total seems to be arrived at by adding (a) the reduction of 546 in the
revenue; (b) the 245 indirect taxes paid by the proprietors; and (c) the 244
millions of direct taxes paid on the reduced revenue. R.L.M.

If, for example, the sovereign tried to maintain the receipts from his direct taxes at 300 *millions*, these taxes, which represent only *one-tenth* of the revenue of 3 *milliards*, would become *one-eighth* of this same revenue, which would be reduced to 2 *milliards* 454 *millions*. Thus the direct taxes would encroach more and more on the revenue, without increasing the sovereign's receipts, to the extent that the indirect taxes reduced the total revenue. Thus the direct and indirect taxes would co-exist without any order, and through their progressive and irregular increase they would both become disastrous for the sovereign and for the nation.

OTHER DAMAGE *of a more serious type caused by the indirect taxes, which remains to be noted.*

It should be emphasized that we have abstracted from four types of damage which we are now going to describe, and which ought to be included, if the details of each can be evaluated, in the computation of the losses caused by the indirect taxes.

FIRST TYPE OF DAMAGE

The kinds of deterioration which they bring about in very rapid progression.

Such, first, is the successive deterioration in landed property, which is a consequence of the decline which the indirect taxes necessarily cause in the revenue of the proprietors of the land—a decline which takes away from these proprietors the means of maintaining and improving their properties.

Such, second, is the successive deterioration in enterprises and profitable work, in which people do not venture to employ visible wealth, which always runs the risk of being valued and used as the basis for the assessment of arbitrary indirect taxes.

Such, third, is the successive deterioration, proceeding in geometrical progression, caused by the spoliation of the advances of cultivation, which is a fatal consequence of arbitrary and anticipatory increases in the indirect taxes which are levied or which fall on the farmers during the term of their leases.

SECOND TYPE OF DAMAGE

The monetary fortunes which are increased by the profits of the financiers who farm out the indirect taxes, and which check or upset the circulation of money and prevent its annual return to agriculture.

THIRD TYPE OF DAMAGE

The residence of wealthy financiers in the capital, which shifts consumption further away from the places where production is carried on. This leads to high transport costs which fall as a loss on the price of products in sales at first hand, and consequently on the revenue of the proprietors of the land, who themselves, especially if they come from distinguished families, also withdraw to the capital with the aim of using their reputations to share in *the favours* of the Court, in order to compensate themselves in part, through the generosity of the sovereign, for the decline in their revenue.

FOURTH TYPE OF DAMAGE

The increase of beggars, which is a consequence of the indirect taxes which destroy wages or subsistence by obliterating part of the reproduction of the nation's annual wealth. This increase of beggars is a large added burden on the cultivators, because they dare not refuse to give alms, being too exposed to the dangers which the discontent of vindictive beggars may draw down upon them. And this added burden is thrown back on to the revenue of the proprietors, who alone can provide for the indemnification of the cultivators, and who are obliged to make this indemnity by the very nature of their proprietorship and by the contracts which they cannot make otherwise than independently with those who farm their land.

These four types of damage have not been included in the calculations associated with the problem which we have just solved: the data are too diverse and numerous to enable us to get an exact idea of them. They could not be made subject to calculation without a very long train of special operations. It is enough for us to have indicated the path which we may follow to bring them all into the same type of computation, when they are known more exactly.

CONCLUSION

We may now ask the landed proprietors if it is not of the utmost importance to them to meet the whole of the direct taxes which determine and safeguard the state of their property, and not, as a result of a misunderstanding of their own interests, to induce sovereigns to have recourse for the state's needs to means which are as ruinous to the revenue of the proprietors, to the sovereigns themselves, and to the whole body of the nation, as indirect taxes.

TRANSLATIONS

IV. THE DIALOGUES AND MAXIMS

A.

THE 'DIALOGUE ON THE WORK OF ARTISANS'[1]

SECOND DIALOGUE

Mr H.

In our last conversation, we confined ourselves to the reasons which have induced you to include trade in the class which you call *sterile*. But this class to which you give the name *sterile*, in contrast to that which you call *productive*, confining as you do the idea of production to the wealth which is generated from the land, must therefore include all the other kinds of work, all the other services which are not directly employed in the regeneration of this wealth and in the marketing of it in sales at first hand. I admit that it would be difficult, in accordance with your division, to include them all under a single general designation other than that which you have chosen; for trade, the sciences, the arts, the magistrature, the military profession, servants, idle rentiers, beggars even, present so many different kinds of object, service, work, and employment, relative to production understood in its most rigorous physical sense, that I cannot visualize any general designation which would be strictly common to them all. It is for this very reason that I find difficulty in accepting your division and the names which you have applied to it in order to convey its meaning; it seems to me to be all the less exact in that you have differentiated the proprietors of the land from the classes which you call *productive* and *sterile*.

---

[1] First published in the *Journal de l'Agriculture, du Commerce et des Finances*, November 1766, and later reprinted in *Physiocratie*. The present translation is from the text of *Physiocratie*, as reproduced in I.N.E.D., II, pp. 885–912. R.L.M.

Mr N.

You should bear in mind, my friend, that in nature everything is intertwined, everything runs through circular courses which are interlaced with one another. The fact that these different movements are necessarily interconnected means that things can be understood, differentiated, and examined only through the medium of abstract ideas which do not cause any adjustment or maladjustment[1] in the physical world, and which comprehend nothing in this complicated network except in a speculative and partial manner. Here each relation can be differentiated only through the causes and effects which characterize it; the more we set out to arrive at precise distinctions, the more we are reduced simply to a few causes and a few effects by means of which, without losing sight of the concatenation[2] as a whole, we get a clear picture of the principal parts through their different functions in the general order of nature. Here, where we are confining ourselves to the physical order which is the most advantageous for men combined together in society, and where we are making an overall examination of the employments of men which conduce to public welfare, we differentiate them on the basis of their most noticeable and distinct causes and effects, in order to subsume them under primary general classes. It is only through the medium of such abstractions that we can examine and appraise the mutual relations between these different classes of men and work in the social order, and give them the designations which conform most closely to their functions, in order to express ourselves in exact terms in the detailed working-out of economic science.

The idea of *production*, or of *regeneration*, which here forms the basis of the differentiation between the general classes of citizens, is confined within physical limits which are so rigorously reduced to reality that they no longer conform to the vague expressions used in ordinary language. But it is not for the natural order to conform to a language which expresses only confused and ambiguous ideas; it is for the expressions to conform to the exact understanding of the natural order, in distinctions which are rigorously regulated by reality.

I note that the differentiation between the *productive class* and the *sterile class*, understood in this way, appears to you to remove the possibility of placing any other class in between them, for it would seem that there is no middle position between affirmative and negative, between a *productive class* and an *unproductive class*. This is true in those cases where all other relations are excluded; but in the present case you should easily be able to see (1) that the pro-

---

[1] *Qui n'arrangent ni ne dérangent rien.* R.L.M.
[2] *Enchaînement.* R.L.M.

prietors, who make none of the advances and do none of the work of cultivation at all, so that we cannot include them in the *productive class*, nevertheless began by making the first advances necessary to put their land in a cultivable state, and still remain charged with the maintenance of their patrimony, so that we cannot confuse them with the *sterile* class either; and (2) that there is a continual intercourse between the two extreme classes, which is carried on through the medium of the receipts and expenditure of an intermediary class. Thus the social order necessarily presupposes this third class of citizens, who originally laid the foundations of cultivation, who are its guardians, and who as *proprietors* distribute the net product.

It is under this last aspect in particular that we have to consider this *mixed* class in relation to the other two; the intercourse between the latter is a consequence of the intercourse which it itself carries on with these classes. Thus the differentiation of the *class of proprietors* must necessarily be made from the very outset if we are to follow clearly and uninterruptedly the course of the inter-communication between the different parts of the social order. So this differentiation, far from bringing possible confusion into your ideas, ought on the contrary to give unity and order to them.

Mr H.

That might be the case if, like you, I confined production solely to the wealth generated from the land. But I must tell you that I always see true production in the goods made by artisans, in spite of all the disquisitions which for some time past have been published with the aim of making this production disappear.

Mr N.

Nobody has attempted to make the production of the goods created by the labour of artisans disappear; for what you see is undoubtedly the production of these very goods. But you should have observed that in the disquisitions you are talking about it is not a question of production of this sort, i.e. a simple production of forms which the artisans give to the materials used in their goods—but of a *real* production of wealth. I say *real*, for I do not wish to deny that there is an addition of wealth to the raw materials used in the goods created by artisans, since their labour does in fact increase the value of the raw materials used in their goods.[1]

---

[1] What Quesnay is trying to say here is that the mere creation of utility of form by a manufacturer does not constitute 'real production' in the Physiocratic sense of that expression. Nor does the mere addition of value to the raw materials constitute 'real production': the essential attribute of 'real production', as the subsequent argument makes rather more clear, is that a *surplus* value should be

Mr H.

You make an admission here, my dear friend, which seems to me to be conclusive in favour of my opinion, and I believe that it ought to put an end to further discussion between us. But this admission at the same time fills me with a certain suspicion which prevents me from giving way completely to the prepossession which first attracted me towards my viewpoint. For I do not imagine that you are ready to rest your case with this first argument, by means of which you are no doubt intending to put aside completely the vulgar notions which uselessly confuse the question. But I confess to you that I do not see where this argument can lead you.

Mr N.

You are mistaken, my dear friend, if you think that my aim is to put aside the vulgar notions of which you have just spoken: that would not be the quickest way to settle the issue between us; and I hope you will forgive me if I tell you frankly that I believe it is these very notions which are imposing upon you yourself, and that you would go on opposing me continually if I did not begin by demonstrating their internal contradictions,[1] in order to prepare you to be on your guard against the dominant fallacy into which they have led you. Admit frankly, now, that you would claim that a shoe-maker who has made a pair of shoes has produced an increase of wealth, since the market value of this pair of shoes greatly exceeds that of the leather which the shoe-maker has employed. Now it is market value which gives to products the quality of wealth; and you believe that you can derive from this fact an incontrovertible argument in support of the view that the shoe-maker's labour constitutes production, in support, that is, of the *reality* of a true production of wealth.

Mr H.

According to your own principles, would not such an argument be decisive? If these are the vulgar notions against which you want to put me on my guard, I see that on the contrary I ought to hold myself on guard against certain tempting subtleties which could put me in difficulties, although I am not disposed to abandon a truth which seems to me self-evident in the extreme.

---

yielded—i.e. that the value of the final product should exceed the value of the raw materials by an amount greater than the value of the subsistence goods consumed in creating it. R.L.M.

[1] *Si je ne commençais par les mettre en opposition avec eux-mêmes.* R.L.M.

Mr N.

So I was not wrong in believing that we should inevitably have to go over the vulgar notions, of which you thought I wanted to keep our discussion free. In fact I know of no others at all which can be put forward in support of the production of wealth by the work of artisans; this is the thesis which you are undertaking to maintain: thus it is also these same notions which you would have brought forward if I had not taken care at the beginning to state them to you and to unfold the ambiguities concealed in the language which is commonly used to express them. But do not be afraid, my dear friend, that my aim is the fraudulent one of having recourse to certain subtleties in order to put you in difficulties. I propose to remain fully in the open with you as we go forward. I believe that the further we proceed in the full light of day, the more will you find that you are in familiar territory, and still more will you be astounded at the road by which we shall have travelled there; for this road is very well known to you, and you have gone over it a number of times, up to the spot at which we are going to arrive; but you have not given enough attention to the different things which have presented themselves to your notice.

We have to distinguish an *adding together* of items of wealth which are combined with one another, from a *production* of wealth. That is, we have to distinguish an increase brought about *by combining* raw materials with expenditure on the consumption of things which were in existence prior to this kind of increase, from a *generation* or creation of wealth, which constitutes a renewal and *real* increase of renascent wealth.[1]

Those who do not make a distinction between this true increase of wealth and this false one fall without noticing it into continual contradictions when they are arguing about the alleged production of wealth which results from the work of artisans.

They agree that the more that can be saved in costs or in costly work, without causing any harm, in the manufacture of artisans' goods, the more profitable will this saving be, as a result of the reduction in the price of these goods. But they nevertheless believe that the production of wealth, which results from the artisans' work, consists in the increase of the market value of their goods. These contradictory ideas exist together in the same mind and continually

---

[1] *Il faut distinguer une* addition *de richesses réunies, d'avec une* production *de richesses; c'est-à-dire une augmentation* par réunion *de matieres premières et de dépenses en consommation de choses qui existaient avant cette sorte d'augmentation, d'avec une* generation, *ou creation de richesses, qui forment un renouvellement et un accroissement réel de richesses renaissantes.* R.L.M.

clash with one another there, without the mind being aware of this discord.

The costly labour of the lace-maker adds an increase of market value to the thread which constitutes the raw material of the lace. Therefore, people conclude, the labour involved in making the lace has produced an increase of wealth. The same thing is believed of the labour of painters who execute highly priced pictures; for the more highly paid is the labour of artists and artisans, the more *productive* it appears.

This drinking-glass costs only *one sou*, and the raw material which is used to make it is worth *one-quarter of a sou:* the glass-maker's labour quadruples the value of this raw material. Here, therefore, is a production of wealth, which has brought about a three-fold increase: so that it would be very advantageous, according to you, to find a method of making such a glass which involved using the labour of two workers for a year; and still better if it involved using the labour of four workers for two years. Consequently you would also tell us that it would be very disadvantageous if a machine were invented which made beautiful lace and fine pictures without any cost, or at a very low cost. In actual fact, the invention of printing gave rise to very serious arguments about the reduction in work for the scriveners; nevertheless, when everything had been thoroughly considered, printing was brought fully into operation. So, my dear friend, reconcile your ideas, if you can, with all these contradictions; otherwise the question of the alleged production of wealth through the labour of artisans no longer appears worthy of any attention.

Mr H.

You do not realize, my friend, that you are putting yourself in the same difficulty with regard to the work of the *productive* class. Are not attempts also made to save as much as possible on this work? Are we to conclude from this that it is not *productive*?

Mr N.

Conversations are often marked by detours and digressions.

It would seem, my dear friend, that you are trying to escape from the difficulty by means of another difficulty, which, as between ourselves, will soon be cleared away. But before we concern ourselves with it, let us finally settle the question of the alleged production of wealth through industrial work. I think that you will not persist further in confusing this production with that of the forms given to their goods by artisans, artists, builders, handicraftsmen, manufacturers, etc. Do you still have any other arguments to bring forward, then, in support of your opinion?

Mr H.

I quite understand that we should not confuse the production of wealth, which may result from the labour of artisans, with the production of their goods, or with the increase in price added to it by the costs of the labour, which is in fact always inseparable from the expenditure required for the subsistence of the workers. But it is this expenditure itself which results in the production of wealth which the artisans' industry brings about, for it is this expenditure which procures the sale of the products of the land and which maintains their prices. And according to you yourself it is the market value of products in their sale at first hand which gives them the quality of wealth, and which is also the measure of the wealth annually produced by the territory. This expenditure of which I am speaking expands consumption and increases competition among purchasers, thus increasing the price of the products and consequently the annual wealth of the nation, population, and consumption. It is in this very circle, then, that the real production of wealth due to industrial work consists.

Mr N.

In relation to the circle which you describe here, you leave out one quite essential matter—that of making known to us its origin and dimensions. Do you think that it can extend further than the annual reproduction, which is itself the measure of the nation's annual expenditure? Do you not see that on the contrary this measure limits the expenditure which *pays for* the artisans' work, and consequently regulates the consumption which these artisans are able to *make payment for* to the productive class?

It is self-evident that all we have here is a circulation of wealth without any increase, a circulation which is regulated by the measure of the nation's annual expenditure; a measure which is equal to that of the wealth which is annually generated from the territory. Thus the work of artists and artisans cannot extend beyond the portion of expenditure which the nation can employ on it, in proportion to the measure of the total expenditure which it can annually make.

This work, then, cannot increase the wealth which the nation annually spends, since it is itself limited by the measure of this wealth, which can be increased only through agricultural work and not through the expenditure involved in artisans' work. Thus the origin, the principle, of all expenditure and all wealth is the fertility of the land, whose products can be increased only through these products themselves. It is the land which provides the advances to the cultivator who renders it fertile in order to make it produce more. The artisan can contribute to this only by making certain implements which are necessary for turning over the land, and which in the absence of the artisan the cultivator would make for himself. No matter who the worker may happen to be, it is necessary that the land should have produced in advance what he has consumed for his subsistence: thus it is not his labour which has produced this subsistence. Nor has the consumption of the subsistence produced anything either, since this consumption is only a destruction of wealth produced in advance by the land. The worker who sought to do more work in order to increase his wages or his consumption would do so in vain, for he cannot extend them beyond the products which are at present available for his consumption, for that of the cultivator, and for that of all the other men who make up the nation.

So you should note that it is not the demand of the artisans, who can make payment only with the wages they have received, which regulates the price of products. It is the need for the products and their quantity itself which determine their market value.

Mr H.

You are not unaware, my friend, that there are certain goods whose price greatly exceeds the value of the costs: such are pictures by great painters, and all the other goods made by artists who are pre-eminent in their professions.

Mr N.

You could also add to these the goods made by those artisans to whom the government grants exclusive privileges. For these pre-eminent artists of whom you speak enjoy the same prerogative, since there are so few of them that competition between them does not force them to lower the price of their labour, to the benefit of those who buy their work. But do not confuse this with the labour of those whose professions demand very long and costly studies, for then you would be forgetting to take these high expenses into account in the price of their goods.

Mr H.

Take those goods made by artisans which last for a number of years—buildings, furniture, pictures, etc.: do they not also constitute part of the total of a nation's wealth? Do not these goods, therefore, represent a real production of wealth, which has a market value for those who possess them? They have paid for them, certainly, but they can resell them; and sales and purchases always assume twofold wealth, since there is an exchange of an item of wealth of one value for another item of wealth of equal value. Does the expenditure of idle men produce such wealth?

Mr N.

My dear friend, what you are here calling production of wealth is only preservation of wealth. The expenditure of those who buy these goods is not for immediate consumption, but for lasting enjoyment. But neither of these two kinds of expenditure is more advantageous than the other, so far as those who engage in this expenditure are concerned; and the very kind which you believe to be less advantageous, owing to the immediate consumption, such as expenditure for daily subsistence, is more indispensable than the other and consequently preferable to it. How then can you claim to prove to us that the labour of a painter produces more than the labour of a baker? A highly priced picture does, I admit, represent great wealth, because the painter has made the purchaser of the picture pay very highly for his labour. Thus if it were not for the high price of the labour, the picture, although an admirable one, would represent only a small amount of wealth. Beautiful drawings would also be highly priced if a method had not been found of reproducing them at a low cost through engraving and printing. And do you think that the reduction in the price of these goods means a reduction in the amount of wealth in a nation? Does not this reduction in price, on the contrary, procure for the nation the advantage of being able with the same expenditure to increase its enjoyments and vary them as it wishes, which is the true object of expenditure, extending even to expenditure on consumption and subsistence? You would agree, I think, that *the perfection of economic conduct consists in obtaining the greatest possible increase in enjoyments through the greatest possible reduction in expense.* But what becomes then of your alleged real production of wealth through the work of artisans?

Mr H.

Ah! my friend, the more you explain your ideas, the more contradictions I detect in your economic science. Does it not teach us that wealth is procured through expenditure, and that the expenditure of each man operates to the benefit of other men? And on the other hand it tells us that *the perfection of economic conduct consists in the greatest [possible] reduction in expense.* This perfection seems to me, in consequence of your own principles, to mean the extinction of a kingdom's prosperity and population. I know that if I looked to my own individual interest I should want to enjoy a great deal with little expense, and that each person as an individual thinks the same. But individual interest is in contradiction with general interest, and is so inconsequent that it would destroy itself if the natural order had not put obstacles in the way of its doing so; that is, if these individual interests themselves, by means of the reciprocity between them, did not resist their own destruction. Men take so short-sighted a view of things, and their greed is so avid, that they would continually go astray if they did not set one another back on the right path through the necessity which faces them all of tending blindly towards the general good. Could it not also be your individual interest, then, which inspires this fine maxim of yours, *to obtain the greatest possible increase in enjoyments through the greatest possible reduction in expense*?

Mr N.

I ought to add something else, my friend; for not only do I ask for *the greatest possible reduction in expense*, but also *the greatest possible reduction in disagreeable[1] labour with the greatest possible enjoyment*. It seems to me that this desire is general among men; those who can rightfully obtain this advantage profit from it as much as they can, and they do this, too, without detrimentally affecting the general welfare. The total amount of the expenditure which is paid out to the artisans, who are necessarily obliged to work in order to obtain their subsistence, is always more limited than the needs which make labour imperative for them. The rich, by virtue of their possessions, are the distributors of the expenditure with which they pay the workers' wages; they would do them a great deal of harm if they worked to earn what they spend in this way,[2] and they would do harm to themselves if they devoted themselves to disagreeable labour which would mean a reduction in their enjoyments; for anything which is disagreeable means a deprivation of satisfying enjoyments. Thus they *would not obtain the greatest possible increase in enjoyments through the greatest possible reduction in expense*. It is no less true, however, that in order to combine these two things advantage is taken of the

[1] *Pénible*. R.L.M.
[2] However, a distinction must again be made between workers who are simply artisans and workers who are husbandmen. If the proprietors gave themselves up to agricultural enterprises and devoted their wealth to them, they would expand the total quantity of products, which would increase the sum total of expenditure, in the beginning to the benefit of the proprietors themselves, whose wealth would be increased, and afterwards to the benefit of the other classes of citizens, not excepting the artisans, who would all share in the expenditure of this increase in products and wealth. From this there would follow from the very first moment a greater degree of well-being for the population, and soon a greater population. In addition, in all countries where agriculture and the quantity of the territory's products are not at their highest possible level, the proprietors are obliged, in their own interest and in that of all their fellow-citizens, scrupulously to economize as much as possible in their expenditure on pure consumption, in order to devote the proceeds of this economy to *productive* expenditure, to expenditure which improves their estates, which increases the products of their land and raises their value.

competition of those who vie with one another in offering their labour;[1] that advantage is taken of this, I say, in order to save as much expense as possible and to extend enjoyments as much as possible. But this saving also has its limits: all labour is inseparable from expense, and people devote themselves to it only in order to satisfy their needs. Competition, it is true, lowers the price of labour, but the gain which one has to procure through one's labour in order to satisfy one's needs calls a peremptory halt to the unregulated decline in the price of labour which is encouraged by competition. Thus the maxim *to obtain the greatest possible increase in enjoyments through the greatest possible reduction in expense* is regulated by the sovereign and immutable laws of the physical order which is most advantageous to men combined together in society. Thus if you follow out in detail the interconnection and application of the principles of economic science you will no longer detect any contradictions in it.

Mr H.

Even if I agreed with you on these principles, so far as internal trade is concerned, would it not always be true that manufactured commodities constitute a branch of trade between nations?

Mr N.

A branch, agreed; or one could say an offshoot. But to trade is not to produce.

Mr H.

Your replies are not at all satisfactory. Generalities, plausible maxims, and *metaphysico-geometrical* abstractions are the subterfuges which you always resort to when arguing with those who are not as practised as you are in this kind of discussion. If you spoke frankly, you would admit as everyone does that what we have here is the sale and production of the worker's commodity, and that it is the worker's labour which has produced the market value of this commodity.

Mr N.

My replies, my friend, appear abstract to you only because you have not yet seen quite clearly that the market value of these commodities consists simply of the very value of the raw material and of the subsistence which the worker has consumed during his labour, and that the sale of this market value which the worker repeatedly carries on is at bottom only a resale of what has already been

[1] *On profite de la concurrence de ceux qui s'entre-disputent le travail.* R.L.M.

produced.[1] Is it your aim, then, to make me believe that *to resell* is *to produce*? I could then come back at you in my own turn and say that your intention was extremely captious.

Mr H.

My intention is not captious at all, for I believe quite sincerely that TO RESELL, WITH PROFIT, IS TO PRODUCE.

Mr N.

You will accuse me once again of replying only with general maxims if I repeat to you that *trade is only an exchange of value for equal value*, and that so far as these values are concerned there is neither loss nor gain as between the contracting parties.

Mr H.

This definition of trade, reduced to the form of a general maxim, is only an abstraction leaving out of account a host of circumstances which in the course of trade procure a real profit for one or other of the contracting parties, and often for both. And without wandering from the point of the question we are arguing about, you envisage the manufacturer as a trader who resells what has already been produced;[2] but I maintain that by virtue of his sales themselves he is a purchaser of our products, since in his resale trade he sells abroad the value of the country's products which he has consumed during his labour.

Mr N.

What do you claim to conclude from that? For my part, I can never see anything in this trade but the exchange of value of equal value, without any production, even though circumstances render this exchange profitable to one or other of the contracting parties, or even to both. In fact, it must always be assumed that it is profitable to both; for both sides procure for themselves the enjoyment of wealth which they can obtain only through exchange. But there is never anything here but an exchange of an item of wealth of one value for another item of wealth of equal value, and consequently no real increase in wealth at all.

Mr H.

Since you agree that in the absence of exchange they would not procure for themselves the wealth which they can obtain only through

[1] *Un commerce de revendeur*. R.L.M.   [2] *Un marchand revendeur*. R.L.M.

exchange, let us apply this admission to external trade in manufactured commodities. The worker, through the sale of his goods abroad, obtains money to buy your products for his subsistence: surely it is very profitable to him to procure his subsistence through this trade, and the money which he obtains from abroad in order to buy your products, which you need to sell, is also very profitable to you.

Mr N.

The products which I need to sell, and which the artisan needs to buy, are in existence before I sell them and before the artisan buys them. Thus our trade in these products, in the form of sales and purchases, by no means generates them. Thus it is by no means productive of the things which I need to sell and which the artisan needs to buy.

Mr H.

I was not expecting this reply. The question at issue between us does not concern the production of which you are speaking. It concerns another kind of production, the production of wealth. An item of exchangeable produce is wealth in proportion to its market value. And the buyer contributes as much as the seller to the market value of produce. Thus the artisan is a producer of wealth if the gain which he obtains through the sale of his goods abroad contributes, in proportion to its magnitude, to increase the price of the product which you sell to him.

Mr N.

You are bringing up again a question which was fully discussed in our earlier conversation, when it was shown that the price of exchangeable products depends neither on the buyer nor on the seller. If it depended on the buyer, the latter would not contribute to the increase, for he has an interest in buying at the lowest possible price. If it depended on the seller, he alone would be the producer of the market value of the product which he sells, for he alone has an interest in selling at the highest possible price. Nevertheless the one is obliged to buy at a price higher than that at which he has an interest in buying, and the other is obliged to sell at a lower price than he would like. Thus there are other decisive conditions determining prices which force them to sacrifice their interests in their sales and purchases; thus their trade is by no means productive of the wealth or market value of the products which they exchange between themselves, since the commodity and the money which pays for it have both had their price established prior to the exchange.

Mr H.

I acknowledge this truth just as you do; but do you not also agree with me that the more our artisans earn from the sales which they make of their goods abroad, the more of our products they are able to buy? And a greater competition among buyers is one of the conditions which cause the market value of products to increase; thus the profitable trade of our artisans with foreign countries then becomes productive of an increase in wealth, or in the market value of our products.

Mr N.

There is no question that *the more our artisans earned from the sales which they made of their goods abroad, the more of our products they would be able to buy,* and this might be a matter requiring some consideration in a country whose trade in products was suffering from a lack of markets. But wherever external trade in produce is un-obstructed, this advantage happily destroys the meagre source of help of which you speak, for it is incapable of bringing about any change in the general price which is current among the trading nations. In that case your objection would combine two contradic-tory assertions. The competition among the artisans, which expanded purchases a little more, could not cause an increase in the price of products, for this slight effect would always be counteracted by another kind of competition, i.e. by the imports associated with external trade, which would be attracted by the increase in sales brought about by the increase in the purchases of our artisans. Thus the increase in price would be checked by competition among the sellers, which would always be proportionate to the competition of the buyers. On the other hand, if the artisans' expenses became greater, the price of their goods would increase; foreigners would no longer find it profitable to buy them, and our artisans would no longer have the advantage of competition in their external trade. I am sure you will not advocate the ridiculous expedient of closing our ports to prevent trade in the territory's products, with the aim of affording our manufacturers a low cost of living; you are too concerned with the sale of our products not to perceive all the disadvantages of so gross a blunder. Thus your objection offers nothing more than a tissue of incompatible conditions.

Mr H.

I am aware of the general advantages of freedom of trade in products; but surely you do not believe that full freedom of competition should be extended to include external trade in manufactured commodities; for it can hardly be doubted that it would not be profitable to us if our artisans sold their goods to other nations, and that it would be disadvantageous to buy them from foreign artisans.

Mr N.

I do not understand the niceties of this arrangement. You want to be a trader in manufactured commodities whose sale, according to you, would not be advantageous. Thus you have completely changed your opinion since a moment ago on the question of the market value of artisans' goods and on the advantages of this branch of foreign trade, since you believe that it is disadvantageous to buy the goods of artisans of other nations. If this disadvantage is a real one, will foreign countries buy the goods of your artisans? Your branch of trade seems to me to be highly dubious, for there must be at least two to enter into trade.

Mr H.

The greater skill and dexterity of our artisans induce foreign countries to buy their goods.

Mr N.

You have a fine exclusive privilege there: but is it all-embracing and everlasting? Do you not rather think that by virtue of the taste for different kinds of goods which nations have, a mutual trade in their goods grows up between them, and that consequently this branch of trade can be extended only through free competition? We shall let you think about putting this little matter in order if you want to; but you will hardly trouble yourself with it: *De minimis non curat praetor.*

Mr H.

But on your part it seems to me that you trouble yourself very little with money, which is obtained only through trade.

Mr N.

You are not to know that in fact I give it very cursory consideration: I am more concerned with the nation's opulence. For when you are rich you do not stand in need of money, and you have substitutes for it. Recollect that one of our friends, a very rich man, who had no money at all, then bought a very large piece of land. His lack of money raised no obstacle to this acquisition; through the medium of his bills the land was soon paid for; and through the medium of bill upon bill of his wealthy creditors he had a great number of payments made to him, only one of which involved ready cash.

Mr H.

Is it not more worth while to employ our fellow-citizens than foreigners?

Mr N.

Yes, they are preferable, so long as we do not lose anything in remunerating their labour; for if not, it is preferable to employ not only foreigners, but also animals, and even machines which can profitably be substituted for them; and the profit from this, which increases disposable wealth, always turns to the advantage of the country's population.

Mr H.

The horses and machines which are preferred to men, in order to economize on costs, do not carry our money out of the kingdom. The horses which are employed consume the produce which is used to feed them and contribute to its sale; and they are themselves commodities, trade in which is profitable to us. But if we preferred Savoyards rather than the kingdom's inhabitants to reap our harvests, they would carry off into their country the money which we paid them, to the detriment of the inhabitants of our countryside whom we ought to have employed, and who would have spent their remuneration with us, so that our money would not have gone out of the kingdom. It is just the same when we buy the goods of foreign artisans, even when they sell them to us at a cheaper price than that at which we could buy them from our artisans. The objection which I am putting forward here has also been made to you a number of times in connection with foreign merchants, in the case of free competition in trade, and it seems to me that you have not given a precise reply to it.

Mr N.

Coined money is meant to circulate among nations, as it does among the inhabitants of each nation; it goes out of a kingdom and comes back into it through the continual intercourse of trade. It has no other use than that of facilitating the exchange of produce, by serving as an intermediary token between sales and purchases, for the object with which an exchange is decisively concerned is not money at all. Thus, in the case where money is exchanged, on the basis of value for equal value, we procure for ourselves without incurring any loss what we need to buy, and what we need to buy is always preferable to the money. In exchanges we sell and we buy, and in order to facilitate exchanges money is always present between sales and purchases. Money cannot be wanting in any country unless that country carries on no exchanges of movable commodities. Thus it is not money which we ought to think about, but rather the exchanges of the things which are to be sold and those which are to be bought, for it is in these exchanges themselves that the advantage which the contracting parties wish to procure for themselves resides. It is true that they express values in terms of money, because money serves them as a measure in which to state the value of exchangeable things; but they know very well that the greater part of exchanges, and above all the most substantial ones, are conducted without the actual intervention of money; promises to pay, properly validated and in writing, are accepted in exchanges, where they are traded like money itself, without the contracting parties suffering any damage through the absence of money. Thus a nation's interest in exchange is not bound up with money, but with the advantage it can procure for itself through exchange. Let us make abstraction from money, then, in the use of money itself, so that we may concern ourselves only with the advantage which can be procured through the use of money, and which makes money circulate continually among nations and among the inhabitants of each nation.

Mr H.

Your arguments are very plausible; but they by no means alter the fact that in the assumed case it would be very hard for me to make abstraction from the money which the Savoyards carry away from us.

Mr N.

Why do we give them our money?

Mr H.

Because we prefer that they should reap our harvests rather than the inhabitants of our countryside.

Mr N.

Why do we prefer them?

Mr H.

Because we pay less for their labour.

Mr N.

As a result of this preference, then, can the husbandman procure for himself a reduction in his expenses?

Mr H.

Yes, but it is to the detriment of the inhabitants of our countryside.

Mr N.

This reply is very vague: you might as well say that all economies in costs are injurious to those who would have benefited from the expenditure of the costs, forgetting about those who benefit from the economies in these costs. But if we bear in mind the interests of both groups, we shall have to decide whether we ought to remedy one injury with another injury, or allow full freedom for expenditure to take its course, in conformity with the interests of those who engage in it. Natural law declares in favour of these latter, for the lawful disposal of the use of their property appertains to them. Moreover, we should take note of the fact that economies in expenditure do not mean an absolute loss of expenditure, but merely a distribution of expenditure which is to the advantage of those who benefit from it, and which is also to the advantage of those who distribute this expenditure, in conformity with their interests. If others gain from the expenditure of what has been saved, and if those who engage in expenditure also gain from this saving, you will find that it is in no way harmful to society, and that if it is injurious to some it is advantageous to others. Thus it is for those who live on the wages which are distributed by means of expenditure to distribute themselves in comformity with the distribution of expenditure; and this state of affairs does not fail to come about, without the government concerning itself with it. For this is certainly not a matter for the government: it is only freedom of choice of occupations or professions itself which can regularly bring about this state of affairs.

Mr H.

I must say, my friend, that this reply, so well adapted to your general principles, is not satisfactory, for it does not prove that there is the same quantity of expenditure available for those members of the nation who live on the wages provided by the expenditure engaged in in the kingdom, since the Savoyards have taken part of these wages away from them. It can also be argued that there is not the same quantity of expenditure, for these same wages which the

Savoyards have earned are spent in Savoy. I am quite willing to make abstraction from our money which goes to a foreign country, but I am not willing to forget the wages which are taken away from our fellow-citizens.

Mr N.

Your importunity is holding up the continuation of the explanation which should make your objection disappear completely, but it at least discloses accurately the difficulty which remains to be cleared up, and brings us back to the source of expenditure, which is itself the source of wages. It is the cultivators and the proprietors who originally distribute all the expenditure and all the wages; thus the more they are able to increase the amount of wealth which is used for expenditure, the more wages they will put into circulation, and the more they will increase the revenue of the sovereign. We must not lose sight of these two matters; you are at present concerning yourself only with keeping inside the kingdom all the wages which can be distributed there by the expenditure, without examining the manner of employing the expenditure which is most advantageous to the prosperity and power of the state. But if you recall that all reductions in the cost of cultivation, which do no harm to cultivation itself, or which may or must expand it, represent an increase of revenue for the proprietors and the sovereign, and that this increase represents an addition to disposable expenditure which ensures the nation's power and increases wages, this will present you with two elements to be included in the calculations, the result of which will cause your difficulties to disappear.

If there is a gain to be made by giving preference to the Savoyards in reaping our harvests, this gain will mean a reduction in the costs of cultivation, an increase in revenue, and consequently an increase in disposable expenditure for the nation. If, on the other hand, the costs of cultivation were to increase to the detriment of the revenue, neither the state nor the nation would be compensated at all for this loss; for expenditure on costs is definitely not disposable expenditure. Expenditure on costs does, it is true, distribute wages, but disposable expenditure also distributes them. And even if the reduction in expenditure on costs appeared to subtract more from wages than the increase in disposable expenditure added to them, you could not conclude from this that this subtraction from wages was disadvantageous to the nation, if its disposable expenditure then came to be employed in a more advantageous manner. For as cultivation became less costly, the profit due to the economies in expenditure on costs would naturally be devoted by the cultivators to expanding their operations, and this would increase the product and the revenue. Thus in actual fact there would be no subtraction from expenditure, and there would be more revenue, which would soon assure the nation of much higher wages than those which it enjoyed before the Savoyards brought the price of labour down. And from the very first moment of the economies in costs, the nation, possessing a greater total of disposable wealth, would be more powerful and lead a less precarious existence.

Here we have imperceptibly come back again to the employment of working animals and machines, the repair of roads, the transport of commodities by means of rivers, canals, etc., for the purpose of reducing the high cost of the wages which would be paid to men and which are avoided by these different methods. Their result is an increase in revenue, i.e. in disposable expenditure, which constitutes the nation's opulence and which is distributed in the kingdom in the form of wages.

Expenditure on costs, although it provides wages, by no means brings about this state of opulence, in which we spend liberally and as we please without impoverishing ourselves. For expenditure on costs cannot be laid out at will so long as it is earmarked for this purpose, from which it cannot be diverted without bringing to a halt the labour which is meant to receive it unless other methods are substituted for this labour. And this brings us back again to the desirability of making economies in expenditure on costs to the greatest extent possible without detrimentally affecting the annual reproduction of the nation's wealth; and also for the purpose of increasing this reproduction, which alone provides for all the different kinds of expenditure, increases enjoyments, and assures the state's power. Thus you see that your objection would make us travel round perpetually in the same circle, which would perpetually reduce it to an absurdity, for it would extend to all the methods which were employed to reduce costs through cutting down on wages which encroached upon the revenue of the land. And according to your view one would always have to conclude that the whole nation ought to be engaged in work which increased expenditure on costs without increasing the annual reproduction of wealth and without leaving any revenue for disposable expenditure.

Mr H.

You will at least agree that the whole of the expenditure of the artisans, and of the whole class which you call *sterile*, returns to the class of cultivators, and that it is this expenditure which maintains the price of the products of the land. And it is in terms of the very price of these products that you calculate the returns of the cultivators and the revenue of the proprietors—in short, everything which you call *wealth* annually regenerated from the land. But could you even attribute the quality of wealth to them in the absence of their market value, i.e. if they were not exchangeable for other wealth of equal value—I mean for other wealth which, making abstraction from the raw materials, is itself wealth or products annually re-generated through the work of the artisans? In this exchange, everything which can be called wealth, on both sides, is given this name only because it is mutually paid for with wealth of equal value. The goods of the artisans are paid for, and it is for this very reason that these products constitute wealth. The products of agriculture are also paid for, and is it not once again for this reason that these products constitute wealth? What difference, then, do you detect between the products of industry and the products of agriculture? Even though you do find some difference here (for in actual fact differences always exist, even between one individual and another individual of the same species), what conclusions can you draw from it relative to the point of the question we are arguing about, when the specific conditions, which we ought to agree on, are essentially the same on both sides?

Mr N.

As I have already told you, all these arguments are simply based on ambiguities of language; and if I had to conform to this inexact language I would say as you do that the goods of the artisans con-stitute products, and that these products constitute wealth with which the artisan is able to pay for the products of agriculture. But permit me to remind you that all the members of the *sterile* class who receive rewards[1] but who do not make any goods at all, the beggars even, and the thieves, who cannot be suspected of producing wealth, also pay for the products of agriculture, by means of the money which they have secured for themselves, with wealth of equal value. Moreover, we have agreed that the smaller the degree to which the artisans' products constitute *wealth*—I mean the greater the economies which can be made in the expenditure which produces them and raises their price—the smaller will be the degree to which wealth of this nature represents a burden to those who exchange the products of the land for this wealth. And yet, my friend, you still ask me what difference I detect between the products of industry and the products of agriculture which can lead me to conclude that the former does not represent a true *generation* or *creation* of wealth. Has this difference, which has just been argued and discussed between us from opposing points of view and in the fullest detail, already escaped you?

[1] *Tous les salariés de le classe* stérile. R.L.M.

Mr H.

You are always saying that the agents of the sterile class have to be paid in order that they should be able to pay for the products which they buy from the productive class. Here we are then, you and I, caught up in a vicious circle, for I say similarly that the agents of the sterile class themselves also have to pay in order that they should be able to be paid. Thus on both sides everyone is paid and everyone pays.

Mr N.

It is true that the agents of the sterile class pay for the products which they buy from the productive class: you can even say in addition, if you want to, that these purchases have a favourable effect on the sale and the price of the products. But does it follow from this that the same money which pays for the products which they buy is also used by them to pay themselves their *wages*? Would you not then be assuming that money is used for two purposes in a single act of trade?[1] For the money with which the agents of the sterile class have paid for the products they have bought has been exchanged with the productive class on the basis of value for equal value; the sterile class has received as much from the productive class as the productive class has received from the sterile class; and you would claim in addition that the sterile class would also pay itself its wages with the money which it has employed in the purchase of products, so that its transactions with the productive class would be such that it would have to have both the commodity which it has bought and the money with which it has paid for it. Would this not mean that the productive class handed over the commodity to it for nothing? In that case the sterile class would not reimburse itself, which would be the opposite of what you are trying to prove to me.

What you were meaning, no doubt, is that when the sterile class has exchanged its money with the productive class, on the basis of value for equal value, this money belongs to the productive class, and the latter in its turn employs it in making payment to the sterile class for the services or goods which it receives from it. This, according to your idea, is the circle or process of circulation followed by this money, which shifts in turn from one proprietor to another, all these proprietors being on an equal basis[2] and reciprocally returning the money to one another.

But here it is not a question simply of money, for money is not

---

[1] *Ne supposeriez-vous pas alors un double emploi dans un même acte de commerce?* R.L.M.

[2] *Qui sont les mêmes.* R.L.M.

consumed; we should also say something about the products which are consumed by the sterile class, which are annually regenerated by the productive class, and which the latter sells to the former. And we should also note that it is not even true that the productive class gives back to the sterile class the money which it receives from it, for it gives it to the proprietors of the land to pay the revenue which it owes to them. Thus this money follows a different course from that which you have supposed: it does not move in a continuous circle, single and reciprocal, between the sterile class and the productive class. Besides, it is not on the circulation of this money, as I have already observed, that we ought to fix our attention: if we did we should be forgetting the object which is essential to us—the annual distribution of the products which are annually regenerated through the work of the productive class.

Once again, then, make abstraction from money, and consider only this distribution, which can actually be carried out without the intervention of money. For the productive class could pay in products themselves for the services and goods which it receives from the sterile class. It could pay in the same way the revenue of the proprietors, who would also pay in products the wages of the sterile class. And then there would remain for the productive class only that portion of its harvest which it itself requires for expenditure on the work necessary to regenerate each year the same reproduction, which would also be distributed in the same way each year among the three classes. You are aware that this distribution used to be carried out in this manner in the great and prolific empire governed by the Incas.[1]

You can see from this form of distribution, which in actual fact is the real distribution of the annual products and consumption among the three classes, that this distribution terminates directly and completely in consumption, and begins over again with reproduction. Thus this distribution does not involve any return to the productive class, and your circle disappears.

Run your eyes over the *Tableau Economique*, and you will see that the productive class supplies the money with which the other classes come to buy its products from it, and that they return this money to it when they come back in the following year to make the same purchases from it. Without any great effort of imagination, you could picture these pieces of metal to yourself as so many tickets which denote the share which each should have in the annual apportionment of the products; for the productive class regularly gives back these same tickets in order that the apportionment of the following year should be denoted in the same way. Thus what you call price in trade between different nations will appear to you in the

---

[1] Cf. Quesnay's *Analyse du Gouvernement des Incas du Pérou*, I.N.E.D., II, pp. 913 ff. R.L.M.

case of each individual nation merely as the measure which regulates
the distribution among citizens of the subsistence which is generated
from the territory through the work of the cultivators, whose own
share is merely regulated in the order of this distribution of the
products which are annually consumed, and whose work you can
easily distinguish from work and services aimed at conveying,
preparing, and diversifying enjoyments or consumption. Thus there
is no circle to be seen here other than that of expenditure followed
by reproduction, and of reproduction followed by expenditure,
a circle which is run through by means of the circulation of the
money which measures the expenditure and the reproduction. You
should therefore stop confusing the measure with the thing measured,
and the circulation of the one with the apportionment of the other.

Mr H.

It has been very well said in the *Theory of Taxation*[1] that 'all men are
husbandmen, because all contribute, each in his own occupation, to
save the husbandman's time. The tailor makes the husbandman's
coat; the husbandman is not obliged to leave his plough in order to
work at making his clothing; the tailor's wife occupies herself with
housekeeping, so that the tailor is never diverted from his work',
etc., etc., etc.

Mr N.

This metaphor, to be found in the book from which you are quoting,
to which you have seen the sterile class precisely distinguished from
the productive class, should not lead you into error. It combines
together, true enough, productive labour and the labour which is
necessary for enjoyment, by means of the conditions which cause
them to resemble one another; but do you not see that to save the
husbandman's time in this way is to increase his productive labour,
which should then generate both his own subsistence and that of the
tailor? Thus the tailor subsists only by virtue of the increase in the
productive labour of the cultivator. Thus if the cultivator were to
interrupt his labour in order to make his clothing himself, he would
no longer generate the subsistence of another man; for the time
which he employed in this sterile labour would be stolen from his
productive labour. Thus the tailor's labour, which prevents this
disarrangement, necessarily assumes double productive labour on
the cultivator's part in order to enable this artisan to subsist, which
clearly proves that the latter's labour is actually sterile.

---

[1] *Théorie de l'Impôt*, by Mirabeau. R.L.M.

Mr H.

I am beginning to see that in fact the artisans' goods constitute wealth only by virtue of the combination of other items of wealth which were already in existence prior to the manufacture of these goods; and that, the quality being the same, the less they cost in terms of these items of wealth—i.e. *the less they constitute wealth—the more beneficial they are.* But I come back again to the objection I have already put before you concerning the economies which are also made, as far as possible, in the agricultural work which generates wealth from the land. Is not their purpose the same—to make this wealth cost less wealth, i.e. *to make it constitute less wealth?* In that case, what becomes of the distinction which you turn to such account in support of your opinion?

Mr N.

This distinction, which you do not understand, can be shown to you very clearly.

All men who work consume in order to subsist. But consumption destroys subsistence goods. Thus it is necessary that they should be regenerated. And it is the cultivator's labour which regenerates not only the subsistence goods which he himself has destroyed but also those destroyed by all the other consumers. The artisan's labour, on the other hand, merely procures for him a right to share in the consumption of the subsistence goods which are regenerated through the labour of the cultivator.

Thus you see that we have to divide the reproduction generated by the cultivator into two portions, namely, the portion which provides for his own subsistence, and the portion which is in excess of this subsistence. Whence it follows that if it is possible, without detrimentally affecting the total reproduction, to cut down on the first portion, the second will be correspondingly increased. For example, if we assume that the reproduction is 20, the cultivator's expenses 10, and the surplus 10, then if the expenses can be cut down to 8 the surplus will be 12.

The prices of products are regulated, irrespective of the costs of cultivation, by the quantity and by the competition of purchasers, whose needs are always greater than the total amount of the reproduction. Thus the economies which are made in the cultivator's expenses, although they increase the portion which is in excess of the costs, do not bring down the price, and consequently the reproduction *does not constitute less wealth.*

In the artisan's goods, on the other hand, there is no addition of wealth over and above his expenses at all, as has been proved. Thus the more economies which are made in his expenses, *the less do his goods constitute wealth.*

These points, which are no doubt familiar to you, ought to enable you, my friend, to understand the difference which exists between the effect of the expenses involved in cultivation and that of the expenses of the artisans, and above all between the value of the wealth which is generated through the labour of cultivation and the value of the artisans' goods. To some extent we can make a comparison between the artisan and the cultivator with reference to the value of their expenses, since the expenses of both should be taken into account in calculations relating to the economic order; but a comparison between the artisan and the cultivator cannot be made with reference to the fruits of their labour. The difference is so obvious that no further explanation of it is necessary to dispose of your objection about the effects of economies in the expenses involved in the artisans' goods and economies in the expenses involved in the work of cultivating the land. It is the expense of the labour which determines the price of the artisans' goods, and the competition of the latter sets limits to the expense of their labour. It is not the same, I repeat, with the price of the products of the land, which is determined not only by the expenses of cultivation but also by many other causes which are capable of maintaining the market value of the products, notwithstanding economies in the costs of cultivation. The product of the artisan's labour is worth only the expense: if it cost more a loss would be involved.[1] The product of the cultivator's labour exceeds the expense; the more it exceeds it the more profitable it is and the more it increases the nation's opulence. Thus the comparison which formed the basis of your objection disappears, and your objection with it; for the more we can economize on the expenses involved in the cultivation of the land, without detrimentally affecting the reproduction, the more net product or revenue there is for the proprietors of the land, whose expenditure is based on the purchases which are made from the *productive* class, and from the *sterile* class, and by the *sterile* class from the *productive* class, in order to enable the same revenue and the same expenditure to be regenerated. This is the distinction which you cannot see *and which I turn to such account,* you say, *in support of my opinion.*

These observations, which are palpably self-evident, ought to put an end to all disputes concerning the sales and prices of products, the wages and consumption of wage-earners of whatever kind, workers,

---

[1] In other words, the price of the artisan's product, under competitive conditions, tends to equal the cost of the raw materials plus the cost of the subsistence goods which it is necessary for the artisan to consume while he is making the product. If the price were higher than this, then *the purchaser* would incur the 'loss' referred to by Quesnay. R.L.M.

manufacturers, artists, merchants, carriers, hired men, etc. *The more highly you pay them, the more each of them will be able to expand his consumption. But then there will be fewer wage-earners and fewer consumers competing with one another for the purchase of your products, since the total quantity of wages is limited. Thus the more highly you paid the wage-earners of the productive class, the less you would be able to pay to the sterile class; and for the same reason the more highly you paid the sterile class, the less you would be able to pay to the productive class.* Everything here is subject to strict rules, in connection with which argument should yield to calculation. Calculate, then, and you will no longer say that high costs, paid over to the wage-earners, expand the consumption and consequently the sales and the market value of products. You will see that this argument, which would seem to you to be decisive in individual cases considered in an abstract way, turns out to be overthrown in the general order of things. You will come round again to the necessity of accepting the greatest possible freedom of competition in all branches of trade, in order to cut down as far as possible on the burdensome costs involved in them. As soon as you have calculated the effects of this general freedom prescribed by natural right, by virtue of which *each person should have the legal power to render his situation as good as he possibly can, without infringing upon the rights of others*, it will become self-evident to you that it is an essential condition of the growth of public and private wealth. You will fear, you will repel all opinions which could lead to injury being done to this sacred freedom, which can be regarded as the epitome of all the rights of man. You will then pass judgement on the system which you at first defended—i.e. that of the people who would assimilate the so-called production which results from the work of the *sterile* class with the real production which results from the work of the *productive* class. You will see that if this system were confined to an abstraction pure and simple, it would be reduced to a prejudice which is empty, trifling, and contradicted by self-evident facts; but that as soon as people have a mind to draw practical conclusions from it (which is the main aim of its defenders) it becomes a dangerous and treacherous error, which unhappily has been only too fruitful of unjust prohibitions, cruel reprisals, ruinous exclusions, burdensome monopolies, and destructive privileges. You will finally recognize that this *system*, which self-evidently has only the choice of being either *futile* if no real use is made of it, or *disastrous* if it is taken as a principle of conduct, can in both cases be upheld only thanks to a vague and inexact language, in which the most different ideas are expressed in the same words. I do you the justice of believing that you are not among those who have sought to profit from the obscurity of this ambiguous language in order to confuse the subject of the debate and keep light from impinging on the dispute to which we have been devoting ourselves. The matter we are discussing is too important, and you are too strongly devoted to the truth, for you to have recourse to this petty deceit. It is only a confusion of ideas, difficult in themselves to unravel in a science which is still little known and obscured by private interests and dominant prejudices, which has led you to defend seriously a delusive opinion; but you are now no doubt aware that the general prepossession which sanctions it will soon give place to the truth.

B.

THE 'GENERAL MAXIMS
FOR THE ECONOMIC GOVERNMENT
OF AN AGRICULTURAL KINGDOM'[1]

I

That there should be a single sovereign authority, standing above all the individuals in the society and all the unjust undertakings of private interests; for the object of dominion and allegiance is the security of all and the lawful interest of all. The view that there should be a balance of forces in government is a disastrous one, leaving scope for nothing but dissension among the great and the oppression of the small. The division of societies into different orders of citizens some of whom exercise sovereign authority over the others destroys the general interest of the nation and ushers in the conflict of private interests between the different classes of citizens. Such a division would play havoc with the order of government in an agricultural kingdom, which ought to reconcile all interests for one main purpose—that of securing the prosperity of agriculture, which is the source of all the wealth of the state and that of all its citizens.

II

That the nation should be given instruction in the general laws of the natural order, which constitute the form of government which is self-evidently the most perfect. The study of human jurisprudence is not sufficient to make a statesman; it is necessary that those who are destined for administrative positions should be obliged to make a study of the natural order which is most advantageous to men combined together in society. It is also necessary that the practical knowledge and insight which the nation acquires through experience and reflection should be brought together in the general science of government, so that the sovereign authority, always guided by what is self-evident,[2] should institute the best laws and cause them to be scrupulously observed, in order to provide for the security of all and to attain to the greatest degree of prosperity possible for the society.

---

[1] Translated from the text of *Physiocratie*, as reproduced in I.N.E.D., II, pp. 949–76. R.L.M.

[2] *Toujours éclairée par l'évidence.* R.L.M.

III

That the sovereign and the nation should never lose sight of the fact that the land is the unique source of wealth, and that it is agriculture which causes wealth to increase.[1] For the growth of wealth ensures the growth of the population; men and wealth cause agriculture to prosper, expand trade, stimulate industry, and increase and perpetuate wealth. Upon this abundant source depends the success of all branches of the administration of the kingdom.

IV

That the ownership of landed property and movable wealth should be guaranteed to those who are their lawful possessors; for SECURITY OF OWNERSHIP IS THE ESSENTIAL FOUNDATION OF THE ECONOMIC ORDER OF SOCIETY. In the absence of surety of ownership the territory would remain uncultivated. It would have neither proprietors nor farmers to make the expenditure necessary to improve and cultivate it, if protection of funds and products were not guaranteed to those who make the advances of this expenditure. It is the security of permanent possession which stimulates labour and the employment of wealth in the improvement and cultivation of the land and in commercial and industrial enterprises. It is only the sovereign power which guarantees the property of its subjects which has a right to the first share of the fruits of the land, the unique source of wealth.

V

That taxes should not be destructive or disproportionate to the mass of the nation's revenue; that their increase should follow the increase of the revenue; and that they should be laid directly on the net product of landed property, and not on men's wages, or on produce, where they would increase the costs of collection, operate to the detriment of trade, and destroy every year a portion of the nation's wealth. That they should also not be taken from the wealth of the farmers of landed property; for THE ADVANCES OF A KINGDOM'S AGRICULTURE OUGHT TO BE REGARDED AS IF THEY WERE FIXED PROPERTY REQUIRING TO BE PRESERVED WITH GREAT CARE IN ORDER TO ENSURE THE PRODUCTION OF TAXES, REVENUE, AND SUBSISTENCE FOR ALL CLASSES OF CITIZENS. Otherwise taxation degenerates into spoliation, and brings about a state of decline which very soon ruins the state.[1]

[1] See note on p. 238 below. R.L.M.

VI

That the advances of the cultivators should be sufficient to enable the greatest possible product to be annually regenerated by expenditure on the cultivation of the land; for if the advances are not sufficient, the expenses of cultivation are proportionately higher and yield a smaller net product.[1]

VII

That the whole of the sum of revenue should come back into the annual circulation, and run through it to the full extent of its course; and that it should never be formed into monetary fortunes, or at least that those which are formed should be counterbalanced by those which come back into circulation.[2] For otherwise these monetary fortunes would check the distribution of a part of the annual revenue of the nation, and hold back the money stock of the kingdom to the detriment of the return of the advances of cultivation, the payment of the artisans' wages, and the consumption which ought to be carried on by the different classes of men who follow remunerative occupations. Such an interception of the money stock would reduce the reproduction of revenue and taxes.

VIII

That the government's economic policy should be concerned only with encouraging productive expenditure and trade in raw produce, and that it should refrain from interfering with sterile expenditure.[2]

IX

That a nation which has a large territory to cultivate, and the means of carrying on a large trade in raw produce, should not extend too far the employment of money and men in manufacturing and trading in luxury goods, to the detriment of the work and expenditure involved in agriculture;[3] for more than anything else THE KINGDOM OUGHT TO BE WELL FURNISHED WITH WEALTHY CULTIVATORS.[4]

X

That no part of the sum of revenue should pass into the hands of foreign countries without return in money or commodities.

[1] See note on p. 242 below. R.L.M.
[2] See note on p. 244 below. R.L.M.
[3] See note on p. 246 below. R.L.M.
[4] See note on p. 247 below. R.L.M.

XI

That the desertion of inhabitants who would take their wealth out of the kingdom should be avoided.

XII

That the children of rich farmers should settle down in the countryside, so that there are always husbandmen there; for if they are harassed into abandoning the countryside and settling in the towns, they take there their fathers' wealth which used to be employed in cultivation. IT IS NOT SO MUCH MEN AS WEALTH WHICH OUGHT TO BE ATTRACTED TO THE COUNTRYSIDE; for the more wealth is employed in cultivation, the less men it requires, the more it prospers, and the more revenue it yields. Such, for example, in the case of corn, is the large-scale cultivation carried on by rich farmers, in comparison with the small-scale cultivation carried on by poor *métayers* who plough with the aid of oxen or cows.[1]

XIII

That each person should be free to cultivate in his fields such produce as his interests, his means, and the nature of the land suggest to him, in order that he may extract from them the greatest possible product. Monopoly in the cultivation of landed property should never be encouraged, for it is detrimental to the general revenue of the nation.[2] The prejudice which leads to the encouragement of an abundance of produce of primary necessity in preference to other produce, to the detriment of the market value of one or the other, is inspired by short-sighted views which do not extend as far as the effects of mutual external trade, which makes provision for everything and determines the price of the produce which each nation can cultivate with the most profit. AFTER THE WEALTH EMPLOYED IN CULTIVATION, IT IS REVENUE AND TAXES WHICH ARE THE WEALTH OF PRIMARY NECESSITY in a state, in order to defend subjects against scarcity and against the enemy, and to maintain the glory and power of the monarch and the prosperity of the nation.[3]

---

[1] See note on p. 248 below. R.L.M.
[2] See note on p. 249 below. R.L.M.
[3] See note on p. 250 below. R.L.M.

XIV

That the breeding of live-stock should be encouraged;[1] for it is live-stock which provides the land with the manure which procures abundant crops.

XV

That the land employed in the cultivation of corn should be brought together, as far as possible, into large farms worked by rich husbandmen; for in large agricultural enterprises there is less expenditure required for the upkeep and repair of buildings, and proportionately much less cost and much more net product, than in small ones. A multiplicity of small farmers is detrimental to the population. The population whose position is most assured, and which is most readily available for the different occupations and different kinds of work which divide men into different classes, is that maintained by the net product. All economies profitably made use of in work which can be done with the aid of animals, machines, rivers, etc., bring benefit to the population and the state, because a greater net product procures men a greater reward for other services or other kinds of work.

XVI

That no barriers at all should be raised to external trade in raw produce; for AS THE MARKET IS, SO IS THE REPRODUCTION.[2]

XVII

That the marketing and transport of produce and manufactured commodities should be facilitated, through the repair of roads and the navigation of canals, rivers, and the sea; for the more that is saved on trading costs, the more the territory's revenue increases.

XVIII

That the prices of produce and commodities in the kingdom should never be made to fall; for then mutual foreign trade would become disadvantageous to the nation.[3] AS THE MARKET VALUE IS, SO IS THE REVENUE: *Abundance plus valuelessness does not equal wealth. Scarcity plus dearness equals poverty. Abundance plus dearness equals opulence.*[4],[5]

---

[1] See note on p. 253 below. R.L.M.
[2] See note on p. 255 below. R.L.M.
[3] See note on p. 257 below. R.L.M.
[4] Cf. the formulation on p. 84 above. R.L.M.
[5] See note on p. 257 below. R.L.M.

XIX

That it should not be believed that cheapness of produce is profitable to the lower classes;[1] for a low price of produce causes a fall in the wages of the lower orders of people, reduces their well-being, makes less work and remunerative occupations available for them, and destroys the nation's revenue.

XX

That the well-being of the latter classes of citizens should not be reduced; for then they would not be able to contribute sufficiently to the consumption of the produce which can be consumed only within the country, which would bring about a reduction in the reproduction and revenue of the nation.[2]

XXI

That the proprietors and those engaged in remunerative occupations should not give themselves over to sterile savings, which would deduct from circulation and distribution a portion of their revenue or gains.

XXII

That no encouragement at all should be given to luxury in the way of ornamentation to the detriment of the expenditure involved in the operations and improvement of agriculture, and of expenditure on the consumption of subsistence goods, which sustains the market for raw produce, its proper price, and the reproduction of the nation's revenue.[3]

XXIII

That the nation should not suffer any loss in its mutual trade with foreign countries, even if this trade were profitable to the merchants who made gains out of their fellow-citizens on the sale of the commodities which were imported. For then the increase in the fortunes of these merchants would bring about a deduction from the circulation of the revenue, which would be detrimental to distribution and reproduction.

XXIV

That people should not be taken in by a seeming advantage in mutual trade with foreign countries, through judging it simply with reference to the balance of the sums of money involved and not examining the

---

[1] See note on p. 257 below. R.L.M.
[2] See note on p. 258 below. R.L.M.
[3] See note on p. 259 below. R.L.M.

greater or lesser profit which results from the particular commodities which are sold and purchased. For the loss often falls on the nation which receives a surplus in money, and this loss works to the detriment of the distribution and reproduction of the revenue.

XXV

That complete freedom of trade should be maintained; for THE POLICY FOR INTERNAL AND EXTERNAL TRADE WHICH IS THE MOST SECURE, THE MOST CORRECT, AND THE MOST PROFITABLE FOR THE NATION AND THE STATE, CONSISTS IN FULL FREEDOM OF COMPETITION.

XXVI

That less attention should be paid to augmenting the population than to increasing the revenue; for the greater well-being which a high revenue brings about is preferable to the greater pressure of subsistence needs which a population in excess of the revenue entails; and when the people are in a state of well-being there are more resources to meet the needs of the state and also more means to enable agriculture to prosper.[1]

XXVII

That the government should trouble itself less with economizing than with the operations necessary for the prosperity of the kingdom; for very high expenditure may cease to be excessive by virtue of the increase of wealth. But abuses must not be confused with simple expenditure, for abuses could swallow up all the wealth of the nation and the sovereign.

XXVIII

That the administration of finance, whether in the collection of taxes or in the expenditure of the government, should not bring about the formation of monetary fortunes, which steal a portion of the revenue away from circulation, distribution, and reproduction.

XXIX

That means to meet the extraordinary needs of a state should be expected to be found only in the prosperity of the nation and not in the credit of financiers; for MONETARY FORTUNES ARE A CLANDESTINE FORM OF WEALTH WHICH KNOWS NEITHER KING NOR COUNTRY.

[1] See note on p. 259 below. R.L.M.

XXX

That the state should avoid contracting loans which create rentier incomes, which burden it with devouring debts, and which bring about a trade or traffic in finance, through the medium of negotiable bills, the discount on which causes a greater and greater increase in sterile monetary fortunes. These fortunes separate finance from agriculture, and deprive the countryside of the wealth necessary for the improvement of landed property and for the operations involved in the cultivation of the land.

NOTES ON THE MAXIMS

Note on Maxim III
(The land is the unique source of wealth, and it is agriculture which causes wealth to increase)

Mutual trade with foreign countries brings in commodities which are paid for by the nation's revenue in money or in bartered goods. Thus we do not have to put this down as a separate item in the detailed account of a kingdom's revenue, since that would constitute double-counting. House-rent and income derived from interest on money must be regarded in the same way; for from the point of view of those who pay them these constitute expenditure which is drawn from another source, with the exception of income charged on land, where the liability is placed on a productive fund; but this income is included in the product of the revenue of the land. Thus it is the land and the advances of the entrepreneurs of cultivation which are the unique source of the revenue of agricultural nations.[1]

Note on Maxim V

(That taxes should not be destructive, etc.)

A properly organized tax, i.e. a tax which does not degenerate into spoliation by reason of a bad form of assessment, should be regarded as a portion of revenue taken out of the net product of the landed property of an agricultural nation; for otherwise it would not be subject to any rule keeping it in proportion with the nation's wealth, nor with the revenue, nor with the situation of tax-paying subjects; it could imperceptibly ruin everything before the administration became aware of it.

The net product of landed property is distributed to three proprietors—the state, the possessors of land, and the tithe-owners. It is only the portion of the property belonging to the possessor which

[1] Cf. the similar passage on p. 122 above. R.L.M.

is transferable, and its selling price is no more than in proportion to the revenue which it produces. The ownership of the possessor, therefore, does not extend any further than this. Thus it is not he who pays the other proprietors who have shares in the property, since their shares do not belong to him, he has not acquired them, and they are not transferable. Thus the possessor of the property should not regard ordinary taxes as a charge laid on his portion, for it is not he who pays this revenue: it is the portion of the property which he has not acquired and which does not belong to him which pays it to those to whom it is due. And it is only in cases of necessity, cases where the security of property is endangered, that all the proprietors should in their own interests make contributions out of their portions to the temporary subsidy which the pressing needs of the state may require.

But it must always be borne in mind that in all cases the contribution should be assessed only on the revenue, i.e. on the annual net product of landed property; and not on the advances of husbandmen, or on labourers,[1] or on the sale of commodities, for otherwise it would be destructive. On the advances of husbandmen it would represent not taxation but spoliation, which would wipe out reproduction, cause the land to deteriorate, and ruin the farmers, the proprietors, and the state. On the wages of labourers and the sale of commodities it would be arbitrary, and the costs of collection would exceed the tax and be thrown back in an unregulated way on the revenue of the nation and that of the sovereign. We have to distinguish here between taxes assessed and taxes received;[2] taxes assessed would be three times taxes received, and would encroach upon taxes received themselves; for in all state expenditure taxes assessed on commodities would be paid for out of taxes received. Thus such taxes would be delusive and ruinous.

The assessment of taxes on labourers who live off their wages is strictly speaking nothing more than an assessment on their labour, which is paid by those who employ the workers, in the same way that an assessment on the horses which plough the land would really be nothing more than an assessment on the expenses of cultivation themselves. Thus an assessment on men rather than on the revenue would be borne by industrial and agricultural costs themselves; it would be thrown back on the revenue of landed property in a way which involved a double loss, and would rapidly lead to the wiping out of tax receipts. Taxes assessed on commodities should be regarded in the same way, for they would also be borne, in a way which involved an absolute loss, by the revenue, by the tax receipts, and by the expenses of cultivation, and would entail enormous charges which it would be impossible to avoid in a large state.

[1] *Hommes de travail.* R.L.M.
[2] *Il faut distinguer ici l'imposition d'avec l'impôt.* R.L.M.

Recourse to assessments of this kind, however, must necessarily be had by small maritime states which get their living by means of re-export trade, the latter being inevitably subjected to taxation in these states which have no territory at all. And it is almost always regarded as a temporary expedient in large states where agriculture has fallen into such a state of decline that the territory's revenue could not provide for the payment of the taxes. But then this insidious expedient means an added burden which reduces the people to forced economies in consumption, causes labour to be checked, wipes out reproduction, and finishes by ruining subject and sovereign.

People have often talked about establishing a tax payable in kind from the harvest in the form of a tithe; this kind of assessment would certainly be proportionate to the total product of the harvest, costs included; but it would not bear any relation to the net product. The more inferior the land was, and the poorer the harvest, the more burdensome, unjust, and disastrous it would be.

Thus taxes should be laid directly on the net product of landed property; for in whatever manner they may be assessed in a kingdom which draws its wealth from its territory, they are always paid by landed property. Thus the form of assessment which is the most simple, the most regular, the most profitable to the state, and the least burdensome to the tax-payers, is that which is made proportionate to the net product and laid directly on the source of continually regenerated wealth.

The simple establishment of an assessment on the source of revenue, i.e. on the net product of the land which constitutes the nation's revenue, becomes very difficult in a kingdom where for want of advances agriculture has fallen into decay, or at least into such a deteriorated state that no cadastral survey would yield results which were permanent and properly adjusted to the qualities of the land, which is badly cultivated and whose product, having become very small, no more than corresponds to the wretched state of cultivation; for the improvement of cultivation which better administration could bring about would immediately render the survey very unreliable.[1]

An assessment which was established uniformly on the land, on its produce, on men, on their labour, on commodities and on working animals, would represent a series of six equal assessments, laid on top of one another, all supported by the same base, with each nevertheless being paid separately. But all these together would provide the sovereign with much less revenue than a simple real[2] tax estab-

[1] Cf. above, pp. 184–5. R.L.M.

[2] The word 'real' (*réel*), as applied to the tax on the net product, is evidently meant to imply that the proceeds of such a tax would really accrue in their entirety to the sovereign, and not be subject, as other forms of assessment allegedly would, to deductions on account of such things as high costs of collection and detrimental effects on agricultural production. R.L.M.

lished solely and costlessly on the net product, and equal in its extent to the six assessments which might be regarded as real. This tax, which is indicated by natural law and which would greatly increase the revenue of the sovereign, would nevertheless cost the nation and the state five times less than the succession of six assessments just described, which would destroy all the territory's produce and would seem likely to cut out any possibility of restoring order. For modes of assessment which are in fact illusory from the point of view of the sovereign and ruinous from that of the nation come to appear to the vulgar mind more and more inevitable in the proportion that the decline of agriculture increases.

Nevertheless we must at least begin by doing away as soon as possible with the arbitrary assessments laid on the farmers of the land, for unless we did so this ruinous kind of assessment would end by completely wiping out the kingdom's revenue. The assessment on landed property which is the most difficult to regulate is that which is laid on small-scale cultivation, where there is no rent to serve as a measure, where it is the proprietor himself who provides the advances, and where the net product is very small and uncertain. This type of cultivation, which is carried on by *métayers* in areas where taxation has destroyed the farmers, and which is the last resort of ruined agriculture, has to be treated very carefully, for a small tax burden robs it of its advances and completely wipes it out. Thus we should be careful to distinguish land which is reduced to this small-scale cultivation, and which relatively to its product is worked at high cost and often without any profit, with land where large-scale cultivation is carried on by rich farmers, who guarantee the proprietors a fixed revenue which can serve as an exact rule for a proportional assessment. This assessment should be paid by the proprietor, and not by the farmer, if it is not deducted from the rent, as happens naturally when the farmer is informed of the amount of the tax before his lease is drawn up. If the needs of the state necessitate increases in taxes, they should be laid solely on the proprietors; for the government would be contradicting itself if it required the farmers to fulfil the obligations of their leases, while it made it impossible for them to meet these obligations by reason of the unforeseen tax which it laid upon them. In all cases the payment of taxes ought to be guaranteed by the value of the landed property itself, and not by that of the wealth employed in cultivation, which cannot escape depradation if it is made to perform any public service other than that of regenerating the wealth of the nation and the sovereign, and which ought never to be diverted from this natural and necessary function. The proprietors, with this rule fixed for them by the government, would take good care, in order to safeguard their revenue and the taxes, to let their land only to rich farmers; and this policy would ensure the success of agriculture. The farmers, no longer subject to anxiety about an assessment during the term of their leases, would increase in numbers; small-scale cultivation would disappear in one case after the other; and the revenue of the proprietors and the taxes would be proportionately increased owing to the increase in the produce of the landed property cultivated by rich husbandmen.

A nation exists[1] which has been able to consolidate its power and ensure its prosperity by exempting agriculture from all assessments. The proprietors, upon whom the taxes are laid, bear the burden of temporary subsidies during war-time; but the work of cultivating the land is never slowed down, and the market for landed property and its market value are always ensured by freedom of trade in raw produce. In this nation, too, agriculture and live-stock breeding do not suffer any decline during the longest and most costly wars; and when peace comes the proprietors find that their land has been well cultivated and well kept up, and their high revenue well maintained and well safeguarded. From this it is easy to see the difference which exists between an excessive tax and a spoliatory one; for according to the way in which it is assessed, a tax may be spoliatory without being excessive, or excessive without being spoliatory.[2]

Note on Maxim VI

(That the advances of cultivation should be sufficient.)

It must be noted that the most fertile land would be worth nothing without the wealth necessary to provide for the expenses involved in cultivation, and that the decline of a kingdom's agriculture should be ascribed not to the idleness of men but to their poverty. If owing to a mistaken government policy the advances of cultivation yielded only a small net product, costs would be high, there would be little revenue, and the population would consist almost entirely of lower-class people working in the countryside, without any profit to the state, at a poor type of cultivation which obliged them to live in wretchedness.

In former times, in a kingdom of *this* kind,[3] the annual advances regenerated on the average a net product, taxes on the husbandman included, of only about *twenty-five* per *hundred*,[4] which was distributed between tithes, taxes, and the proprietor, after deducting the annual returns of the husbandman. If the original advances had been sufficient, cultivation would easily have been capable of yielding a *hundred* net product and even more per *hundred* annual

---

[1] Quesnay probably has England in mind here. R.L.M.
[2] 'Excessive' = *exorbitant*, and 'spoliatory' = *spoliatif*. R.L.M.
[3] Quesnay clearly has France in mind. R.L.M.
[4] See above, p. 121. Cf. the statement on p. 112. R.L.M.

advances. Thus the nation had to bear a *deficit* of at least four-fifths in the net product of its annual advances, without taking into account the loss of revenue involved in the employment of the land which was used to make up for the costs of a poor type of cultivation, and which was allowed to lie fallow in rotation for several years in order to restore it and put it once again in a position to produce a meagre harvest. At that time the majority of the inhabitants lived in poverty, and their activities brought no profit to the state. For *as the net product of advances over and above expenses is, so is also the net product of the labour of the men who generate it; and as the net product of landed property is, so is the net product available for revenue, taxation, and the subsistence of the different classes of men in a nation.* Thus the more insufficient the advances are, the less profitable the men and the land are to the state. Husbandmen who make a wretched living from a thankless type of cultivation serve only to maintain profitlessly the population of a poor nation.

In this kingdom taxes were almost all laid arbitrarily on farmers, workers, and commodities. Thus they bore directly and indirectly upon the advances of the expenditure involved in cultivation, which charged landed property with about 300 millions for the ordinary taxes, and as much again for administration, costs of collection, etc. And in recent years, judging from the total of the tax of one-tenth on productive property and from an examination of the product of the land, the produce of the soil did not yield to the nation more than about 400 millions of net revenue, including the tithes and other ecclesiastical revenues: a deplorable product for a large and splendid territory and a large and hard-working population! The export of corn was forbidden; production was limited to the nation's consumption; half the land lay fallow; the planting of vineyards was forbidden; internal trade in corn was subjected to an arbitrary system of regulation; the sale of corn from province to province was continually hindered; and the market value of produce was always uncertain.

The advances of productive expenditure were successively carried off by the arbitrary taxes and the indirect charges, leading to the wiping-out of reproduction and the taxes themselves; the children of the husbandmen abandoned the countryside; the excessive burden of taxes on produce raised its natural price and brought about a heavy increase in the nation's expenditure by adding to the prices of commodities and wage costs; and this in turn caused a falling-off in the returns of the farmers, the net product of landed property, taxes, cultivation, etc. The spoliation brought about by the portion of the taxes which was arbitrarily laid on the farmers, moreover, caused a progressive decline, which, when combined with the absence of freedom of trade, led to land being cultivated on a small-scale basis and allowed to lie fallow. The extent of the decline was such that the expenses of cultivation did not produce more than 25 per cent, territorial taxes included; and even this was only due to the gains from the large-scale cultivation which still existed over a quarter of the kingdom.[1] We shall not follow out here the course of this rapid process of decline: it is sufficient to calculate the effects of so many destructive causes, one arising from another, in order to foresee its fatal consequences.

All these irregularities and abuses have been recognized; and the glory of redressing them was reserved for a more enlightened minister. But the needs of the state and particular circumstances do not always harmonize with the views put forward concerning the reforms which good administration in political economy may require, even though these reforms are very necessary and very urgent from the point of view of the common benefit of the sovereign and the nation.

Note on Maxim VII

(*The fortunes which come back into circulation.*)

By the fortunes which come back into circulation we should understand not simply those fortunes which are destroyed, but also those sterile or idle fortunes which become active, and which are employed, for example, to form the advances of large enterprises in agriculture, trade, and profitable manufactures, or to improve landed property whose revenue comes back into circulation each year. Indeed, it is by virtue of these active fortunes, when they are properly used in business, that a state possesses stability, and that it is secure in its possession of great wealth which is used each year to regenerate great wealth, to maintain its population in comfort, and to ensure the prosperity of the state and the power of the sovereign. But we should not regard in the same way the monetary fortunes which are drawn from interest on money and which are not charged on productive funds, nor those which are employed in the acquisition of useless offices, privileges, etc.; their sterile circulation by no means prevents them from being burdensome fortunes which undermine the nation.

Note on Maxim VIII

(*Refrain from interfering with sterile expenditure.*)

The work involved in making manufactured and industrial commodities for the nation's use is simply something which costs money,

[1] See the article *Corn* in the Encyclopedia for the example of a nation which loses every year four-fifths of the product of its cultivation.

and not a source of revenue. It cannot yield any profit through sale abroad, except only in countries where manufacturing labour is cheap because of the low price of the produce which serves for the subsistence of the workers; a condition which is very disadvantageous so far as the product of landed property is concerned. Thus, such a condition should not be found in states with a free and unobstructed external trade which keeps up the sales and the prices of raw produce, and which happily does away with the small profit which could be obtained from an external trade in manufactured commodities, where the gain would be based on the loss which would result from the low prices of the produce of landed property. Here the net product or revenue accruing to the nation is not confused with the gains of the merchants and manufacturing entrepreneurs; these gains, from the point of view of the nation, ought to be ranked as costs. It would not be sufficient, for example, to have rich husbandmen, if the territory which they cultivated were to produce for them alone.

There are poor kingdoms where the greater part of the over-abundant luxury manufactures are kept going by means of exclusive privileges, and lay the nation under contribution through prohibitions forbidding it to use other manufactured commodities. These prohibitions, which are always harmful to the nation, are still more disastrous when the spirit of monopoly and error which has engendered them causes them to be extended to cultivation and trade in the produce of landed property, where the most energetic competition is absolutely necessary to expand the wealth of nations.

I shall not speak here of re-export trade, to which small maritime states are fated. A large state should not abandon the plough in order to become a carrier. It will never be forgotten that a minister of the last century,[1] dazzled by the trade of the Dutch and the glitter of luxury manufactures, brought his country to such a state of frenzy that no one talked about anything but trade and money, without reflecting on the true employment of money or on a country's true trade.[2]

This minister, whose good intentions were so worthy of esteem but who was too much a prisoner of his ideas, tried to bring about the generation of wealth from the work of men's hands, to the detriment of the very source of wealth, and put the whole economic constitution of an agricultural nation out of gear. External trade in corn was stopped in order to bring about a low cost of living for the manufacturer; and the sale of corn inside the kingdom was subjected to an arbitrary system of regulation which cut off trade between provinces. The protectors of industry, the justices in the towns, in order to procure corn at a low price, ruined their towns and pro-

---

[1] Colbert. R.L.M.
[2] Cf. the similar passage on p. 123 above. R.L.M.

vinces through poor calculation by causing a gradual decline in the cultivation of their land. Everything tended to bring about the destruction of the revenue of landed property, manufactures, trade, and industry, which, in an agricultural nation, can be maintained only through the produce of the soil. For it is this produce which provides trade with a surplus for export, and which pays revenue to the proprietors and wages to the men engaged in remunerative activities. Different causes bringing about the emigration of men and wealth quickened the pace of this course of destruction.

Men and money were diverted from agriculture and employed in manufactures of silk, cotton, and foreign wool, to the detriment of the manufacture of home-produced wool and the expansion of flocks and herds. Luxury in the way of ornamentation was encouraged, and made very rapid progress. The administration of the provinces, harassed by the needs of the state, no longer offered any security in the countryside for the ready employment of the wealth necessary for the annual reproduction of wealth, which caused a large part of the land to be reduced to small-scale cultivation, to be left lying fallow, and to become valueless. The revenue of the proprietors of landed property was uselessly sacrificed to a mercantile trade which could make no contribution to taxes. It became virtually impossible for agriculture to provide for them, depressed and overburdened as it was; their coverage was extended more and more to include men, food, and trade in raw produce; they were increased through the expenses of collection and through the destructive plundering of the reproduction; and a system of finance grew up around them which enriched the capital with the spoils of the provinces. Traffic in money lent out at interest created a very important kind of revenue based on money and drawn from money, which from the point of view of the nation was only an imaginary product, eluding taxation and undermining the state. This revenue based on money, and the appearance of opulence, maintained by the splendour of ruinous luxury, imposed upon the vulgar, and reduced further and further the reproduction of real wealth and the money stock of the nation. Unhappily, alas, the causes of this general disorder remained unknown for too long a time: *inde mali labes*. But today the government has accepted more enlightened principles; it knows where the resources of the kingdom are to be found, and the means of restoring abundance to it.

Note on Maxim IX

(Not to extend the employment of money and men in manufacturing and trading in luxury goods to the detriment of the work and expenditure involved in agriculture.)

A nation ought to carry on the production only of those manufactured commodities for which it possesses the raw materials; and it should purchase from abroad such manufactured commodities as can be bought at a price lower than the cost which would be involved if the nation made them itself. Through these purchases mutual trade is stimulated; for if nations tried to buy nothing and sell everything, this would do away with external trade and the advantages of the export of raw produce,[1] which is infinitely more profitable than that of manufactured commodities. An agricultural nation should facilitate an active external trade in raw produce, by means of a passive external trade in manufactured commodities which it can profitably buy from abroad. This is the whole secret of trade: do not be afraid that by incurring this cost you will become *a tributary of other nations.*

Note on the Same Maxim

(*More than anything else, the kingdom ought to be well furnished with wealthy cultivators.*)

The borough of *Goodmans-chester*, in England, is renowned in history for escorting its king with the most worthy procession, having accompanied his passage with 180 ploughs.[2] This magnificent display[3] is likely to appear completely absurd to our townsmen, accustomed as they are to frivolous ornamentation. We still see stupidly conceited men who are ignorant of the fact that it is wealthy husbandmen and wealthy merchants engaged in rural trade who stimulate agriculture, who conduct its operations, who control, who direct, who are independent, who safeguard the nation's revenue, and who, after the proprietors who are distinguished by their birth, titles, and learning, constitute the most honourable, praiseworthy, and important order of citizens in the state. It is these worthy inhabitants of the countryside, however, these masters, these patriarchs, whom the bourgeois knows only under the contemptuous title of *peasants*, and from whom he even wants to take away the schoolmasters who teach them to read and write, to bring security and order into their businesses, and to extend their knowledge of the different aspects of their calling.

An education of this type, it is claimed, fills them with vanity and makes them fond of going to law: should legal protection be allowed to these earthy men,[4] who presume to set themselves up in haughty

---

[1] Cf. the similar passage on p. 124 above. R.L.M.

[2] Cf. I.N.E.D., II, p. 717: 'The king, when passing through this province [Chester], was accompanied by the inhabitants with a great procession of yoked ploughs, in order to assure him of their gratitude by means of the most expressive testimony of their success in agriculture.' R.L.M.

[3] *Faste.* Cf. pp. 317–8 ff. below. R.L.M.   [4] *Ces hommes terrestres.* R.L.M.

opposition to those who, by virtue of the elevated rank which their residence in the city gives them, ought to enjoy a special distinction and superiority which are bound to overawe the rustics? Such are the absurd claims made in his vanity by the townsman, who is nothing but a hireling paid by the wealth of the countryside. *Omnium autem rerum ex quibus aliquid acquiritur, nihil est AGRICUL-TURA melius, nihil uberius, nihil dulcius, nihil homine libero dignius.* Cicero, *De Officiis. Mea quidem sententia, haud scio an nulla beatior esse possit, neque solum officio, quod hominum generi universo cultura agrorum est salutaris, sed et delectatione, et saturitate, copiaque omnium rerum quae ad victum hominum, ad cultum etiam Deorum pertinent.* Cicero, *De Senectute.*

OF ALL THE OCCUPATIONS BY WHICH GAIN IS SECURED, NONE IS BETTER THAN AGRICULTURE, NONE MORE PROFITABLE, NONE MORE DELIGHTFUL, NONE MORE BECOMING TO A FREEMAN.[1] . . . FOR MY PART, AT LEAST, I AM INCLINED TO THINK THAT NO LIFE CAN BE HAPPIER THAN THAT OF THE FARMER, NOT MERELY FROM THE STANDPOINT OF THE DUTY PERFORMED, WHICH BENEFITS THE ENTIRE HUMAN RACE, BUT ALSO BECAUSE OF ITS CHARM, AND THE PLENTY AND ABUNDANCE IT GIVES OF EVERYTHING THAT TENDS TO THE NURTURE OF MAN AND EVEN TO THE WORSHIP OF THE GODS.[2]

Note on Maxim XII

(To attract wealth into the countryside, for the purpose of extending large-scale and avoiding small-scale cultivation.)

In large-scale cultivation one man alone drives a plough drawn by horses, which does as much work as three ploughs drawn by oxen and driven by six men. In the case of small-scale cultivation, because of a lack of the original advances required for the introduction of large-scale cultivation, the annual expenses are excessive in relation to the net product, which is almost zero, and ten or twelve times more land is employed to no purpose. When the proprietors lack farmers in a position to meet the expenses of proper cultivation, the advances are made at the expense of the land, almost entirely to no purpose; the produce is almost all consumed during the winter by the labouring oxen, and a part of the land is left aside for their pasturage during the summer; and the net product of the harvest is so nearly

---

[1] Cicero, *De Officiis* (Loeb Classical Library edn., 1938), p. 155. English translation by Walter Miller. R.L.M.

[2] Cicero, *De Senectute* (Loeb Classical Library edn., 1938), p. 69. English translation by W. A. Falconer. R.L.M.

valueless that the smallest tax makes it necessary to give up these remnants of cultivation, which in fact happens in many places simply by reason of the poverty of the inhabitants. It is said that there is a poor nation which is reduced to this small-scale cultivation over three-quarters of its territory, and in which, in addition, more than a third of the cultivable land is going to waste. But the government is engaged in stopping the course of this decline and in providing the means for setting things right again.[1]

Note on Maxim XIII

(Never to encourage monopoly in cultivation, and to allow each person the freedom to give his fields over to what suits him.)

As a result of interested attitudes[2] it was believed for a period that it was necessary in France to restrict the cultivation of vineyards in order to increase the cultivation of corn, at the very time when external trade in corn was prohibited, when trade suffered even from restrictions on the passage of corn between the provinces of the kingdom, when the greater part of the land was lying fallow because the cultivation of corn on it was confined to the internal consumption of each of the provinces of the kingdom, and when the destruction of the vineyards was increasing to a greater and greater degree the amount of land lying fallow. The provinces which were distant from the capital, moreover, were obliged to make representations in order to resist the extension of the cultivation of corn, which for lack of a market was going to waste in their districts: this was bringing about the ruin of the proprietors and the farmers, and wiping out the taxes with which the land was burdened. Thus everything was conspiring to bring about the deterioration of the two main branches of cultivation in the kingdom, and to destroy more and more the value of landed property; and one section of the proprietors of the land, to the detriment of the others, was aiming at exclusive privileges in cultivation. These were the disastrous effects of prohibitions and impediments to trade in the produce of landed property, in a kingdom where the provinces are linked with one another by rivers and seas, where the capital and all the other towns can easily be supplied with the produce of all parts of the territory, and where facility of export guarantees a market for the surplus.

The cultivation of vineyards is the most wealthy branch of cultivation in the French kingdom, for the net product of an *arpent* of land given over to vineyards, valued on an average basis, is about three times that of an *arpent* of the best land given over to the cultivation of corn. It should also be noted that the expenses which

---

[1] Cf. the similar passage above, p. 122. R.L.M.
[2] *Des vues particulières.* R.L.M.

are included in the total product of each branch of cultivation are more advantageous in the case of the cultivation of vineyards than in that of the cultivation of corn, because in the cultivation of vineyards the expenses provide, with profit, much greater wages for men; because the expenditure for vine-props and casks facilitates the sale of wood; and because the men engaged in the cultivation of vineyards are not employed in it at harvest-time, when they can very usefully be drawn on by husbandmen in order to gather in the corn. In addition, when this class of men, paid for its work by the land, becomes very numerous, it widens the market for corn and wine, and maintains their market value, in the proportion that cultivation is extended and the expansion of cultivation increases wealth. For the increase in wealth increases the number of people in all the classes of men in a nation, and this increase in population maintains the market value of the produce of cultivation on all sides.

It should be noted that an unobstructed external trade in raw produce, released from burdensome duties, is very advantageous to a nation with a large territory, where the pattern of cultivation can be varied in order to obtain different assortments of highly-valued products, above all those which cannot be produced in neighbouring countries. Since the sale of wines and spirits abroad is for us a privileged trade, owing to the nature of our soil and our climate, it should receive special protection from the government. Thus it should not be subjected, for taxation purposes, to a useless multiplicity of duties, which are very harmful to the sale of these products, with which a large part of our external trade, capable of maintaining the kingdom's opulence, is concerned. The tax should be simple and unique, and charged on the land which produces this wealth. In considering the question of compensation for the loss of general tax revenue,[1] account should be taken of the fact that the sale of these items of wealth to foreign countries has to be ensured by means of a favourable price; for then it will be seen that the state is fully recompensed for its action in moderating the taxes on these items by the favourable influence of this trade on all the other sources of wealth in the kingdom.

Note on the Same Maxim

(After the advances employed in cultivation, it is revenue and taxes which are the wealth of primary necessity, and which ensure the prosperity of the nation.)

In what does the prosperity of an agricultural nation consist? IN LARGE ADVANCES TO PERPETUATE AND INCREASE REVENUE AND TAXES; IN A FREE AND UNOBSTRUCTED

---

[1] *Dans la compensation de l'imposition générale.* R.L.M.

INTERNAL AND EXTERNAL TRADE; IN THE ENJOYMENT OF THE ANNUAL WEALTH FROM LANDED PROPERTY; AND IN AMPLE MONETARY PAYMENTS OF REVENUE AND TAXES. An abundance of products is obtained through large advances; consumption and trade maintain the sales and market value of the products; the market value is the measure of the nation's wealth; the wealth regulates the contributions which can be levied, and provides the money which pays them. This money ought to circulate in trading transactions: it ought never to be accumulated in a country to the detriment of the use and consumption of the annual product, which ought through reproduction and mutual trade to perpetuate true wealth there.

Coined money is a form of wealth which is paid for by other forms of wealth, *which is for nations a token intermediating between sales and purchases*, and which no longer contributes to the perpetuation of a state's wealth when it is kept out of circulation and no longer returns wealth for wealth. Thus the more it is accumulated the more it costs in terms of wealth which is not renewed, and the more it impoverishes the nation. Thus money is an active and really profitable form of wealth in a state only so far as it continually returns wealth for wealth, because money in itself is only sterile wealth. It possesses no utility for a nation other than its employment in sales and purchases, and in the payment of revenue and taxes, which puts it back into circulation in such a way that the same money continually and by turns meets these payments and fulfils its function in trade.

Thus the total money stock of an agricultural nation is only about equal to the net product or annual revenue of its landed property, for when it stands in this proportion it is more than sufficient for the nation's use. A greater quantity of money would not be a useful item of wealth for the state at all. Although taxes are paid in money, it is not money which provides them: it is the wealth annually regenerated from the land. It is in this renascent wealth, and not as the vulgar believe in the nation's money stock, that the prosperity and power of a state consist. You can never make up for the successive renewal of this wealth with the money stock; but in trade the money stock is readily made up for with written pledges, guaranteed by the wealth which is possessed in the country and transported abroad. Greed for money is an ardent passion among individuals, because they are greedy for the form of wealth which represents other forms of wealth. But this kind of greed, which draws money away from its proper employment, ought not to be a passion indulged in by the state. A great quantity of money in a state is to be desired only so far as it is proportionate to the revenue, and denotes in this way a state of opulence which is perpetually being renewed, and the enjoyment of which is effective and fully guaranteed. Of such a type was the abundance of money which, in the reign of Charles V, called *The Wise*, followed upon an abundance of the other forms of wealth in the kingdom. We can see this from the items of wealth which are set out in this prince's huge inventory, independently of a reserve of 17 millions (about 300 millions according to the present value of our money) which was held in his treasury. This great quantity of wealth is still more remarkable when we recall that the estates of the kings of France at this time did not include one-third of the kingdom.

Thus money does not constitute the true wealth of a nation, the wealth which is consumed and regenerated continually, for money does not breed money. It is true that an *écu* which is properly employed can cause wealth worth two *écus* to be generated, but then it is production and not money which has increased. Thus money should not remain in sterile hands. So it is not a matter of such indifference to the state as people believe whether money goes into Peter's pocket or into Paul's, for it is essential that it should not be taken away from the man who employs it to the benefit of the state. Strictly speaking, money which is employed in this way in a nation has no owner at all: it belongs to the needs of the state, which cause it to circulate for the purpose of reproducing the wealth which enables the nation to subsist and provides contributions for the sovereign.

This money must not be confused with the funds which are the subject of the ruinous traffic in loans at interest, and which escape the contributions which all annual revenue ought to pay to the state. Money held to meet needs,[1] I maintain, has in the case of all individuals a destination to which it decisively belongs. That which is destined for the payment of current taxes belongs to the taxes; that which is destined to meet the need for some purchase belongs to this need; that which invigorates agriculture, trade, and industry belongs to this employment; and that which is destined to pay a debt which has fallen due or a loan which is about to expire belongs to this debt, etc., and not to the man who possesses it. It is the nation's money, and no one is entitled to hold it back, because it belongs to no one; yet it is money dispersed in this way which constitutes the main part of the money stock of a really opulent kingdom, where it is always employed to the benefit of the state. People do not even hesitate to sell it for the same price that it has cost, that is, to allow it to go abroad for the purchase of commodities which are required; and foreign countries too are not unaware of the advantages of this trade, in which the requirements of exchange make it necessary that money should be employed in the purchase of commodities and com- modities in the purchase of money. For money and commodities constitute wealth only in proportion to their market value.

[1] *L'argent de besoin.* R.L.M.

The quantity of money which is diverted and kept back from circulation is small, and it is soon exhausted when borrowing increases a little. It is this idle money, however, which deludes the rabble; it is this which the vulgar regard as the nation's wealth and as an important means for meeting a state's needs—even those of a great state which in actual fact can be opulent only as a result of the net product of the wealth which is annually generated from its territory, and which, so to speak, causes money to be regenerated by renewing it and continually accelerating its circulation.

Moreover, when a kingdom is wealthy and thriving as a result of trade in its products, it has, as a result of its intercourse, wealth in other countries, and paper everywhere takes the place of money for it. The abundance of its products and their sale thus assure to it everywhere the use of the money stock of other nations; and money is never lacking, either, in a kingdom which is properly cultivated, for the purpose of paying to the sovereign and the proprietors the revenue provided by the net product of the exchangeable produce which is annually regenerated from the land. But although money is never lacking for the purpose of paying this revenue, we must not make the mistake of believing that taxes can be imposed on the circulation of money.[1]

Money is a form of wealth which steals away on sight. Contributions can be imposed only on the source of disposable wealth, always renascent, palpable, and exchangeable. It is there that the revenue of the sovereign is generated, and there, moreover, that he can find assured means for meeting the urgent needs of the state. Thus the government's gaze should not stop short at money, but should extend further and fix itself upon the abundance and market value of the produce of the land, in order to increase the revenue. It is in this part of visible and annual wealth that the state's power and the nation's prosperity consist; it is this which binds and attaches the subjects to the land. Money, industry, and mercantile trade and traffic constitute only an artificial and independent realm, which in the absence of the produce of the land would be only a republican state: Constantinople itself, which has control over no such produce, but is reduced to the movable wealth associated with the re-export trade, gains from it, in the midst of despotism, considerable ability and independence in its intercourse and in the free state of its commercial wealth.[2]

Note on Maxim XIV

(To encourage the breeding of live-stock.)

[1] See what we have said about taxes above, pp. 238 ff.

[2] This last sentence will be more comprehensible if it is read in conjunction with the passage from the *Philosophie Rurale* translated above, pp. 63–4. R.L.M.

This advantage is brought about through the sale, employment, and use of wool in the kingdom, through the high consumption of meat, milk foods, butter, cheese, etc., above all through that which ought to be engaged in by the lower classes, who are the most numerous. For it is only in proportion to this consumption that markets for live-stock can be found and that people breed them; and it is the manure which the live-stock provides for the land which procures abundant harvests, as a result of the breeding of the live-stock itself. This abundance of harvests and live-stock removes all anxiety about famine in a kingdom which is so fruitful of subsistence goods. The food which live-stock provides for men in such a kingdom reduces their consumption of corn, so that the nation can sell a greater quantity of it abroad and continually increase its wealth by means of its trade in so valuable a product. In this way, therefore, the comfortable circumstances of the lower classes necessarily contribute to the prosperity of the state.

The profit from live-stock is confused with the profit from cultivation so far as the proprietor's revenue is concerned, since the rent payable for the lease of a farm is fixed in proportion to the product which it can yield through cultivation and through the raising of live-stock, in countries where the farmers' advances are not exposed to the danger of being wiped out by arbitrary taxes. But when taxes are laid on the farmer, the revenue from the land falls into a decline, because farmers do not dare to make advances for the purchase of live-stock, fearing that this live-stock, which consists of visible things, will draw a ruinous tax down upon them. Thus for want of a sufficient number of live-stock to provide manure for the land, cultivation declines, and the costs of working poor land swallow up the net product and wipe out the revenue.

The profit from live-stock contributes to the product of landed property to such a degree that the one is procured as a result of the other, and these two parts should not be separated when reckoning the value of the products of cultivation, calculated in accordance with the proprietors' revenue. For the net product which provides the revenue and the taxes is procured more by means of the live-stock than by means of the labour of men, whose returns if they worked alone would barely cover the cost of their subsistence. But large advances are necessary for the purchase of live-stock: that is why the government ought to be more concerned with attracting wealth to the countryside than with attracting men. Men will not be lacking if there is wealth there; but without wealth there is a general decline, the land becomes valueless, and the kingdom is left without resources and power.

Thus there must be complete security for the ready employment of wealth in the cultivation of the land, and full freedom of trade in produce. The wealth which gives birth to wealth ought not to be burdened with taxes. The farmers and their families, moreover, ought to be exempted from all personal contributions, to which wealthy inhabitants in essential occupations should not be subjected, in case they carry off into the towns the wealth which they employ in agriculture, in order to enjoy there the privileges which an un-enlightened government, in its partiality towards town-dwelling hirelings, would grant them. The comfortably-placed bourgeois, above all the retail traders who make money only at the expense of the public and whose over-abundance in the towns is burdensome to the nation—these bourgeois, I say, would find in an agriculture which was protected and honoured sounder and less servile businesses in which to settle their children than those which are to be found in the towns. Their wealth, when brought back to the countryside, would render the land fertile, increase wealth, and ensure the prosperity and power of the state.

There is one point which should be made about the noblemen who cultivate their property in the countryside. There are many of them who do not own a sufficient quantity of land for the employment of their ploughs or their abilities, so that they are subjected to a loss on their expenditure and their activities. Would it take away from the dignity of the nobility to allow them to rent land for the purpose of extending their cultivation and activities to the benefit of the state, especially in a country where the burden of taxes (having become improper) was no longer laid either on persons or on cultivators? Is it unseemly for a duke and peer to rent a mansion in a town? The payment of rent for a farm does not involve any dependence upon anyone, any more than does the payment made for a coat, an annuity, or the rent of a house. Further, it should be noted that in agriculture the possessor of the land and the possessor of the advances necessary for cultivation are both equally proprietors, and that on this account there is equal dignity on each side. The noblemen, by extending their agricultural enterprises, would contribute through this activity to the prosperity of the state, and they would find there the means to main-tain their expenditure and that of their children in the military profession. At all times the nobility and agriculture have been linked together. In free nations, the rent of land, relieved of arbitrary and personal taxes, is in itself a matter of complete indifference. Have the dues attached to property, to which noblemen themselves are subject, ever degraded either the nobility or agriculture?

Note on Maxim XVI

(As the market is, so is the reproduction.)

If external trade in corn and other raw produce is stopped, agriculture is limited by the state of the population, instead of the population being increased through agriculture. The sale of raw produce abroad increases the revenue from landed property; this increase in revenue increases the proprietors' expenditure; this increase in expenditure attracts men into the kingdom; this increase in population increases the consumption of raw produce; this increase in consumption and the sales abroad both accelerate the advance of agriculture, population, and revenue.

As a result of a free and unobstructed export and import trade, corn always commands a more equal price, for the most equal price is that which is current among trading nations. This trade all the time smooths out the annual inequalities in nations' harvests, by supplying in turn those which are suffering from a scarcity with the surplus of those which have plenty, and this always and everywhere brings products and prices back to almost the same level. That is why trading nations which have no land to till are just as sure of their bread as those which cultivate large territories. The slightest price-advantage in a country attracts the commodity to it, and equality is continually re-established.

It has been shown that, independently of foreign sales and an increase in price, the constant equality of prices alone increases the revenue from the land by more than one-tenth; that it increases and safeguards the advances necessary for cultivation; that it avoids excessively high prices which reduce the population; and that it prevents agriculture from wasting away through its produce becoming valueless. The prohibition of external trade, on the other hand, is the reason why necessaries are often lacking; why agriculture which is too closely proportioned to the needs of the nation causes prices to vary to the extent that good and bad years cause harvests to vary; why this limited agriculture leaves a large part of the land going to waste without yielding any revenue; why the uncertainty of the market causes anxiety to the farmers, halts expenditure on cultivation, and lowers the level of rent; and why this decline increases more and more, to the extent that the nation suffers from an insidious measure which ends by ruining it completely.

Suppose that for the purpose of avoiding any lack of corn we imagined that the sale of it abroad was forbidden, and also that merchants were prevented from filling up their warehouses in abundant years in order to make up for bad years; that it was forbidden, I say, to expand these free stores, where competition between merchants wards off monopoly, enables husbandmen to sell their produce in abundant years, and maintains abundance in sterile years. We should have to conclude, on the basis of these timorous administrative principles, so alien to an agricultural nation which can enrich itself only through the sale of its produce, that we should also restrict as much as possible the consumption of corn in the country, by reducing the food of its lower classes to potatoes, buckwheat, acorns, etc.; and that we should adopt so improper and ruinous a measure as to prevent the transport of corn from provinces where it is abundant to those which are suffering from scarcity and those whose supplies are depleted. What abuses, what monopolies, this arbitrary and destructive policy would bring about! What would become of the cultivation of the land? What would become of the revenue, the taxes, men's wages, and the strength of the nation?

Note on Maxim XVIII

(A low price for raw produce would render trade disadvantageous to the nation.)

If, for example, we buy from abroad a certain quantity of commodities for the value of one *setier* of corn priced at 20 livres, two *setiers* of it would be necessary to pay for the same quantity of this commodity if the government forced the price of corn down to 10 livres.

Note on the Same Maxim

(As the market value is, so is the revenue.)

A distinction should be made in a state between goods which have use value but which have no market value, and wealth, which has both use value and market value. For example, the savages of Louisiana used to enjoy many goods, such as water, wood, game, and the fruits of the earth, which did not constitute wealth because they had no market value. But after a number of branches of trade were opened up between them and the French, the English, the Spaniards, etc., a part of these goods has acquired market value and has become wealth. Thus the administration of a kingdom ought to aim at procuring for the nation at one and the same time the greatest possible abundance of products and the greatest possible market value, because with the aid of great wealth it procures for itself through trade all the other things it may need, in the proportions appropriate to the state of its wealth.

Note on Maxim XIX

(Cheapness of produce is not advantageous to the lower classes.)

A high price[1] of corn, for example, provided that it is constant, is more advantageous to the lower classes in an agricultural kingdom

[1] *Cherté*. See above, p. 93. R.L.M.

I

than a low price. The daily wage of a labourer is fixed more or less naturally on the basis of the price of corn, and normally amounts to a twentieth of the price of one *setier*. On this basis, if the price of corn were constantly at 20 livres, the labourer would earn about 260 livres in the course of the year. He would spend 200 livres of this on corn for himself and his family, and would have 60 livres left over for other needs. If on the other hand a *setier* of corn were worth only 10 livres, he would earn only 130 livres. He would spend 100 livres of this on corn, and would have only 30 livres left over for other needs. It is for this reason that we observe that provinces where corn is dear are much more populous than those where it is at a low price.

The same benefit is received in the case of all other classes of men, in the case of the gains of the cultivators, the revenue of the proprietors, the taxes, and the prosperity of the state. For in these cases the product of the land amply compensates for the addition to the cost of wages and food. It is easy to convince oneself of this by making a calculation of the expenses and the increase in produce.[1]

Note on Maxim XX

(That the well-being of the lower classes should not be reduced.)

In order to justify the harassment of the inhabitants of the countryside, the extortioners have put forward as a maxim that it is necessary that the *peasants should be poor, so as to prevent them from being idle.* The contemptuous bourgeois have readily adopted this cruel maxim because they pay less heed to other more peremptory maxims—namely that the man *who is unable to save*[2] *anything does only just as much work as is necessary to earn him his food; and that in general all men who can save are industrious, because all men are greedy for wealth.* The real cause of the idleness of the oppressed peasant is that wages and employment are at too low a level in countries where restrictions on trade render produce valueless, and where other causes have ruined agriculture. Harassment, a low price of produce, and a gain which is insufficient to stimulate them to work, render them idle men, poachers, vagabonds, and robbers. Thus enforced poverty is not the way to render the peasants industrious: it is only a guarantee of the ownership and enjoyment of their gains which can put heart into them and make them diligent.

Ministers who are guided by feelings of humanity, by superior education, and by more far-seeing views, indignantly reject hateful and destructive maxims which lead only to the devastation of the countryside. For they are not unaware of the fact that it is the wealth

---

[1] Cf. e.g. the calculation above, pp. 168 ff. R.L.M.

[2] *Conserver.* R.L.M.

of the inhabitants of the countryside which gives birth to the wealth of the nation. POOR PEASANTS, POOR KINGDOM.

Note on Maxim XXII

(A high level of expenditure on the consumption of subsistence goods sustains the proper price of produce and the reproduction of the revenue.)

What is said here with reference to a high level of expenditure on the consumption of raw produce applies to agricultural nations. But we should consider the small trading nations which have no territory in a different light; for their interest obliges them to be sparing in all types of expenditure in order to conserve and increase the fund of wealth which is necessary for their trade, and in order to carry on their trade at less cost than other nations, with the aim of being able to secure for themselves the benefits of competition in sales and purchases abroad. These small trading nations should be regarded as the commercial agents of the large states, because it is more advantageous to the latter to trade through their intervention than to burden themselves with different branches of trade which they would carry on at greater expense and from which they would draw less profit than if they brought about a high degree of competition of foreign merchants within their borders. For it is only through the greatest possible degree of competition, open to all the merchants in the world, that a nation can be sure of securing the best price and the most advantageous market for the products of its territory, and of preserving itself from the monopoly of the country's merchants.

Note on Maxim XXVI

(To pay less attention to increasing the population than to increasing the revenue.)

The desire of all nations to be powerful in war, coupled with ignorance of the resources required for waging war, which are regarded by the vulgar as consisting only of men, have led to the belief that the strength of a state consists in a large population. It has never been sufficiently understood that in order to carry on a war not nearly such a large number of men is required as one would think at first sight; that very large armies must be, and normally are, much more fatal to the nation which exhausts itself in employing them than to the enemy whom they engage in combat; and that the military section of a nation can neither subsist nor take action except through the instrumentality of the tax-paying section.

Some superficial thinkers imagine that great wealth in a state is obtained as a result of an abundance of men; but their view springs from the fact that they forget that men can obtain and perpetuate wealth only by means of wealth, and only to the extent that a proper proportion exists between men and wealth.

Nations always believe that they do not have enough men: it is not perceived that there are not enough wages to maintain a larger population, and that men without means are of benefit to a country only to the extent that they receive assured gains there which enable them to live by their work. In the absence of gains or wages, it is true, a section of people in the countryside may generate for their subsistence certain very low-priced products which do not demand large expenses or protracted labour, and which one does not have to wait a long time before gathering in. But these men, these products, and the land on which they are grown, are worth nothing to the state. In order that the land should yield a revenue, work in the countryside must render a net product over and above the wages paid to the workmen, for it is this net product which enables the other classes of men who are necessary in a state to subsist. This should not be expected from poor men who work the land with their hands, or with other insufficient resources; for they can procure subsistence for themselves alone only by giving up the cultivation of corn, which demands too much time, too much labour, and too much expense to be carried on by men who are destitute of means and reduced to obtaining their food from the land simply by the work of their hands.

Thus it is not to these poor peasants that you should entrust the cultivation of your land. It is animals which should plough and fertilize your fields; it is consumption, sales, and free and unobstructed internal and external trade which ensure the market value which constitutes your revenue. Thus it is wealthy men whom you should put in charge of the enterprises of agriculture and rural trade, in order to enrich yourselves, to enrich the state, and to enable inexhaustible wealth to be generated. With the aid of this wealth you may enjoy in abundance the products of the land and the arts, maintain powerful defences against your enemies, and provide amply for the expenses of public works devoted to the conveniences of the nation, to the facilitation of trade in your produce, to the fortification of your frontiers, to the maintenance of a formidable navy, to the beautification of the kingdom, and to the procuring for working men of wages and gains which attract them into the kingdom and keep them there. Thus the political administration of agriculture and of trade in its produce is the foundation of the department of finance, and of all the other branches of administration in an agricultural nation.

Large armies are not sufficient to provide a powerful defence. The soldier must be well paid if he is to be well disciplined, well trained, energetic, happy, and fearless. War on land and sea employs other resources besides men's strength, and demands other expenditure much greater than that necessary for the soldiers' subsistence. Thus it is much less men than wealth which sustains a war, for so long as wealth is available to pay the men well, men will not be lacking as reinforcements for the army. The more wealth a nation possesses for the purpose of enabling wealth to be annually regenerated, the less men does this annual reproduction employ, the more net product it yields, and the more men the government has at its disposal for services and public works; and the more wages there are to enable them to subsist, the more useful are these men to the state by virtue of their occupations, and by virtue of their expenditure, which causes their pay to be brought back into circulation.

Battles which are won simply by killing men, without causing any other damage, do little to weaken the enemy if he still has the wages of the men he has lost, and if they are sufficient to attract other men. An army of 100,000 well-paid men is an army of a million men, for no army to which men are attracted by the pay can be destroyed. It is then up to the soldiers to defend themselves bravely; they are the ones who have most to lose; for they will not lack bold successors fully prepared to face the dangers of war. Thus it is wealth which sustains the honour of the troops. The hero who wins battles, who takes cities, who acquires glory, and who is the soonest exhausted, is not the conqueror. The historian who confines himself to a description of marvellous happenings in his account of military exploits does little to instruct posterity about the results of decisive events in war, if he allows himself to ignore the state of the basic resources and policy of the nations whose history he is writing. For it is in the permanent well-being of the tax-paying section of a nation, and in the patriotic virtues, that the permanent power of a state consists.

One should consider in the same light the public works which facilitate the increase of wealth, such as the construction of canals, the putting into order of roads, rivers, etc., which can be carried out only as a result of the comfortable situation of tax-payers who are in a position to meet these expenses without detrimentally affecting the annual reproduction of the nation's wealth. Otherwise works of such an extensive character, although very desirable, would as a result of ill-regulated taxes or continual *corvées* become ruinous enterprises, whose consequences would not be made up for by the utility of these resource-straining[1] and burdensome works: for it is not easy to make up for the decline of a state. Destructive causes, which increase more and more, render all the vigilance and exertions of the administration useless, when attention is devoted only to keeping the effects in check instead of going back to the causes. This is fully proved, for the time, by the author of the book entitled *A Detailed Account of*

[1] *Forcés.* R.L.M.

France under Louis XIV,[1] published in 1699. This author dates the beginning of the kingdom's decline back to the year 1660, and he examines its course down to the time when his book was published. He shows that the revenue from landed property, which was formerly 700 millions (1400 millions in terms of our money today) diminished by one-half between 1660 and 1699. He notes that it is not to the level of taxes but to the injurious form of assessment and the disorder which it brought about that this huge decline must be attributed. One is bound to impute the continuation of this contraction to the continuation of the same form of administration. The assessment became so irregular that under Louis XIV it rose to more than 750 millions but yielded to the royal treasury only 250 millions,[2] which meant that the tax-payers were deprived every year of the enjoyment of 500 millions, without taking into account the annual deterioration caused by the arbitrary *taille* which was imposed on the farmers. The increased and ruinous taxes on all kinds of expenditure spread out as a result of *repompement*[3] over the expenditure of the taxes themselves, to the detriment of the sovereign, for whom a large part of his revenue became illusory. Thus we see that by a better form of administration tax revenue could have been greatly increased in a very short time, and the subjects could have been enriched, by abolishing such destructive impositions, and by reviving external trade in corn, wine, wool, cloth, etc. But who would have dared to attempt such a reform at a time when no one had any conception of the economic administration of an agricultural kingdom? At that time it would have been considered as overthrowing the pillars of the building.

[1] By Boisguillebert. R.L.M.

[2] See *Memoranda on the General History of Finance,* by M. D. de B. [D'Eon de Beaumont. R.L.M.]

[3] See note (1) on p. 198 above. R.L.M.

PART TWO
ESSAYS

Part Two

ESSAYS

I

PROBLEMS OF THE *TABLEAU ECONOMIQUE*[1]

Economists have now been interpreting Quesnay's *Tableau Econo-mique* for two centuries. The first interpreter was Quesnay himself: hearing that Mirabeau was 'bogged down' in the original version of the 'zigzag', Quesnay sent him a long letter explaining its mechanism[2] —a letter which was soon to grow into the 'Explanation'[3] included in the 'third edition'. As the 'Little Book of Household Accounts'[4] reached larger audiences through Mirabeau's extended treatment in the sixth part of the *Friend of Mankind*,[5] through the *Rural Philosophy*,[6] and, later, through Quesnay's *Analysis*,[7] *First Economic Problem*,[8] and *Second Economic Problem*,[9] interest in this remarkable analytical device grew apace. At this stage, however, apart from the *ex cathedra* pronouncements of Quesnay and Mirabeau themselves, there was little in the way of interpretation of the *Tableau:* the Physiocratic rank-and-file, with the exception of Baudeau, tended to leave the explanation and development of the *Tableau* to their acknowledged masters; and their adversaries, with the exception of Forbonnais, usually contented themselves with satire and abuse.

Interest in the *Tableau* declined as the influence of the Physiocrats themselves declined. The publicity given to the *Tableau* by Smith[10] was more than counterbalanced by his rather patronizing critique of the Physiocratic system as a whole; and Physiocratically-inclined economists like Garnier, Spence, Chalmers, and Malthus were

[1] This essay is an amended and enlarged version of an article published in *Economica*, November 1960. I am grateful to the editors of *Economica* for their permission to reproduce it in this volume.

[2] Translated above, pp. 115 ff.   [3] Translated above, pp. 128 ff.

[4] See above, p. 117.

[5] References to *L'Ami des Hommes* in the present essay are to the sixth volume of the edition stated to be published '*A la Haye, chez Benjamin Gilbert*', the date of this volume being 1762.

[6] References to the *Philosophie Rurale* in the present essay are to the 1764 edition from which the extracts appearing above have been translated.

[7] Translated above, pp. 150 ff.   [8] Translated above, pp. 168 ff.

[9] Translated above, pp. 186 ff.   [10] *Wealth of Nations*, Book IV, chapter 9.

interested more in the under-consumptionist implications of the general theory of the Physiocrats than in the *Tableau* and the uses to which it could be put.[1] In 1846, however, Daire published his two volumes of selections from the Physiocratic literature, including Quesnay's *Analysis, First Economic Problem*, and *Second Economic Problem*, as well as Baudeau's *Explanation*, and the ball was set rolling once again.[2] Marx subjected Quesnay's *Analysis* to an exhaustive study in the early 1860s,[3] laboured in the hot July of 1863 to substitute a new *Tableau* for Quesnay's,[4] and later, in 1878, published a detailed critique of some comments on the *Tableau* made by the unfortunate Dühring.[5] Since then several generations of scholars have been at work, notably Oncken, Bauer, Schelle, Higgs, and Weulersse,[6] a number of important documents have been discovered, and with the revived interest in aggregative and general equilibrium analysis in our own time there have been several new interpretations.[7]

The purpose of the present essay is to make a contribution to the solution of a number of problems relating to the *Tableau* which still remain outstanding, in spite of the work of these scholars. These problems can be grouped under two main headings—first, certain historical problems relating in particular to the influence of Cantillon on Quesnay, and to the nature of the three 'editions' of the *Tableau* which Quesnay apparently brought out in 1758-59; and second, certain problems of interpretation and methodology associated with the various formulations of the *Tableau* and its use as a tool in dynamic welfare analysis.

I

The general influence of Cantillon on Quesnay was, I believe, first noted by Marx,[8] and in more recent years attention has been drawn

[1] See my essay on pp. 313 ff. below. See also the articles by J. J. Spengler in the *Journal of Political Economy*, Vol. LIII, nos. 3–4, September–December 1945.

[2] Eugène Daire, *Physiocrates*, Paris, 1846.

[3] See *Theories of Surplus Value*, London, 1951, pp. 67 ff.

[4] See *Correspondence of Marx and Engels*, London, 1936, pp. 153–6.

[5] See F. Engels, *Herr Eugen Dühring's Revolution in Science*, London, n.d., pp. 268–78. The chapter in which the relevant passages appear was written by Marx.

[6] References to the main works of these scholars will be found in the extensive bibliography at the end of Vol. I of I.N.E.D.

[7] See e.g. H. Woog, *The Tableau Economique of François Quesnay*, Berne, 1950; L. Fishman, *A Reconsideration of the Tableau Economique*, in *Current Economic Comment* (University of Illinois), Vol. XX, February 1958, no. 1, pp. 41 ff.; and A. Phillips, *The Tableau Economique as a Simple Leontief Model*, in *Quarterly Journal of Economics*, Vol. LXIX, February 1955, no. 1, pp. 137 ff.

[8] *Capital*, Vol. I (Foreign Languages Publishing House, Moscow, 1954), p. 555, footnote.

by other writers to the intellectual affiliation between Cantillon's picture of circulation in his *Essay* and Quesnay's picture in the early Encyclopedia articles and in the *Tableau* itself.[1] Certainly some considerable intellectual influence seems to have impinged on Quesnay between the time when he wrote his first Encyclopedia article, *Farmers* (published in January 1756), and the time when he wrote his second, *Corn* (published in November 1757). *Farmers*, an impressive plea for the introduction into France of large-scale capitalist agriculture on the English model, contains very little that can properly be called an anticipation of basic Physiocratic theory: vague statements to the effect that the countryside is the 'source of the true wealth of the state'[2] hardly compensate for the lack of anything really resembling the later concepts of net product and exclusive productivity.[3] In *Corn*, however, there is a quite startling change of atmosphere: the net product appears for the first time,[4] together with the doctrine of exclusive productivity in embryo form,[5] the doctrine of the dependence of the merchants and the artisans on the revenue,[6] and the idea that trade and manufacture are really only branches of agriculture;[7] and in the *Maxims of Economic Government* at the end of the article[8] the theory becomes much more precise.

Cantillon's *Essay* appeared in the middle of 1755;[9] and Quesnay himself specifically refers in *Corn* to Cantillon's recognition of certain 'fundamental truths', notably that 'the revenue of the king, the clergy, and the proprietors, and the gains of the farmer and of those whom he employs, turn into expenditure, which is distributed to all the other estates and to all the other occupations'.[10] There seems to be little doubt that one of the main *theoretical* influences working on Quesnay (and also, of course, on Mirabeau)[11] at this stage was that of Cantillon. This is borne out not only by the well-known parallels between Cantillon's account of the circulation process[12] and Quesnay's, but also by one rather curious and striking feature of

---

[1] See e.g. Jevons's essay on Cantillon, reprinted in the Royal Economic Society's edition of Cantillon's *Essai* (1931), *passim.*; H. Higgs, *The Physiocrats* (1897), pp. 16 ff.; and the introductory essays in the I.N.E.D. edition of Cantillon's *Essai* (1952), *passim.*

[2] I.N.E.D., II, p. 462.

[3] Cf. Du Pont's vastly exaggerated remarks on *Fermiers* in his *Notice Abrégée* (Oncken, p. 150).

[4] I.N.E.D., II, p. 462.   [5] Ibid., p. 472.

[6] Ibid., pp. 472-3.   [7] Ibid., p. 481.

[8] Translated above, pp. 72 ff.

[9] See the I.N.E.D. edition of the *Essai*, p. xxxvi.

[10] I.N.E.D., II, p. 482.

[11] See above, p. 16.

[12] The main elements of Cantillon's account will be found in Chapter XII, Part One, and Chapter III, Part Two, of the *Essai*.

Corn which so far as I know has not hitherto been noticed in this connection.

The point is this. The main burden of the relevant passages in Cantillon's *Essay* is that 'all the classes and inhabitants of a State live at the expense of the Proprietors of Land'.[1] Now the Physiocrats were later to argue, when their theory was more fully formulated, that the main reason for this was that the only truly 'disposable' or 'net' part of the national income was received (and spent) by the proprietors. Cantillon, however, does not argue in this way at all. His view is that the farmers, as well as the proprietors, also receive an income which is truly 'net', at any rate in part. The farmer, Cantillon argues, normally makes 'three Rents', each 'rent' being roughly equal to one-third of the produce of his farm. The first represents the 'true Rent' which he pays to the proprietor; the second represents compensation for his costs and subsistence expenses; and the third represents a net income 'which ought to remain with him to make his undertaking profitable'.[2] In effect what he is saying is that the 'net product' of the land (in the Physiocratic sense) includes not only the 'first rent' accruing to the proprietor, but also the 'third rent' representing the farmer's net profit. It is no doubt for this reason that Cantillon argues that 'the three Rents of the Farmer must . . . be considered as the principal sources or so to speak the mainspring of circulation in the state'.[3]

Now the interesting thing about *Corn* is that Quesnay in this article, but hardly anywhere else in the whole of his later writing, adopts this Cantillonian approach and assumes that the farmer shares in the net product.[4] This is fairly clear from two of his arithmetical calculations which show how the net product is divided up between the proprietor, the *taille*, and the farmer;[5] and also from certain other passages in the article.[6] It is true that the two calculations concerned could conceivably be regarded as relating to certain special conditions in which Quesnay even in his later writings admitted that the farmer might receive extra gains during the course of his lease, thus in effect sharing *temporarily* in the net product (until the extra gains crystallized out into rent).[7] But taking the evidence as a whole, it

---

[1] *Essai* (Royal Economic Society edition), p. 15.

[2] *Essai* (Royal Economic Society edition), p. 121. Cf. ibid., p. 43, where the third rent' of the farmers is described as 'the Profit of their Undertaking'.

[3] Ibid., p. 123. Cf. also the following passage on p. 45: 'If we examine the Means by which an Inhabitant is supported it will always appear in returning back to the Fountain-Head, that these Means arise from the Land of the Proprietor either in the two thirds reserved by the Farmer, or the one third which remains to the Landlord.'

[4] The other occasions on which he does so, or appears to do so, are described below, pp. 299 ff., in a rather different connection.

[5] I.N.E.D., II, pp. 463 and 475.

[6] See e.g. I.N.E.D., II, pp. 480, 482, and 505.   [7] See below, pp. 301 ff.

seems more plausible to say that Quesnay, at this stage in the evolution of his thought, was implicitly defining the term 'net product' so as to include not only the proprietor's rent but also the farmer's profit.[1] And this may, I think, be taken as an important indication of the extent of Cantillon's influence on Quesnay at this stage in his intellectual development.

Cantillon's inspired hints about the circulation of money and goods in a predominantly agricultural kingdom developed under their own momentum in Quesnay's mind once he had absorbed them. It is no doubt as true as it is trite to say that the parallel between this economic circulation and the circulation of the blood presented itself to Quesnay very forcibly: Quesnay's medical writings, after all, as one recent commentator has said, were 'truly haunted by circulation';[2] and the Physiocrats occasionally drew this parallel themselves. But however this may be, there is at least one very *Tableau*-like passage in *Men*,[3] and with the further substantial development of basic Physiocratic theory in *Taxation* Quesnay no doubt felt ready to present the results of his theoretical and practical research in summary form. The result was the successive 'editions' of the *Tableau Economique* which Quesnay appears to have brought out in 1758-59.

Du Pont tells us that the 'first edition' of the *Tableau* was printed at Versailles in 'a very fine edition in 4to'. He adds that copies of it are no longer to be found 'except in the hands of the individuals to whom they were given'. So far as the date of its publication is concerned, he says that Quesnay told him several times that it was definitely December 1758, but that Mirabeau, who was equally sure about it, told him that it was 1759 and not even the beginning of that year.[4] A copy of the 'first edition' was sent by Quesnay to Mirabeau, under cover of a letter which is now in the *Archives Nationales*,[5] but no copy of the 'edition' itself has to my knowledge yet been found. However, a manuscript draft of a *Tableau* with a base of 400 livres, accompanied by a set of 22 'Remarks', all in Quesnay's handwriting, exists in the *Archives Nationales*,[6] and most modern commentators

---

[1] Cf. the passage in the 'second edition' of the *Tableau* (translated above, p. 121, footnote) where Quesnay assumes that in a kingdom dominated by small-scale cultivation the net product includes a share accruing to the farmer 'for his gain, the interest on his advances, and his risks'. This passage is further discussed below, pp. 300 ff.

[2] I.N.E.D., I, p. 202 (article by Jean Sutter). It is probable that certain other physical analogies were of almost equal importance—notably the biological analogy (the concept of reproduction) and the mechanical analogy (the concept of the economic 'machine').

[3] I.N.E.D., II, pp. 541-2. Cf. also above, pp. 92-3.

[4] Oncken, pp. 125-6, footnote. For a possible explanation of the discrepancy in the dates, see below, p. 272, footnote (2).

[5] Translated above, p. 108.　　　　　　　　[6] Translated above, pp. 109 ff.

have accepted this as a draft of the 'first edition'. Whether this is in fact so or not cannot be finally determined until a copy of the 'first edition' comes to light, but it seems reasonable to assume at any rate that the 'first edition' did not differ very substantially from this draft.[1]

The 'second edition' of the *Tableau* seems to have followed a few months after the 'first'. In his letter to Mirabeau explaining certain aspects of the 'first edition' of the *Tableau*, Quesnay announced that he would be sending him an amended and enlarged (but not too greatly enlarged) 'second edition', in which the base would be raised to 600 livres.[2] Two copies of a compilation corresponding reasonably well to this description are extant, one in the *Archives Nationales* and the other in the *Bibliothèque Nationale*.[3] This compilation consists, like the 'first edition', of a *Tableau* with explanatory comments at either side,[4] followed by a set of remarks, now increased in number to 23, retitled *Extrait des Oeconomies Royales de M. de Sully*, and supplemented by a number of new notes.[5]

So far as the 'second edition' is concerned, a number of commentators were rather seriously misled by the publication in 1894, by the British Economic Association, of a collection of documents from the *Archives Nationales* which was represented to be a facsimile of the 'second printed edition' of the *Tableau*. This collection consists of (a) an engraved *Tableau*, base 600, with a reference at the foot to an 'explanation on the following page';[6] (b) an 'Explanation of the *Tableau Economique*', with corrections in Quesnay's hand;[7] (c) the printed *Tableau*, base 600, which appears in the compilation described in the last paragraph; and (d) the *Extrait des Oeconomies Royales de M. de Sully* which appears in the compilation described in the last paragraph. It was perhaps natural enough, in the first flush of discovery of these documents in the *Archives*, that this collection should have been identified with the 'second edition' referred to in Quesnay's letter to Mirabeau. But there are certain curious features of the collection, when one looks at it as a whole, which ought surely to have suggested even then that it was most unlikely that the four documents together should have constituted a single 'edition', whether the 'second' or any other.[8] The most reasonable hypothesis

---

[1] We know from a letter from Quesnay to Mirabeau (translated above, pp. 115 ff.) that the *Tableau* of the 'first edition' started off with a revenue of 400 livres, which no extant version of the *Tableau* other than the manuscript draft does.

[2] See above, p. 117.   [3] See above, p. 118.

[4] A photographic reproduction of this *Tableau* appears above, between pp. 112 and 113 (Plate 3).   [5] Translated above, pp. 250 ff.

[6] A photographic reproduction of this *Tableau* appears above, between pp. 112 and 113 (Plate 4).

[7] Translated above, pp. 128 ff.

[8] The words 'see the explanation on the following page' at the foot of (a) suggest that (a) and (b) were intended to be linked with one another; and (c) and

was in fact that documents (c) and (d) constituted the true 'second edition', and that documents (a) and (b) were of a later date. But if this was so, for what purpose were documents (a) and (b) prepared?[1]

This mystery was partially solved by Schelle's discovery, in 1905, of a copy of what he called the 'third' or 'definitive' edition of the *Tableau*. Unfortunately, to add to the chapter of accidents, this copy disappeared after Schelle's death and so far as I am aware has not yet been rediscovered. But judging from Schelle's not very adequate description of it, it consisted of: (i) an engraved *Tableau*, base 600 livres, probably identical with or similar to (a) in the British Economic Association's edition; (ii) an 'Explanation', probably identical with (b) in the British Economic Association's edition, with the corrections made by Quesnay 'included in the text or put in a printed erratum'; and (iii) a set of numbered maxims, similar in form to (d) in the British Economic Association's edition, but with 24 maxims instead of 23, and a number of extensive additions (particularly to the notes) and amendments.[2] It is rather surprising that Schelle did not draw one fairly obvious conclusion from his discovery—that (a) and (b) in the British Economic Association's edition were actually prepared by Quesnay for the 'third edition', and were not in fact included in the true 'second edition' at all.

The best guess one can make, then, in the light of the somewhat unsatisfactory evidence, is that Quesnay issued three 'editions' of the *Tableau* in 1758–59. The 'first edition', probably printed at Versailles in December 1758, consisted of a *Tableau*, base 400, and a set of 22 'Remarks', the whole being similar in form and content to the manuscript draft in the *Archives Nationales*. The 'second edition', probably printed early in 1759, consisted of (c) and (d) in the British Economic Association's edition—a *Tableau*, base 600 livres, and a set of 23 maxims. The 'third edition', probably printed some time before the middle of 1759, was as described by Schelle—a

---

(d) are *physically* linked with one another in the case of both the extant copies. But were (a) and (b) intended to be linked with (c) and (d)? The evidence is surely all against this. If (a), (b), (c), and (d) together constituted a single 'edition', what could have been the reason for the inclusion of (c), since a great deal of the explanatory comment in the latter is duplicated in (b) and the *Tableau* itself is duplicated in (a)? There are also certain differences in spelling (*Economique* in (a) and (b) and *Oeconomique* and *Oeconomies* in (c) and (d); a difference in the figures for the total reproduction in the two *Tableaux* (interest is included in (a) but not in (c)); and certain features of the pagination, etc., which are inexplicable on the assumption that the four documents together constituted a single 'edition'.

[1] (a) is almost identical in content with the first *Tableau* in the sixth part of *L'Ami des Hommes* (p. 179 of Vol. VI, 1762 edition), but the words 'see the explanation on the following page' suggest that it was not prepared for that work. In *L'Ami des Hommes* most of the content of (b) reappears, but it is scattered through Mirabeau's own extensive commentary.

[2] See above, pp. 126 ff.

Tableau, base 600 livres (probably (a) of the British Economic Association's edition), an 'Explanation' (of which (b) in the British Economic Association's edition is probably a proof copy), and a set of 24 maxims. It seems likely that very few copies of the 'first edition' and the 'second edition' were printed, but a rather greater number of copies of the 'third edition'. The copy which Forbonnais describes[1] seems to have been that of the 'third edition'; Du Pont probably had a copy of this edition before him when writing his *Short Note*;[2] and it was clearly this edition of which Mirabeau made such extensive use in the sixth part of the *Friend of Mankind*.

II

The graphical models used by Quesnay and Mirabeau to display the working of the economic machine changed their character as the

[1] See Forbonnais, *Principes et Observations Oeconomiques* (1767), Vol. I, pp. 161–2: 'The *Tableau Economique* is a kind of genealogical tree, in which it has been sought to express the course of the circulation and to portray it visually.

This celebrated *Tableau* appeared for the first time five or six years ago, in the form of a little printed book in quarto format, which was sent to only a small number of persons. Following upon a succinct explanation, which contained only the analysis of the system of national wealth already put forward in the article *Corn* in the Encyclopedia, the author presented a short exposition of this same system in the form of 24 general maxims. A large number of notes, of greater length than the text, repeated in large part, or developed, what had already been said in the articles *Farmers* and *Corn* in the Encyclopedia on the subject of political oeconomy, that is, on agriculture, trade, and finance. This exposition was entitled *Extract from the Royal Economic Maxims of M. de Sulli*, whether because the author believed himself to be imbued with his spirit, or whether he wanted to gain credit for his system by the use of this revered name.'

[2] The implication of Du Pont's account of the origins of the *Tableau* in his *Notice Abrégée*, in my opinion, is that he simply did not know of the existence of the (true) first and second editions. The 'first edition' which he purports to describe is said to contain an *Explication* giving an account of the manner in which the wealth of a nation can be calculated, and 24 maxims—characteristics which suggest that he was in fact describing the (true) 'third edition'. This 'third edition', which evidently received a wider circulation than the earlier ones, probably became known to the Physiocrats as the 'first edition'. (It is noteworthy, for example, that Du Pont in his *Notice Abrégée* refers to the sixth part of *L'Ami des Hommes* as containing 'the second explanation of the *Tableau*' (Oncken, p. 157).) This may explain the curious discrepancy (above, p. 269) in the dates of the publication of the 'first edition' given to Du Pont by Quesnay and Mirabeau respectively. When Quesnay said that the date was December 1758 he was probably referring to the (true) 'first edition'; when Mirabeau said that the date was 1759, and not even the beginning of that year, he was probably referring to the (true) 'third edition', which had by then become known to the Physiocrats as the 'first edition'. These dates fit in fairly well with the internal evidence— notably the reference in Quesnay's letter to Mirabeau of the latter's dissertation for the prize offered by the Society of Berne (above p. 117), and certain figures in one of the notes to the *Explication* (above, p. 134).

Physiocratic system was developed,[1] but the general purposes of the models always remained the same—to display the relation between 'expenditure and products' in a way which was easy to grasp, and to enable a clear estimation to be made of the 'organization and disorganization' which government policy could bring about.[2] To fulfil these purposes, Quesnay believed, it was necessary (a) that the models should concentrate, first, on the distribution of the revenue by the class of proprietors to the productive class and the sterile class,[3] and, second, on the mutual exchanges between the productive class and the sterile class; and (b) that the models designed to show the 'disorganization' should be related to a basic model showing the circulatory system in a 'state of prosperity'. Let us consider first the leading characteristics of this basic model, around whicn most of the subsequent attempts at interpretation have centred.

The essential qualitative assumption of the basic model is that the kingdom concerned is 'fully cultivated by the best possible methods',[4] by which Quesnay meant not only that all the kingdom's territory has been brought under cultivation, but also that large-scale capitalist agriculture, using the most productive methods then available, has been widely introduced. It is important to appreciate that the data selected on the basis of this assumption were not utopian: they were in fact drawn from the detailed calculations made by Quesnay in his Encyclopedia articles and elsewhere of the product and revenue which French agriculture was actually capable of producing, given the widespread use of certain existing techniques and forms of socioeconomic organization.[5] The situation envisaged is one of zero net

[1] In the first three editions of the *Tableau* and in *L'Ami des Hommes* the 'zigzag' form was employed. In the *Philosophie Rurale* the 'zigzag' receded into the background, use being mainly made of a simplified *'précis'*. In the *Analyse* a new *'formule'* was developed, which was employed in the *Premier Problème Economique* and the *Second Problème Economique*. These different models are described in more detail below.

[2] Above, p. 108.

[3] The 'revenue', or 'net product', is the amount by which the value of the annual output of agriculture exceeds the costs incurred in producing that output. In the *Tableaux* of the first three editions and in the first *Tableau* of *L'Ami des Hommes* the revenue is reckoned net of taxes and tithes, so that it takes the form of land rent alone. Thus the 'class of proprietors', to whom the revenue accrues, is in effect assumed to consist solely of the landowners. In the later *Tableaux* taxes and tithes are normally included in the revenue, so that the class of proprietors is assumed to consist of the landowners, the sovereign, and the clergy. The 'productive class' consists of all those engaged in agriculture, and the 'sterile class' of all those engaged in non-agricultural pursuits, mainly manufacture and commerce.

[4] Above, p. 151.

[5] The most useful comparison which can be made here is that between the statistical data brought together in the seventh chapter of the *Philosophie Rurale* and the data employed in the basic *Tableaux* of the *Philosophie Rurale* and the *Analyse*.

investment, in which the national product is reproduced every year without increase or diminution. This does not imply that Quesnay imagined that the economy would develop into a stationary state: the situation envisaged was certainly in some respects similar to what we might call today a state of bliss, but not a state which was incapable of being improved upon by further increases in productivity in the future.[1] It is also assumed that the main social and economic reforms advocated by the Physiocrats have been introduced—e.g. that competition is free, and that the removal of restrictions on foreign trade has resulted in the formation of a 'proper price' for agricultural produce.[2] So far as the activities of the sterile class are concerned, however, it is assumed that these are still organized on an artisan rather than on a capitalist basis.[3]

The general form which the *Tableau* assumes in the first three editions and in the sixth part of the *Friend of Mankind* is as follows:[4] The quantitative assumptions here are as follows: The 'annual advances' (working capital) of the productive class are 2000, and its 'original advances'[5] (not shown in the *Tableau* itself) are usually taken to be five times the annual advances—i.e. 10,000. The annual advances 'reproduce 100 per cent'—in other words when employed in production they yield a total product which is sufficient to refund the annual advances and to provide in addition a revenue equal to the annual advances. The total annual reproduction is thus 4000, and the revenue is 2000. The annual advances of the sterile class are 1000, and the value of their annual product is 2000. The class of proprietors spends one-half of its revenue with the productive class and one-half with the sterile class. The receipts of the productive class and the sterile class are distributed according to the same simple

[1] See the interesting *Tableaux* in the *Philosophie Rurale* (Vol. II, pp. 156 ff.) illustrating an imaginary state of affairs in the future, when society has managed to surpass the ratio of revenue to advances assumed in the basic *Tableau*. Cf. also above, p. 149.

[2] Cf. above, p. 151. The maxims associated with the *Tableau* are really statements of the policy assumptions upon which the data of the *Tableau* are based.

[3] This statement is true of Quesnay and Mirabeau, but not so true of Baudeau and Turgot.

[4] See p. 275. In order to facilitate comparison, and for the sake of convenience, I have made all the basic *Tableaux* described in the present essay start with a 'base' (i.e. revenue) of 2000 (millions). In actual fact the base was 400 in the first edition; 600 in the second and third editions and in the first *Tableau* of *L'Ami des Hommes*; 1050 in the remaining *Tableaux* of *L'Ami des Hommes* (taxes and tithes having now been included in the revenue); and 2000 in the *Philosophie Rurale* and the *Analyse*. The proportions between the key quantities, however, and thus the general pattern of distribution, remained substantially the same throughout.

[5] The 'original advances' comprise all the expenses incurred by the agricultural entrepreneurs prior to their receipt of the returns from the first harvest. They thus consist mainly, but not exclusively, of expenditure on fixed capital.

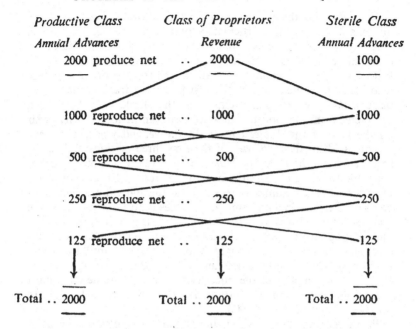

pattern, one-half always being spent within the class concerned and one-half with the other class.

This form of the *Tableau*, then, illustrates the following activities and exchanges which take place during the course of a year: The employment of the productive class's 2000 annual advances in production yields a revenue of 2000 which is paid to the class of proprietors in the form of rent. The class of proprietors uses this 2000 to buy 1000 food from the productive class and 1000 manufactured goods from the sterile class. 500 of the 1000 thus received by the productive class is used to buy manufactured goods from the sterile class; and 500 of the 1000 thus received by the sterile class is used to buy food from the productive class. One-half of the sum of 500 thus received by each of these two classes is sent back to the other, and the process of exchange between the two classes continues in this way to the limit of the geometrical progression. The total receipts of the sterile class, 2000, are equal to the value of its total product. The total receipts of the productive class, 2000, represent a refund of its annual advances, and the employment of these advances in production yields an equal amount of net revenue, represented in the *Tableau* by the sums directed to the central column at each stage in the process. The total of the revenue reproduced is naturally 2000, so that the whole process can be started again at the same level, and conducted according to the same pattern, in the following year.

The *Tableau* in this form is quite easy to follow, and displays in an illuminating way the particular activities and exchanges which Quesnay believed to be essential to the proper understanding of the economic process as a whole. It is obvious, however, that certain features of the process have been abstracted from in order to reduce it to its simplest elements. In the first place, the transactions taking place *within* the productive class and the sterile class have been abstracted from: it is only the inter-sectoral transactions which appear on the face of the *Tableau* itself. In the second place, as I have already said, in the *Tableaux* of the first three editions and in the first *Tableau* of the *Friend of Mankind* the revenue is reckoned net of taxes and tithes.[1] In the third place, the interest of 10 per cent which Quesnay usually assumes is received by the agricultural entrepreneurs on their original and annual advances is abstracted from in the *Tableau*.[2] In the fourth place, the *Tableau* abstracts from the agricultural entrepreneurs' wages of management and rewards for risk-bearing, which are not brought into the picture until the *Rural Philosophy*.[3] In the fifth place, and finally, the *Tableau* obviously abstracts from a part of the purchases which the sterile class must necessarily make from the productive class if it is to be able to produce a total output of 2000.[4]

Two important points about the situation depicted in the basic *Tableau* must be appreciated if the problems involved in its interpretation are to be fully solved. In the first place, the total value of the sterile class's output is not arbitrary, but is conceived to be determined by the total amount spent on manufactured goods by the

---

[1] See n. (3) on p. 273 and n. (4) on p. 274 above.

[2] In the *Tableau* of the third edition Quesnay includes interest of 10 per cent on the original advances in the calculation of the total annual reproduction at the foot; and in the *Explication* he includes interest at 10 per cent on both the original and the annual advances in his detailed calculation of the total annual reproduction. Mirabeau's *Tableaux* in *L'Ami des Hommes* usually include interest at 10 per cent on both original and annual advances in the calculations of the total annual reproduction at the foot. It was not until the *Analyse* that interest was included in the actual *Tableau* itself.

[3] See below, pp. 279 ff.

[4] In the *Explication* Quesnay says that one-half of the receipts of the sterile class is spent with the productive class in the purchase of products for its subsistence, for raw materials for its goods, and for foreign trade, the other half being spent within the sterile class itself for its maintenance and for the restitution of its advances (above, p. 129). And the *Tableau* in fact shows one-half of the receipts of the sterile class (i.e. 1000) being used in purchases from the productive class. (The remaining 3000 of the annual reproduction of 4000 is consumed as to 1000 by the proprietors, as to 1000 by the productive class itself, and as to 1000 by the live-stock of the productive class: see above, pp. 129-30.) But it is clear that part of the sterile class's purchases from the productive class is being abstracted from here, since the basic Physiocratic assumptions regarding the constitution of the value of the sterile class's output make purchases of 2000 from the productive class necessary if that output is to be 2000.

proprietors and the productive class[1]—in this case 2000. This is the most significant sense in which the sterile class is envisaged to be 'dependent' upon the other two classes. In the second place, certain crucial assumptions are specifically made concerning the distribution of the total population of the kingdom between the three classes and the relative levels of their *per capita* personal consumption.[2] The class of proprietors is usually assumed to constitute one-quarter of the population, the productive class one-half, and the sterile class one-quarter; the personal consumption *per capita* of the productive class is equal to that of the sterile class,[3] and one-half that of the class of proprietors;[4] and in the case of each class consumption is equally divided between food and manufactured goods.

The general form which the *Tableau* assumes in the *Rural Philosophy* is usually as follows:

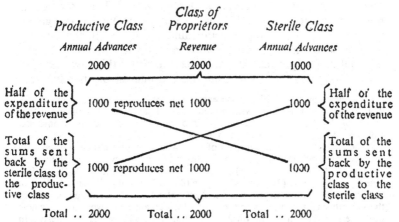

This formula is aptly described as a '*Précis* of the results of the distribution depicted in the *Tableau*'. It omits the geometrical progressions of the zigzag, concentrating on the final results of the

---

[1] This is clearly implied in the first three editions of the *Tableau* and in *L'Ami des Hommes*, and is specifically stated in the *Philosophie Rurale*, Vol. I, p. 81. The annual advances of the sterile class are always assumed to be equal to one-half of the total value of its output; and it is also assumed, of course, that no 'net revenue' at all is yielded as a result of the sterile class's activities.

[2] For statements of these assumptions, see the *Tableaux* of the first and second editions; the *Explication* (p. 130 above); *L'Ami des Hommes* (p. 188); and the *Analyse* (p. 161 above).

[3] Strictly speaking, it is the *per capita* consumption of the *wage-earners* of the productive class which is equal to that of the sterile class: the consumption of the agricultural entrepreneurs, as will be seen later, is higher. But this fact is abstracted from in the *Tableau*.

[4] If the proprietors consume 2000, then these two conditions obviously imply that the productive class must consume 2000 and the sterile class 1000.

transactions, and it provides a much less clumsy tool for dealing with the 'disorganization' than the full zigzag *Tableau*.[1] Abstraction is still made in the *précis* itself of the transactions taking place within the productive and sterile classes, of the farmers' interest and other rewards, and of part of the sterile class's purchases from the productive class, but the two latter points at any rate are dealt with fairly satisfactorily in the accompanying text. In particular, a number of the problems of interpretation which have subsequently arisen are cleared up in the seventh chapter, which seems to have been largely written by Quesnay himself and which has been unduly neglected by most modern interpreters.[2]

In the first place, the mystery of the deficit in the sterile class's purchases from the productive class is cleared up: it is now stated specifically that the sterile class uses its annual advances of 1000 to buy raw materials from the productive class.[3] This transaction, however, still remains outside the *Tableau* itself; but it is recognized that the total annual reproduction must go up by 1000 above the level of 4000 shown in the *Tableau* in order to provide these raw materials.[4] The productive class's receipts from this raw materials transaction, it is now said, comprise the interest on its advances.[5]

[1] The new formula, which represents a sort of half-way house towards the final formula of the *Analyse*, was no doubt arrived at as a result of the experience of *L'Ami des Hommes*, where the full *Tableau* turned out to be a somewhat cumbersome and unnecessarily complex weapon of analysis.

[2] The question of the authorship of the seventh chapter is not quite as easy to solve as the editor of the I.N.E.D. edition of Quesnay's works (which includes the text of the seventh chapter) appears to assume. (See I.N.E.D., II, p. 687, note (1), p. 688, note (3), and p. 725, note (8).) It is true that in the first draft of the *Philosophie Rurale* in the *Archives Nationales* (M. 779) a substantial part of the seventh chapter appears in the hand of an amanuensis, whereas the whole of the rest of the draft is in Mirabeau's hand, but this in itself is not decisive. In the second and third drafts, however, Quesnay's notes and additions are very extensive indeed, and it seems very likely that the operative portions of the central part of the chapter were in fact contributed by Quesnay. The best guess one can make is that Mirabeau wrote most of the first part of the chapter (up to the end of the first paragraph on p. 693 of I.N.E.D., II), and virtually the whole of the final section (pp. 725-8 of I.N.E.D., II), and that Quesnay contributed most of the remainder.

[3] This is first stated at the foot of the *précis* on p. 104 of Vol. I. The total purchases of the sterile class from the productive class are now 2000, consisting of 1000 food (Vol. I, p. 89) and 1000 raw materials, all of which (or so it would at first sight appear) are used up by the sterile class in manufacturing its total product of 2000. Quesnay's original attempt to bring the sterile class's sales abroad into the picture is given up, at any rate at this particular stage of the analysis. It is still stated, however (Vol. I, pp. 89–90), that one-half of the sterile class's receipts (i.e. 1000) is spent within the sterile class in the purchase of manufactured goods. Since the sterile class's total product of 2000 is all sold to the proprietors and the productive class, this raises the vexing problem of where the sterile class gets its own manufactured goods from. See below, pp. 282 ff.

[4] Vol. I, p. 104. [5] Ibid., p. 305.

Since the full amount of this interest is assumed to be spent every year on real goods,[1] it would appear that the annual reproduction ought to go up by a further 1000, to 6000, in order to provide these goods. In fact, however, there is no indication in the *Rural Philosophy* that it actually does so: the figures for the total annual reproduction obstinately remain at 5000, which has given rise to some bewilderment among the interpreters. Actually the solution of this problem is extremely simple: the total annual reproduction remains at 5000 because the 1000 fodder for the live-stock which was included in the early *Tableaux*[2] is now abstracted from.[3] The total annual reproduction of 5000, in real terms, is now made up as follows: 1000 food sold to the proprietors; 1000 food consumed *in natura* by the productive class;[4] 1000 food sold to the sterile class; 1000 raw materials sold to the sterile class; and 1000 produce on which the interest is spent.[5] If one wants to see the animals fed, nothing is easier: just add 1000 for fodder to the total reproduction, the annual advances, and the returns.[6] Nothing happens to the revenue or to the pattern of circulation depicted in the *Tableau*.

It is only when the costs of fodder are reinstated in this way in the annual advances, however, oddly enough, that the normal rewards accruing to the agricultural entrepreneurs (over and above the interest on their advances) can come into the picture. The interest, although Mirabeau on one occasion incautiously described it as an 'honest profit',[7] and Quesnay once hinted that it might contain a net element,[8] was normally regarded merely as a sort of amortization-and-reserve fund. It was recognized, of course, that the entrepreneurs

---

[1] See e.g. the calculation in ibid., p. 331.

[2] See the *Explication*, p. 130 above.

[3] Quesnay states this specifically in the *Analyse* (p. 162 above), referring the reader to the seventh chapter of the *Philosophie Rurale*.

[4] The fact that this 1000 food does not 'enter into trade' but is consumed *in natura* is made clear by Quesnay in the *Premier Problème Economique* (p. 170 above).

[5] A statement by Quesnay in the *Analyse* (p. 154 above) has led a number of commentators to take the view that the interest is spent on manufactured goods. This is not, however, a logical conclusion from Quesnay's statement; nor would it be physically possible under the conditions assumed in the *Tableau*, since the agents of the productive class have to consume 1000 food and 1000 manufactured goods for their maintenance; and only 1000 manufactured goods in all are purchased by the productive class. Quesnay, I think, visualized these 'interest goods' (as I shall call them from now on) as consisting essentially of agricultural produce of various kinds—live-stock for replacing losses, stocks of seed, etc., to meet emergencies, and subsistence for men employed to repair buildings, machines, etc. See in this connection Marx, *Theories of Surplus Value*, p. 69.

[6] The returns = the annual advances + the interest. The total annual reproduction = the returns + the revenue.

[7] *L'Ami des Hommes*, pp. 169–70.

[8] In the *Analyse*, p. 155 above.

might be able to earn net profits during the course of their leases if
(for example) there was a rise in the price of produce; but these extra
gains were assumed to crystallize out into rents when the leases
came up for renewal, and the Physiocrats generally denied that the
normal income of the agricultural entrepreneur contained anything
really resembling our modern category of 'pure' or 'net' profit.[1] In
the seventh chapter of the *Rural Philosophy*, however, Quesnay
recognizes that the normal income of the agricultural entrepreneur
includes a 'reward due for the trouble, work, and risks of his enterprise'.[2] So far, he says, in discussing the farmer's returns he has
abstracted from this reward, the reason being that it is mixed up in
the expenditure of the farmer's annual advances and in the product
of the live-stock which he keeps for profit as a sort of accessory or
side-line to his main business, that of the cultivation of corn.
Quesnay's idea seems to be that the product yielded by this live-stock
returns to the farmer the costs of the fodder required by all the
animals on his farm, *including that required by his working horses.*
Thus although an item for 'fodder for horses' will appear in the
annual advances which are refunded to him out of the proceeds of
the harvest, he will in effect already have been compensated for this
item out of another account—that of the live-stock he keeps for
profit. Thus this amount remains with him, and represents the
'reward due for his personal employment'.[3] Quesnay's language
suggests that he regarded this reward as a sort of superior wage-of-
management-plus-payment-for-risk-bearing rather than as a 'net
profit' in the modern sense: he could hardly have admitted the
existence of a truly 'net' element in the normal income of the farmer
without driving a large hole through basic Physiocratic theory and
policy. It is interesting to note, however, that Quesnay visualizes
the reward as varying with the number of 'ploughs'[4] of land employed
by the farmer: a man with two ploughs of land gets twice as much
reward as a man with one. Since the 'trouble, work, and risks' of a
farmer with two ploughs of land are unlikely to be twice as great as
those of a farmer with one, we may perhaps regard this as Quesnay's
nearest approach to the modern concept of net profit on capital.
In the average case where two ploughs of land are assumed to be
employed, Quesnay estimates the reward at 1200 livres per farmer,
which includes living costs of 600. The normal living costs of the
productive class as a whole have already been taken account of
in the annual reproduction, but strictly speaking the surplus of
reward over living costs should be matched by a corresponding
increase in the annual reproduction, since all incomes in the world

---

[1] This question is dealt with in more detail in the second essay below, pp. 297 ff.
[2] *Philosophie Rurale*, Vol. I, p. 313.
[3] Ibid.   [4] *Charrues*. See above, p. 131, note (2).

of the *Tableau* are assumed to be fully spent in one way or another during the course of the year. But Quesnay abstracts from this surplus in the *Tableau*,[1] either because he feels that its inclusion would complicate its mechanism unduly[2] or because he does not wish to meddle further with such dangerous thoughts; and I shall follow his example in the remainder of this essay.

We are now in a position to explain the final formula of the *Tableau* worked out by Quesnay in the *Analysis*, to solve the problem of where the sterile class gets its own manufactured goods from, and to give a complete picture of the process of circulation shown in the *Tableau* in both real and money terms.

The general form assumed by the *Tableau* in the *Analysis* is as follows:

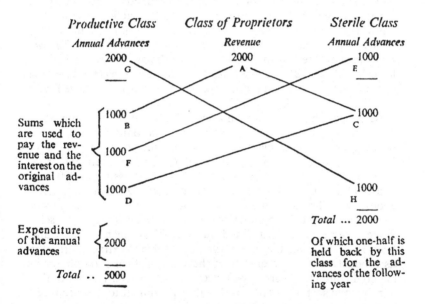

In this extremely ingenious formula, Quesnay managed at last to include the raw materials transaction and the payment of the farmers' interest in the *Tableau* itself. The thing is perfectly comprehensible so far as it goes. AB represents the purchase of 1000 food by the

---

[1] He includes the reward, however, in the striking calculation of the total reproduction and expenditure which follows this discussion—a calculation which more than any other in the whole of Quesnay's work reveals him as the great master of conjectural statistics which he was.

[2] Its inclusion would, of course, cause a change in inter-sectoral trade, since one-half of the reward, in accordance with the normal Physiocratic assumptions, would be spent with the sterile class.

proprietors from the productive class, and AC the purchase of 1000 manufactured goods by the proprietors from the sterile class: these two transactions provide the proprietors with the food and manufactured goods they require. EF represents the purchase of 1000 raw materials by the sterile class from the productive class; and CD the purchase of 1000 food by the sterile class from the productive class: these two transactions provide the sterile class with the raw materials and food it requires. GH represents the purchase of 1000 manufactured goods by the productive class from the sterile class: this transaction provides the productive class with the manufactured goods it requires. The sums at B, F, and D represent the receipts of the productive class from its sales to the proprietors and the sterile class; the sums at C and H represent the receipts of the sterile class from its sales to the proprietors and the productive class. The total receipts of the productive class from these transactions enable it to pay the revenue and obtain the interest; the total receipts of the sterile class enable it to recoup its costs. This is all that the *Tableau* really tells us: there are a number of other things, however, which we have to tell the *Tableau* if we are to obtain a complete idea of the process of circulation, and it is here that the interpreters have found their happy hunting-ground.

Before we deal with this, however, let us dispose of the great problem which has worried everyone from Baudeau onwards— where does the sterile class get its own manufactured goods from? If we assume, as would appear from the *Tableau* itself and from Quesnay's running commentary, that the sterile class buys 1000 food and 1000 raw materials, uses them up in making 2000 manufactured goods, and sells the whole of this output to the other classes, from where does it get the manufactured goods which it requires itself? Some commentators (e.g. Baudeau, and following him Marx and Beer) have suggested that the sterile class is able to extract a price for its products which is higher than the value of their food-plus-raw-material content. Others have suggested that the sterile class is able to produce a sort of 'net product' of its own, similar to that produced by the productive class. Neither of these explanations will wash, however: the first runs so counter to the assumption of free competition on which the *Tableau* is based, and the second runs so counter to the basic doctrine of exclusive productivity, as to make it inconceivable that Quesnay should in fact have adopted either of them.

The solution becomes very simple if we remember (a) that although Quesnay in the *Analysis* assumes a closed economy,[1] the economy is not in actual fact closed, and its trade is largely conducted by the sterile class; and (b) that the number of people in the sterile class is

---

[1] Above, p. 162.

one-half that in the productive class, so that the total personal consumption of the sterile class must be one-half that of the productive class.[1] Now the total personal consumption of the productive class is 1000 food and 1000 manufactured goods: the total personal consumption of the sterile class must therefore be 500 food and 500 manufactured goods. Thus, although the sterile class appears on the face of the *Tableau* to have 500 too little manufactured goods, it is clear that *it has 500 too much food*. The solution to the problem now becomes fairly obvious: the 1000 'food' purchased by the sterile class actually consists of 500 food for the personal consumption of the sterile class and 500 food (and other produce) which the sterile class exchanges abroad for foreign manufactured goods.[2] The necessary exchanges may of course be made in a number of different ways: one simple way, which seems reasonably consistent with the relevant texts, is incorporated in the complete account of the circulatory process which now follows.

In this account we assume that the total annual reproduction is 6000,[3] and that at the beginning of the circulatory process it is in the hands of the productive class in the following form: 1000 interest goods; 1000 raw materials for sale to the sterile class; 500 food and 500 produce for export for sale to the sterile class; 1000 food for sale to the proprietors; 1000 food for consumption *in natura* within the productive class; and 1000 fodder for the horses. We assume that the total money stock is 2000, that half of this is in the hands of the sterile class and half in the hands of the productive class, and that the process begins with the sale of the 1000 raw materials by the productive class to the sterile class.[4]

---

[1] See above, p. 277.

[2] Some such notion is surely implied in the *Explication* (above, pp. 129–30), in *L'Ami des Hommes* (p. 186), and in the *Philosophie Rurale* (Vol. I, p. 332).

[3] 6000 instead of the usual 5000, because we are bringing fodder for the horses back into the picture. There is no merit whatever in abstracting from it.

[4] A problem is involved here over which much ink has been spilt. Quesnay and Mirabeau state in a dozen places that the money stock is equal to the revenue (i.e., in this case, 2000); and Quesnay makes it clear in the *Analyse* (above, pp. 152 and 158) that the sterile class begins the process with its annual advances of 1000 in its hands in the form of money. This naturally implies that the other 1000 of the money stock is in the hands of the productive class, since the proprietors are assumed to possess nothing at the beginning of the process except their claim to 2000 revenue. A number of commentators have argued that under these circumstances the total money stock must in fact be 3000, with 2000 of this in the hands of the productive class, since the process must start with the payment of the revenue of 2000 by the productive class to the proprietors and its distribution by the latter between the productive class and the sterile class. But does the process really have to start with these transactions? Quesnay certainly says in the *Analyse* (above, p. 156) that the total reproduction is shared '*d'abord*' between the productive class and the proprietors; but he also uses the word '*d'abord*' in connection with the raw materials transaction (above, p. 152).

At the beginning, then, the holdings of the three classes are as follows:

Productive Class	Class of Proprietors	Sterile Class
1. 1000 money	Claim to 2000 revenue	1000 money
1000 interest goods		
1000 raw materials		
(for sterile class)		
⎰ 500 food and		
⎱ 500 produce for export		
(for sterile class)		
1000 food		
(for proprietors)		
1000 food		
(for productive class)		
1000 fodder		

The sterile class now buys 1000 raw materials from the productive class, so that the holdings become:

Productive Class	Class of Proprietors	Sterile Class
2. 2000 money	Claim to 2000 revenue	1000 raw materials
1000 interest goods		
⎰ 500 food and		
⎱ 500 produce for export		
(for sterile class)		
1000 food		
(for proprietors)		
1000 food		
(for productive class)		
1000 fodder		

The productive class pays 2000 money to the proprietors for the revenue, and the sterile class works up its 1000 raw materials into 2000 manufactured goods, so that the position becomes:

Productive Class	Class of Proprietors	Sterile Class
3. 1000 interest goods	2000 money	2000 mfd. goods
⎰ 500 food and		
⎱ 500 produce for export		
(for sterile class)		

I see no reason at all why we should not assume that the process starts with the raw materials transaction, in which case the thing can be made to work perfectly well with only 2000 of money. This does not contradict the Physiocratic assumption of the 'dependence' of the sterile class: the real essence of this 'dependence', as I have explained on pp. 276–7 above, consists in the fact that the size of the sterile class's annual product is determined by the total expenditure of the two other classes on manufactured goods. The matter is of much less importance than the attention paid to it would seem to warrant, since (as Quesnay was well aware) the effectiveness of the money stock depends not only on its size but also on its velocity of circulation. I suppose, however, that there is some merit in trying to make our account of the process conform as far as possible to Quesnay's own assumptions.

1000 food
  (for proprietors)
1000 food
  (for productive class)
1000 fodder

The prerequisites of the main inter-sectoral exchanges are now completed, and these exchanges themselves begin with the purchase by the proprietors of 1000 food from the productive class and 1000 manufactured goods from the sterile class. The situation now becomes:

Productive Class	Class of Proprietors	Sterile Class
4. 1000 money	1000 food	1000 money
1000 interest goods	1000 mfd. goods.	1000 mfd. goods
$\begin{cases} 500 \text{ food and} \\ 500 \text{ produce for export} \end{cases}$		
(for sterile class)		
1000 food		
(for productive class)		
1000 fodder		

The sterile class now buys the 500 food and 500 produce for export from the productive class, so that we then have:

Productive Class	Class of Proprietors	Sterile Class
5. 2000 money	1000 food	1000 mfd. goods
1000 interest goods	1000 mfd. goods	500 food
1000 food		500 produce for export
(for productive class)		
1000 fodder		

The sterile class now exchanges its 500 produce for export, by means of overseas trade, for 500 manufactured goods of foreign origin, so that the holdings become:[1]

Productive Class	Class of Proprietors	Sterile Class
6. 2000 money	1000 food	1500 mfd. goods
1000 interest goods	1000 mfd. goods	500 food
1000 food		
(for productive class)		
1000 fodder		

[1] In actual fact the 500 imported manufactured goods would probably be of a luxury character, and thus would be sold to the proprietors, instead of being consumed by the sterile class and the productive class as my scheme implies. This point could be dealt with easily enough by assuming that at stage 2 the sterile class buys, say, only 500 raw materials instead of 1000, spending the remaining 500 of its 1000 money on produce for export which it forthwith exchanges for foreign manufactured goods. The latter would then be sold to the proprietors (along with 500 of the sterile class's own manufactured goods) at stage 4. Alternatively, it could be assumed that one-half of the raw materials purchased by the sterile class at stage 2 is exported in exchange for foreign manufactures. But the consequential adjustments in the items and transactions would make the model unnecessarily complex: such a degree of refinement is hardly necessary.

Productive activity now begins in the productive class. To explain what happens it is useful at this stage to divide the productive class into entrepreneurs and wage-earners. The entrepreneurs hire the wage-earners and pay them their annual wages of 2000, half in the form of money and half in the form of food.[1] The position now becomes:

Productive Class		Class of Proprietors	Sterile Class
Wage-earners	*Entrepreneurs*		
7. 1000 money	1000 money	1000 food	1500 mfd. goods
1000 food	1000 interest goods	1000 mfd. goods	500 food
	1000 fodder		

The wage-earners of the productive class now buy 1000 manufactured goods from the sterile class, bringing the position to:

Productive Class		Class of Proprietors	Sterile Class
Wage-earners	*Entrepreneurs*		
8. 1000 food	1000 money	1000 food	1000 money
1000 mfd. goods	1000 interest goods	1000 mfd. goods	500 food
	1000 fodder		500 mfd. goods

As production proceeds in the productive class, the non-monetary holdings of the different classes are consumed. The wage-earners of the productive class consume their 1000 food and 1000 manufactured goods. The entrepreneurs use their 1000 money to buy the 1000 interest goods from one another; employ these goods in the replacement and repair of their fixed capital, stocks, etc.; and feed the 1000 fodder to their horses. The proprietors consume their 1000 food and 1000 manufactured goods. The sterile class consumes its 500 food and 500 manufactured goods.[2] When the harvest appears, the position returns to that displayed at stage 1 above, and the whole process can take place over again. This scheme, I think, fulfils all the basic conditions of the *Tableau*, reduces the items abstracted from to a minimum, and is reasonably consistent with Quesnay's accounts of what actually happens.

[1] The assumption that half the wages is paid in the form of food accords with Quesnay's statement that 1000 food is consumed *in natura* within the productive class and thus does not 'enter into trade'. If, however, one wished to assume that the wages were paid entirely in money, 1000 of this money would simply be paid back to the entrepreneurs in return for 1000 food, so that the position would become identical with that shown in 7. As stated above, we are abstracting from the surplus of the farmers' reward over their living costs: the living costs themselves, we may conveniently assume, are included in the wages of 2000 paid to the wage-earners.

[2] Thus enabling it, after it has purchased 1000 raw materials at the beginning of the next round, to produce 2000 manufactured goods.

III

If the *Tableaux* of the first three editions and the *Analysis* were primarily designed to explain and display the situation in the state of bliss, most of the *Tableaux* in the *Friend of Mankind*, the *Rural Philosophy*, and the two *Economic Problems* were designed to illustrate the operation of causes leading to movements away from or towards this state of bliss. These causes were conceived to be largely due to changes in government policy, but it was also recognized that they could be due to changes in 'private' factors, notably tastes.[1] Let us begin by considering the Physiocrats' treatment of the effect of a change in tastes of a particular type.

Suppose, says Quesnay in the *Explanation*, that the proprietors decided to indulge in luxury in the way of ornamentation, and began to spend more than half their revenue with the sterile class and less than half with the productive class: the immediate result, he argues, would be a reduction in the revenue, and if this change in tastes continued the nation would very soon be ruined.[2] This situation was illustrated by Mirabeau in the *Friend of Mankind* with the aid of the original zigzag formula, in the following way: Starting from the state of bliss, we assume that the proprietors suddenly decide to increase their expenditure on the products of the sterile class by one-fifth, and that the productive class and the sterile class follow their bad example. The productive class now sends three-fifths of its receipts to the sterile class, instead of one-half, and the sterile class sends two-fifths of its receipts to the productive class, instead of one-half. The *Tableau* then, as Mirabeau puts it, 'has lost its equilibrium',[3] and appears in the form in which it is reproduced on the following page.

The total receipts of the productive class from the inter-sectoral transactions have been reduced from 2000 to 1684, and the revenue is naturally reduced to the same amount. The receipts of the sterile class, however, have been increased from 2000 to 2211.

But, it might be asked, does not the increase in the sterile class's receipts go quite a way towards compensating for the bad welfare effects of the reduction in the productive class's receipts? The treatment of this objection in the *Rural Philosophy* is a good example of the way in which the Physiocrats dealt with such problems of welfare. It is admitted that the receipts of the sterile class will rise substantially *in the first year*. But what about the subsequent years? In the second year the revenue will be smaller, so that the amount spent by the proprietors with the sterile class, and therefore the receipts of the

---

[1] Cf. the classification given by Mirabeau in *L'Ami des Hommes*, pp. 231–2.

[2] Above, pp. 128–9.

[3] *L'Ami des Hommes*, p. 232. The relevant *Tableau* will be found facing p. 231. Cf. the treatment of the same problem in the *Philosophie Rurale*, in terms of the *précis* (Vol. III, pp. 29 ff.).

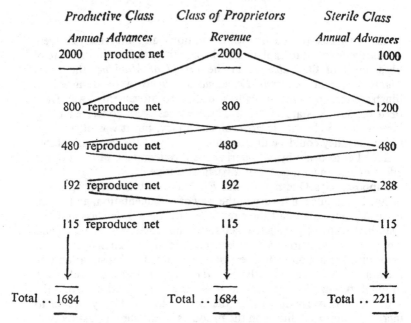

Productive Class	Class of Proprietors	Sterile Class
Annual Advances	Revenue	Annual Advances
2000 produce net	2000	1000
800 reproduce net	800	1200
480 reproduce net	480	480
192 reproduce net	192	288
115 reproduce net	115	115
Total .. 1684	Total .. 1684	Total .. 2211

latter class, will be reduced as compared with the first year.[1] Eventually, as the process continues, the receipts of the sterile class will fall back to their level in the state of bliss and then begin to decline below this level. From a static point of view, looking at the first year only, it would appear that the gains of the sterile class should to some extent offset the losses of the productive class. From a dynamic point of view, however, looking at the process as it continues over several years, everyone will lose; and nothing can arrest the process of decline, other things being equal, except an increase in the propensity to consume agricultural produce.[2] Arithmetically, all that is involved in the analysis of the position of the sterile class is the simple fact that if a sum rises from x per cent of a to y per cent of a, it will eventually drop below its original level if a continuously decreases. Economically, of course, much more than this is involved: nothing less, indeed, than the whole basic Physiocratic theory of the exclusive productivity of agriculture and the dependence of the sterile class on the expenditure of the other two classes (particularly that of the proprietors) and thus on the size of the revenue.[3]

[1] A *Tableau* is drawn to show the position in the second year (*Philosophie Rurale*, Vol. III, pp. 35–6).

[2] A '*Tableau inverse*' is drawn to show the effects of such an increase (*Philosophie Rurale*, Vol. II, pp. 45–7).

[3] Cf. Mirabeau, *L'Ami des Hommes*, p. 253: 'We see in the *Tableau* that nothing can move except through the revenue, that it is it which sets the whole circulation going.'

The 'public' as distinct from the 'private' causes of movements away from or towards the state of bliss were mainly sought by the Physiocrats in the fields of trade and taxation policy. If restrictions on trade in raw produce (both internal and external) were eased, it was assumed, the price of the produce and thus the size of the revenue would be increased, whereas if these restrictions were tightened up the reverse would happen.[1] Again, if the Exchequer increased the proportion of 'direct' taxes on the revenue to 'indirect' taxes on men, commodities, or consumption, the revenue would rise, whereas any move in the opposite direction would cause a decline in the revenue.[2] The data of the basic *Tableau* representing the state of bliss were selected on the assumption of the existence both of free trade and the single tax, and various *Tableaux* were constructed to show the departures from this optimum situation which would occur if these conditions did not in fact obtain. At bottom, of course, the purpose of these *Tableaux* was to show that the main reason for the failure of the French economy to reach the state of bliss depicted in the basic *Tableau* was the failure of the government to take the necessary steps to see that these conditions were fulfilled.

Perhaps the best illustration of the interesting techniques employed by the Physiocrats to analyse these cases is provided by Quesnay's *First Economic Problem*, which deals with the effects of a rise in the price of produce brought about by an assumed restoration of free trade.[3] The problem is framed at the outset in welfare terms: would the advantage to sellers caused by the rise in prices outweigh the disadvantage to buyers?[4] Quesnay starts with a situation in which the ratio of the revenue to the productive class's annual advances is assumed to be much lower than in the basic *Tableau*, and the productive class's annual advances are assumed to be burdened with heavy indirect taxes. He now assumes that the price of produce rises by one-sixth above its present level as a result of the restoration of free trade, and traces out its economic effects, arriving eventually at a *Tableau* which shows that the receipts of all three classes have substantially increased.[5] In money terms all classes are better off, but, as Quesnay recognizes,[6] the *Tableau* tells us nothing about what has happened in real terms. The full solution of the welfare problem thus involves a further calculation, in which Quesnay places side by side the money expenditure of the different classes and the 'measures' of

[1] The reasons for the assumption that free trade would lead to a rise in the price of French produce are set out in Quesnay's early Encyclopedia articles.

[2] 'Indirect' taxes, in the Physiocrats' terminology, are all taxes other than those laid directly on the net product of the land.

[3] Translated above, pp. 168 ff. Similar problems are dealt with in terms of the zigzag in *L'Ami des Hommes* and in terms of the *précis* in the *Philosophie Rurale*.

[4] Above, p. 168.   [5] Above, p. 173.

[6] Above, pp. 174.

K

real product which each can purchase. The general conclusion reached is that the proprietors and the sterile class will be better off in real terms as a result of the price rise, and that the productive class will be no worse off (and will, indeed, be better off during the term of its leases, until its extra gains crystallize out into rents).

Finally, let us take a less arduous illustration of the use of the *Tableau* in the analysis of the 'disorganization' caused by a taxation policy different from that advocated by the Physiocrats. Starting from the state of bliss, we assume that 50 is levied in the form of 'personal taxes', one-half on the agents of the productive class and one-half on the agents of the sterile class. We may illustrate this case, as was done in the *Rural Philosophy*, with a *Tableau* of the simple *précis* type:[1]

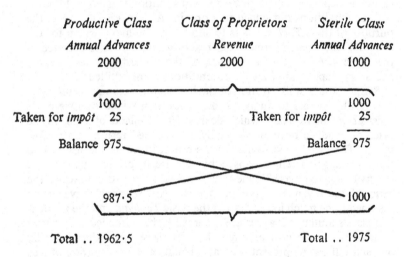

	Productive Class	*Class of Proprietors*	*Sterile Class*
	Annual Advances	*Revenue*	*Annual Advances*
	2000	2000	1000

```
              1000                                    1000
Taken for impôt   25            Taken for impôt       25
          ──────                                  ──────
    Balance 975                            Balance  975

           987·5                                   1000

   Total .. 1962·5                          Total .. 1975
```

The key assumption here is that the productive class's annual advances remain for the time being at 2000, so that its purchases from the sterile class remain at 1000. The taxes, however, in effect abstract 25 from the sterile class's receipts from the proprietors, reducing them to 975. The total product of the sterile class is thus reduced to 1975, so that its annual advances will be reduced to one-half of this sum, i.e. 987·5. (Here, it will be observed, two successive periods are in effect telescoped into one *Tableau*, contrary to the usual Physiocratic practice.) The total annual reproduction is now no longer 5000, but 4950, made up as follows:

[1] *Philosophie Rurale*, Vol. II, pp. 270–1. Similar problems are analysed in *L'Ami des Hommes* in terms of the zigzag, and in the *Second Problème Economique* in terms of the *formule*.

The advances of the productive class	2000
The portion of the revenue (net of taxes) which passes directly to the productive class	975
The total of the sums sent back to the productive class by the sterile class (as shown in the *Tableau*)	987·5
The sum received by the productive class when the sterile class uses its annual advances to buy raw materials (not shown in the *Tableau*)	987·5
Total	4950

Since the returns of the productive class are still 3000, this leaves only 1950, instead of 2000, for the revenue. If the productive class is obliged, as it normally will be, to pay the full 2000 to the proprietors, it will have to reduce its annual advances by 50 in the succeeding period, so that the revenue reproduced (assuming a continuance of the same ratio between annual advances and revenue) will also be reduced by 50.

We have now considered the way in which the Physiocrats used the zigzag, the 'formula' and the *précis* to analyse the three main types of 'disorganization' with which they concerned themselves. Once the mechanism of the basic *Tableau* is understood, there is no real difficulty in understanding the *Tableaux* used to analyse the 'disorganization'. The problem of interpretation therefore reduces itself to the problem of the connection between the *Tableau*-type of analysis and certain methods of analysis which have been developed in our own times.

The Physiocrats' methods of dealing with the different types of 'disorganization', as I have described them above, may appear to smack somewhat of special pleading. And it is indeed true that the *Tableau* was mainly used by Quesnay and Mirabeau to provide a sort of arithmetical confirmation of the validity of the leading Physiocratic battle-cries. Down with luxury in the way of ornamentation!— the *Tableau* shows the dreadful things which happen when the propensity to consume manufactured luxuries increases. Down with restrictions on trade!—the *Tableau* shows the increase in welfare which will result from the abolition of these restrictions and the consequential rise in prices. Down with 'indirect' taxes!—the *Tableau* shows that they are borne by the revenue anyway, so why not lay all taxes directly on the revenue and save the unpleasant consequences which the 'indirect' form of imposition brings in its train? The

Tableau was certainly designed by Quesnay with these policy proposals uppermost in his mind, and it cannot be properly understood
unless its connection with these policy proposals is fully appreciated.
But the *general approach* to the analysis of economic phenomena
which the *Tableau* reflects and embodies is of much wider significance;
it can obviously be employed in other contexts, where the policy
proposals involved, and also the basic theoretical assumptions, are
quite different from those of the Physiocrats.[1] It is these general
aspects of the *Tableau*-type of analysis, naturally enough, which are
of most interest to present-day economists, and we must therefore
conclude this essay on the *Tableau* with a brief study of four different
parallels which have recently been drawn between the *Tableau* and
certain modern methods of analysis.

The first parallel is that between the *Tableau* and the Walrasian
general equilibrium system. The *Tableau*, says Schumpeter, 'was the
first method ever devised in order to convey an *explicit* conception
of the nature of economic equilibrium'.[2] There is an important sense
in which this is true: Quesnay did, after all, visualize the economic
process as a whole, each part being conceived as dependent upon and
interconnected with every other part, with the different parts being
held together by means of mutual exchanges. But the parallel should
not be carried too far. For, in the first place, Quesnay did not say
merely that everything in the economic universe depends upon everything else: he also broke the chain of causes at a particular point,
isolating a certain set of factors which he regarded as exercising a
primary determining influence on the total situation. Most present-
day economists, of course, would want to say that he broke the chain
at the wrong point,[3] and many would want to say that there was
really no need for him to break it anywhere. The fact remains,
however, that he *did* break it, and this must be regarded as an
important qualification of the parallel which we are now considering.
In the second place, the 'equilibrium' depicted in the basic *Tableau*
is an 'equilibrium' of a rather special kind. The system is certainly
conceived to be 'in equilibrium' in the sense that the different
branches of the economy support one another and get just what they
need from one another by means of exchange, in such a way that at
the end of the year the whole process can be exactly repeated. But the
'equilibrium' depicted in the *Tableau* is hardly stable: at the best it is
neutral, and at the worst it is unstable. Quesnay did not imagine that

---

[1] The most obvious example, of course, is provided by Marx's famous reproduction schemes, which seem to have owed their origin to Marx's study of
the *Analyse*.

[2] *History of Economic Analysis*, p. 242.

[3] It is the 'wrong' point today, certainly; but it may well have been the 'right'
point in France in the middle of the nineteenth century.

there were any forces inherent in the system which would pull it back towards this 'equilibrium' situation if it should happen to depart from it: on the contrary, the whole purpose of the exercise was to show that this situation could be reached only as the result of certain specific government policies and the direction of private expenditure along certain specific lines, and that once it had been reached the slightest relaxation of these conditions would cause at the best the re-establishment of 'equilibrium' at a lower level of output, and at the worst (and more usually) a progressive decline in output and productivity.

The second parallel is that between the general approach in the *Tableau* and the modern 'Keynesian' approach. Once again there is an important element of truth in this parallel: the general 'equilibrium' of which I have just spoken was certainly conceived as an equilibrium of economic aggregates, much in the Keynesian manner.[1] It is also true that Quesnay concerned himself greatly with the reductions in output which were associated with the different types of 'disorganization', although before we draw any over-hasty Keynesian parallels here we should remember (a) that the main types of 'disorganization' were conceived as being caused by faulty government policy and the improper direction of expenditure by the proprietors rather than by any inherent defect in the economic mechanism itself; and (b) that the main emphasis was usually placed on reductions in ouput rather than on reductions in employment.[2] The analogy sometimes drawn between the mechanism disclosed in the zigzag and the Keynesian multiplier-type of analysis is to my mind rather formal: the zigzag certainly shows in an impressive way that the expenditure of one man's income generates income for another man, which in turn generates income for another, and so on, but the important point is surely that in spite of this 'multiplier' effect the income of the nation as a whole (and of each class in it) is conceived, at any rate in the state of bliss, to remain precisely the same from year to year. More striking, I think, are the analogies which can be drawn between the Keynesian and Physiocratic analyses of the effects of hoarding, and between the Keynesian concept of under-employment equilibrium and the Physiocratic notion that the process of decline may stop at a 'fixed point' and remain at that point for some time in the absence of 'external shocks'.[3]

The third parallel is that between the general method of analysis of the Physiocrats, as reflected in the *Tableau*, and the modern 'dynamic,

---

[1] Cf. Schumpeter, op. cit., p. 243.

[2] In the latter respect, speaking very broadly, the Physiocratic analysis was essentially long-term: population was simply conceived to adjust itself to alterations in output.

[3] See the *Philosophie Rurale*, Vol. II, pp. 141 ff.

methods of analysis. The basic *Tableau*, of course, represented a 'static' situation, in the sense that it depicted a system with a circular flow; but the *Tableau*-type of analysis was mainly used in connection with an essentially 'dynamic' problem—that of the movement of the system as a whole away from or towards the state of bliss represented in the basic *Tableau*. From this point of view, it is quite correct to visualize the *Tableau*-type of analysis as the first deliberate attempt ever made to construct a dynamic welfare economics. Essentially, however, if we must employ modern labels, the *general method* used in the analysis of this 'dynamic' problem was closer to that of comparative statics, or to that of the Robertsonian period analysis, than to any of the methods which most modern economists would want to call truly 'dynamic'. The range of the *Tableau* itself is in fact limited to the analysis of the effects of a once-over change occurring in a given year in a given situation. For example, if the proprietors' propensity to consume manufactured goods increases in year 2 as compared with year 1, we can draw up a *Tableau* which will show how the situation at the end of year 2 differs from that at the end of year 1. If in year 3 the proprietors' propensity to consume manufactured goods still remains at its year 2 level, we have to draw up another *Tableau* which will show how the situation at the end of year 3 differs from that at the end of year 2. All we are really doing here is to assume that the once-over change which we analysed in relation to year 2 is repeated in year 3. We can, of course, if we want to, make generalizations about the nature and direction of the alterations in the general situation which will occur over a period of years as a result of these repeated changes, but if we do so we will have arrived at them by a general method of analysis which seems to me to be essentially 'static' rather than 'dynamic' in character. There is one important qualification to be made here, however: with the Physiocrats this 'static' method of analysis was closely associated with, and largely inspired by, a general (semi-'materialist') theory of socioeconomic development, which some modern economists would want to call 'dynamic' in character.

The fourth and last parallel is that between the *Tableau* and the Leontief input-output system. It is easy enough to arrange the data of the basic *Tableau* in the form of a three-industry closed Leontief model, as follows:[1]

---

[1] This is a slightly modified version of the table given by A. Phillips, op. cit., p. 141. The main figures relate to the money values of input and output, but I have put in brackets the real constituents of each item in order to facilitate comparison with the accounts of the basic *Tableaux* given above. The model does not of course show the transaction in which the sterile class uses its 500 'produce for export' to buy foreign manufactured goods; and fodder is once again abstracted from.

PRODUCING 'INDUSTRY'	PURCHASING 'INDUSTRY'			Total Production
	I Productive Class	II Class of Proprietors	III Sterile Class	
I. Productive Class	2000 (1000 food; 1000 interest goods)	1000 (food)	2000 (1000 raw materials; 500 food; 500 produce for export)	5000
II. Class of Proprietors	2000 (rental services)	0	0	2000
III. Sterile Class	1000 (manufactured goods)	1000 (manufactured goods)	0	2000
Total Purchases	5000	2000	2000	9000

Quesnay would certainly have raised his eyebrows at this model, which effectively conceals the difference between the surplus-producing capacity of the productive class and that of the sterile class, and obliges us to assume that the proprietors produce 'rental services' in return for their revenue; but there is no doubt that the model does provide an effective way of explaining the actual mechanism of the *Tableau* to economists who are unfamiliar with Physiocratic ways of thought. I doubt, however, whether the parallel is very significant in itself: the Physiocratic aggregates, after all, can readily be translated into the terms of *any* other model which deals with the equilibrium of similar aggregates, provided that the appropriate modifications are made in the basic theoretical assumptions.[1]

One general point of some importance does, however, emerge from this comparison with the Leontief system. The particular feature of the *Tableau* which makes the comparison possible is the fact that Quesnay *gave specific values* to his aggregates—values which were by no means arbitrary, but based on a careful study of such statistics as were then available of national income, sector incomes, productivity, population, etc. The *Tableau* is far from being the ideal and airy thing which it is sometimes made out to be: on the contrary, it is one of the most striking examples in the whole history of economic thought of

[1] Cf., for example, the well-known comparison between the reproduction schemes of Quesnay, Marx, and Keynes made by Shigeto Tsuru in his appendix to Sweezy's *Theory of Capitalist Development*.

the achievement of a harmonious unity between abstract theory and concrete investigation.[1] And if we add that it also embodied a fairly advanced understanding of the key causal significance of relations between socio-economic groups, it should become clear that it is not only economic antiquarians who can benefit from its study.

[1] It is interesting that Leontief singled out this point for emphasis in his speech at the Quesnay bi-centenary celebrations at the Sorbonne in June 1958. (See *Bi-centenaire du 'Tableau Economique' de François Quesnay*, Paris, 1958, p. 38.)

II

THE PHYSIOCRATIC CONCEPT
OF PROFIT[1]

The most significant theoretical advance which Adam Smith made over the work of his predecessors was undoubtedly his inclusion of profit on capital as a constituent element in the supply price of commodities. Before Smith, speaking very broadly, 'profit' had usually been regarded either as a mere synonym for 'gain', or as a sort of superior wage, or as a surplus over cost whose level varied (as Steuart put it) 'according to circumstances'.[2] With one bold stroke Smith cut through the difficulties involved in these earlier approaches to the problem. He postulated profit as the income of the class of employers of labour—the third of 'the three great, original and constituent orders of every civilized society';[3] he argued that competition would tend to reduce this profit to 'an ordinary or average rate' on the capital employed;[4] and he included profit at this 'natural' rate along with wages and rent (at *their* 'natural' rates) in the supply price of commodities.[5] What was more, he was careful to distinguish profit from wages of management,[6] and to emphasize that after sufficient had been set aside as a compensation for 'the occasional losses to which every employment of stock is exposed' and for payment of interest to the lender (if any), there still normally remained a 'neat or clear' surplus, out of which new capital could be accumulated.[7] Profit, in other words, was not only a constituent part of the supply price of commodities: it also constituted, on an aggregative view, an important part of the 'net revenue' of society.

The present essay discusses the contribution made by the French Physiocrats to the development of this Classical concept of profit. The main problem here revolves around an apparent contradiction in the work of the Physiocrats which has never been properly resolved and which can be stated as follows: The Physiocrats stoutly maintained not only the plausible thesis that land rent was an income in the nature of a surplus, but also the much less plausible thesis that

[1] This essay is an amended version of an article published in *Economica*, February 1959. I am grateful to the editors of *Economica* for their permission to reproduce it in this volume.
[2] Steuart, *Political Oeconomy* (1767), Vol. I, p. 182.
[3] *Wealth of Nations* (Cannan edn.), Vol. I, p. 248.
[4] Ibid., p. 57. [5] Ibid., pp. 57–8.
[6] Ibid., pp. 50–1. [7] Ibid., pp. 97–9.

land rent was the *only* income in the nature of a surplus, all other returns to the agents of production being merely compensation for costs.[1] Yet at the same time their theoretical system can properly be said to have been a 'capitalist' system,[2] in the sense that its whole *raison d'être* was the advocacy of a state of affairs in which economic activity, particularly in agriculture, would be conducted by wealthy entrepreneurs motivated by a desire for profit. References to the large surpluses over cost obtainable by entrepreneurs under certain circumstances abound in the Physiocratic literature, from the first days of the school to the last. How then, if at all, can these two aspects of the Physiocratic system be reconciled? In what follows it will not be denied that in a certain sense the contradiction was a real one. It will be suggested, however, that in the work of the founders of the school (Quesnay and Mirabeau) the contradiction remained latent owing to their adoption of certain assumptions concerning the nature and sources of profit; that the contradiction emerged to the surface only when economic developments rendered these assumptions implausible; and that the later history of Physiocratic theory consisted largely of attempts to solve the contradiction, in the course of which substantial advances towards the Classical concept of profit were made.

II

Let us consider first the place which the 'profit' of the agricultural entrepreneur occupied in Quesnay's theoretical system. The best starting-point here is his *Analysis* of the *Tableau Economique*. In the *Analysis*, as we have seen, the nation is divided into the usual three socio-economic classes: the productive class (those engaged in agriculture, including both entrepreneurs and wage-earners); the class of proprietors (the landlords, sovereign, and clergy, who receive the net product in the form of rent, taxes, and tithes respectively); and the sterile class (those engaged in non-agricultural employments, including both entrepreneurs and wage-earners).[3] The nation in question is assumed to be one in which the main reforms advocated by the Physiocrats have been adopted, namely, the universal application of large-scale capitalist agriculture; the establishment of free trade in corn, which ensures the 'proper price' for agricultural produce; the institution of the single tax, which frees the agricultural entrepreneur from tax burdens; and the complete fulfilment by the class of proprietors of their duty to provide the advances necessary for the improvement of their land, the development of transport facilities, etc.[4] Under these conditions, it is assumed that the produc-

---

[1] Cf. Schumpeter, *History of Economic Analysis*, p. 238.
[2] Cf. Weulersse, II, p. 684.   [3] Above, pp. 150–1.
[4] Above, pp. 151, 153, and 160.

tive class, employing original advances of 10 and annual advances of 2, will produce a harvest of 5. This harvest will be sufficient, after setting aside 2 for the replacement of the annual advances and 1 for interest on the original advances, to yield a net product or net revenue of 2 to the class of proprietors. On the basis of these assumptions, as we have seen, the *Tableau* shows how the flow of income between the three classes will result in the needs of each being satisfied. In the particular case analysed by Quesnay, agriculture, wealth, and population remain in the same state without increase or decline (i.e. net investment is zero); but he hastens to add that a different set of data will produce a different result.[1]

Now in all this there is no specific mention of the 'profit' of the agricultural entrepreneur. How then does this 'profit' fit into Quesnay's theoretical scheme? It is at least conceivable, of course, that Quesnay simply forgot about the existence of this type of income when writing his *Analysis*, or that he regarded it as quantitatively insignificant; but in view of the great emphasis laid on agricultural profit in Quesnay's work taken as a whole (and particularly in his early Encyclopedia articles) this seems hardly likely. There are therefore four possibilities: (1) that the farmer's profit is included in the net product; (2) that it is included in the interest received by the farmer on his original advances; (3) that under the conditions postulated in the *Analysis* no profit would in fact be earned by the farmers; or (4) that it is included in the farmer's annual returns along with the ordinary costs of cultivation.

The first possibility might at first sight hardly seem worth while exploring, in view of the Physiocrats' very frequent and positive insistence on the fact that the net product consists *solely* of the income of the class of proprietors. Yet at least twice in Quesnay's early work, and (perhaps) once in his later work, this identification of the net product with the income of the class of proprietors breaks down, and the farmer's 'profit' is included, along with the landlord's rent, in the net product. The first occasion on which this occurs is in *Corn*, in connection with two arithmetical calculations to which I have already drawn attention in the previous essay.[2] Quesnay here begins by discussing what he calls the 'state of the large-scale cultivation of corn' which exists in certain northern provinces of France. The net product per *arpent* of land cultivated in this manner is estimated by Quesnay at 17 liv. 8s. Out of this sum the farmer must pay his rent, and 'he must also pay the *taille* out of this same sum, and find in it a gain to enable him to subsist'. So the 17 liv. 8s. is divided up as follows:[3]

---

[1] Above, p. 157.   [2] Above, p. 268.

[3] The arithmetic here is obviously shaky, but this does not affect the point at ssue.

For the proprietor	3/5, or 10	7	7	
For the *taille*	1/5, or 3	9	6	17 liv. 8s.
For the farmer	1/5, or 5	9	6	

Quesnay adds in a footnote that he is not basing his calculation on the actual level of the *taille*, but rather assuming an assessment which 'leaves some profit for the farmer and a revenue for the proprietor'.[1] In this context, then, the net product is evidently being defined so as to include not only the landlord's rent and the *taille*, but also a 'profit' for the farmer.

The second occasion where the identification breaks down is in the *Extract from the Royal Economic Maxims of M. de Sully* included by Quesnay in the 'second edition' of the *Tableau*. The eighth maxim reads as follows: '8. That the advances of the farmers are sufficient to enable the expenses of cultivation to reproduce at least 100 per cent; for if the advances are not sufficient, the expenses of cultivation are proportionally higher and yield less net product'. To this maxim there is appended the following interesting note:

'In a kingdom of this kind the advances produced, on the average, apart from taxes, only about 20 per cent, which was distributed to the tithes, the proprietor, and to the farmer for his gain, the interest on his advances, and his risks. Thus there was a *deficit* of three-quarters in the net product.'[2] Here again the net product is clearly being defined so as to include certain rewards accruing to the farmer.

The third occasion, where the proper interpretation is rather more doubtful, is in the *Dialogue on the Work of Artisans*. There are two relevant passages. If there is a reduction in the wages cost of cultivation, says Quesnay in the first of these, then 'the profit due to the economies in expenditure on costs would naturally be devoted by the cultivators to expanding their operations, and this would increase the product and the revenue'.[3] In the second passage, which occurs a few pages later, Quesnay says:

'Thus you see that we have to divide the reproduction generated by the cultivator into two portions, namely, the portion which provides for his own subsistence, and the portion which is in excess of this subsistence. Whence it follows that if it is possible, without detrimentally affecting the total reproduction, to cut down on the first portion, the second will be correspondingly increased. For example, if we assume that the reproduction is 20, the cultivator's expenses 10, and the surplus 10, then if the expenses can be cut down to 8 the surplus will be 12.'[4]

[1] I.N.E.D., II, p. 463. Cf. the footnote on p. 464. The second of the two relevant calculations appears on p. 475.

[2] Above, p. 121.   [3] Above, pp. 221-2.   [4] Above, p. 227.

If one can legitimately identify the 'surplus' in the latter passage with the net product, then if the two passages quoted are read together it seems to follow that in Quesnay's view a reduction in the wages bill would allow the farmer to share in the net product.

Can it be said, then, on the basis of the passages I have quoted, that in Quesnay's view the farmer's profit was included in the net product? I do not think so. For one thing, the passages are very isolated: I have not been able to find any others of similar import in Quesnay's work. Then again, the first of the passages is very early; the second seems to occur in this particular version of the Maxims only;[1] and the interpretation of the third, as I have said, is rather doubtful. It seems better, as I have suggested in the previous essay,[2] to put down Quesnay's early inclusion of the farmer's 'gain' or 'profit' in the net product to the influence of Cantillon.

It might seem at first sight as if Quesnay could be rescued from the charge of inconsistency in the following manner: The two calculations in *Corn*, it might be argued, refer respectively (a) to a situation where profits are being earned by a relatively small group of agricultural entrepreneurs who have as it were stolen a march on their rivals in the introduction of certain technical innovations, and (b) to a situation where profits are earned by the farmers as a result of the higher and steadier price which the Physiocrats believed would result from the restoration of free trade in corn. And the third passage quoted above, it might be added, refers to a situation where profits are being earned by the farmers through economies in the agricultural wages bill. Now it would be perfectly reasonable for Quesnay to argue that profits of this character constituted a part of the net revenue of society at any given moment, while at the same time arguing that in the long run these profits must either disappear or crystallize out into rents for the proprietors. Thus, it might be concluded, it is not necessarily inconsistent to say in one place that profits of this character are included in the net product, and in another place, where a more long-period view is being taken, to say that they are not so included. And there is indeed evidence, which will be reviewed later in this essay, to suggest that Quesnay did in fact think of the problem of agricultural profit at least partly in such terms as these. Such an interpretation, however, seems a little strained in the light of the second passage quoted above, where none of the special circumstances just described are assumed to apply, and where nevertheless a compensation for the farmer's 'gain, the

---

[1] The reference to the division of the net product does not occur in the 'first edition'; and the version appearing in *Physiocratie*, significantly enough, divides the net product among the *dixme*, the *impôt*, and the proprietor, making no reference to the farmer (see above, p. 242).

[2] Above, p. 269.

interest on his advances, and his risks' is unequivocally included in the net product.

Consider, then, the second possibility mentioned above—that Quesnay conceived the 'profit' of the agricultural entrepreneurs to be included in the interest they received on their original advances. This possibility must, I think, be fairly definitely rejected. Quesnay was by no means the most consistent of writers, but the general impression one receives from his comments on the farmer's interest, taking them as a whole, is that he regarded it basically as the compensation for a cost incurred by the farmer. We meet the concept first in *Farmers*, where the following item is included in a list of the farmer's expenses:

'For the interest on the amount of expenditure employed in the purchase of horses, ploughs, carts, and other ground advances which wear out,[1] which, abstracting from live-stock, can be estimated at 3000 livres; thus the interest is at least.................. 300 livres'[2]

The concept was further clarified as time went on, but this association of the interest with 'advances which wear out' was fairly consistently maintained. In Quesnay's description in *Corn* of the 'state of small-scale cultivation of corn', for example, the proprietor who supplies oxen to the *métayer* is assumed to be entitled to collect interest at 10 per cent on the price of the oxen, 'by reason of the risks and the loss on the sale of these oxen when they are old and thin'.[3] In the early formulations of the *Tableau*, again, where the interest is analysed separately in order to avoid undue complications,[4] Quesnay makes it clear that the reason why the interest should amount to at least 10 per cent is that 'the products of agriculture are subject to disastrous accidents which, over a period of ten years, destroy at least the value of one year's harvest', and that 'these advances require a great deal of upkeep and renewal.'[5]

The most extended treatment which Quesnay ever gave to this matter is that in the *Analysis*. The interest on the original advances is no longer analysed separately but is formally included in the returns shown in the *Tableau*; and Quesnay gives the following explanation of 'why this interest is necessary':

'(1) The fund of wealth employed in cultivation which constitutes the original advances is subject from day to day to a wearing-away which demands continual repairs, absolutely necessary if this important fund is to remain intact and not to move progressively towards complete annihilation. . . .

---

[1] *Autres avances foncières qui périssent.* R.L.M.   [2] I.N.E.D., II, p. 443.
[3] I.N.E.D., II, p. 467.   [4] Above, p. 129.
[5] Above, p. 132.

(2) Cultivation is inseparable from a number of serious accidents which sometimes almost completely destroy the harvest; such are frost, hail, blight, floods, mortality among live-stock, etc., etc. If the cultivators did not have any fund in reserve, it would follow that after such accidents they would be unable to pay the proprietors and the sovereign, or unable to meet the expenses of their cultivation in the following year. . . .

The interest on the advances of the cultivators' enterprises ought therefore to be included in their *annual returns*. It enables them to face these serious accidents and the day-to-day maintenance of the wealth employed in cultivation, which requires to be constantly kept in repair.'[1]

In the light of this very explicit statement, which was repeated with an equal lack of ambiguity by Mirabeau,[2] the second possibility must, I think, be ruled out of court. It should be noted, however, that immediately following the passage just quoted Quesnay went on to develop his argument in a way which left a loophole for later Physiocrats who were anxious to include a net element in the farmer's interest. This is a point which can most suitably be left over until the next section of the present essay.

Before considering the third and fourth possibilities, let us briefly examine the main contexts in which Quesnay speaks specifically of the agricultural entrepreneur's profit and the circumstances in which it will in fact accrue to him. Three more or less separate cases can be distinguished:

1. Entrepreneurs who operate large-scale cultivation will normally earn higher profits than those who operate small-scale cultivation. 'There is . . . more profit', says Quesnay, 'for the *farmer* who carries on cultivation with horses than for the *métayer* who carries on cultivation with oxen'.[3] This is one of the basic themes of *Farmers*, and it is continued in *Corn*. 'It is true', writes Quesnay in the latter article, 'that a farmer who is limited to the employment of one plough cannot aspire to a considerable gain; it is only those who are wealthy enough to set up larger enterprises who can draw a high profit and improve the land to the maximum with the aid of the expenditure which they are in a position to undertake.'[4]

2. Entrepreneurs will profit if the price of their product rises (as a result, for example, of the establishment of free trade in corn) during the course of their leases. The ultimate benefit of this rise in

[1] Above, pp. 154-5.
[2] *Philosophie Rurale*, Vol. II, pp. 90-1. Cf. also Baudeau, in Daire, *Physiocrates*, Vol. II, p. 825.
[3] I.N.É.D., II, p. 434.
[4] Ibid., p. 482. Cf. Mirabeau, *Philosophie Rurale*, Vol. I, p. 34.

price will normally accrue to the proprietors in the form of higher rents, but the short-term benefits for the farmer will often be considerable and important:

'First, the farmers of landed property profit up to the renewal of their leases from the constant increase in the prices of products which occurs during the term of these leases. And this gain is most fruitful, most profitable, and most necessary in a nation whose agriculture is in need of extension and improvement. For farmers, if they are not oppressed, never leave their occupation; the profits which they make increase the wealth which they employ in cultivation, which is greatly to the advantage of agriculture. And these profits, which increase the number of wealthy farmers, promote at the time of the renewal of the leases a greater degree of competition between them, which then assures to the proprietors and the sovereign the full return of the net product—not only that which results directly from the increase in prices, but also that additional amount which is generated by the more ample means of the farmers; for we know that wealth is the great and principal implement of cultivation, and that a wealthy farmer can often profitably rent land at a rate one-third or one-half above that which a poor farmer could pay only with difficulty and at the risk of ruining himself.'[1]

3. Entrepreneurs will profit, again during the course of their leases, if they manage to reduce the costs of cultivation. This is illustrated by the remarks quoted near the foot of p. 300 above, and by a further comment of Quesnay's to the effect that:

'The product of the artisan's labour is worth only the expense: if it cost more a loss would be involved. The product of the cultivator's labour exceeds the expense; the more it exceeds it the more profitable it is and the more it increases the nation's opulence.'[2]

Now these three types of profit will clearly persist only so long as large-scale cultivation is not universal (case 1) or only up to the renewal of the farmers' leases (cases 2 and 3). Thus if we construct a model of the economy in which large-scale cultivation is assumed to be universal, and which is sufficiently long-period to enable us to assume that any temporary above-average profits have crystallized out into rents, we can plausibly abstract from these types of profit in our model. This, in my opinion, is precisely what Quesnay did in the basic *Tableau*. Thus the third of the four possibilities noted above leads us much further in the direction of an adequate solution of the apparent contradiction than the first and second. But it does not lead us all the way there. There remains the fourth and final possibility that some form of 'profit' may be included in the annual returns along with the ordinary costs.

---

[1] Above, pp. 180-1.   [2] Above, p. 228.

Here the crucial passage is to be found in the *Rural Philosophy*. Since it has been analysed in the previous essay,[1] I shall not deal with it in detail here. Suffice it to say that it indicates that Quesnay took over the traditional idea that the agricultural entrepreneur normally received a sort of 'wage' which was rather higher than that paid to his employees—a 'wage' which was included, along with the wages of his employees, in the costs of cultivation, and which was recompensed with the other costs out of the proceeds of the harvest. The next historical step—which Quesnay himself did not really take[2] but which some of his Physiocratic followers approached rather more closely—was to recognize that this superior 'wage' (together with certain other elements of entrepreneurial income) included a portion which in fact constituted a clear or net surplus and which under competitive conditions tended to bear a more or less regular proportion to the amount of capital employed.

So much for the 'profit' of the agricultural entrepreneur. The question of the place which the 'profit' of the industrial and commercial entrepreneur occupied in Quesnay's system is rather more easy to answer. It is not true to say that Quesnay was unaware of the importance of capital investment in manufacture,[3] but we can at least say that he regarded investment in agriculture as far more important. Agriculture in the basic *Tableau* is assumed to be more or less subordinated to the capitalist mode of production, and the class of proprietors is assumed to appropriate the net product which it yields; but manufacture is still visualized as being conducted by and large by what we would call today 'workers on their own account'. The market value of manufactured commodities, therefore, is regarded as being made up solely of the value of the raw materials employed plus the value of the subsistence goods which the worker consumes while he is working them up.[4] If the artisan economizes on his costs, Quesnay argues, the result will not be increased profits for him, but merely a corresponding reduction (due to competition) in the price which he will obtain for his commodity. If the farmer economizes on his costs, on the other hand, the result will (eventually) be an increase in the net product, since according to Quesnay there are 'many other causes which are capable of maintaining the market value of the products, notwithstanding economies in the costs of cultivation'.[5] This last remark no doubt begs a whole host of questions,[6] but Quesnay's comparison here does at least bring out very forcibly the nature of the model of the industrial sector which he employed. We can hardly blame him for employing it: it provided

---

[1] Above, pp. 279 ff.   [2] Except to the extent noted above, p. 280.
[3] Cf. e.g. above, pp. 100–1, 134, and 183.
[4] Cf. above, pp. 72–3, 96, and 105.   [5] Above, p. 228.
[6] The main one is dealt with below, pp. 387 ff.

a pretty fair approximation to the actual state of French industry at the time when Quesnay's ideas were developed. And the model was, after all, the common property of most of the economists of the day—including, it is worth noting, the Adam Smith of the *Glasgow Lectures.*

Quesnay was of course quite aware of the fact that under certain circumstances those engaged in non-agricultural pursuits might receive more than a subsistence income. This he explained primarily in terms of the existence of some form or another of monopoly. 'The goods made by those artisans to whom the government grants exclusive privileges', and 'pictures by great painters, and all the other goods made by artists who are pre-eminent in their professions', he admitted, will often sell at a price which 'greatly exceeds the value of the costs'. The reason for this is said to be that the workers concerned are so few in number that 'competition between them does not force them to lower the price of their labour, to the benefit of those who buy their work'.[1] In another place, much less convincingly, Quesnay tried to explain the 'big fortunes' acquired by large commercial and industrial enterprises as a sort of gathering together or accumulation of 'gains similar to those of small merchants' and the 'small profits which are derived from the labour of a large number of workers'.[2] This is a poor argument, but it is quite understandable that the existence of such net gains should not have worried Quesnay unduly at this stage in the development of his doctrine. Not only were such gains often in actual fact due to the existence of some form of exclusive privilege, but they were also quantitatively insignificant compared with the net gains regularly yielded in agriculture. And, in addition, once the primacy of agriculture and the expenditure of the class of proprietors was granted, any net gains made by industry could be plausibly explained as being in some significant sense 'paid out of' the net product—a sort of 'net product in reverse', as Weulersse describes it.[3]

To sum up Quesnay's views on this subject, then, one can probably say that he recognized the existence of entrepreneurial profits, both in agriculture and in manufacture, but reconciled it with his doctrine that land rent was the sole income in the nature of a surplus by:

(a) including in the returns of the agricultural entrepreneur a sort of superior 'wage' for what he called his 'trouble, labour, and the risks of his enterprise';

(b) treating any agricultural 'profit' over and above this 'normal' amount as essentially temporary in character, and therefore assuming that it could legitimately be abstracted from in the long-period analysis of an economy in which large-scale cultivation was universal; and

[1] Above, p. 210.   [2] Above, p. 73.   [3] Weulersse, I, p. 290.

(c) using a model of the industrial sector which assumed that industry was carried on by workers on their own account, so that any 'profit' which in fact emerged could be regarded either as the result of monopoly or as a 'net product in reverse'.

Thus it can hardly be said that Quesnay himself, as distinct from his disciples, contributed very much *directly* to the formation of the crucial Smithian idea that the supply price of a commodity normally included a 'net or clear' profit which bore a more or less regular proportion to the capital employed.

III

In spite of this, Quesnay's view of profits was rather more sensible and consistent than is commonly appreciated, given the assumptions of the basic *Tableau* and the particular model of the economy which he employed. But the contradiction of which I have spoken above remained latent in his system, and in the course of the development of Physiocracy it gradually emerged to the surface—as a result partly of the general march of economic events in the latter half of the eighteenth century, partly of the putting into effect of some of the very reforms which Quesnay himself had advocated, and partly of the cogent criticisms put forward by the Physiocrats' opponents. One can put the essential point simply, if perhaps too mechanically, as follows: With the rise of Smith's third 'constituent order' (the capitalist class), and the gradual subordination of both agriculture and manufacture to the capitalist mode of production, there is an appreciable increase in the accumulation of new capital out of profits, and in the mobility of capital between different employments. This means that economists become obliged to recognize (a) that in the normal case, even under conditions of free competition, the 'profit' of the entrepreneur includes a net element which is not merely a compensation for paid-out costs; and (b) that the man who employs capital in one occupation will normally receive roughly the same rate of net reward (other things being equal) as the man who employs it in any other occupation. But if these facts are to be recognized and embodied in the theoretical model one employs to analyse the economy, how can this be done within the framework of a system, like that of Quesnay, which assumes that land rent is the only income in the nature of a surplus and that non-agricultural occupations are 'sterile'? This was the basic difficulty which the later Physiocrats had to face.

As I have said, Quesnay in one place left a loophole for his followers. Continuing the remarks on the farmer's interest in the *Analysis*, he says:

'. . . . A fund which is as advantageous to the nation as that of the advances of its cultivation ought in itself to bring in net to the farmers, who combine their work and the use of their intelligence with it, an annual interest at least as high as that which is paid to idle rentiers.

The total amount of this interest is spent annually, because cultivators never allow it to remain inactive; for in the intervals when they are not obliged to use it for repairs, they do not fail to put it to profit in order to increase and improve their cultivation, without which they would be unable to provide for serious accidents. That is why interest is included in the total of annual expenditure.'[1]

Quesnay's mode of expression here is typically imprecise, but there is at least a hint that the interest may possibly contain an element which is truly net and which may under certain circumstances be available for accumulation. Even before the *Analysis* appeared, Du Pont had attempted to justify a 10 per cent rate of interest not only by reason of the high rate of loss and depreciation to which the farmer's capital was subject, but also by reason of the fact that 'all labour is worthy of a reward, and . . . it would be neither just nor safe that the type of labour which is the most troublesome, and upon which all other types of labour depend, should be deprived of the thing to which they all aspire'.[2] And Quesnay's significant comparison in the *Analysis* between the interest of the farmers and that received by the 'idle rentiers' must have been a direct incitement to revisionism. The Comte d'Albon, indeed, writing in 1775, shortly after Quesnay's death, went so far as to attribute to him the view that the returns must not only replace the annual advances and provide for the maintenance intact of the original advances, but must also yield 'a kind of interest on the capitals which have been employed in these advances, so that the occupation of cultivator may be no less profitable than the carrying-on of any other occupation could have been'.[3] I do not think that Quesnay himself did actually hold this view, but the fact that Albon could attribute it to him in the *Nouvelles Ephémérides* is an indication of the extent to which the ideas of the school had been developed during the years immediately preceding Quesnay's death.

Mercier de la Rivière, in his *Natural and Essential Order of Political Societies* (1767), made at least three amendments to the Physiocratic canon as Quesnay had presented it. First, he emphasized that the farmer must receive a net reward *at least* (Mercier's

---

[1] Above, pp. 155–6.

[2] *De l'Exportation et de l'Importation des Grains* (1764), pp. 3–4. The quotation is translated from the 1911 reprint (ed. E. Depitre), p. 2.

[3] Oncken, p. 55. Cf. the radically different interpretation of Quesnay's interest doctrine given in an *Eloge* by the Marquis de Mesmon (Oncken, p. 102).

italics) as great as that which he would get if he employed his capital
in another occupation.[1] Second, in his analysis of the constituents of
what he called the 'necessary price' (i.e. supply price) of a manufactured commodity, he included not only the cost of the raw material
and the expenses of the artisan and the merchant, but also 'the
interest which he [the merchant] ought to receive on [his] advances;
. . . the reward due for the trouble which he personally takes; . . .
the value of the different risks to which his trade exposes him'.[2]
Third, in connection with this last item, he affirmed that 'these risks
do not, however, materialize equally for all merchants, and from the
differences which are found in these accidents are bound to arise
differences in their profits'.[3] Mercier has obviously travelled some
distance towards the Smithian concept, but he has not yet arrived at
it. Much more radical alterations were made by Baudeau and
Turgot, who were the main agents in the attempted reform of
Physiocracy.

Baudeau's chief contribution lay in his firm recognition of the
importance of the class division between entrepreneurs and wage-
earners. He still maintains the basic Physiocratic distinction between
the productive class and the sterile class, but he emphasizes, in a way
which Quesnay never did, the economic significance of the division
of each of these classes into those who 'guide and direct the work'
and those who 'do it under their orders'.[4] This division, he makes
clear, is just as important in manufacture as it is in agriculture.[5]
He waxes lyrical over the great benefits which accrue to society when
there emerges 'a leader who knows how to, wants to, and is able to
operate on a large scale',[6] and calls, much more specifically than
most of his predecessors, for the application of capital and capitalist
methods to manufacture.[7] In addition, he emphasizes that the
returns received by the agricultural entrepreneur must include not
only a refund of paid-out costs of cultivation and an amount for the
upkeep and repair of the original advances, but also, as well as these
amounts, 'a just compensation for the advances, trouble, and
danger; for we cannot expect that a class which is numerous, wealthy,
and well-informed will advance large capitals, give itself continuously
a great deal of trouble, and expose itself to great risks, without
drawing this just compensation'.[8] Baudeau also makes it fairly clear
that he visualizes the income of the industrial entrepreneur as

---

[1] *L'Ordre Naturel*, p. 223.   [2] Ibid., pp. 428–9.   [3] Ibid., p. 431.
[4] *Première Introduction à la Philosophie Economique* (1910 edn., ed. A. Dubois),
p. 47.
[5] Cf. e.g. ibid., pp. 66–7.   [6] Ibid., p. 67.
[7] Cf. e.g. ibid., p. 68: 'The establishment of great and vigorous workshops
under the direction of wealthy and hard-working leaders thus tends to procure
for the same price a greater sum of more pleasant enjoyments.'
[8] Ibid., p. 116.

including a similar element;[1] and even in the net product, he maintains, there are two portions which should be exempt from the single tax—the just interest on the money which the proprietor has already spent either in putting his land into a cultivable state or in purchasing it, and a fund to cover the amounts which he customarily spends in maintenance and repair.[2] Finally, although Baudeau still uses the word 'sterile' to describe the class engaged in non-agricultural pursuits, the distinction between 'productive' and 'sterile' is virtually attenuated by him into a purely chronological one.[3]

Turgot's brilliant analysis of the employment of capital in industry and agriculture opened up even wider possibilities. Capital, writes Turgot, can be employed in five different ways—in purchasing a landed estate; in taking a lease of an estate and cultivating it as a tenant-farmer; in investment in industry; in investment in commerce; or in making loans at interest. The first type of investment yields the least revenue, because if the farmer is solvent there is little risk and the collection of the revenue involves little trouble. Making loans at interest usually brings in a rather larger reward than investment in a landed estate, since the debtor may become insolvent and therefore the owner of the capital will not 'content himself with an interest equal to the revenue of the land which he might buy with the same capital'. Money invested in farming, commerce, and industry, however, must necessarily yield a higher rate of return than in the two other fields, since the entrepreneur must 'draw a profit to recompense him for his care, his labour, his talents and his risks, and to furnish him in addition with that wherewith he may replace the annual wear and tear of his advances'. What Turgot calls 'a sort of equilibrium' establishes itself between all these different employments of capital, since funds will flow towards the most lucrative field of investment, and this 'necessarily alters in each of these employments the relation between the capital and the annual produce'.[4] This analysis obviously makes considerable inroads into the doctrine of the sterility of manufacture (Turgot preferred to call industrial workers 'stipendiaries'), and is very reminiscent of Adam Smith's account of the consequences of capital mobility in the *Wealth of Nations*.

Inevitably, the views expressed by men like Baudeau and Turgot were grafted on to the main body of Physiocracy, and eventually even ascribed to Quesnay himself. Du Pont, surveying in the days of his old age the rise of Classical economics, saw clearly that it was

[1] Cf. e.g. *Première Introduction*, p. 67.
[2] *Explication sur le Vrai Sens du Mot Stérile*, reprinted in Daire, *Physiocrates*, Vol. II, at p. 871.
[3] *Explication*, pp. 868 ff.
[4] *Reflections on the Formation and the Distribution of Riches* (Ashley edn., 1898), pp. 81–5.

Quesnay's emphasis on capital accumulation which constituted, historically speaking, the most important feature of his work. In his extraordinary obituary of Quesnay's grandson, written in 1805, Du Pont purports to give a summary of the views of the founder of Physiocracy, but lays hardly any stress on the doctrine of sterility or the notion of the dependence of manufacture upon agriculture. He takes as his theme—or rather as Quesnay's theme—the maxim 'have respect for capital'. 'The increase of capital', he writes, 'is thus the principal means of increasing labour, and the greatest concern of society'. Land *and capital* are the sources of wealth. Agriculture, it is true, is still vaguely conceived as the only 'productive' occupation, but respect is due to *all* capital—and to all capitalists—whether in agriculture or in any other sphere. Summing up what he now believes to have been the essence of Quesnay's doctrine, Du Pont writes: 'Respect for freedom and property demands that men and capitalists remain complete masters of the employment of their advances and their time, provided that there does not result from this any hindrance to freedom or damage to anyone's property'. The taxes should never be permitted to encroach upon 'the advances which the work requires, which ought to be refunded with profit to the entrepreneurs, if we do not want to dry up or obstruct the source of labour and wealth'.[1] One is irresistibly reminded of the way in which certain of the followers of Ricardo began their discussion of value by affirming that Ricardo had said the last word on this subject, and then happily proceeded to modify his doctrine out of all recognition.

But the framework of traditional Physiocratic theory was too rigid to contain these new ideas for long. Even in the work of Turgot, who was more a fellow-traveller of the Physiocrats than a Physiocrat *pur*, the difficulties are evident. The main problem which has to be faced, of course, is the reconciliation of the idea that the agricultural net product is the only true form of surplus with the manifest fact that anyone who employs capital, in whatever occupation, normally receives a reward which at least appears to contain an element of true surplus, and out of which new capital can be accumulated. Turgot was quite unequivocal in his recognition of this fact. Entrepreneurs, he says, normally receive profits proportionate to their advances, their talent, and their activity, and have a surplus over and above their subsistence which they save in order to plough it back into their enterprises.[2] Should not these profits, then, be put on a par with the revenue received by the proprietors of the land? Turgot answers this question in the negative, but is obviously rather hard put to it to

---

[1] The *Nécrologue* is reprinted in Oncken, pp. 801 ff. Another example of the tendency discussed in this paragraph is to be found in Du Pont's note to Turgot's *Eloge de Gournay*, reprinted in Daire's edition of Turgot's *Oeuvres*, pp. 266–8.

[2] *Reflections*, p. 97.

defend his answer. There are two main lines of defence which he adopts. First, he argues, even though new capitals are indeed formed by saving out of profits, these profits always come ultimately from the land, since they are all paid 'either from the revenue, or as part of the expenditure which serves to produce the revenue'. They are in effect only 'the accumulation of the part of the values produced by the land that the proprietors of the revenue, or those who share it with them, can lay by every year without using it for the satisfaction of their wants'.[1] Second, an important part of these profits is merely compensation for a sort of opportunity cost: the returns on capital in any employment must be sufficient to yield an income at least as great as that which can be earned in any other employment, since otherwise the capital will be transferred to that other employment. Interest on money lent may appear at first sight to be truly 'disposable', Turgot argues, but it is not really so: if the state tried to appropriate it by means of taxation, the lender would simply withdraw his money.[2] The agricultural entrepreneurs must receive a return sufficient to pay 'a profit equal to the revenue they could acquire with their capitals without labour', or they will not employ their wealth and their toil to cultivate another man's land.[3] And the industrial entrepreneur must receive a profit sufficient to compensate him 'for what his money would have been worth to him if he had employed it in the purchase of an estate'.[4]

But both these lines of defence are purely formal. The first in effect assumes what has to be proved; and the second, however useful it may be in an analysis of general equilibrium, says merely that capital has a supply price. It is fairly evident, on Turgot's own showing, that profit on capital does in fact include an element which is 'disposable' in the original Physiocratic sense of that word—a point which Hume, in a little-known letter to Turgot,[5] was quick to seize upon. With Turgot, Physiocracy begins to burst its seams: the framework of concepts elaborated by Quesnay can no longer accommodate the basic economic phenomena of capitalist society. Turgot, however, went much further in preparing the way for Adam Smith than any of his predecessors or contemporaries: with him, the 'necessary price' came to include, as it was to do with Smith, a 'normal' return on capital, part of which was available for accumulation. It remained only to remove the Physiocratic integument, and the way was clear for the emergence of the *Wealth of Nations*.

---

[1] *Reflections*, p. 98.   [2] Ibid., pp. 92–3.   [3] Ibid., pp. 55–6.
[4] Ibid., p. 53.
[5] *The Letters of David Hume*, ed. J. Y. T. Grieg, Vol. II, p. 94.

III

PHYSIOCRACY AND THE EARLY
THEORIES OF UNDER-CONSUMPTION[1]

The economists of the school of Adam Smith, when confronted with the unorthodox doctrines concerning the relationship between consumption and production which began to appear as the eighteenth century ended, immediately sensed their Physiocratic quality. Say, for example, in the lengthy section of his *Treatise* devoted to consumption, said this about them:

'Many people, seeing that in the aggregate production is always equal to consumption (for it is clearly necessary that what is consumed should have been produced), have imagined that to encourage consumption is to favour production. The *Economists*[2] were imbued with this idea, and turned it into one of the fundamental principles of their doctrine. *Consumption is the measure of reproduction*, they said; i.e. *the more that is consumed, the more that is produced*. And, since production enriches people, it was concluded that a state enriched itself through its consumption, that saving was in direct contradiction to public prosperity, and that the most useful citizen was the one who spent the most.'[3]

And James Mill, in his reply to Spence, went even further, attributing to the Physiocrats something like a developed under-consumptionist theory of crisis:

'The Economistes and their disciples express great apprehensions lest capital should increase too fast, lest the production of commodities should be too rapid. There is only, say they, a market for a given quantity of commodities, and if you increase the supply beyond that quantity you will be unable to dispose of the surplus.'[4]

To what extent were such statements concerning the Physiocratic affiliations of the new theories correct? It is obvious enough that *some* connection existed, if only because of the fact that most of the early under-consumptionists, even when they were not out-and-out Physiocrats, had strong leanings in that direction. But what was the

---

[1] This essay is an amended version of an article which appeared in *Economica*, August 1951. I am indebted to the editors of *Economica* for permission to reproduce it here.

[2] *Les Economistes*—a title often given at this period to the French Physiocrats.

[3] Say, *Traité d'Economie Politique* (1st edn., 1803), Vol. II, pp. 358–9. Cf. ibid., p. 366.

[4] James Mill, *Commerce Defended* (2nd edn., 1808), p. 80.

exact nature and significance of the relationship? The present essay is an attempt to answer these questions. It begins with a brief account of the doctrines relating to consumption held by the French Physio-crats; it then passes to an examination of the theories of under-consumption put forward by Spence, Sismondi, Malthus, Chalmers, and others; and it concludes with some comments on the place of the early under-consumptionists in the history of economic thought.

I

Say was hardly justified in ascribing to the French Physiocrats, without serious qualification, the idea that 'to encourage consumption is to favour production'. In so far as they did accept some such doctrine as this, they confined its application to a sphere much more limited than Say's comments would suggest. And Mill was clearly quite wrong in asserting that they expressed great apprehensions 'lest capital should increase too fast, lest the production of commodities should be too rapid'; when they did express any apprehensions concerning the accumulation of capital (as distinct from the forma-tion of monetary hoards), these were almost always to the effect that capital was not increasing fast enough. The Physiocrats were primarily interested in the problem of the maximization of the rate of increase in national wealth. The prosperity of the country, they believed, depended to a large extent upon the size of the 'disposable revenue', or surplus over paid-out costs of production, which was yielded in agriculture, and upon the proportion of this net revenue which was annually converted into capital. The Physiocratic theory of consumption was directly related to this fundamental view of the economic problem. In essence, it amounted to a set of administrative rules and moral precepts designed, first, to assist in increasing the monetary value of the produce of agriculture, and second, to bring about a proper balance between productive and unproductive expenditure out of the net product. Under the first heading the Physiocrats considered the effect of consumption on the 'proper price' of agricultural produce, and under the second the so-called theory of luxury.[1]

The net product, which according to the Physiocrats was yielded only in agriculture, was the mainspring of the country's economic

---

[1] It is convenient to consider the two theories separately, but they were of course intimately related. The whole rationale of the distinction between *faste de décoration* and *faste de consommation* lay in the effect which the latter type of expenditure was conceived to have on the price of agricultural produce and thus on the value of the net product. The most convenient collections of the relevant texts are to be found in Weulersse, I, pp. 484–95, and René Gonnard, *Histoire des Doctrines Economiques* (5th edn.), pp. 54–8. A useful summary is also to be found in the introduction by A. Dubois to the 1912 reprint of Baudeau's *Principes de la Science Morale et Politique sur le Luxe et les Loix Somptuaires* (1767).

life and the key to its increasing prosperity. But the value of the net product varied not only according to the physical productivity of agriculture but also according to the market price of agricultural produce. The higher the price of corn, other things being equal, the greater the net product. All possible measures should therefore be taken to raise the price of produce above its then relatively low level, to make it less subject to fluctuations, and to extend the market for the produce. The main measure which was called for, in the Physiocrats' opinion, was of course freedom of trade, both internal and external, in agricultural produce. But the Physiocrats also laid considerable emphasis on the importance of increasing the internal consumption of agricultural produce, and occasionally described the beneficial effects of an extended consumption in terms so extravagant as almost to warrant Say's criticism.[1]

The measures they proposed for increasing the internal consumption of agricultural produce were many and varied. It was suggested, for example, that those manufactures which employed home-grown raw materials should be encouraged; that the lower classes should be made as well off as possible so that they would be able to buy more produce and pay a higher price for it; and that disposable revenue should never be accumulated in the form of monetary hoards. And the Physiocrats had plausible answers ready for those who objected, on the one hand, that low prices rather than high prices were beneficial to the common people, and on the other hand, that with higher prices the purchaser lost as much as the vendor gained so that no net profit was yielded. To the first group of critics they replied in the words of the nineteenth *General Maxim* of *Physiocracy* that:

'*It should not be believed that cheapness of produce is profitable to the lower classes;* for a low price of produce causes a fall in the wages of the lower orders of people, reduces their well-being, makes less work and remunerative occupations available for them, and destroys the nation's revenue.'[2]

And to the second group Quesnay suggested that the increase in the price of agricultural produce would induce a sort of Physiocratic multiplier effect throughout the economy:

'Those who do not follow the circulation of the wealth of a state to its full extent may object that dearness is advantageous only to the sellers, and that it impoverishes the buyers. . . . Dearness, according to this idea, can never under any conditions mean an increase in the state's wealth.

But do not dearness and abundance of agricultural produce increase the profits of the cultivators, and the revenues of the king, the proprietors, and the recipients of the tithes? Does not this

---

[1] Cf. Gonnard, op. cit., p. 54.   [2] Above, p. 236.

wealth itself also cause an increase in expenditure and gains? Do not the labourers, artisans, manufacturers, etc., get paid for their time and their goods in proportion to the cost of their subsistence? The more revenue there is in a state, the more do trade, manufacture, the arts, the crafts, and the other occupations become necessary and remunerative.'[1]

To raise agricultural prices was one way of increasing the net product and national prosperity. The same problem could also be tackled from another angle: rules could be laid down concerning the manner in which the net product ought to be disposed of by those to whom it accrued in the first instance. The net product was 'disposable' only in the sense that it represented a clear surplus over production costs in a given period of working: the manner in which it was actually expended was far from being a matter of indifference to society. The Physiocrats were well aware of the fact that a large number of the landed proprietors of their day were spending their rents on the luxuries and dissipations of the cities rather than on the improvement of their estates, and much of their argument was directed towards bringing about a reversal of this state of affairs.[2]

The Physiocrats' theory of luxury was in effect an attempt to evaluate the various ways of spending the net product according to the effect which they might be expected to have on the size of future net products, and thus on the size of future national incomes. The concepts which they evolved in this connection were rather more complicated than those employed by Smith and his successors in their discussions on the productive and unproductive expenditure of revenue, since the Physiocrats had to take account of the fact that one type of seemingly unproductive expenditure—that on agricultural produce—might exert a stimulating effect on the economy per medium of the 'proper price' which it would help to bring about. In the earlier Physiocratic writings on this point, particularly those of Quesnay, there is a certain amount of vagueness and ambiguity, which was not entirely cleared up until Baudeau synthesized the theory in 1767 in the columns of the *Ephémérides*. His first job was to give an adequate definition of luxury:

'We call Luxury that subversion of the natural and essential order of national expenditure which increases the total of unproductive expenditure to the detriment of that which is used in production, and at the same time to the detriment of production itself.'[3]

---

[1] Above, p. 87.
[2] 'The wealthy and their wealth', complained Baudeau, 'no longer dwell in our villages; they have fled far from our fields, which can never be rendered fertile except through their opulence' (op. cit., p. 20).
[3] Baudeau, ibid., p. 14.

But whether any particular act of expenditure on consumption goods out of the net product comes within the category of luxury necessarily depends upon the state of agriculture at the time in question. If agriculture is flourishing, then it is sufficient if the proprietor does not actually reduce the amount he spends annually on the improvement of his land, as a result of his expenditure on consumption. If, on the other hand, agriculture is in a state of decline, then it is the duty of the proprietor to put aside a substantial portion of the net product each year in order to increase his expenditure on the improvement of his land. In either case, however, a certain portion of the net product should be annually earmarked for use as capital in the improvement of the land; and to the extent that the proprietor in fact spends this portion on goods for his own personal consumption he is committing the crime of luxury.[1] Luxury, in other words, is defined with reference to the degree of capitalization of agriculture, and not with reference to the nature or amount of goods consumed.

But not all expenditure on luxury goods constitutes luxury. It is necessary to make a clear distinction between conspicuous consumption (*faste*) and luxury (*luxe*). *Luxe* is very often *faste*, but *faste* is not necessarily *luxe*. In particular, *faste* is not *luxe* when it represents expenditure out of that part of the net product which is morally as well as legally 'disposable'. Conspicuous consumption, in other words, is not luxury when it does not detrimentally affect the capitalization of agriculture. But some kinds of conspicuous consumption are preferable to others, so that a further distinction has to be made between conspicuous consumption in the way of consumption (*faste de consommation*) and conspicuous consumption in the way of ornamentation (*faste de décoration*). Generally speaking, the former is to be preferred to the latter. *Faste de consommation*—i.e. the conspicuous consumption of primary produce—is healthy in so far as it helps to secure the 'proper price'. *Faste de décoration*—i.e. the conspicuous consumption of manufactured products—is less healthy, since, although the expenditure ultimately finds its way back to the productive class, it does so burdened with all sorts of commercial costs. A hierarchy of permissible expenditure out of the net product was thus erected. The most admirable type of expenditure was, of course, capital expenditure in agriculture. Until a state of something like capital saturation in agriculture is reached, as much as possible of the net product should be spent in improving the land. When agriculture is in a state of decline, *faste de décoration* is little better than a theft from society. The next most patriotic type of expenditure is *faste de consommation*, which should be so directed as to return their wealth to the productive class as quickly as possible. Third, there is *faste de décoration*, when this does not constitute

[1] Baudeau, *Principes*, pp. 14, 19, and 31–2.

luxe. Baudeau somewhat grudgingly permits this type of expenditure to the proprietor 'who contents himself with not doing evil, and who prefers to the pleasure of conducing to public welfare that of satisfying his inclinations or whims'.[1]

Now it is fairly clear that there was very little in this Physiocratic theory of consumption which could have been of any direct use to an under-consumptionist. Consider, for example, two of the major themes which we find in the work of the under-consumptionists of the early nineteenth century—that increased investment somehow brings about a relative diminution of demand, and that a failure on the part of the proprietors to spend their surplus on manufactured goods will cause a hiatus in the circulation process. There is obviously little support to be found in French Physiocratic writings for either of these two propositions. The theory of luxury, with its distinction between productive and unproductive expenditure out of revenue, was much more useful to Smith and Ricardo than it was to the under-consumptionists. And from the theory of the 'proper price' the under-consumptionists could garner little except a few rather vague aphorisms concerning the stimulating effect of increased consumption—aphorisms which the British under-consumptionists could have found (and sometimes in fact did find) much nearer home. The clear connection between Physiocratic concepts and theories of under-consumption in the early nineteenth century therefore remains as a puzzle which we must try to solve.

II

Some modern commentators—Keynes, for example—have thought to detect in Mercantilist writings the beginnings of a long tradition of concern about the effect upon employment of 'the insufficiency of the propensity to consume'.[2] It is certainly true that most Mercantilist writers were well aware of the fact that changes in the pattern and intensity of demand might radically affect the disposition of the social labour force. Their works abound with statements of the 'spending is good for trade' type.[3] But these were generally more

---

[1] *Baudeau*, op. cit., p. 32.

[2] Keynes, *General Theory*, pp. 358 ff. 'It is no new thing', Keynes writes, '. . . to ascribe the evils of unemployment to . . . the insufficiency of the propensity to consume.' But after the publication of Mandeville's *Fable*, Keynes asserts, the doctrine expressed in that work 'did not reappear in respectable circles for another century, until in the later phase of Malthus the notion of the insufficiency of effective demand takes a definite place as a scientific explanation of unemployment'. Cf. D. H. MacGregor, *Economic Thought and Policy*, chapter 4, *passim*.

[3] E.g. Berkeley asked 'Whether the industry of the lower part of the people doth not much depend upon the expense of the upper?', and Barbon praised 'liberality in the rich'. These and a number of similar statements are quoted in E. S. Furniss, *The Position of the Laborer in a System of Nationalism*, pp. 56–62. See also E. A. J. Johnson, *Predecessors of Adam Smith*, pp. 289–97.

discriminating than is sometimes suggested today. 'Liberality in the rich' was praiseworthy only if it was a disciplined liberality. Just as the Physiocrats, believing that the source of wealth lay in agriculture, condemned any consumption which had a detrimental effect on the supply of capital to agriculture, so the Mercantilists, believing that the source of wealth lay in a favourable balance of trade, condemned any consumption which worsened the foreign trade position. Mun, for example, declared that the commonwealth is no better than 'an unthrift who spends beyond his means' when 'through Pride and other Excesses they do consume more forraign wares in value than the wealth of the Kingdom can satisfie and pay by the exportation of our own commodities'.[1] However, 'the pomp of Buildings, Apparel, and the like' on the part of the rich is not necessarily to be condemned: 'if it be done with curious and costly works upon our Materials, and by our own people, it will maintain the poor with the purse of the rich, which is the best distribution of the Common-wealth.' But, Mun adds drily, 'if any man say, that when the people want work, then the Fishing-trade would be a better employment, and far more profitable; I subscribe willingly'.[2] The employment of the people in useful arts and manufactures, it was generally agreed, was an essential ingredient of national strength, and demand was an important factor in stimulating employment. But employment was not wanted for its own sake, and demand should therefore be directed only into those channels where the production which it fostered would be conducive to the growth of national wealth and prosperity. The emphasis placed by the nineteenth-century under-consumptionists on the salutary effects of consumption was entirely different from this both in purpose and in quality—which is hardly surprising, since they and the Mercantilists lived in two quite different economic worlds.

The Mercantilist literature, however, contains not only positive injunctions in favour of spending, but also positive condemnations of 'frugality', 'thrift', 'saving', and so on. So common are these that Heckscher is able to speak of the Mercantilists' 'deep-rooted belief in . . . the evil of thrift'.[3] It cannot be too strongly emphasized, however, that in the majority of cases what was being condemned was simply *hoarding*, the withdrawal of money income from circulation. In one passage Mun speaks of a man taking a 'Frugal course' and putting half his revenue 'in his Chest',[4] and this, I think, was the sort of activity which the Mercantilists usually had in mind when they spoke of the evils of 'frugality' and 'saving'. The Physio-

---

[1] *England's Treasure by Forraign Trade* (1933 reprint), p. 26.
[2] Ibid., p. 60. [3] *Mercantilism*, Vol. II, p. 208.
[4] *England's Treasure*, p. 5. Mun himself did not condemn this type of frugality, but surely both he and those who did condemn it (e.g. Mandeville) were talking about much the same phenomenon.

crats had much the same idea when they urged that the rich should not indulge in 'sterile saving, which would deduct from circulation and distribution a portion of their revenue or gains'.[1] *Sterile* saving (i.e. hoarding), as distinct from saving which was transformed directly or indirectly into investment, was regarded by the Physiocrats as harmful because it disrupted the general process of circulation and had a detrimental effect on employment and business activity.[2] This belief has been accepted by all subsequent schools of economic thought, including not only the early under-consumptionists, but also their opponents—even those who held most rigorously to Say's Law.[3] The controversies between Spence and Mill and between Malthus and Ricardo were conducted throughout on the explicit assumption, not that hoarding was harmless, but that it was a pathological phenomenon whose existence could safely be ignored. Spence and Malthus, in other words, meant by 'frugality' something quite different from what the Mercantilists meant by it.

The Mercantilist emphasis on consumption had necessarily to give way before the Classical emphasis on accumulation, which was first systematized in Britain in the *Wealth of Nations*. The new attitude was not, of course, unheralded: French Physiocracy was, in the broadest sense, a theory of capital accumulation, and Smith no doubt learned much from Francis Hutcheson, whose account of profit and accumulation was somewhat similar to his[4] and who consistently castigated *The Fable of the Bees*. But Smith's greatest teacher was the society in which he lived. He possessed that peculiar faculty, given only to the very great, of being able to discern in the world about him those features which although not preponderant now are destined to become so as the result of a process of social development. Writing on the eve of the industrial revolution, Smith foresaw the vital role which capital accumulation was to play in Britain in the near future. And since capital can be accumulated only by means of parsimony—i.e. by saving out of disposable revenue— the prodigal begins to appear in Smith's pages as a public enemy and the parsimonious man as a public benefactor.

This does not mean, however, that Smith believed consumption to

---

[1] Above, p. 121.

[2] It should be noted here that the Physiocrats were not always as careful as they might have been in distinguishing 'sterile' saving from the non-sterile variety: in some of their more dogmatic statements on this subject they undoubtedly laid themselves open to the charge of a general anti-saving bias. Turgot in particular castigated certain of them for confusing saving and hoarding: cf. e.g. the letter from Turgot to Du Pont quoted in the 1898 edn. of Turgot's *Reflections* (ed. Ashley), p. 112.

[3] Cf. D. H. MacGregor, op. cit., pp. 111 ff.

[4] *A System of Moral Philosophy* (1755 edn.), Vol. I, chapter 7 (particularly pp. 328–9), and Vol. II, chapter 13 (particularly pp. 71–3).

be unimportant. On the contrary, he insisted that 'consumption is the sole end and purpose of all production'.[1] He was careful to contrast parsimony, not with consumption *per se*, but with 'prodigality'. 'Prodigality' was not just conspicuous consumption, but conspicuous consumption which encroached upon capital. It was not just *faste*, but *luxe*. At the end of his chapter on accumulation, too, he discusses in detail the case of those individuals 'whose expense just equals their revenue'—i.e. those who are neither prodigals spending more than their revenue nor frugal people spending less. Smith does not suggest that they alter their ways and become frugal; all he does is to argue that expenditure by them on durable commodities is likely to 'contribute more to the growth of public opulence' than expenditure on things which are consumed immediately.[2] And, finally, Smith points out—no doubt addressing himself to those Mercantilists of his own day who still confused hoarding with accumulation—that:

'What is annually saved is as regularly consumed as what is annually spent, and nearly in the same time too; but it is consumed by a different set of people. That portion of his revenue which a rich man annually spends is in most cases consumed by idle guests, and menial servants, who leave nothing behind them in return for their consumption. That portion which he annually saves, as for the sake of the profit it is immediately employed as a capital, is consumed in the same manner, and nearly in the same time too, but by a different set of people, by labourers, manufacturers, and artificers, who re-produce with a profit the value of their annual consumption'.[3]

Nevertheless, it was Smith's emphasis on the social value of accumulation and the moral value of parsimony, rather than his remarks on consumption, which caught the imagination of the generation which followed him. That generation grew up at a time when capital accumulation and real income were beginning to increase rapidly and hand in hand; when accumulation was fast becoming the province of the capitalists rather than of the landed proprietors; and when the political conflict between the capitalists and the landed proprietors was beginning to come to a head. Those whose sympathies lay with the new economic and political order seized on Smith's theory of accumulation to bolster up their approval, and some of them, going further than Smith himself had ever done, maintained that there was no limit to the amount of capital which could be accumulated in a country. Those who feared or were suspicious of the new order, on the other hand, asserted that there were definite limits to the accumulation of capital. Each group produced a theory of consumption to support its opinion. The first

---

[1] *Wealth of Nations* (Cannan edn.), Vol. II, p. 159.
[2] Ibid., Vol. I, pp. 328–31.   [3] Ibid., p. 320.

L

nailed its colours to the mast of Say's Law. The second argued that an over-rapid accumulation might be checked by a deficiency of effective demand, and that 'unproductive consumers' (such as landlords, stockholders, and clergymen), although they now contributed little to accumulation, might still play a useful social role by helping to maintain demand at the requisite level. This is obviously a greatly over-simplified account of the motives and content of a long and complicated controversy (for example, the last remark hardly applies to Sismondi!), but it does, I suggest, provide us with a useful frame in which to set the actual events.

III

William Spence seems to have been the first, at least in England, to put forward a more or less coherent under-consumptionist case. But there had already been a certain amount of softening-up. Smith himself, for example, had stated several times that profits tended to fall as accumulation increased.[1] Edmund Burke, in a remarkable passage in his *Reflections on the Revolution in France*, had argued that 'the idle expences of monks' were useful in helping 'to distribute the surplus product of the soil'—an argument which was essentially based on the Physiocratic scheme of circulation.[2] Germain Garnier, the French follower of the Physiocrats and translator of Adam Smith, had stated in his *Summary of the Principles of Political Economy* (1796) that although an individual's wealth would certainly increase through saving, that of a nation could increase only per medium of an expanded consumption;[3] and in the notes to his translation of Smith he had argued that in old countries, like those of Europe, in which capital had been accumulating over several centuries, there was an annual excess of produce 'the superabundance of which would

---

[1] *Wealth of Nations*, Vol. I, pp. 89, 91, and 335. Cf. *Edinburgh Review*, October 1804, pp. 113 ff.

[2] Burke, *Select Works* (Clarendon Press edn., 1886), Vol. II, pp. 189–90. 'In every prosperous community', Burke writes, 'something more is produced than goes to the immediate support of the producer. This surplus forms the income of the landed capitalist. It will be spent by a proprietor who does not labour. But this idleness is itself the spring of labour; this repose the spur to industry.' The idle monks and abbots, Burke proceeds, even though they do nothing but sing in the choir, are as usefully employed as if they worked from dawn to dusk in those 'pestiferous occupations, to which by the social oeconomy so many wretches are inevitably doomed. . . . I am sure that no consideration, except the necessity of submitting to the yoke of luxury, and the despotism of fancy, who in their own imperious way will distribute the surplus product of the soil, can justify the toleration of such trades and employments in a well-regulated state. But for this purpose of distribution, it seems to me, that the idle expences of monks are quite as well directed as the idle expences of us lay-loiterers'. Spence made good use of this passage: see his *Tracts on Political Economy* (1822), pp. 162 and 257–8.

[3] Cited in Say, *Traité*, Vol. II, p. 397.

obstruct the circulation, if it were not absorbed by a consumption proportionate to it'.[1] And Lauderdale, in his influential *Inquiry*, had strongly attacked Smith's emphasis on parsimony, stressed the regulating role of demand, and insisted that 'accumulation of capital must at all times have its bounds'.[2]

Napoleon's threat of blockade may have been the occasion for the appearance of Spence's pamphlet, but it was hardly the cause. Spence himself admitted this in his rejoinder to Mill's *Commerce Defended*. Erroneous opinions in political economy, he said, 'can be eradicated only by a frequent recurrence, whenever temporary topics have directed the public attention to the subject, to the great principles of the science'.[3] And Mill, too, was fully conscious of what was really at stake. He was in fact substantially in agreement with Spence's low estimate of the value of Britain's commerce, and regarded this question as something of a side issue. 'Had Mr Spence directed his efforts', Mill wrote, 'to moderate our ideas of the value of commerce, without teaching other doctrines which, first, were false, and next led to practical conclusions of the most dangerous tendency, he might have been of service to his country'.[4] Spence had maintained that there were definite limits to the accumulation of capital, and that the then fashionable emphasis on the importance of parsimony was therefore misplaced. And, what was worse, he had maintained that even though the landlords and other unproductive classes now tended to spend rather than to save their revenue, they still performed a

---

[1] *Recherches sur la Nature et les Causes de la Richesse des Nations* (1802), Vol. V (translator's notes), pp. 240–2. This statement, like that in the *Abrégé*, aroused the anger of Say (*Traité*, Vol. II, pp. 178–9) and probably inspired the first important statement of 'Say's Law' (ibid., pp. 175–9). The parallels between this controversy and the later controversies between Spence and Mill and between Malthus and Ricardo are extremely interesting.

[2] *Inquiry into the Nature and Origin of Public Wealth* (1804), p. 265 and *passim*, Lauderdale has some claim to be regarded as the earliest British under-consumptionist. Although his first main example of accumulation 'pushed beyond its due bounds' was a case of accumulation in excess of *physical need* (pp. 212 ff.), his discussion contained the elements of a theory of under-consumption which might have been capable of more general application (pp. 216–8). And consideration of his second example—suggested by contemporary Sinking Fund proposals—led him to formulate a number of general principles curiously similar to those subsequently put forward by Spence and Malthus (see e.g. pp. 251–2 and 265–7). Spence, indeed, acknowledged Lauderdale's priority on the Sinking Fund question (*Tracts*, p. 81, footnote), and James Mill agreed that 'his Lordship's arguments . . . are merely those of Mr. Spence extended. They are drawn from the same source, and applied to the same end' (*Commerce Defended*, 2nd edn., 1808, p. 96, footnote). But Lauderdale was hardly a Physiocrat: the most that can be said on this point is that his strictures on the Physiocrats were rather less severe than his strictures on Smith. See, however, Haney, *History of Economic Thought* (1st edn.), p. 301.

[3] *Tracts*, p. 69.

[4] *Commerce Defended*, pp. 107–8.

useful social function—and, indeed, that their continued and
progressively increasing expenditure was essential to prosperity. Mill
immediately recognized that these doctrines were actually an attack
on the new order by a partisan of the old.

Spence was probably the first to see clearly that the Physiocratic
pattern of production and demand, as displayed in Quesnay's
Tableau, could with appropriate modifications provide the framework
for a theory of under-consumption which would at the same time
serve as a critique of capitalism and a vindication of the unproductive consumption of the landlords. The Physiocratic scheme provided,
first, the notion that the 'real value' of manufactured commodities
was precisely equal to the value of the raw materials and subsistence
goods which had been physically used up in their manufacture, so
that any net profit yielded on capital employed in manufacture
must be conceived as arising in the process of exchange rather than
in the process of production. It provided, secondly, the basic idea
that those employed in the manufacturing trades were subsisted by
and dependent upon the expenditure of the agricultural surplus by
the landed proprietors.[1] From these two principles it was quite
legitimate to conclude, as Spence did, that the net income of the
manufacturing capitalists was not an original but a derived revenue,
and that any accumulation of capital out of their profits 'would be at
the expense of the land proprietors'.[2] But it was *not* legitimate to
conclude, as Spence also did, that in European societies 'expenditure,
not parsimony, is the province of the class of land proprietors, and
. . . it is on the due performance of this duty, by the class in question,
that the production of national wealth depends'.[3] The French
Physiocrats would have repudiated this suggestion (within the limits
defined in the first section of this essay), since it was precisely
'parsimony' on the part of the proprietors—i.e. the sinking of a large
portion of the net product in agricultural improvements—that they
were most anxious to encourage. They clearly regarded such
'parsimony' as constituting a transfer and not a diminution of
demand.

It is important that Spence's argument should be reproduced in a
little more detail, since several of the points he makes will be met with

---

[1] Spence recognized that they might also draw subsistence from the portion
of the surplus received by the farmers, but argued that 'the class of farmers may
. . . be considered, with relation to the net *profit* they make, as belonging to the
class of land proprietors' (*Tracts*, p. 28, footnote)—thereby by-passing one of
the central difficulties of French Physiocracy. Spence was by no means a consistent Physiocrat: he argued, for example, that even though all taxes fell ultimately upon the land, the land was *not* 'the only proper source of taxation'
(*Tracts*, pp. 140–1). When politics conflicted with Physiocracy, Spence always
allowed politics to prevail.

[2] *Tracts*, pp. 13–16.   [3] Ibid., p. 32.

again later. In European societies, he says, it is a condition essential to the creation of national wealth:

'that the class of land proprietors, expend the greater part of the revenue which they derive from the soil. They are the agents, through whose hands the revenue of the society passes, but in order that wealth and prosperity should accrue to the community, it is absolutely necessary, that they should spend this revenue. So long as they perform this duty, everything goes on in its proper train'.

Smith's arguments in favour of parsimony, Spence proceeds, 'seem to be intended to maintain, that fresh capital may be profitably employed, in manufacturing goods which nobody will buy: for, certainly, no purchasers could be found for the goods brought into existence by the employment of new capital, if all the members of the society were to convert the greater part of their revenue into capital'. And Spence gives an example designed to show what would happen if the proprietors 'ceased to expend':

'Let us make the supposition that fifty of our great land owners, each deriving 20,000 *l.* a year from his estates, which they had been accustomed to spend . . . resolved not to spend, but to save, the 1,000,000 *l.* which their revenue amounted to. Is it not self-evident, that all those members of the manufacturing and unproductive classes, who had, directly, or indirectly, been accustomed to draw the revenue destined for their subsistence, from the expenditure of this sum, would have their power of consuming the produce of the earth diminished, by the whole amount of this 1,000,000 *l.*?'

Spence goes on to consider the evil effects of this 'saving scheme', and then tries to answer the obvious objection that 'as this supposed sum would not be hoarded, . . . but would be lent on interest: It would still be employed in circulation, and would still give employment to manufacturers'. To this objection he replies:

'It should be considered, that money borrowed on interest, is destined, not for expenditure, but to be employed as capital; that the very circumstance of lessening expenditure, decreases the means of the profitable employment of capital, and, consequently, that the employment of the sum alluded to as capital, would in no degree diminish the hardships of those who had been deprived of the revenue derived from its expenditure.'

Spence's argument closes with an attempt to show that for the 'constantly progressive maintenance of the prosperity of the community' it is necessary not only that the class of proprietors should spend, but also that 'this class should go on progressively increasing its expenditure'. Prosperity will induce an increased population—

and 'how is this increased population to be subsisted, unless the class, from whom the revenue of the whole is derived, proportionably increases its expenditure?' Two final conclusions are drawn—first, that the increase of luxury is absolutely essential to the well-being of European countries, and second, that 'all taxes, however levied, in the end fall upon the soil, and are eventually borne by the land proprietors'.[1]

Mill's reply to all this can be conveniently divided into two parts. First, he draws on Adam Smith in order to attack Spence's key proposition—the idea that the act of saving, even when the savings are invested, somehow reduces the volume of effective demand. 'Let not Mr Spence be alarmed', says Mill:

'Let him rest in perfect assurance, that the whole annual produce of the country will be always very completely consumed, whether his landholders choose to spend or to accumulate. . . . No man, if he can help it, will let any part of his property lie useless and run to waste. . . . That part, however, which is destined for future profit, is just as completely consumed, as that which is destined for immediate gratification.'

Second, Mill attacks Spence's assertion that a country can have too much capital. 'A nation always has within itself a market equal to all the commodities of which it can possibly have to dispose', Mill contends, and puts forward his well-known version of 'Say's Law' as proof:

'The production of commodities creates, and is the one and universal cause which creates a market for the commodities produced. . . . If a nation's power of purchasing is exactly measured by its annual produce, as it undoubtedly is; the more you increase the annual produce, the more by that very act you extend the national market, the power of purchasing and the actual purchases of the nation. Whatever be the additional quantity of goods therefore which is at any time created in any country, an additional power of purchasing, exactly equivalent, is at the same instant created; so that a nation can never be naturally overstocked either with capital or with commodities; as the very operation of capital makes a vent for its produce. . . . It may be necessary, however, to remark, that a nation may easily have more than enough of any one commodity, though she can never have more than enough of commodities in general. The quantity of any one commodity may easily be carried beyond its due proportion; but by that very circumstance is implied that some other commodity is not provided in sufficient proportion.'[2]

[1] Quotations from *Tracts*, pp. 29–36.
[2] Quotations from *Commerce Defended*, pp. 65–8. It should be noted that

Spence's rejoinder to Mill's attack is not particularly impressive. He insists that it was his aim 'not to argue against the accumulation of capital in general, but against its accumulation in excess, and particularly by the class of land owners'. He seems to admit the principle of the Smith-Mill 'saving is spending' argument, but denies its relevance to the question at issue. 'We can come to a solid determination', he asserts, 'only by putting an extreme case—by inquiring what would be the result if *all* the land holders were to save their revenue'. If they employed their savings as agricultural capital, then 'the system of society must undergo a total change. All the manufacturers and idlers, which comprise five-sixths of the community, must become cultivators, or they must starve'. But such a scheme would be 'stark nonsense': the landholders would obviously refuse to 'employ their revenue in feeding twelve millions of people to do work which may be performed by two millions'. If, on the other hand, they employed their savings as manufacturing capital, 'then all the manufacturing capital before existing, would be useless', while if they did not employ it themselves but lent it to the master-manufacturers it would be impossible for employment to be found for so much additional capital 'at the moment when those who are to employ it have lost customers for their articles to the same amount'. So far as Mill's formulation of 'Say's Law' is concerned, Spence frankly confesses that he is unable to understand it. Does Mill mean to assert, he asks, 'that capital may be employed *ad infinitum* in producing new manufactures, while no addition is made to agricultural capital'? He has little difficulty in disposing of this suggestion:

'Additional capital can be employed in new manufactures only when there are fresh hands to be engaged. Now, how could Mr Mill support his increased population, if there were no increase of food provided for them? Half of his manufacturers might make shoes, and the other half coats; but while they were starving for want of

---

Mill's two arguments are logically distinct. The first, the 'saving is spending' argument, states that unhoarded savings are spent—i.e. that accumulation, or saving-*plus-investment*, does not reduce the total volume of demand. The second 'Say's Law' proper, states that in the last analysis supply and demand must always be equal and that therefore a general glut of commodities is impossible. It is obviously possible to accept the 'saving is spending' argument while rejecting 'Say's Law'. It is true, of course, that an acceptance of 'Say's Law' implies an acceptance of the 'saving is spending' argument; but it is *not* true that 'Say's Law' implies 'the notion that if people do not spend their money in one way they will spend it in another' (Keynes, *General Theory*, p. 20). 'Say's Law' assumed that hoarding was unlikely; it did not imply that it was impossible. The villain of the piece is not so much 'Say's Law'—which, after all, was not an integral part of the Classical theoretical structure—but the neo-Classical theory of interest, to which the Classical economists properly so-called did not subscribe. Cf. D. H. MacGregor, op. cit., pp. 111–18.

bread, it would be a poor consolation to tell them that they might exchange one for the other.'[1]

This idea, that the extension of manufacture is limited by the size of the agricultural surplus, was perfectly familiar, having been popularized in Britain by writers like Cantillon, Steuart, Paley, and Malthus; and Mill would not have dreamed of disputing it as a general principle. It was, of course, true that a nation could have too much of a *particular type* of capital. But Mill—and Ricardo, whose friendship with Mill began at the time of the publication of *Commerce Defended*—refused to be converted to the view that it could have too much of capital *in general*.

IV

Although the 'temporary topics' which had provided the occasion for Spence's pamphlet soon ceased to agitate the mind of the public, the theoretical problems associated with the idea of under-consumption continued to be debated during the next decade. Chalmers, for example, argued that 'It is the degree of expenditure . . . which imposes a limit on the use and extension of capital, and if universal accumulation were to go on, the increase of capital and diminution of expenditure would reduce the profit to a mere nothing, and all further inducement to accumulation would cease'.[2] Interesting accounts of certain aspects of the problem were contained in the works of Buchanan and Mrs. Marcet.[3] Malthus and Ricardo corresponded with one another on the general glut question in 1814, and at the same time the new theory of rent was worked out—a theory which enabled Ricardo to blame the falling rate of profit on a factor which operated outside the economic system itself. Simon Gray, in his unduly neglected work *The Happiness of States*, gave a surprisingly 'modern' account of the effects which 'stagnations in the foreign market' might have on demand and employment at home, and the remedies which should be applied to meet the situation.[4] And after the crisis of 1815 Robert Owen hastened to popularize the notion that the cause of all the trouble lay in the fact that the productive power of the nation had increased enormously 'without increasing the power of consumption in the same proportion'.[5]

---

[1] Quotations from *Tracts*, pp. 152–62.

[2] *Enquiry into the Extent and Stability of National Resources* (1808), p. 237. Chalmers at this time believed that there was 'little danger' of this happening.

[3] Buchanan, *Observations on the Subjects Treated in Dr. Smith's Inquiry* (1814), pp. 75–9; Jane Marcet, *Conversations on Political Economy* (1816), chapter 22, *passim*.

[4] *The Happiness of States* (1815), pp. 83–91.

[5] *The Life of Robert Owen* (1858), Vol. IA, p. 110. Cf. also pp. 54–5 and 213–6, ibid., and the Owenite pamphlet *Mr. Owen's Arrangements, etc.* (1819), *passim*.

But the next really important event in the history of theories of under-consumption was the publication in 1819 of Sismondi's *New Principles of Political Economy*. Whereas Spence, Malthus, and Chalmers wrote on behalf of the landlords and 'unproductive consumers', Sismondi, although by no means a socialist,[1] wrote on behalf of the proletariat. His main aim was to emphasize and explain the disproportion between production and consumption which appeared to have become chronic in the modern world. He never ceased to castigate those economists who maintained that consumption was 'a force without limits, always ready to swallow up an infinitely large product'.[2] Nothing was easier, he believed, than for production and consumption to get out of step with one another.

Sismondi's treatment of this theme can perhaps be discussed under two separate headings without unduly distorting his meaning. First, he interested himself in the social and economic causes of those rigidities, immobilities, time-lags, and other frictions which prevented equilibrium being reached as smoothly and painlessly as it was assumed to do in the works of the 'chrematistical' economists. He never sought seriously to deny that under capitalism there were powerful tendencies towards a state of equilibrium: he was too earnest a disciple of Smith for that. What he did deny was that this equilibrium could ever in fact be achieved, under the institutional set-up peculiar to modern capitalism, except at the cost of appalling suffering for the working people. And the frictions which caused economic dislocations, he believed, were inherent in rather than excrescent upon the modern industrial system. The impossibility of accurately forecasting the demand for one's product, the comparative immobility of specialized labour and fixed capital, the displacements caused by the introduction of machinery, and even the difficulty of adjusting population to revenue—all these were conceived by Sismondi to be essentially modern phenomena, associated almost exclusively with industrial capitalism.[3]

Another contemporary work with under-consumptionist tendencies (see pp. xvii–xx, 365–7, 386–90, etc.)—David Laurie's *Treatise on Finance* (1815)—is referred to by D. H. MacGregor, op. cit., p. 122, footnote.

[1] Marx and Engels, in the *Communist Manifesto*, after a generous appraisal of the positive elements of Sismondi's teaching, say that it 'aspires either to restoring the old means of production and of exchange, and with them the old property relations and the old society, or to cramping the modern means of production and of exchange within the framework of the old property relations that have been, and were bound to be, exploded by those means. In either case, it is both reactionary and utopian. Its last words are: corporate guilds for manufacture; patriarchal relations in agriculture'. (Quoted from the centenary edn. of the *Manifesto* (London, 1948), p. 39.)

[2] *Nouveaux Principes* (1st edn., 1819), Vol. I, p. 78.

[3] Ibid., Vol. I, pp. 301–13, and Vol. II, pp. 256–65; *Etudes sur l'Economie Politique* (1837), Vol. I, pp. 142–54.

Second, Sismondi sought to penetrate even further below the surface of economic reality in order to reveal certain more general and deep-seated tendencies towards under-consumption. Here, like Marx, he was convinced that the fact that the labourer had been dispossessed of his means of production was the key to a proper understanding of the forces at work. 'We are now', he wrote in his *Studies*, 'and it has never been sufficiently noted, in a condition of society which is absolutely new, and of which we have as yet no experience at all. We are tending to separate completely every kind of property from every kind of labour, to break the whole connection between the day-labourer and the master, and to take away from the first every kind of participation in the profits of the second'. This separation of property and labour forced the labourer into a state of dependence upon the capitalist, so that his income tended always to be reduced to the minimum of subsistence. The income of the capitalists and landed proprietors, on the other hand, tended to increase as time went on, and this ever-widening inequality of distribution made a smooth adaptation of production to demand absolutely impossible:

'The same revenue is indeed employed by the rich and by the poor, but it is not employed in the same manner. The first replaces much less labour than the second; it is much less favourable to population, and consequently serves much less towards the reproduction of wealth. . . . If the same revenue is distributed between ninety-nine very poor families, and one very rich one, the encouragement which they will give to national industry will be infinitely less. . . . It is also worthy of note that, while the effect of the increase of capitals is in general to concentrate work in very large manufactories, the effect of great wealth is to exclude almost completely the products of these very large manufactories from the consumption of the rich. Every time an object, previously produced by the skill of a worker, becomes the product of a blind mechanism, it loses something of its perfection, and also of its reputation, in the eyes of fashion. . . . Thus, then, through the concentration of fortunes in the hands of a small number of owners, the internal flow is more and more contracted, and industry is more and more reduced to seeking an outlet in foreign markets, where greater revolutions threaten it.'[1]

Once property and labour had been separated, the system of competition replaced that of associative effort. Under conditions of capitalist competition, production tended to be regulated not according to the actual demand for one's product (which could never be exactly determined) but according to the size of one's capital,

[1] Translated from *Etudes*, Vol. I, pp. 91–2, and *Nouveaux Principes*, Vol. I, pp. 329–42.

with the result that there was a permanent tendency towards over-production. Each producer would strive to produce more and to sell at a lower price than his competitors; he would seek to reduce his costs of production by paying less rent to the landlord, less interest to the rentier, and less wages to the labourers; and he would actually succeed in reducing these payments, since the impact of the increased output on the market would lower the price of the product for all producers. As a result of such operations there would be a constant tendency for output to increase and for consuming power to diminish or at least not to increase in the same proportion—a tendency which would be intensified by the displacement of labour due to the intro-duction of machinery and by the extension of bank credit. To this argument it might be objected that the additional capital employed to increase production would in fact be spent, and that demand would accordingly increase proportionately with production. It was quite true, Sismondi admitted, that invested savings were spent; but since the price per unit of the factors of production tended to diminish as production increased, it was still true to say that 'consumption will never increase at the same rate as production'.[1]

Sismondi was free from any desire to apologize for the 'unproduc-tive consumers' of his day, and he did not commit the vulgar error of supposing that invested savings remained unspent. And it seems at first sight that he also succeeded in emancipating himself from those Physiocratic ideas in which most of the other early under-consump-tionists were still to some extent entangled. The theoretical basis upon which Sismondi built, for what it was worth, was taken from Smith rather than from Quesnay. The influence of Physiocratic ways of thought is much less obvious in Sismondi's case than in, say, Spence's, since Sismondi deliberately attempted to discard the Physiocratic framework. Yet there are certain aspects of his work which on closer examination seem to suggest that we would be unwise to place Sismondi too far outside the Physiocratic pale. There is, to begin with, his marked preference for an agricultural over a manufacturing economy, and the distinctly Physiocratic tone of some of the passages in which he states it.[2] Again, the dependence of the manufacturing sector upon the agricultural sector, and the importance of achieving a proper 'balance' between them, are often emphasized.[3] And some-times he even seems to accept the idea that the incomes of the

[1] *Etudes*, Vol. I, pp. 144–51; *Nouveaux Principes*, Vol. I, pp. 374–84. There was, of course, no real reason why monetary demand *should* increase propor-tionately with physical productivity. Sismondi seems to have modified his views on this subject after an interview with Ricardo: see the long note commencing on p. 81 of Vol. I of the *Etudes*.

[2] E.g. *Nouveaux Principes*, Vol. I, pp. 150–2. Cf. M. Tuan, *Sismondi as an Economist*, p. 47.

[3] *Nouveaux Principes*, Vol. I, pp. 292, 296–300, 372–3, etc.

manufacturing classes are ultimately paid out of the net product accruing to the proprietors and cultivators.[1] In themselves such passages are not particularly significant: similar remarks—although not often in such profusion—are quite frequently to be found in the works of contemporary authors who can scarcely be accused of any attachment to Physiocracy. But it will be argued in the last section of this essay that their occurrence in Sismondi's work was not fortuitous, and that his treatment of some of the leading under-consumptionist themes was strongly influenced by ways of thought which were essentially Physiocratic.

V

It is quite possible that Malthus borrowed more from Sismondi than he was prepared to acknowledge. Some of the leading ideas of Book Two of the *Principles of Political Economy* may well have owed their origin to passages in the *New Principles*.[2] But there are at least two features of Malthus's approach, quite apart from the obvious political divergences, which mark it off sharply from Sismondi's and which it is necessary to consider if Malthus's particular brand of under-consumption theory is to be placed in its proper perspective.

In the first place, Malthus's leanings towards Physiocracy were much more direct and conscious than were Sismondi's. Book Three of the second edition of the *Essay on Population* contained, indeed, some of the most Physiocratic passages which had appeared in British economic writing since Cantillon. Malthus pointed out that Smith's definition of the wealth of a nation as 'the annual produce of its land and labour' involved a dangerous abstraction from the physical characteristics of the commodities produced. 'Wealth' according to Smith's definition might increase while the condition of the labouring poor actually worsened. For example, if a nation's savings over a period were invested solely in manufacture and not in agriculture, its 'power of supporting labourers' would at best remain static, and even if the poor retained the same command over the

---

[1] E.g. *Etudes*, Vol. II, pp. 246–7.

[2] For example, Malthus's idea that the consumption of the labourers employed in making a commodity can never alone furnish an adequate market for it, and the broad conclusions he drew from this idea, are clearly foreshadowed in chapters 4 and 5 of Book Two of the *Nouveaux Principes*. And the fact that an increase in accumulation must be preceded by an increase in the national revenue if over-production is to be avoided is emphasized strongly by Sismondi in chapters 3 and 4 of Book Four. Cf. M. Tuan, op. cit., pp. 56–7 and 66–7. Cf. also Marx's comments, in his *Theorien über den Mehrwert*, on Malthus's alleged plagiarism from Sismondi (translated in my *Marx and Engels on Malthus*, pp. 158 ff.).

necessaries and conveniences of life a greater proportion of them than before would be employed in manufacture, an occupation much more unhealthy and precarious than agriculture. Malthus then went on to compare the Physiocrats' definition of wealth with that of Smith, and although he criticized the Physiocrats in certain respects he adopted a number of their basic premises. For example, he said that manufactures, strictly speaking:

'... are no new production, no new creation, but merely a modification of an old one, and when sold must be paid for out of a revenue already in existence, and consequently the gain of the seller is the loss of the buyer. A revenue is transferred, but not created.'

He proceeded to contrast the 'surplus produce of the cultivators', which was measured by rent, with a 'net monied revenue, arising from manufactures': whereas the former would support all those people in the nation who did not labour on the land, a 'net monied revenue' of the same extent would simply 'throw the country in which it existed into an absolute dependence upon the surplus produce of others'. Then again, he asserted that 'Land, in an enlarged view of the subject, is incontrovertibly the sole source of all riches'; that the system of the Physiocrats was the only one 'by which commerce and manufactures can prevail to a very great extent, without bringing with them, at the same time, the seeds of their own ruin'; that 'the surplus produce of the land is the fund which pays everything besides the food of the cultivators'; that English commerce and manufactures (whose 'shewiness' blinded people to the true position) were really the consequence rather than the cause of 'the wealth, power, and prosperity of England'; and that the superiority of England over France lay primarily in the 'great surplus produce' which English agriculture produced and which 'enables her to support such a vast body of manufactures, such formidable fleets and armies, such a crowd of persons engaged in the liberal professions, and a proportion of the society living on money rents, very far beyond what has ever been known in any other country of the world'. And, finally, he insisted that whichever of the two definitions of wealth was adopted:

'... the great position of the Economists will always remain true, that the surplus produce of the cultivators is the great fund which ultimately pays all those who are not employed upon the land. Throughout the whole world, the number of manufacturers, of proprietors, and of persons engaged in the various civil and military professions, must be exactly proportioned to this surplus produce, and cannot in the nature of things increase beyond it. ... In proportion as the labour and ingenuity of man, exercised upon the land, have increased this surplus produce, leisure has been given to a greater number of persons to employ themselves in all the inventions which embellish civilized life. And though, in its turn, the desire to profit by these inventions, has greatly contributed to stimulate the cultivators to increase their surplus produce; yet the order of the precedence is clearly the surplus produce.'

It is true that many of these statements were eventually purged as the *Essay* proceeded through its successive editions, but there is no doubt that Malthus retained to the end at least three of the leading ideas—that agriculture was superior to manufacture, that the agricultural surplus held a key position in the economy, and that it was dangerous to abstract from the physical characteristics of the commodities produced when framing one's basic model.[1]

In the second place, Malthus's theory of value was much more developed and much more closely integrated with his under-consumption theory than Sismondi's. Sismondi had contented himself with distinguishing between what he called the 'intrinsic value' and the 'relative value' of a commodity—'the one is established by production; the other by competition'.[2] Malthus, on the other hand, deliberately set out to attack not only the labour theory as Ricardo had developed it but also the very foundations of the Smith-Ricardo concept of value. Adam Smith, rejecting the old 'physical cost' concept of value and the Mercantilist idea of 'profit upon alienation', had identified exchange value with 'natural price'—that is, a price sufficient to cover the costs of production *including profit at the customary rate*. Under conditions of competitive equilibrium, when supply and demand were assumed to balance, all commodities tended to sell at a value equivalent to this 'natural price', although deviations of the actual 'market price' from the value or 'natural price' of the commodity might be caused by temporary discrepancies between supply and demand. If, then, relative prices tended to be determined by relative costs of production, what determined costs of production?

---

[1] Quotations from *Essay* (2nd edn., 1803), pp. 420–42. A number of important changes were made in this part of the work in the third and fourth editions, many of them designed to weaken the links with Physiocracy. During the gap of ten years between the fourth and fifth editions, Spence's pamphlet appeared, claiming Malthus as a fellow-traveller of the Physiocrats, and Ricardo criticized the Physiocratic chapters in personal conversation with Malthus. Possibly these events—and, of course, contemporary economic developments—were responsible for the radical rearrangement and rewriting of these chapters in the fifth edition of 1817. The last passage quoted above was the only one which survived without substantial amendment—and even in that the substance of the first sentence was omitted.

[2] *Noveaux Principes*, Vol. I, pp. 281–6. The context shows clearly that Sismondi, like Malthus, was anxious to use the distinction as the basis for a demonstration that the realization of a surplus over cost was largely dependent upon the conditions of demand.

As is well known, Smith never really answered this question, since he relegated the 'labour embodied' explanation to the 'early and rude state of society': Ricardo, on the other hand, argued that the 'labour embodied' explanation was valid (at any rate up to a point) in modern society as well. Malthus began his attack on this structure by arguing that the prices of monopolized commodities and agricultural products —'a class of commodities of the greatest extent'—were almost always 'determined upon a principle distinct from the cost of production'. And even in the case of manufactured products, where 'the existing market prices much more frequently coincide with the costs of production', Malthus argued that our experience shows us:

'. . . that any alteration in the proportion of the demand to the supply quite overcomes for a time the influence of these costs; and further, when we come to examine the subject more closely, we find that the cost of production itself only influences the prices of these commodities, as the payment of this cost is the necessary condition of their continued supply in proportion to the extent of the effectual demand for them.'

If this be true, Malthus concluded, 'it follows that the great law of demand and supply is called into action to determine what Adam Smith calls natural prices, as well as what he calls market prices'.[1] It follows, too, that the quantity of labour either commanded by or embodied in a commodity cannot *determine* the value of the commodity, although it may be capable of use as a *measure* of its value. In Malthus's opinion the value of a commodity was *determined* by supply and demand, and its best *measure* was the amount of labour the commodity would command. Now if the commodity is to be sold at a profitable price, the amount of labour which it commands must be greater than the amount of labour which is embodied in it, the excess representing the profit yielded. And it is obvious that the consumption of the labourers directly employed in the production of the commodity cannot alone furnish an adequate demand for it: the selling price, if a profit is to be earned, must exceed the wage-costs. If one adopts this way of looking at the process of production and exchange one may easily be led, as Malthus was, to assert that the size of the excess—and, indeed, its very existence—is dependent upon the effective demand for the product exercised by those who are not directly employed in its production.[2] And a bias towards Physiocracy will encourage this view, if only because the idea that

---

[1] *Principles* (2nd edn., 1836), pp. 70–1.
[2] Malthus did not deny that the state of cultivation of the land ultimately and in the last resort governed profits. But he relegated this cause to the status of a 'limiting principle', and postulated 'the state of the demand and the supply' as the 'regulating principle'. Cf. Malthus's *Principles*, pp. 271–82.

profits (at least in manufacture) do not originate in the process of production but are somehow paid out of the incomes of the purchasers is of the essence of the Physiocratic framework.

Malthus believed that this line of thought could provide an effective answer to the 'saving is spending' argument with which Ricardo, Say, and Mill were endeavouring to protect themselves against the under-consumptionist attack. Malthus, it must be emphasized, always meant saving-*plus-investment* when he spoke of 'accumulation', 'parsimony', or 'saving'. 'No political economist of the present day', he wrote, 'can by saving mean mere hoarding.'[1] By 'saving' Malthus meant exactly what all the British Classical economists meant by it—the employment of 'productive' instead of 'unproductive' labourers out of the net revenue.[2] It could not, therefore, be denied that when additional savings were made they were in actual fact transferred to and spent by the labourers who were employed by them; but, as we have seen, it *could* be denied that the demand of these workers alone was sufficient to enable the product to be sold at a profitable price. Whence, then, was the necessary extra demand to come? It could hardly come from the capitalists, since by hypothesis they were saving-and-investing more and therefore spending less on personal consumption. It seemed obvious to Malthus that the extra demand could only come from the community's 'unproductive consumers'—the landlords, stockholders, menial servants, clergymen, etc., who consumed but did not produce and who were therefore capable of maintaining 'such a balance between produce and consumption as will give the greatest exchangeable value to the results of the national industry'. It followed that if saving-and-investment increased rapidly without a 'previous increase in the value of the national revenue' (the most potent cause of which was an increase in the expenditure of unproductive consumers), a number of commodities would be produced which could not be sold at a profit-

---

[1] *Principles*, p. 38.

[2] Malthus makes this perfectly clear in literally dozens of places, and it would not be necessary to insist upon the point here were it not that a certain amount of misunderstanding seems to exist among modern commentators. Mr O'Leary, for example (*Journal of Political Economy*, Vol. L, pp. 910–11), is puzzled by the fact that Malthus did not state definitely anywhere that hoarding plays 'a significant role in aggravating a deficiency in effective consumer demand'. Mr O'Leary seems to feel, however, that Malthus must have meant it even if he did not definitely say it, and, on the very slightest textual evidence, concludes that 'in Malthus' theory excessive savings cause a damming-up of idle purchasing power, but he was not altogether clear as to where the damming-up process takes place'. There is, however, another possible solution to the mystery—that Malthus's argument was simply a bad one. It is amusing, in the light of certain modern discussions on this point, to read Malthus's own comments on an author who identified saving with hoarding: see *Essay* (1st edn., 1798), pp. 282–4 and 295–7.

able price. This glut of commodities would cause such a reduction of profits 'as very greatly to diminish both the power and the will to save'.[1]

This somewhat precarious thesis Malthus endeavoured to support with all the subsidiary arguments he could muster. Accumulation, he admitted, was certainly a *condition* of the increase of wealth, but by itself it did not afford an adequate stimulus to that increase. Those who believed the contrary, he remarked (with some justice), 'have considered commodities as if they were so many mathematical figures, or arithmetical characters, the relations of which were to be compared, instead of articles of consumption, which must of course be referred to the numbers and wants of the consumers'. They have also failed to take into consideration 'the influence of so general and important a principle in human nature, as indolence or love of ease'. They have assumed that 'the consumption of the labourers employed by those whose object is to save, will create such an effectual demand for commodities as to encourage a continued increase of produce'. They have assumed that in the process of saving all that was lost by the capitalist is gained by the labourers—but if the general glut that follows over-accumulation creates unemployment, how can Ricardo be right in saying that in such a case 'the check to the progress of wealth would be but temporary'? Obviously a 'previous increase in the value of the national revenue' is required, both to give the necessary stimulus to accumulation and to make that accumulation 'effective in the continued production of wealth'. The causes most favourable to this increase in value are 'the division of landed property', 'internal and external commerce', and, last but not least, 'the maintenance of an adequate proportion of the society employed in personal services, or otherwise entitled to make a demand for material products without contributing directly to their supply'. The capitalists have the power but not the will to consume their revenue, since 'the great object of their lives is to save a fortune' and therefore 'they could not afford an adequate market to each other by exchanging their several products'. In the class of unproductive consumers 'the landlords no doubt stand pre-eminent', but 'if they were not assisted by the great mass of individuals engaged in personal services, whom they maintain, their own consumption would of

---

[1] Quotations from *Principles*, pp. 413, 365, and 315. There is not a great deal in common between Malthus's theory and those which are generally associated with the Keynesian analysis today. Not only does Malthus deliberately assume that savings are automatically invested, but he also implies that an increase in investment will widen and not narrow a gap between effective demand and supply. If Ricardo committed a gross heresy in arguing that demand for commodities is not demand for labour, surely Malthus committed an even grosser one in arguing that demand for labour is not—or at least is not sufficient—demand for commodities.

itself be insufficient to keep up and increase the value of the produce'.[1]

Ricardo had admitted, in his *Principles*, that 'If every man were to forego the use of luxuries, and be intent only on accumulation, a quantity of necessaries might be produced, for which there would not be any immediate consumption. Of commodities so limited in number, there might undoubtedly be a universal glut'. But this was as far as he was prepared to go, and even this case, he believed, did not 'impugn the general principle'.[2] If such a thing happened (which was, to say the least, extremely unlikely), 'profits would be low because wages would be high', and in any event the condition would only be temporary since the principle of population would eventually rectify matters.[3] And Ricardo emphasized that he had only admitted that '*of commodities so limited in number*' there might be a universal glut. But, in actual fact:

'Would only such a limited number of commodities be produced? Impossible, because the labourers would be glad to consume conveniences and luxuries if they could get them, and in the case supposed to promote the very object of the masters it would be their interest to produce the commodities for which their labourers had the will and power to pay.'[4]

Ricardo's attitude on this point is typical of his attitude to the whole of Malthus's argument. In his own reasoning he always assumed, first, that the pattern of class demand would automatically change as class income varied, and, second, that production would speedily adapt itself to any marked change in the pattern of demand. Malthus, on the other hand, often appeared to base his belief in the possibility of a general glut either on the assumption that the pattern of class demand (particularly working-class demand) might remain unaltered for long periods in spite of changes in income, or on the assumption that production would fail to adapt itself to changes in the pattern of demand. An 'inordinate passion for accumulation', Malthus wrote, will inevitably lead to a supply ot commodities beyond what the 'structure and habits' of society will permit to be profitably consumed.[5] Ricardo was not prepared to allow that the 'structure' (of production) and 'habits' (of consumption) under competitive capitalism were as rigid as Malthus supposed, but the real difference between the two men lay deeper than this. It was not so much that they differed over the degree of rigidity of the 'structure and habits' of their own society, as that they each en-

---

[1] Quotations from *Principles*, pp. 361–7, 320, 322, 326, 365–6, 372, and 400
[2] *Principles* (Sraffa edn.), p. 293.
[3] *Notes on Malthus* (Sraffa edn.), p. 303.
[4] Ibid., p. 313.   [5] *Principles*, p. 325.

visaged their own society *in terms of a different assemblage of 'structure and habits'*. Whereas Ricardo's model was built on the basis of concepts and patterns appropriate to a developed capitalist society, Malthus on occasions still tended to think in terms of certain ideas and relationships which were appropriate to an older type of society—a society which was essentially Physiocratic in character.

VI

The last two under-consumptionist works to be considered in this essay—the anonymous pamphlet *Considerations on the Accumulation of Capital, etc.* (1822) and Thomas Chalmers' *Political Economy* (1832)—need not detain us long.

The *Considerations* does little more than echo Malthus, and its only real virtue lies in the fact that its complete lack of subtlety exposes in a rather startling manner a number of the contradictions implicit in Malthus's contribution. The basic assumptions are the same: that a commodity must command more labour than is embodied in it, that value is determined by supply and demand, that the workers will never demand anything but necessaries even if their income increases,[1] and so on. In two respects the author goes rather further than Malthus: he states in one place that 'the proportion in which the net revenue of a country is saved and spent must be practically the great regulator of profits'; and towards the end of the pamphlet he maintains quite categorically that demand for labour is not demand for commodities.[2] And in one section he outlines with some precision the nature of the 'structure and habits' of the type of economy which both he and Malthus tended to take as their model. It is obviously necessary, he argues, that net revenue should be partly spent unproductively and partly saved if wealth is to increase, but how is the proper proportion between saving and spending to be determined? This must, he answers, 'in every particular country, depend upon its situation and circumstances generally, but more particularly on the fertility of its land'. Enlarging on the latter point, he goes on as follows:

'A country whose soil was of so poor a quality as to yield but little more than sufficient to maintain the cultivators, could not possibly support a very large body of unproductive consumers; while one whose lands were of great natural or acquired fertility would not only be enabled to maintain a considerable body of unproductive labourers, but would absolutely require a much larger unproductive consumption, in order to give the fullest development to its produc-

[1] *Considerations*, pp. 11–12. Cf. Sismondi, *Nouveaux Principes*, Vol. I, pp. 80–1.
[2] *Considerations*, p. 30, and pp. 39 ff.

tive powers. In no country, however, is the land so poor as not to yield some surplus produce; and as the whole of the labouring population cannot, therefore, be employed in raising necessaries, the remainder, if they be productive labourers, must be employed in the production of superfluities, and a proportionate degree of unproductive consumption must be always requisite to give effect to their labours, since, without it, their commodities could not possibly find a market.'

There follows a long Physiocratic passage quoted from Paley, (somewhat similar to the comments on the agricultural surplus made by Malthus in the *Essay*),[1] which the author adduces as an illustration of the doctrine he wishes to lay down—that production cannot be carried 'to its utmost extent' unless 'they who have revenue at their command will give it in exchange for that particular description of commodities which are objects of unproductive expenditure'.[2]

It is clear from all this that we have not come very far from Spence. We are still in a society in which the landlords, cultivators, and 'manufacturers' are the only classes between whom it is deemed necessary to distinguish, and in which the landlords 'support' the manufacturers by presenting the agricultural surplus to them in exchange for the luxuries which they produce. The theory of underconsumption as Malthus and his followers developed it depends to an extent that it is not generally realized upon an essentially Physiocratic view of the pattern of production and demand. This is certainly *one* way of looking at society in all its stages (at least after the establishment of manufactures); but it is hardly the most useful way of looking at a modern society in which the dominating position formerly assumed by land has now been usurped by capital.

With Chalmers, too, we are in the same Physiocratic realm. His division of classes is substantially the same, although he endeavours to bring it a little more up to date by dividing the producers of necessaries into 'agricultural' and 'secondary' producers. His landlords, who 'have a natural superiority over all other classes of men', exchange the agricultural surplus which accrues to them in the form of rent for the luxury goods produced by the so-called 'disposable' population—'disposable' because the landlords may dispose of their services in whatever manner they please. Capital possesses no 'creative and emanating power'; manufacturers play no 'creative part in augmenting the public revenue'; food is the 'chief article of maintenance', and it is therefore obvious that 'principally with the holders of this maintenance, is lodged the power of replacing the outlays of the capitalist'. It is quite clear that Chalmers regards the

---

[1] Quoted above, pp. 333–4.
[2] Quotations from *Considerations*, pp. 19–25.

profits yielded in manufacture as being paid out of the agricultural surplus. Profits are dependent upon, and in fact originate in, the process of exchange.[1] In general, Chalmers follows Malthus fairly closely, extending his analogies and reproducing his illustrations. Value and profit are determined by supply and demand; over-production is possible notwithstanding the fact that 'saving is spending'; the agricultural surplus is the 'original fund out of which are paid the expenses of art, and science, and civilization, and luxury, and law, and defence'[2]—and so on. His differences with Malthus over the general glut question are mainly differences of emphasis. For example, Chalmers' illustrations are usually more extreme than Malthus's, assuming greater and more sudden changes; he gives more attention to the limitations imposed upon the expansion of capital by the state of agriculture; and he lays rather more stress on the mechanisms which ensure a restoration of equilibrium after a dislocation has occurred.[3] It seems obvious that both Chalmers and Malthus were led towards their under-consumptionist conclusions by looking at modern capitalist society in terms of a collection of concepts originally derived from a very different institutional set-up.[4]

VII

The basic Physiocratic structure, then—suitably amended to accord with contemporary changes in economic organization—was always lurking at the back of the minds of the early under-consumptionists. It appealed to them for reasons which were largely political. On the one hand, it appealed to them because the Physiocratic realm represented a fairly close approximation to the type of economy which they most admired. Malthus, Spence, and Chalmers were quite prepared to enter into some sort of compromise with the parvenu capitalist class, but they always hankered after a society in which the landlords would once again assume their rightful place as economic and political leaders of the community. Sismondi would have no truck with landlords: he was anxious to retreat even further back in history to the system of patriarchal cultivation; but the economy which he eulogized was at least one in which agriculture

---

[1] Quotations from *Political Economy*, pp. 63, 80, 557, and 86. Chalmers' views regarding the subordinate position of profits are set out more clearly in his *Enquiry* (1808), particularly in chapters 2 and 4. See below, pp. 359 ff.

[2] *Political Economy*, p. 46.

[3] Ibid., pp. 113–17. Cf. Malthus, *Principles*, p. 433.

[4] The possibility of a general glut was recognized by a number of less important writers at this period. See, for example, John Craig's *Remarks on Some Fundamental Doctrines in Political Economy* (1821), chapter 3; Robert Hamilton's *Progress of Society* (1830), chapter 19; and John Cazenove's *Outlines of Political Economy* (1832), chapter 19.

was predominant and manufacture definitely subsidiary.[1] On the other hand, the Physiocratic structure appealed to them because certain elements of it could be used to bolster up their general critique of capitalism. All of them believed that the unrestricted investment of capital, particularly in manufacture, would inevitably cause (and in fact already had caused) violent dislocations in the economy. And there were at least three ways in which basic elements of the Physiocratic structure could be used to give theoretical backing to this belief. First, the Physiocratic pattern of demand, with its emphasis on the purchase of goods by the landlord class, could be used to suggest that the prosperity of the community was largely dependent upon the continued and increasing expenditure of that class, and that if the landlords accumulated their income instead of spending it on personal consumption serious maladjustments would be brought about. Second, the Physiocratic account of value and profit could be used to draw attention in a more general manner to the idea that profit on capital was essentially dependent upon the effective demand of those who bought the commodities which the capital was employed to produce. Third, the Physiocratic idea of a natural balance between agriculture on the one hand and manufacture and commerce on the other could be used to provide a broad background for the study of economic dislocations. For these reasons, then, the approach of the early under-consumptionists was strongly influenced by their conscious or unconscious adoption of certain Physiocratic ideas. With Sismondi and Malthus we are some-times in the Physiocratic and sometimes in the Ricardian realm. With Spence and Chalmers we are in the Physiocratic realm for almost the whole time.[2]

Eventually, of course, the march of economic events renders the Physiocratic view of the economy implausible, even to those for whom it possesses political attractions. One simple but vastly important phenomenon impresses itself more and more on men's minds as capitalist competition develops in all spheres of production: all commodities which are produced for sale, irrespective of their physical attributes, normally tend to sell at a price which is sufficient not only to cover paid-out costs, but also to provide a profit propor-

---

[1] Rist has drawn attention to the fact that Sismondi sometimes 'reasons as if the nation were composed of agriculturists who buy the manufactured goods they need with the revenue received from the sale of the present year's crop'. See Gide and Rist, *A History of Economic Doctrines* (2nd English edn.), p. 190.

[2] Spence and Chalmers quite consciously made further amendments to the Physiocratic framework in an attempt to bring it more into consonance with the new economic environment. Spence, for example, admitted that the farmer usually shared in the net product. Chalmers introduced his new class of 'secondary' producers, and tried to adapt the basic model so that it could be applied to a country which was partly dependent upon overseas trade.

tioned to the amount of capital employed. It was a consideration of this phenomenon—and certain associated phenomena such as the changes in the source of accumulation and the pattern of demand, and the growth of international trade and factor mobility—which stimulated the construction of a new theoretical system.[1]

The differences between the new system and the Physiocratic system were considerable. The relation between capitalist and worker was no longer abstracted from, but placed at the very foundation of the analysis. Agricultural and manufacturing profits were clearly recognized as two different species of the same genus. Profit, rather than rent, assumed the key position in the economy, and the social surplus was conceived as consisting not of rent alone but of rent and profits. In the field of value, 'exchange value' was identified with equilibrium price and equated to cost of production including profits, and it was assumed that market price oscillated around 'exchange value' according to fluctuations in supply and demand. In the field of distribution, since the social surplus was now conceived to consist of both rent and profits, the question of its apportionment between the landlords and the capitalists for the first time began to assume importance and interest.

There were three special aspects of the new system which brought it sharply into conflict with the early theories of under-consumption. First, it assumed 'that those commodities only will be produced which will be suited to the wants and tastes of mankind, because none other will be demanded'.[2] Since any lack of balance between supply and demand would be swiftly rectified per medium of the price mechanism, it was assumed that demand was merely a *condition* of production and therefore irrelevant to the problem of exchange value.[3] Second, as a necessary consequence, it made abstraction of the physical attributes of commodities. There no longer appeared to be any logical reason for laying emphasis on the physical distinctions between, say, agricultural produce and manufactured goods, and many of the examples imagined by the under-consumptionists of a dislocation of the balance between agriculture and manufacture began to appear as irrelevant. Third, profit was regarded as an income which *originated* in the process of production and was merely *realized* in the process of exchange. It followed that any explanation of profit conducted mainly in terms of supply and demand was bound to appear empty and superficial.

It is easy enough to criticize the assumptions upon which the new

---

[1] The history of the transition from Physiocracy to the new theoretical system is considered in more detail in the next essay.

[2] Ricardo, *Works* (Sraffa edn.), Vol. VI, p. 148.

[3] This conclusion was also dependent upon the further assumption of constant returns to the industry.

system was founded, and to assert that they begged the whole question of under-consumption. But under-consumption was a new phenomenon taking place in a new type of economy, and the general tendencies and features of that economy had to be summed up and generalized theoretically before the nature and causes of dislocations within it could be adequately studied. Ricardo and his disciples did not themselves make such a study, since for reasons which were primarily political they accepted Say's Law. But the example of Marx shows clearly enough that it was at least *possible* to make a profound analysis of under-consumption while at the same time accepting the greater part of the Ricardian economic framework. And if our study of the early under-consumptionists has shown any-thing it is this—that the theoretical apparatus which they used was hopelessly inadequate to the task which they set out to perform.

The early under-consumptionists failed, I believe, not only because their political opinions were reactionary but also because their economic theory was, in the widest sense, *out of date*.[1] It is a mistake to look upon the controversy, as so many have done, merely as a struggle between a 'right' side and a 'wrong' side, or merely as a political squabble disguised as an ideological one. Logic and politics certainly played an important part in determining the position of each individual economist, but the controversy was in essence a part of the wider struggle to establish a new set of theoretical principles which would more closely correspond to the social structure of the time. It provided, in fact, the major field in which this wider struggle was fought out. To say this is not, of course, to say that the *conclusions* of the under-consumptionists were necessarily wrong. To put the label 'Physiocratic' on the foundations of their theory is merely to determine their place in the history of economic thought: it is not to dispose of them.

[1] S. N. Patten, in his article 'The Interpretation of Ricardo' (*Quarterly Journal of Economics*, April 1893), has analysed certain aspects of the Ricardo-Malthus controversy in a manner which bears some resemblance to this. See also J. H. Hollander, introduction to the 1928 edn. of Ricardo's *Notes on Malthus*, pp. xxiii–iv.

IV

PHYSIOCRACY AND CLASSICISM

IN BRITAIN[1]

'That system,' Lauderdale noted in 1805, 'which represents the produce of land as the sole source of the revenue, and the wealth of a nation, has long had its disciples in this country'.[2] Lauderdale and his contemporaries found little difficulty in tracing many instances where earlier British writers had substantially anticipated certain of the basic doctrines of Quesnay. In the early years of the nineteenth century, indeed, it would have been virtually impossible for any British economist to regard Physiocracy as an eccentric, ephemeral, and peculiarly French body of thought. For these were the years of the great debates over the validity of Physiocratic economic principles. Attempts were being made by numbers of publicists to popularize Physiocratic doctrines in various forms; polemics were being written in reply, some of them by men of considerable ability; and there was scarcely an economist writing in Britain at this time who did not feel impelled to give his opinion on the issues at stake.

It was largely in the course of these debates that British political economy was finally purged of the Physiocratic elements which had often characterized it in the past and moulded into something like the form it was eventually to assume in the hands of Ricardo. The present essay begins with a discussion of the broad theoretical and historical relationships between the Physiocratic viewpoint and that adopted by Adam Smith and his followers. It then proceeds to its main task—to examine the nature and significance of the British Physiocratic controversies, with special reference to the manner in which they stimulated the development and refinement of Classical theory during the twenty years prior to the publication of Ricardo's *Principles*.

I

To Quesnay, as to Smith, the fundamental economic problem seemed to be that of the nature and causes of the wealth of nations. Of what

[1] This essay is an amended version of an article published in the *Economic Journal*, March 1951. I am indebted to the editors of the *Economic Journal* for their permission to reproduce it here.

[2] *An Inquiry into the Nature and Origin of Public Wealth*, p. 112. Cf. Dugald Stewart, 'Lectures on Political Economy', in *Collected Works*, Vol. I, at pp. 298–301.

did wealth consist? How was it produced and increased? And, in particular, what action should be taken to maximize its rate of increase? Both Quesnay and Smith believed that it was impossible to answer such questions as these unless one began by making a clear distinction between the two portions into which the annual produce 'naturally divides itself' when it first comes into the hands of those to whom it directly accrues. One portion of the produce (or its value) has to be used to replace or compensate for the items which have been physically used up in the process of production during the period which has just ended. The second portion, the surplus over what Ricardo called 'the absolutely necessary expenses of production',[1] represents the net social gain on the period's working. This surplus is 'disposable' in the sense that it does not have to be expended in *maintaining intact* the productive powers of the community, but may at the option of the community be either consumed 'unproductively' or employed to increase its productive powers.[2] In French Physiocracy the second portion of the produce figured, of course, as the famous 'net product'. In the systems of Adam Smith and his followers it figured variously as the 'net real income', 'net revenue', 'disposable income', or simply 'surplus'.

Upon the size of the social surplus, it was often assumed, the prosperity of the community largely depended. This assumption was based, at least in part, upon the belief that the surplus was one of the main sources from which new capital could be accumulated.[3] The importance of this idea is obvious enough in the *Wealth of Nations*, but it is not so immediately apparent in the work of the French Physiocrats. Yet the Physiocrats' analysis of the various forms of capital was surely one of their most significant contributions to economic thought. Quesnay himself was concerned above all with the application of capitalist methods to agriculture, but this one-sided approach was gradually corrected as the agricultural school founded by Quesnay and Mirabeau increasingly joined forces with the 'sister-school' allegedly founded by Gournay. When Du Pont, Baudeau, and Turgot, who were mainly responsible for removing the feudal trappings from Quesnay's system, began to call energetically for the application of capitalist methods to manufacture as well as to agriculture, the essential character of Physiocracy became easier to discern. But even in the earlier works of the founders of the agricultural school the emphasis on the importance of capital is quite unmistakable. Quesnay's first economic article, *Farmers*, as we have

---

[1] *Principles* (Sraffa edn.), p. 348, footnote.

[2] Cf. J. S. Mill, *Essays on Some Unsettled Questions of Political Economy* (L.S.E. reprint), p. 89.

[3] The question of the accumulation of new capital out of the profit of the farmers is discussed in the second essay in the present volume.

seen, was a plea for the adoption of large-scale cultivation by a small number of wealthy farmers rather than small-scale cultivation by a host of poor *métayers*; and in his second article, *Corn*, he made it clear that he visualized his wealthy farmer not as a superior sort of labourer but as an 'entrepreneur', in something very like the modern sense of that word.[1] It was not so much men who were required in the country, Quesnay always insisted—it was rather wealth.[2] In the *Tableau* the 'great kingdom' was obviously intended to represent a France of the future in which the large-scale cultivation which Quesnay had seen in operation in certain French provinces had been extended throughout the whole realm. And Quesnay also made it clear that the capital required to introduce this large-scale cultivation must come, at any rate in large part, from the net product. 'The more agriculture is in a state of stagnation', he wrote, 'the more one should then devote a portion of the disposable expenditure to building it up again.'[3]

Both Quesnay and Smith, then, and the schools which they represent, were primarily concerned with the scientific analysis of *capitalist production*. Both were interested in securing an increase in national wealth through an extension of capitalist methods, and both realized that freedom of trade, internal and external, was a necessary precondition of this. In their theoretical analyses they both tended to concentrate much of their attention on the question of the origin and disposition of the social surplus, which they regarded as the only possible source of new capital. In this common interest and emphasis they are so sharply distinguished on the one hand from the Mercantilist writers who preceded them,[4] and on the other hand from the Marginalist writers who followed them, that it seems proper for the historian of economic thought to stress their community by treating them as working within a broadly similar framework of aims and concepts. The most convenient name for this framework is probably 'Classicism'. Physiocracy and the type of theory propounded by Smith and his followers are best regarded, I suggest, as two different species of the genus Classicism.[5]

But the differences between these two species of Classical thought were nevertheless profound. The root of the essential difference between them lay in the distinct assumption which each school made concerning the *form* taken by the social surplus. The Physiocrats

---

[1] See I.N.E.D., II, p. 483.   [2] See e.g. p. 234 above.
[3] Above, p. 158.

[4] The opposition of Quesnay and Smith to the Mercantilist approach was often expressed, of course, in the form of an insistence on the importance of penetrating the veil of money in order to uncover the 'real' forces which lay beneath it. Cf. e.g. pp. 217 ff., and 236–7 above.

[5] This view roughly coincides with the original use of the term 'Classical' by Marx. Cf. his *Critique of Political Economy* (Kerr edn.), p. 56.

assumed that the surplus took the form of land rent and land rent alone.[1] The earth is the unique source of wealth; agriculture is productive and manufacture sterile; the net product alone constitutes wealth—such propositions as these are simply different ways of saying that land rent is the only form which the social surplus assumes. As we have seen in the second essay in the present volume, the earlier Physiocrats usually insisted that the entrepreneur's 'profit', in so far as he received one at all, was not a separate, original, and constituent part of the social surplus. When the entrepreneur received a profit which was not reducible to a sort of superior wage, it was usually regarded as the product of some sort of monopoly situation of a greater or lesser degree of permanence, and as being 'paid out of' land rent. This is a view which is likely to be quite extensively held in any society which is passing through a historical stage in which profit on capital is beginning to emerge as a distinct and separate category of income, but does not bear (or is not yet recognized as bearing) any very definite and regular relation to the quantity of capital employed.

Whereas the Physiocrats considered rent to be the only income in the nature of a surplus, then, the Smithian school afforded that status to profit as well as to rent. To Smith himself it seemed clear that that second portion of the annual produce which represented the social surplus over cost consisted of both rent and profits. One part of the produce, he wrote, is 'destined for replacing a capital, or for renewing the provisions, materials, and finished work which had been withdrawn from a capital; the other for constituting a revenue either to the owner of this capital, as the profit of his stock, or to some other person, as the rent of his land.'[2] The Physiocratic controversies which are examined later in this essay resulted in the eventual confirmation of this viewpoint and in the partial elaboration of a set of techniques capable of giving it theoretical expression. And they also stimulated an important advance beyond this viewpoint.

In British economic thought before Adam Smith, those writers who were interested in questions relating to the analysis of the process of production (as distinct from the process of exchange) occasionally adopted a Physiocratic viewpoint—that is, they tended to regard profits (and interest) as being paid out of and dependent upon the rent of land. Cantillon, for example, believed that 'all classes and individuals in a state subsist or are enriched at the expense of the proprietors of land'.[3] A seventeenth-century pamphleteer asserted that the landowners 'are masters and proprietors of the foundation of all the wealth of this nation, all the profits arising out of the ground which

---

[1] I am abstracting here, of course, from taxes and tithes.
[2] *Wealth of Nations* (Cannan edn.), Vol. I, p. 315.
[3] *Essai* (R. E. S. reprint), p. 43.

is theirs.'[1] Petty, and to some extent Locke, seem to have regarded profits as included in rent, and interest as derived from rent.[2] It is easy enough to detect, in some of the earlier efforts to define the Classical framework and to work within it, a definite Physiocratic bias. Why was it, then, that the eventual *systematization* of the Classical attitude in Britain did not assume a Physiocratic form? And why was it that the Classical attitude was *first* systematized in France (where the system could hardly help assuming a Physiocratic form), rather than in Britain, whose economy was considerably more advanced than that of France?

Let us deal with the latter question first. The predecessors of Adam Smith, like Smith himself, were mainly interested in the problem of increasing national wealth, but in the conditions of their time it was only natural that their attention should have been chiefly directed to the relative 'surplus' yielded in foreign trade rather than to the positive surplus yielded in production. The gains from foreign trade were so manifest and so considerable, and their importance as a source of capital accumulation so obvious, that the commercial classes inevitably regarded the prosperity of the country as being largely dependent upon the size of their own profits. And, as Mr Dobb has pointed out, conditions were such that they still found it difficult 'to imagine any substantial profit being "naturally" made by investment in production'.[3] If, therefore, the revenue from the sale of a commodity exceeded the cost of producing or acquiring it, the excess was regarded as originating, not in the process of production, but in the act of exchange. All industrial and commercial profit, in other words, was 'profit upon alienation'. For example, Cary explained that when manufactured goods were sold

[1] Quoted in Beer, *An Inquiry into Physiocracy*, p. 74.

[2] Cf. Marx, *Theories of Surplus Value* (London, 1951), pp. 17 and 29. It should perhaps be pointed out here that I do not regard statements to the effect that the earth is 'properly the fountaine and mother of all the riches and abundance of the world', etc., or panegyrics in praise of the agricultural surplus, as being necessarily Physiocratic, in the sense in which I am using the word—although they may often be associated with a Physiocratic outlook. There is obviously an important sense in which it is universally true to say that all wealth springs from the earth, and that the agricultural surplus 'maintains' all those who do not work on the land. I count as Physiocrats only those who, at a time when profit on capital is a recognized (though not necessarily a regular or normal) category of income, treat it not as an original and independent income but as being in some way dependent upon or 'paid out of' land rent, which alone constitutes the social surplus. This definition, while it leaves us with some difficult border-line cases like Paley and Steuart, at least prevents our having to acknowledge Aristotle and Artaxerxes as pioneers of Physiocracy—which William Spence was quite prepared to do! (See Cobbett's *Weekly Political Register*, December 12, 1807, p. 923.)

[3] *Studies in the Development of Capitalism*, p. 199. Cf. Engels, *Engels on 'Capital'*, pp. 110–11.

abroad 'the necessity and humour of the buyers' sometimes enabled the merchant to sell his commodities at a price greater than the 'true value of the materials and labour'.[1] It was widely realized, of course, that if such a situation were to persist, it was necessary that the seller should be protected as far as possible against competition—a task which the state was expected to undertake.[2] For these reasons, then, in the last century of the Mercantilist era in Britain the economic analysis of production was almost always subordinated to the analysis of exchange. In France, on the other hand, the gains from foreign trade were of little economic importance, and it was possible for the foundations of the Classical analysis, with its emphasis on production, to be laid at a time when the capitalist order was only just beginning to emerge from feudal society.

To answer the other question—why the eventual systematization of the Classical attitude in Britain did not assume a Physiocratic form—it is necessary to ask why the Mercantilist emphasis on exchange gradually gave way in this country to the Classical emphasis on production. Two interrelated developments in the eighteenth century contributed largely to this radical change of viewpoint. First, British merchants began to experience more serious competition in foreign trade, and attention was increasingly directed towards the reduction of costs in the manufactory rather than towards the strengthening of their monopolistic position in the foreign market[3]—a change of attitude which was, of course, greatly encouraged by the contemporary developments in industrial technique. Second, net profit on capital slowly began to emerge as a distinct and normal category of income, receivable at more or less the same rate per cent on capital employed not only in commerce but also in manufacture and agriculture—and receivable, too, even under conditions approaching pure competition. Under these conditions, the notion of 'profit upon alienation' could hardly hope to survive. Economists gradually began to regard profit as *originating* in the process of production and as merely being *realized* in the act of sale. Under these circumstances, economists naturally began to seek for the origin of the social surplus in the sphere of production rather than in the sphere of exchange. But the very conditions which induced this movement towards Classicism were such as to make it virtually impossible for the eventual systematization of the Classical attitude in Britain to assume a Physiocratic form. By the time British economists came to analyse capitalist production, capitalist production itself had

---

[1] John Cary, *An Essay Towards Regulating the Trade and Employing the Poor in this Kingdom* (2nd edition, 1719), pp. 11-12.

[2] M. H. Dobb, op. cit., p. 200.

[3] Cf. E. S. Furniss, *The Position of the Laborer in a System of Nationalism*, pp. 165–7.

developed to such an extent that the basic Physiocratic assumptions seemed quite inconsistent with economic reality.

II

If we look at the *Wealth of Nations* from the vantage point of Ricardo's *Principles* it is not difficult to pick out the concepts which were destined to play the most prominent part in the development of political economy in the early nineteenth century. In the first place, Smith defined clearly the aim of the science. 'Political oeconomy', he said, 'considered as a branch of the science of a statesman or legislator, proposes . . . to enrich both the people and the sovereign.'[1] Second, he suggested that the size of the annual produce per head in any country—the best measure of its degree of enrichment—is regulated by two factors—'first, by the skill, dexterity, and judgment with which its labour is generally applied; and, secondly, by the proportion between the number of those who are employed in useful labour, and that of those who are not so employed'.[2] Third, he insisted that both of these factors are largely dependent upon the quantity of capital—in the first case because the accumulation of capital is not only a historical precondition of the division of labour but also greatly encourages the extension of the division of labour, and in the second case because the number of 'useful and productive' labourers 'is every where in proportion to the quantity of capital stock which is employed in setting them to work, and to the particular way in which it is so employed'.[3]

Smith's main theoretical interest lay, therefore, in the sphere of capitalist production, and particularly in the problems relating to the accumulation of capital. The analytical tools which he developed were designed to deal with the leading questions arising in this sphere. His account of accumulation, for example, is formulated in terms of two basic theoretical concepts—the notion of surplus and the distinction between productive and unproductive labour. The social surplus of product over cost, assuming the dual form of rent and profits, is regarded as the only possible source of funds for accumulation, and labour is described as 'productive' or 'unproductive' according to whether it actually helps to create this surplus or merely shares in it.[4]

[1] *Wealth of Nations*, Vol. I, p. 395.   [2] Ibid., p. 1.
[3] Ibid., pp. 258–9 and 2.
[4] This, I believe, is the basic idea which Smith had in mind when making his distinction. It is surely implied in the very title of the chapter in which he discusses the question—'Of the Accumulation of Capital, or of Productive and Unproductive Labour'. The criterion of distinction usually emphasized by Smith's critics today—that relating to the material or immaterial character of the commodity produced—probably owed its origin to the fact that in Smith's time

In Smith's system, as opposed to that of the Physiocrats, labour employed in manufacture is assumed to be productive—in other words, industrial profit is regarded as being an income in the nature of a surplus. Profit now stands on its own, quite independent of rent—a 'real primitive increase of national wealth', as a later economist was to describe it,[1] originating in the process of production and regularly yielded even under competitive conditions. Smith intuitively recognized, I think, that if profit was to be regarded in this way a new theory of value had to be evolved. Roughly speaking (and with several notable exceptions), previous writers had conceived of the 'value' of a commodity in terms of the physical items which had been used up in order to produce it. The value of a finished commodity equalled the value of the raw materials embodied in it, plus the value of the subsistence goods consumed during the process of production by the men who worked up the raw materials. This crude theory of value—which we can perhaps call the 'physical cost' theory to distinguish it from the Ricardian 'labour cost' theory—was, of course, quite inadequate to deal with the theoretical problems arising out of the new way of looking at profit. In the first place, the physical cost theory implied that the 'value' of what went into the productive process was exactly the same as the 'value' of what came out—that is, it implied that no surplus was yielded *in production*. And in the second place, on the basis of the physical cost theory the existence of profit could be accounted for only by conceiving commodities as being customarily sold *above their value*. But as capitalism developed, and markets became more and more competitive, economists became increasingly impressed by the fact that the actual prices received for a commodity tended to oscillate around a sort of mean or average price, and a new notion of value began to take the place of the old. It began to be felt that value ought to be conceived, not as something which a commodity usually sold *above*, but as something which under competition it tended to sell *at*. The physical cost theory, then, was incapable of giving theoretical expression to the idea of profit as a value-surplus which originated in the activity of production and which was realized when the commodity was sold 'at its value' on a market. A new theory of value had to be developed. Smith's own attempt to develop such a theory was no doubt confused and ambiguous in some respects, but it did at least have the merit of directing inquiry away from the physical cost theory and towards the embodied labour theory eventually adopted by Ricardo. And although Smith eventually decided that the embodied labour theory was inapplicable under conditions of developed capitalism, he did

almost all the labourers employed on a capitalist basis were engaged in the production of material goods.

[1] Daniel Boileau, *Introduction to the Study of Political Economy* (1811). p. 164.

apply it fairly consistently in his account of the origin of profit. 'The value which the workmen add to the materials,' he wrote, 'resolves itself . . . into two parts, of which the one pays their wages, the other the profits of their employer upon the whole stock of materials and wages which he advanced.'[1]

But these aspects of the *Wealth of Nations* appear especially significant only if, as I have suggested, we look at Smith's work from the viewpoint of Ricardo's *Principles*. It is easy to exaggerate the extent of Smith's emancipation from Physiocratic notions. Taking the *Wealth of Nations* as a whole, Smith looks backward towards the Physiocrats almost as often as he looks forward towards Ricardo. In a number of passages, for example, he stresses the primacy of the agricultural surplus. 'It is the surplus produce of the country only,' he writes in his chapter on the natural progress of opulence, 'or what is over and above the maintenance of the cultivators, that constitutes the subsistence of the town, which can therefore increase only with the increase of this surplus produce.'[2] Such statements are not in themselves Physiocratic, but they may easily lead to the adoption of a Physiocratic viewpoint. Smith asserted that the great landed proprietor, when he uses his rent-surplus to purchase manufactured goods from tradesmen and artificers, 'indirectly pays all [their] wages and profits, and thus indirectly contributes to the maintenance of all the workmen and their employers'.[3] And in another passage, which Spence was later to find useful, Smith argued that the produce of 'lands, mines, and fisheries' replaces with a profit not only the capitals required in these spheres 'but all the others in the society'.[4] Smith's leanings towards Physiocracy are even more clearly revealed in his well-known comparison between the productive powers of labour in manufacture and in agriculture. In manufacture the labourers occasion only 'the reproduction of a value equal to their own consumption, or to the capital which employs them, together with its owners profits'; but in agriculture, 'over and above the capital of the farmer and all its profits, they regularly occasion the reproduction of the rent of the landlord'. The generation of this additional surplus in agriculture is ascribed to the fact that it is only

---

[1] *Wealth of Nations*, Vol. 1, p. 50. It should be noted that the Physiocrats did not need a theory of value at all in order to give expression to the idea of *rent* as a surplus. In early agricultural production, as distinct from manufacture, the commodities comprising the input are likely to be qualitatively similar to those comprising the output, so that the creation of the surplus can be plausibly described in *real* terms without the intervention of a value theory. Cf. Malthus, *Principles* (L.S.E. reprint), pp. 262–4; Ramsay, *An Essay on the Distribution of Wealth* (1836), pp. 137–8 and 146; Marx, *Theories of Surplus Value*, p. 46; and M. H. Dobb, *Political Economy and Capitalism*, pp. 31–2.

[2] *Wealth of Nations*, Vol. 1, p. 356.   [3] Ibid., p. 387.

[4] Ibid., p. 266.

M

in agriculture that 'nature labours along with man'.[1] In view of these statements, it is not surprising that Smith should have believed that the interest of the landlords is 'strictly and inseparably connected with the general interest of the society'.[2] Nor is it surprising that his direct critique of Physiocracy at the end of Book IV should have been so unsatisfactory.

In a predominantly agricultural society, it may seem quite natural to regard land rent as the primary and original category of income and profit as a secondary and derivative category. In a developed capitalist economy, on the other hand, in which capital and capitalist organization have been extended to embrace every field of productive activity, including agriculture, it may seem more appropriate to regard profit on capital as the primary and land rent as the secondary income.[3] From this point of view, Smith's thought was essentially transitional. Although he partially succeeded in emancipating profit from its former state of dependence upon rent, he was content merely to afford it an equal status, and did not seek to assert its superiority over rent. In fact, as we have just seen, rent in his system often retained some of its old pre-eminence. Smith's genius enabled him to discern the broad outlines of the capitalist form of economic organization rather in advance of its complete realization, but he could hardly have been expected to anticipate certain fundamental social attitudes which emerged only when the industrial revolution was well under way.

The more abstract sections of the *Wealth of Nations* did not excite much interest until the end of the century. Then, however, a number of factors combined to attract a considerable amount of attention to the question of the origin of capitalist profit and its relation to land rent. The startling increase in productivity and profit in the manufacturing industries and the threat to Britain's commerce during the Napoleonic wars were obviously influential factors. The promulgation of the Malthusian theory of population may perhaps be regarded as another: Malthus had drawn popular attention to the relationship between subsistence and population, and thence to the relationship of dependence between the agricultural surplus and the non-agricultural population.[4] But the most important influence, overlapping the others and in part dictating the attitudes adopted by the participants in controversies over more ephemeral issues, was undoubtedly the sharpening of the political struggle between the recipients of rents and the recipients of profits. This struggle, culminating in the passing of the Reform Bill, may be said to have marked

---

[1] *Wealth of Nations*, Vol. 1, pp. 343–4.   [2] Ibid., p. 248.
[3] Cf. S. N. Patten, 'The Interpretation of Ricardo', *Quarterly Journal of Economics*, April 1893, *passim*.
[4] See e.g. the second edition of Malthus's *Essay* (1803), pp. 435–6.

the consummation of the victory of the capitalist order in Britain. The question of the origin of profit and the nature of the inter-dependence between rent and profit began to be regarded as *politically* significant. If the agricultural surplus was in fact the basic income out of which all the other incomes were ultimately paid, this might be presumptive evidence in favour of special discrimin-atory measures protecting agriculture and the recipients of rent. If, on the other hand, profit on capital—particularly capital employed in manufacture—actually represented 'a real primitive increase of national wealth', there was no longer any necessary presumption in favour of the landed proprietors: if manufacture was truly pro-ductive, it was truly independent.

The first important work to be considered is John Gray's pamphlet *The Essential Principles of the Wealth of Nations*, published in 1797. 'The principal and most essential cause of the prosperity of a state', Gray argues, 'is the ingenuity and labour of its inhabitants exercised upon the fertility of the soil'.[1] Agricultural labour is truly productive —i.e. productive of a surplus; but 'no augmentation of the revenue of society arises from the labour of a manufacturer', since 'the buyer precisely loses not only what the manufacturer gains, but the amount of the wages, and of the price of the raw materials besides'.[2] Adam Smith and other notable writers have been misled into believing that manufacturing labour produces a surplus because of the obvious fact that many master-manufacturers do somehow manage to get rich. But profit actually originates, not in the process of production, but in the act of exchange. 'When the manufacturer ceases to be a seller,' Gray asserts, 'his profits are immediately at a stand, because they are not natural profits, but artificial.'[3]

Two special aspects of Gray's argument deserve comment. In the first place, Gray regards manufacture as unproductive from the point of view of the nation as a whole only if the goods are sold at home. If they are exported, then 'the profit of the exporter becomes the profit of the nation where he lives'—a thorough-going Mercan-tilist conclusion.[4] In the second place, Gray uses Physiocracy not to defend but to attack the landed interests. The labourers in manufac-ture, he says, may be unproductive, but they are at least a necessary and useful class. But the landlords, because they have separated the rent of land from 'the constitutional purpose of the defence of the state', have now rendered themselves 'one of the most unessential and most burdensome classes in society'.[5] Gray was not the only economist to make Physiocratic principles serve radical ends. The idea that the incomes of the landowners were nothing but a mon-

---

[1] *Essential Principles*, p. 4.   [2] Ibid., p. 36.   [3] Ibid., p. 39.
[4] Cf. Davenant, *An Essay on the East-India-Trade* (1697), p. 31.
[5] *Essential Principles*, p. 51.

strous exaction from the produce of the labour of the agricultural workers, and that upon this primary exaction were based the claims of numerous other parasitical elements, became quite common in the radical literature of the period. Charles Hall, Piercy Ravenstone, and Thomas Hopkins were among those who founded their main arguments on this thesis.[1]

Daniel Wakefield, an uncle of Edward Gibbon Wakefield, published a reply to Gray in 1799, of which a second edition, virtually a new work, appeared five years later. The main problem which excited Wakefield's interest was 'whether labour employed in manufacture does produce, as well as labour employed in agriculture, a surplus value'.[2] He personifies agriculture by a 'cultivator' and manufacture by a 'manufacturer', both of whom, at least in the earlier stages of the argument, are assumed to combine in their own persons the qualities of entrepreneur and labourer. The 'cultivator' is apparently assumed to operate with his own 'cattle for work, implements, sheds, &c.' and to rent land from a proprietor, while the 'manufacturer' is assumed 'to exercise his industry on a borrowed capital'. The cultivator during the process of production 'annihilates' certain things in order to obtain his product. He annihilates: (1) 'his own intermediate support, between seed time and harvest'; (2) 'the wear of his stock advances'; and (3) 'the seed sown'. The value of his 'rude produce' will be sufficient to replace the value of the three items 'annihilated' and in addition to provide a 'surplus value, or surplus prodution', divided into 'the profits of his stock, and the rent of his land'. The manufacturer similarly 'annihilates': (1) 'his own intermediate support between the beginning and completion of the manufacture'; (2) 'the wear of his stock advances'; and (3) 'the raw material used'. The value of his 'finished manufacture' will also be sufficient to replace the value of the three items 'annihilated' and in addition to provide a 'surplus value' divided into 'the profits of his stock, and the interest of his capital'.[3] Wakefield believes that this argument proves that 'both rent of land and interest of capital ... are equally caused by the labour and ingenuity of man producing a surplus, or more than his support and expence, whether employed on land, or capital: in agriculture, or manufactures'.[4]

This was not a new argument. It had been anticipated in a casual remark made by Smith,[5] and Alexander Hamilton had used a variant of it as a weapon against Physiocracy in his *Report on Manufactures*

[1] Charles Hall, at least, was quite conscious of the affiliation. In a letter written in 1808 to Arthur Young he complains that Spence and Cobbett 'took their ideas' from his *Effects of Civilisation* (B. M. Addl. 35, 130, f. 128).

[2] *An Inquiry into the Truth of the Two Positions of the French Oeconomists, etc.* (1799), pp. 6–7.

[3] *An Essay upon Political Oeconomy* (1804), pp. 9–11.

[4] *Inquiry*, pp. 14–15.   [5] *Wealth of Nations*, Vol. II, p. 332.

in 1791.[1] And, of course, the analogy between rent and interest is not very happily drawn: if the cultivator operates with his own capital, his net receipts will obviously include a payment for interest,[2] and rent remains as an income of a unique type whose appearance in agriculture alone has still to be explained. But the fact that Wakefield looked at the problem in terms of cost and surplus value led him to put forward a number of subsidiary arguments which are of rather more interest. In the first place, he realized that an adequate answer to the Physiocrats required the intervention of a theory of value, and he endeavoured to supply such a theory himself. The Physiocrats assert, Wakefield argues, that 'the increase of the Manufacturer is only nominal: that, though to him it is an increase, to the community it is only a transfer of produce, from the class of Cultivators to that of Manufacturers'. But, he asks, 'how is it ascertained, that the increase of the Cultivator is not equally nominal?' Surely it is wrong to consider 'not any thing to be valuable but food'. The labour of the manufacturer, like that of the cultivator, yields a surplus value—that is, it is 'worth more in the estimation of the Consumer' than the items annihilated in the process of production. If the estimation of the consumer is not to be taken as evidence of the value of the product, 'what shall be considered as evidence?'[3] Wakefield's attempt to link a subjective theory of value with his main analysis is not particularly successful, but a number of the by-products of his attempt are interesting—notably his concept of 'relative cost' (roughly equivalent to our opportunity cost),[4] his statement that the wages of 'every kind of educated labour' constitutes a 'monopoly price',[5] and his recognition of the fact that anything which the labourers and capitalists receive over and above the supply price of labour and capital is in the nature of a rent.[6] In the second place, Wakefield laid considerable emphasis on the role of *labour* in production. 'All value,' he says, 'is the result of an exertion of human wit and industry,' supporting this contention with extensive quotations from Garnier, Locke, and Priestley. He stresses the fact that even in agriculture and the extractive industries labour plays a prominent and active role—an argument which was to become increasingly familiar during the next decade.[7]

---

[1] *Papers on Public Credit, Commerce and Finance* (ed. S. McKee), pp. 184–5. Hamilton, like Turgot, emphasized the fact that rent may be regarded as interest on the capital sunk in land. The rent paid on land 'advanced' to the farmer by the landlord, therefore, did not differ qualitatively from the interest paid on the capital advanced to the manufacturer.

[2] Wakefield recognized clearly enough that this would be the case if the *manufacturer* worked with his own capital: *Essay*, p. 11.

[3] *Essay*, pp. 12–14.　　　[4] Ibid., pp. 51–3.　　　[5] Ibid., p. 67.

[6] Ibid., p. 69. Cf. Buchanan, *Observations* (1814), pp. 39–41.

[7] Ibid., p. 56 and pp. 40–6. This argument, that labour is very important in

Interest in these problems among economists must have been widespread in the opening years of the nineteenth century. In 1801 William Spence was reading to a literary society a paper in which he maintained 'all the main positions' subsequently taken up in his *Britain Independent of Commerce*.[1] In 1803 Malthus's second edition appeared. Lauderdale's *Inquiry*, with its critique of Physiocracy and its new theory of profit, was published in 1804; and in the same year, apparently, Simon Gray wrote his *Happiness of States*. And Dugald Stewart was including in his influential lectures a long discussion on the distinction between productive and unproductive labour, in which he tended to side with the Physiocrats rather than with Adam Smith. But the publication of Spence's *Britain Independent of Commerce* in 1807, the advocacy of Spence's views by Cobbett in his *Political Register*, and the entrance of Mill, Torrens, and Chalmers into the arena, brought the controversy to the notice of a much wider public.

Spence's work, considered in itself, is not particularly interesting. It caused a great popular stir, of course, largely because Spence put forward the comfortable view that the destruction of Britain's overseas trade by Napoleon would make little difference to national welfare. As an exposition of the theory of Physiocracy it is inferior to Gray's pamphlet. Spence tried to explain the origin of industrial profit by arguing, more or less as the French Physiocrats had done, that the cultivator may give more for a manufactured article than its 'real value'—its 'real value' being conceived (in physical cost terms) as being equivalent to 'the raw produce and food consumed in producing it'.[2] The master-manufacturer may in this manner receive a surplus over his costs of production, and may even be able to accumulate part of his profits and thus acquire great riches—but even then 'the whole of his gains would be at the expense of the land proprietors, and no addition would be made to the national wealth'.[3] Cobbett's extensive advocacy of Spence's views (under the provocative title 'Perish Commerce') did not contribute a great deal towards a solution of the theoretical problem involved, although one of his correspondents was acute enough to realize that its solution depended

---

agriculture, was sometimes associated with another—that nature is very impor, tant in manufacture. Ricardo used it in his *Principles* (*Works*, Vol. I, p. 76 footnote); it is also to be found in Hamilton's *Report on Manufactures* (op. cit., p. 183), and in a review of Lauderdale's *Inquiry* in the *Edinburgh Review*, July 1804, p. 359.

[1] Cf. Spence's letter in Cobbett's *Weekly Political Register*, December 5, 1807, pp. 921–2.

[2] Spence, *Tracts on Political Economy* (1822), p. 148.

[3] Ibid., p. 14.

upon regarding value as being 'constituted by labour, or the difficulty of producing any commodity'.[1]

Torrens's reply to Spence, *The Economists Refuted*, contains some interesting passages which have sometimes been construed as an anticipation of the doctrine of comparative costs,[2] but in general it is much less effective than James Mill's *Commerce Defended*. Mill's chapter on Consumption is a remarkable piece of work. It is quite consciously imbued with the main ideas associated with the mature Classical outlook—that consumption is in an important sense dependent upon production, that the economic progress of society depends upon the accumulation of capital, and that the only possible source of funds for accumulation is the social surplus.[3]

Two more Physiocratic tracts remain to be noticed.[4] One of them, the anonymous pamphlet *Sketches on Political Economy* (1809), has often been commented upon, and little need be said about it here. The author uses Physiocracy (plus a version of the labour theory of value) to attack Lauderdale's theory of the productivity of capital. Capital is merely 'accumulated labour', it is urged, and 'can only reproduce itself without addition'.[5] The most curious thing about the pamphlet is the manner in which the author vacillates between different theories of value. He begins by flirting with something like a subjective theory based on diminishing utility; then he asserts that value 'may safely be defined *labour*' and that 'in the exchange of commodities, the worth of each in relation to the other, is estimated by the time employed in fabricating it';[6] and finally, he seems to discard the labour theory and adopts Spence's Physiocratic concept of 'real value'. The pamphlet, like Wakefield's, at least has the merit of recognizing that to explain surplus value *some* theory of value is necessary.

The other Physiocratic work, Thomas Chalmers' *Enquiry into the*

---

[1] *Register*, January 23, 1808, pp. 130 ff. See also the letter in the issue of February 6, 1808, pp. 218 ff.

[2] See Viner, *Studies in the Theory of International Trade*, pp. 441–4.

[3] *Commerce Defended* (1808), pp. 79, 70–4, and *passim*. The controversy between Mill and Spence is dealt with in more detail above, pp. 322 ff.

[4] Traces of the Physiocratic outlook may be found in the work of men like Thomas Joplin and J. S. Reynolds, as well as in that of a number of the radical economists and Malthusian underconsumptionists. Haney has claimed Egerton Brydges as a Physiocrat, but the allegedly Physiocratic passages are so vague that the claim seems to be hardly justified. (Brydges is more notable for a clear statement of the relation between price and marginal cost—see his *Population and Riches* (1819), pp. 21–2 and *passim*.) The only other out-and-out Physiocrat I have been able to trace was William Reid, who published a defence of Physiocracy in 1833 (*Inquiry into the Causes of the Present Distress*). (See, however, Mark Blaug, *Ricardian Economics*, p. 97, footnote.)

[5] *Sketches*, pp. 19–28.

[6] Ibid., pp. 1–3.

Extent and Stability of National Resources, was published in 1808
It was inspired by the same set of circumstances which stimulated
Spence's pamphlet, but according to Chalmers he did not see the
latter until his own work was nearly completed.[1] Chalmers' intention
was to prove that 'a much larger proportion of the wealth of the
country may be transferred to the augmentation of the public
revenue, and that . . . a much larger proportion of the population of
the country may be transferred to the augmentation of its naval and
military establishments'.[2] His main analysis is divided into three
parts. First, he considers 'the case of a country that carries on no
foreign trade'. He argues that the population of a country consists of:
(1) the *Agricultural Population,* upon whom devolves the labour of
providing food for the whole community; (2) the *Secondary Population,* who are engaged in providing strict necessities other than food
(clothing, housing, etc.) for the whole community; and (3) the
balance, the *Disposable Population.* This third group is 'disposable'
in the sense that it is maintained out of the 'surplus food of the
country', which is, in the first instance, 'at the disposal of its proprietor'.
The proprietor assigns the agricultural surplus to the disposable
population, who, in return, 'contribute in various ways to his comforts
and enjoyments'. The master gives the orders and the servants obey.
If the country carries on no foreign trade, then, it follows from this
view of the economy that the destruction of a particular manufacture
is a matter of little concern. The agricultural surplus—the subsistence
fund for the disposable population—is still in existence, and since 'it
will infallibly be expended' by the landed proprietor, the displaced
workmen will soon be given 'the same maintenance as before, in
another capacity'. All that will happen is that a section of the disposable population will be put on to producing a different commodity. And if the government taxes the landed proprietor, 'and
appropriates to itself part of that fund which is expended on the
maintenance of the disposable population', the position is similar:
the proprietor has to dismiss a section of the disposable population,
but the government will soon re-employ them in another capacity.
If it employs them as soldiers, the country will lose the commodities
they were formerly producing, but will gain in return a different
commodity, which at the present time is far more precious—security
against invasion. 'There is no creative, no inherent virtue in the
manufacture: It is the consumer who contributes the revenue'.[3]

Secondly, Chalmers considers 'the case of a country which carries
on foreign trade, but is subsisted by its own agricultural produce'.
The landed proprietor, it is contended, 'may also conceive a liking for
an article of foreign manufacture'. Owing to the heavy transport

---

[1] *Enquiry,* p. 343. For a further account of Chalmers' work, see above, pp.
340–1.   [2] *Enquiry,* p. 295.   [3] Ibid., chapter I, *passim.*

costs involved, he will not send his surplus produce abroad to pay for the foreign goods—he will instead 'maintain labourers at home, and send over their work as an equivalent'. The idea that those who live by foreign trade form 'an independent interest', and that their wealth 'is an original and not a derived wealth', is simply an illusion. The practical conclusions arrived at in the first case also apply to the second.[1]

Thirdly, Chalmers considers 'the case of a country which has to import agricultural produce'. This is obviously a much more difficult case than the second one, and Chalmers' method of dealing with it is ingenious, although hardly satisfactory. He begins by asserting that 'the inhabitants of a whole country are seldom accumulated to any great degree beyond the limits of its own agricultural produce'.[2] He then suggests, with the aid of a somewhat dubious calculation, that the 'redundant population' of Great Britain (that is, the population subsisted by imported food) 'does not amount to above one-thirtieth of the natural population of the island'.[3] It is true, he admits, that the destruction of Britain's foreign trade would render the redundant population jobless, and reduce the national income. But this is not a cause for despair; their contribution is negligible, and in any event it would probably be quite easy to introduce improvements in agriculture which would increase the surplus of food sufficiently to maintain them.[4]

The passages in which Chalmers discusses the origin of industrial and commercial profit are consistently Physiocratic. It may be asked, he argues, how it is possible to distinguish between 'original and derived wealth' when there appears on the surface to be a 'mutual dependence' between buyers and sellers. It may be asked whether he has not 'all along overlooked a very important element, the profit of our capitalists'. But such criticisms ignore the vital fact that 'the proprietors of the necessaries of life compose the original and independent interest'. And profit is simply a wage for the 'higher species of service' rendered by the capitalist—a wage which, like that of all the others who labour in manufactures, is paid by the 'original proprietors of the necessaries of existence'. The capitalist may secure a profit which is more than sufficient 'to make up to him the maintenance of a labourer', so that he, as well as the landed proprietor, may be able to 'command the services of so many of the disposable population'. But even so, the wealth of the merchant or manufacturer is necessarily derived, whereas that of the landed proprietor is original.[5]

---

[1] *Enquiry*, chapter 2, *passim*.
[2] Ibid., p. 145. Cf. Dugald Stewart, *Works*, Vol. I, p. 270.
[3] *Enquiry*, p. 147.   [4] Ibid., chapter 3, *passim*.
[5] Ibid., chapters 2 and 4, *passim*.

Between Chalmers' *Enquiry* and Ricardo's *Principles* there lies a deep gulf. Whereas Chalmers thinks of the surplus as a flow of *commodities* of a particular type, Ricardo thinks of it as a flow of *value*, and the physical attributes of the commodities produced in the economy become irrelevant to the problem of the increase of wealth. Then again, while both Chalmers and Ricardo regard the power and prosperity of a country as being largely dependent upon the size of its net revenue, Chalmers regards the surplus as consisting of rent alone, and Ricardo regards it as consisting of both rent and profits. And finally, whereas Chalmers treats profit as being paid out of rent, there is an important sense in which Ricardo treats profit as the primary and rent as the derivative income.

Ricardo's *Principles* reflects a new social attitude which had been struggling for adequate theoretical expression for some time. Chalmers himself was haunted by it, and, since his book was written to combat it, often stated it fairly precisely. Manufactures, he said, 'are looked up to as an original and independent interest, as possessing in themselves some native and inherent ability, and as if the very existence of the country depended upon their prosperity and extension'.[1] Again, 'the interest of the country is supposed to be identical with the interest of its traders and shopkeepers; and as profit is the grand source of their revenue, so profit . . . is supposed to be one of the grand sources of the revenue of the public'.[2] As capitalist methods spread throughout the economy, as striking increases in productivity followed one upon the other, and as accumulation came to be made more and more out of profits and less and less out of rents, the idea naturally became current that profits were not just equally as important as rents, but somehow superior to them.

It was more difficult than it might appear to give theoretical expression to this new attitude. For one thing, the claims of agriculture to pre-eminence were hard to dispute. No one could deny that agriculture was historically prior to industry and commerce, and that, at least in the absence of international trade, the size of the agricultural surplus did still effectively limit the extension of industry and commerce. And whereas the production of a surplus in agriculture could easily enough be visualized in physical terms, it was difficult to visualize a similar process taking place in manufacture, where the elements of input and output usually consisted of entirely different commodities. The production of a surplus in manufacture could be visualized only in terms of *value*, which required quite a considerable development in the use of abstraction in economic analysis; and an abstraction from the physical attributes of the commodities produced

---

[1] *Enquiry*, p. 54. Cf. Hollander, *David Ricardo*, p. 16.
[2] *Enquiry*, p. 169.

could become plausible only when the territorial division of labour had become recognized as a normal and natural feature of the world economic scene, and when it had been allowed that 'there is always abundance of food in the world'[1] for which Britain's manufactured exports could be exchanged. For these reasons, it was difficult enough to establish even the independence of profit, let alone its superiority over rent.

Nevertheless, as a result of the Physiocratic controversies, the independence of profit was successfully maintained. It became widely accepted that labour was able to produce a surplus in manufacture as well as in agriculture, and that agriculture was not even *especially* productive. Nature's labour is important in manufacture; man's labour is important in agriculture; rent of land is qualitatively similar to interest on capital; elements akin to rent are found in profit and wages— all these were arguments put forward to prove that there was nothing sacrosanct about rent and nothing unique about agriculture. The next stage was to turn the tables completely on the Physiocrats and to treat profit, rather than rent, as the primary and original income.[2] For this principle to be embodied in a theoretical system, two pieces of apparatus required to be evolved. First, a *theory of value* was needed—a theory which would be free from any bias towards the old physical cost concept, and which was capable of distinguishing between cost and surplus in manufacture as well as in agriculture. Smith and some of the anti-Physiocrats had pointed in the direction of the labour theory which Ricardo was to adopt; and any ties which still existed between the physical cost and embodied labour concepts were decisively broken in Ricardo's first chapter-heading. Second, a *theory of rent* was needed—a theory which would suggest that rent was not an original but a derivative income. Ricardo consistently interpreted his new theory of rent in this way. Whereas Malthus always regarded rent as an agricultural surplus beneficently provided by Nature, Ricardo always regarded it as a deduction from profits—a deduction made possible only because Nature had been *less* beneficent in supplying fertile land than she had been in supplying such things as air and water. Rent, by the operation of natural laws, had come to be a part of the social surplus, but it had gained this position only at the expense of profits. Building on the ground which had been cleared during the Physiocratic controversies, Ricardo was at last able to give precise theoretical expression to the mature Classical outlook.

[1] Quoted by Ricardo, *Works*, Vol. 1, p. 318, footnote.
[2] Buchanan made an attempt to do this in 1814: see his *Observations*, p. 135. Ricardo was apparently impressed by these passages: see *Works*, Vol. I, pp. 398–9.

THE INTERPRETATION OF
PHYSIOCRACY

I

When we speak of the necessity for an 'interpretation' of Physiocracy, what we usually have in mind is the necessity for an approach to the doctrine which will bring out its 'meaning' *in such a way as to throw light upon its 'validity'*. The antiquarian may be interested in the problem of the 'meaning' of Physiocracy for its own sake; but the contemporary economist, living in a different world which he is accustomed to analyse in terms of a different set of concepts, is interested in the problem of 'meaning' mainly for the sake of the light it may throw upon the problem of 'validity'. We adopt one set of concepts today and the Physiocrats in their time adopted another: in what sense, then, can their doctrines be said to be 'false' and ours 'true'—or *vice versa*? This is the basic question which most of us would want an 'interpretation' of Physiocracy to answer.

The majority of historians of economic thought tend to eschew interpretation in the above sense almost completely, and to content themselves with a mere *description* of Physiocracy and a simple *comparison* between Physiocratic and contemporary doctrines. The problem of validity can then be dealt with very easily indeed, if we assume, as most historians of economic thought do, that the contemporary doctrines are substantially 'true'. Physiocracy can be said to be 'false' in so far as it embodied notions different from or opposed to those of contemporary theory (e.g. the doctrine of the exclusive productivity of agriculture), and 'true' in so far as it embodied or anticipated notions similar to those of contemporary theory (e.g. the concept of general equilibrium). Quite often this simple comparison is accompanied by something which bears a formal resemblance to interpretation in the above sense—for example, an explanation of Physiocratic doctrine couched in terms of 'bending the rod the other way';[1] but such explanations are usually put forward

---

[1] Cf. Adam Smith, *Wealth of Nations* (Cannan edn.), Vol. II, p. 162: 'If the rod be bent too much one way, says the proverb, in order to make it straight you must bend it as much the other. The French philosophers, who have proposed the system which represents agriculture as the sole source of the revenue and wealth of every country, seem to have adopted this proverbial maxim; and as in the plan of Mr. Colbert the industry of the towns was certainly over-valued in comparison with that of the country; so in their system it seems to be as certainly under-valued.'

largely by way of charity, as little more than benevolent excuses for what are regarded as basic theoretical 'errors'.

So far as the alleged 'errors' of Physiocracy are concerned, the results of this type of approach are usually completely sterile. All too often it leads merely to the highly unlikely conclusion that men of the calibre of Quesnay and Turgot committed blunders so crass and elementary that we would cheerfully fail a first-year student if he perpetrated them. So far as the 'true' elements in Physiocracy are concerned, however, the case against this type of approach is not quite so clear. In the hands of a competent historian like Schumpeter, it may lead to the emergence of new insights into the history of economic thought in general and into the doctrines of the Physiocrats in particular. For even the most convinced relativist would agree that at any rate in certain branches of economic analysis—and not least in some of those which the Physiocrats cultivated—there has indeed been something which can properly be called 'progress'. It would be merely silly, for example, to argue that one could not legitimately use the term 'progress' when comparing Marshall's demand schedules with Quesnay's.[1] And in cases to which the concept of 'progress' is applicable, the type of approach I am now describing may in fact lead to useful results.

What the question at issue really boils down to, then, is whether one can properly separate those parts of a doctrine to which the concept of progress is applicable from those parts to which it is not. And up to a point—but only up to a point—it seems to me that we can make such a separation. The way I am accustomed to look at the matter, speaking very broadly, is as follows: Economics, in the form in which it has come down to us today, has always been primarily concerned with the analysis of economies based on the system of market exchange. Now these economies have passed through a number of different stages of development, in each of which the data to be analysed and the practical problems to be solved have been to some extent different. The Smithian world and its problems differed in certain important respects from the Physiocratic world; the Keynesian world and its problems from the Marshallian world; and so on. To a large extent the different data and problems of these worlds required the use of different concepts and methods of analysis: the text-book of *Principles* which was useful in one world became out of date to a greater or lesser degree as a new world replaced the old one. In so far as differences in methods of analysis reflect differences in the data and problems of the worlds being analysed, then, it seems to me to be impossible to make comparisons between the 'truth' or 'validity' *of different methods of*

---

[1] For Quesnay's 'demand schedules' (if they can properly be interpreted as such) see I.N.E.D., II, pp. 462, 474, and 532-3.

analysis.[1] The question of 'truth' or 'validity' can be relevant only to the case of *any one individual method of analysis*, and it can be decided only by relating that method of analysis to the data and problems of the world with which it attempts to deal. But the different worlds nevertheless have all of them one and the same basis—the system o f market exchange. And the analysis of this system as such, at least in its broad formal outlines, can up to a point be separated from those concepts and methods of analysis which necessarily change as one world replaces another. Thus in this sphere at any rate—albeit rather a limited one—it *is* possible to talk in terms of 'progress' and to compare the validity of different analyses.

Here, however, we must be careful to make a distinction between the formal analysis of price phenomena in a system based on market exchange, and the *general angle* from which this analysis is approached. Historically, the distinction I want to make here corresponds roughly to that between a 'theory of price' and a 'theory of value'. In the case of the 'theory of price' we can legitimately talk in terms of progress: in the case of the 'theory of value' it seems to me that we cannot.[2] The difficulty here, of course, is that although for purposes of discussion it is possible to make a conceptual distinction between the two, it is almost impossible to make the distinction in actual practice when one is dealing with any specific analysis of price phenomena, since the degree of interdependence between the two is usually so very great. Thus even in this sphere, to which the concept of progress does appear to some extent to be applicable, interpretation should properly precede comparison.

How, then, should we approach this problem of interpretation? Historians of economic thought have long been familiar with the idea that the sets of ideological concepts which it is their business to discuss can usefully be said to be 'conditioned by', 'relative to', or at least in some meaningful sense 'appropriate to' a given socioeconomic structure and its problems. This idea has in fact become something of a commonplace in our own time. It is difficult, indeed, to understand how any historian of economic thought who wants to interpret, and not merely to describe, the work of an author or period can possibly do without it. A historian of music might not, perhaps, find it quite as useful, because a composer's work does not consist directly of an analysis and generalization of the economic experience of his age. But it is of course precisely of this that the basic

---

[1] A view of this kind seems to be implied in Mr. Guillebaud's helpful comparison between the Marshallian and Keynesian worlds in his article *Marshall's Principles of Economics in the Light of Contemporary Economic Thought*, in *Economica*, May 1952, at pp. 115–16.

[2] Some of the reasons are outlined in my article *Is Economics Biased?*, in the *Scottish Journal of Political Economy*, March 1957.

work of an economist does consist. If it does not, he can hardly be called an economist.

The only question, therefore, is that of whether the role which this idea plays in our interpretation should be a leading or subordinate one. Generally speaking, the further back we go in the history of economic thought the more ready we seem to be to grant the idea a leading role. The inhibitions which operate to limit our application of it to our own work are very powerful: every generation of economists naturally believes that its work is more 'scientific', more 'objective', than that of earlier generations, and every individual economist feels strongly that he is in fact an independent agent and not a mere tool of history. But these inhibitions become less powerful the further back we go in history towards theoretical systems radically different from our own. No one objects, at any rate on grounds of methodological principle, to an interpretation of Mercantilism as the economics of the age of state-making, or of Physiocracy as the economic reflection of the difficulties facing French agriculture under the *ancien régime*. If we do object to such interpretations as these, it is either on the grounds that they are too sweeping and indiscriminate, or on the grounds that the systems concerned were in our opinion really reflections of something else.

My own feeling is that at any rate in the case of Physiocracy the questions with which we want our interpretation to deal can be answered satisfactorily only if we grant the idea a leading role. In other words, answers to our questions must be primarily sought, not in the personal predilections of Quesnay and his followers, but in the relation between their doctrines and the facts and problems of what Richard Jones called the 'economical structure'.[1] The interpretation which follows, however, can be judged by no criterion other than whether it gives sensible and consistent answers to the questions about Physiocracy which contemporary economists want to ask. The greatest of all economic principles is that the proof of the pudding is in the eating.

II

The 'economical structure' does not have ideas and cannot write treatises on political economy. But the 'economical structure' can and does set fundamental problems for men and women of goodwill to

[1] Richard Jones, *Literary Remains* (1859), p. 60: 'By the economical structure of nations, I mean those relations between the different classes which are established in the first instance by the institution of property in the soil, and by the distribution of its surplus produce; afterwards modified and changed (to a greater or less extent) by the introduction of capitalists, as agents in producing and exchanging wealth, and in feeding and employing the laboring population.'

solve. How to increase the wealth of nations; how to make the best use of a given stock of scarce resources; how to cure chronic unemployment; how to choose between alternative investment projects in the absence of an interest rate—these are examples of basic problems which various 'economical structures' have set or are setting for economists to solve.

For the Physiocrats, the fundamental problem set by the 'economical structure' of their time was how to increase the national income of an under-developed country like France from a low level to a high one. The aim of political economy, for the Physiocrats, was simply to secure 'the greatest degree of prosperity possible for the society',[1] just as for Adam Smith it was to 'enrich both the people and the sovereign'[2] and for Ricardo to secure 'an abundance of commodities'.[3] That this was in fact the basic problem upon which the Physiocrats intended their political economy to throw light hardly requires detailed demonstration: if any doubt were felt about it, a glance at, say, the General Maxims should be sufficient to remove it.

Today, when 'the revival of interest in the classical questions' has brought 'a revival of the classical theory',[4] few economists would be found to dispute this judgment. We are no longer so inclined as we used to be, for example, to consider the Tableau in abstraction from the basic problem of economic development with which it was designed to deal.[5] One modern commentator, however,[6] has taken a radically different view, claiming that 'Physiocracy is . . . a rationalization of medieval economic life',[7] and that 'Quesnay's main endeavour . . . was to recreate a medieval society which should be of greater permanency and excellence than the old one had been'.[8] The Physiocratic realm, this writer claims, is 'intended by its author to preserve in perpetuity its stable equilibrium'.[9] The 'stable equilibrium' of this society is not disturbed by any 'dynamic class pressing on its limits'; there is 'no urge for expansion'; and there are 'no inventions'.[10] This somewhat bizarre interpretation, which rests largely on a misunderstanding of the nature and functions of the basic Tableau and an almost complete neglect of Quesnay's continuous emphasis on the innovatory activities of agricultural entrepreneurs, is hardly worth much consideration. It is perfectly true, however, that Quesnay's language does at times have a certain 'feudal' flavour which cannot be completely explained by the fact

---

[1] Above, p. 231.   [2] Wealth of Nations, Vol. I, p. 395.

[3] Works (Sraffa edn.), Vol. IV, p. 248.

[4] Joan Robinson, The Accumulation of Capital, p. vi.

[5] See e.g. Lionel Robbins, An Essay on the Nature and Significance of Economic Science, p. 68. For a less sophisticated example of this method of approach to the Tableau, see Alexander Gray, The Development of Economic Doctrine, p. 108.

[6] M. Beer, An Inquiry into Physiocracy.   [7] Ibid., p. 110.

[8] Ibid., p. 167.   [9] Ibid., p. 164.   [10] Ibid., p. 169.

that the inventor of a new science must always to some extent work with concept-material inherited from the past. There is indeed a certain sense in which Physiocracy was a reflection of the contemporary reaction against Colbert and Law, and a sigh for the golden age of Sully. But to see this as the *essence* of Physiocracy, as I shall argue below, is to miss the whole point of it.

In what way, exactly, can the 'economical structure' of Quesnay's time be said to have posed this problem of the development of an under-developed economy? The term 'under-developed', of course, is an essentially relative one. A country may be said to be under-developed either (a) relatively to its own position in the past; (b) relatively to its present potentialities; or (c) relatively to the present position of other countries. And the problem of under-development is unlikely to be put at the head of the agenda for discussion in a country until the fact of its under-development in one or more of these senses has become, to use one of Quesnay's favourite expressions, 'self-evident'. In a more or less static medieval world the problem of under-development is not likely to seize hold of men's minds: such a world may well produce a Utopia or two, but it does not produce a body of scientific theory and policy devoted to the problem of securing 'an abundance of commodities'. By Quesnay's time, however, the fact of France's under-development in each of the three senses I have distinguished had become—or at any rate was believed to have become—fairly obvious. The degree of impoverishment caused by a long succession of wars was such as to encourage the belief that things must have been better at some time in the past. The relative prosperity of certain northern provinces where agricultural entrepreneurs had been particularly active was such as to lead to speculations about the possibility of extending the new methods over the whole of the country. And the relative prosperity of Britain, where the agricultural revolution had proceeded much further than in France, was such as to afford a solid basis for these speculations. Not only was France's under-development a fact, but escape from its under-development was also beginning to appear as a practical proposition. It is no doubt true that the Physiocrats often exaggerated the glories of the past and underestimated the extent to which economic development was in fact proceeding in France in their own century, particularly in the second half of it. But the latter fact should not mislead us: it is precisely in a period when economic development has in fact begun that the problem of making it proceed further and faster comes to attain its greatest significance in men's minds. The improvements in productivity in the northern farms had much the same 'demonstration effect' on Quesnay as the improvements in productivity in the Glasgow factories were having at about the same time on Adam Smith.

The key to the task of securing 'an abundance of commodities', then, appeared to Quesnay to be the widespread introduction of large-scale agriculture under the direction of capitalist entrepreneurs. The two main obstacles standing in the way of this in contemporary France were believed to be, first, the arbitrary and oppressive tax system, which fell with particular severity on the farmer, and, second, the corn laws, which prevented a 'proper price' being obtained for the farmer's product. It was upon these crucial practical problems, then, that the 'pure theory' of the Physiocrats was primarily designed to throw light. The doctrine of the exclusive productivity of agriculture, and the *Tableau Economique*, were 'oriented' towards these problems in much the same way as Keynes's key concepts were 'oriented' towards the problem of unemployment.[1]

Before proceeding to discuss the nature of this orientation, let us pause to salute the achievement of the Physiocrats in recognizing that the formulation of a theoretical model of the economy was a necessary prerequisite to the solution of such problems as these. With the Physiocrats, for the first time in the history of economic thought, we find a firm appreciation of the fact that the 'areas of decision' open to policy-makers in the economic sphere have certain limits, and that a theoretical model of the economy is necessary in order to define these limits.[2] We are unfree, the Physiocrats in effect proclaimed, so long as we do not understand the necessities by which we are bound in our society; and we can understand these necessities, in a society as complex as ours, only if we use the methods of simplification, selection, and generalization in our analysis of it.[3] It was in their recognition of this vital fact that the Physiocrats took the decisive step leading from politics to political economy.

III

If the methods of analysis developed in connection with the natural sciences are to be usefully applied to an economic system, that system must possess two characteristics. In the first place, the various parts of which it is composed must be integrated and co-ordinated with one another to a degree which is sufficient to enable the system to be visualized as a single entity. In the second place, the nature of the tie linking the constituent parts together must be such that the net results arising from the confluence of human activities are sufficiently regular, and sufficiently independent of the will of individual men, to be regarded as being 'subject to law'. The emergence of 'political

---

[1] Cf. Rogin, *The Meaning and Validity of Economic Theory*, p. 16.
[2] Cf. B. S. Keirstead, *The Theory of Economic Change*, p. 32.
[3] Cf. above, pp. 204 ff.

economy', or 'economics', as a general system of theoretical principles, had to await the entry on to the historic scene of an economic order possessing both these characteristics.

The key factor here was of course the development of *market exchange*. So long as market exchange was the rule only in more or less separate and isolated corners of the economy, or in individual spheres of activity like international trade, political economy as a general body of theoretical principles could hardly have been expected to emerge. Once the sphere of operation of market exchange had widened to cover virtually the whole area of the economy and the whole range of economic activities, however, the situation was radically transformed. The fundamental tie linking men together in the 'ordinary business of life' was now such that this business could plausibly be regarded as 'subject to law'. It had at last become possible for the analytical methods developed in connection with the natural sciences to be successfully applied to the study of the economic behaviour of men in society.

One of the great achievements of the economists of the eighteentht century was to recognize this possibility, and to act upon it.[1] In Britain the nature and significance of the new tie binding men to one another were fairly easily discernible: not only was the development of market exchange proceeding quite rapidly, but the contrast between the new tie and the old system of feudal ties which it was in a sense replacing was a vivid and obvious one. Looking at eighteenth century British economic literature as a whole, one is impressed by the extent to which men whose viewpoints were in certain other respects quite dissimilar—Mandeville, Cantillon, Steuart, and Smith, for example—took a common view of the basic economic structure of the new 'commercial society'.[2] In France, however, where the development of market exchange was proceeding much more slowly, and within the framework of an economic system which was still essentially feudal, the nature of the new 'commercial society' which was coming into being must have been more difficult to grasp. It is some measure of Quesnay's genius that he managed under these circumstances to grasp it as firmly as he did.

'The whole magic of well-ordered society', it is stated in the *Rural Philosophy*, 'is that each man works for others, while believing that he is working for himself'.[3] Here the essential nature of the tie linking men to one another in a society based on market exchange is accurately and succinctly expressed. 'No man who lives in society,' writes Quesnay in a very Smithian passage in *Corn*, 'provides for all his needs with his own labour; he obtains what he lacks through the

---

[1] Cf. Robbins, *Robert Torrens and the Evolution of Classical Economics*, p. 234.
[2] For examples, see my *Studies in the Labour Theory of Value*, pp. 37–42.
[3] Above, p. 70.

sale of the produce of his labour. Thus everything becomes exchange-able, everything becomes wealth through the medium of mutual trade between men'.[1] For the products of men's separate labours to become exchangeable in this way, it is of course necessary that the products should possess utility. Quesnay was fairly clear on this point,[2] and also on the more sophisticated point that the fact of exchange presupposes a gain in utility to both the contracting parties.[3] But Quesnay also recognized clearly that the exchange relations between the contracting parties were governed by the *prices* of the commodities exchanged, and that these prices normally bore little relation to the utilities of the commodities. Prices, in short, depended on causes which were 'independent of men's will'. They were not 'arbitrary' or merely the result of 'agreement between the contracting parties',[4] but were subject to objective laws which it was one of the main functions of political economy to ascertain.[5] And Quesnay was also reasonably clear on the point that the regularities observable in the field of price-phenomena were due to the fact that men normally behaved in a regular way when confronted with prices: they sought to buy in the cheapest market and to sell in the dearest.[6] The desire for 'the greatest possible reduction in disagreeable labour with the greatest possible enjoyment', says Quesnay, is 'general among men.'[7]

The exchange economy, then, came to be visualized as a kind of gigantic machine, whose motive force was the desire of men to maximize their receipts and minimize their costs, and whose belts and levers were the activities of individual economic subjects who in effect worked for one another by producing products which they exchanged on a market. Since the prices of the products so exchanged were governed by causes 'independent of men's will', the behaviour of the machine was not 'arbitrary', but in some significant sense 'subject to law'. So commonplace has this type of conceptual approach to the economy become in our own time that it is perhaps difficult for us to appreciate what a tremendous intellectual achieve-ment its original development represented.

Something will be said below about the actual content of some of

[1] Above, p. 83.   [2] Above, p. 90.
[3] Above, p. 214.   [4] Above, p. 90.
[5] To economists brought up on the subjective approach to value theory, the eighteenth-century separation of use value from exchange value sometimes appears merely as a simple error, which delayed for many years the formulation of a 'true' theory of value. To the economists who made the separation, however, it appeared to be necessary in order to clear the way for the application of scientific method to the study of the exchange economy. From a historical view-point, paradoxically enough, the separation was a necessary precondition for the development of *any* general theory of value, whether a cost theory or a utility theory.
[6] Above, p. 215.   [7] Above, p. 212.

the objective laws to which the Physiocrats believed their economy to be subject. In the present section, where I am confining myself to the question of the nature of the Physiocrats' general methodological approach to economic phenomena, the only comment which seems called for is one on the language in which they often formulated these laws—the language of the 'natural order'. The point here is that the Physiocrats tended to visualize the laws which they discovered as being 'natural' not only in the sense that they expressed necessary regularities deriving from the actual economic facts, but also in the sense that they expressed the will of God and therefore represented a sort of absolute ideal towards which men should properly aim. It would be quite wrong to dismiss the divine and ideal elements in their formulations, which were evidently of considerable importance to the Physiocrats themselves, as mere verbal camouflage. On the other hand, it would be equally wrong to suggest, as so many commentators have in fact done, that their ideas about 'natural law somehow lay *at the basis* of their economic analysis, so that their economics must be said to have been derived from their philosophy.[1] To suggest this is to miss the whole point of the Physiocrats' quite revolutionary approach to the interrelation between the 'physical' and the 'moral'. For them, the 'moral' had to be derived from the 'physical', and not *vice versa*. As Du Pont put it, with remarkable clarity, in the course of a discussion of Quesnay's early Encyclopedia articles:

'Undoubtedly their most distinctive characteristic is that whereas all the other moralists have set out from the *natural right* of man in order to lead up to the rules of his actions, the author set out from the calculated interest[2] of men in order to arrive at the results which their natural right rigorously prescribes. Moral and political writers have often caused the *justice* of some of the natural laws which they discussed to be very fully appreciated; but they have always been at a loss to discover the physical *sanction* of these laws. M. Quesnay began by stating their physical and imperative sanction, and this led him to a recognition of their *justice*.'[3]

The essential point here, as Schumpeter has said, is that 'neither the theological nor the naturalist element was really the point from which they started. They merely expressed the results of economic

---

[1] Cf. e.g. Gide and Rist, *A History of Economic Doctrines* (2nd English edn.), p. 25: 'The essence of the Physiocratic system lay in their conception of the "natural order".'

[2] *Intérêt calculé*. R.L.M.

[3] Du Pont, *Notice Abrégée*, in Oncken, at p. 152. For a number of other fairly specific statements of this principle, see Weulersse, II, pp. 106–10. As Weulersse states (p. 117), 'in 1760 it was materialism, and not deism, which was an innovation'. Cf. below, pp. 376–7.

analysis in this theological or naturalist form *after* they had established them'.[1] We will not go far wrong in our interpretation of the work of the Physiocrats, then, if we take their 'natural laws' to be essentially the objective laws operating in an economy based on market exchange in which the Physiocratic policy prescriptions have been put into effect. When they spoke about the necessity of instructing the people in 'the general laws of the natural order',[2] what they meant was simply that instruction should be given in the methods, arguments, and results of Physiocratic economic analysis.

Now the dependence of men upon one another in an exchange economy has two aspects, each of which was emphasized by different authors for different purposes during the eighteenth century. On the one hand, men as consumers are dependent upon the reciprocal services performed by men as producers; on the other hand, men as producers are dependent upon the reciprocal demands exercised by men as consumers. Those economists who were interested in the productive potentialities of the division of labour, for example, like Smith, tended to emphasize the first aspect; those who were interested in the influence of demand on the paths of development followed by an economy, like Steuart, tended to emphasize the second aspect. The Physiocrats, however, were not normally concerned to afford special emphasis to either of these two aspects: their concern throughout was simply the analysis of the particular forms which the general interdependence of production and demand assumed in the society of their time—the 'general system of expenditure, work, gain, and consumption', as Quesnay called it.[3] The close attention which they gave to the study of this 'general system' was no doubt partly the result of mere analytical curiosity; but to a much greater extent it was the result of their endeavours to find a valid criterion by which to judge the particular policy proposals which they were concerned either to justify or to condemn.

The essential point here, which is of some importance in the interpretation of the Physiocrats' analysis of the 'circular flow', can be explained in the following way. It was one of Quesnay's commonest complaints that the defenders of certain policies which he regarded as misguided, such as, for example, the imposition of 'indirect' taxes or restrictions on the export of corn, saw only the immediate effects of these policies on particular areas or groups: they never traced out their long-run effects on the economy as a whole. Now the economy as a whole, when its constituent parts were linked by means of the mechanism of market exchange, was an extremely complex and delicate organism, in which any disturbance to one part communicated itself sooner or later to all the other parts through a

[1] Schumpeter, *Economic Doctrine and Method*, pp. 49–50.
[2] Above, p. 231.   [3] Above, p. 82.

complicated process of reciprocal action and interaction. A disturbance in production brought about a disturbance in demand, and
vice versa, because of the close mutual interdependence which
existed between the volume and pattern of production and the volume
and pattern of demand. How, then, was one to trace out the full
effects of the disputed policies in such a way as to enable a valid
judgment to be formed about their utility? The best way of doing
this, the Physiocrats in effect argued, was to conceive the process of
the mutual interaction of production and demand as constituting,
in any given year,[1] a sort of 'circle';[2] to examine the way in which
the particular policy concerned, when its full effects were taken into
account, would affect the *dimensions* of the 'circle'[3] in future years;
and to pass judgment on the utility of the policy concerned according
to whether it resulted in an expansion or contraction in these dimensions. The Physiocrats' analysis of the 'general system of expenditure,
work, gain, and consumption', in other words, was conducted not
so much for its own sake as for the light which the Physiocrats
believed it could throw on the burning policy issues of their times.

But to leave the matter there would be to neglect another very
important aspect of the methodology of the Physiocrats. Quesnay
was concerned, as he put it himself, not only with the question of the
'dimensions' of the circle, but also with the related question of its
'origin'.[4] It is to this question of the 'origin' of the circle, indeed,
that Quesnay's most comprehensive statement of his methodological
approach, the *Dialogue on the Work of Artisans*, is largely devoted.
The main thing to bear in mind when reading this fascinating
document is that Quesnay (Mr N.) and his *alter ego* (Mr H.) are
both agreed on the necessity for postulating the circle as an analytical
device, and on the necessity for judging policies according to the
criterion of whether their ultimate effect is to enlarge or reduce the
dimensions of the circle. What they are arguing about, at bottom,
is whether it is necessary to *break* the circle at some definite point[5]—
i.e. to regard some particular factor or aspect of the circular process
as 'primary' in the sense that it can be said to govern or determine
both the general pattern of the process as a whole and the direction
and extent of changes in the level at which the process takes place.
Quesnay's main argument in the *Dialogue* was designed to emphasize

[1] The year was taken as the basic time-unit, of course, not merely for the sake
of analytical convenience, but also because it was the natural period to select in
an economy in which agricultural production still predominated.

[2] It is interesting to note in passing the way in which the 'circle', in one form
or another, dominated Quesnay's intellectual activity during the whole of his
life. His medical writings were largely concerned with the circulation of the blood;
his economic writings with the 'circular flow'; and his mathematical research at
the close of his life with the geometry of the circle.

[3] Cf. above, p. 209.   [4] Above, p. 209.   [5] Cf. above, p. 292.

and justify his view that it was indeed vitally necessary to pick out such a key factor in the process, and, in examining the results of different policies, to visualize these policies as operating on the economy as a whole *through their effects on this key factor*. It was not enough, in other words, in order to deal adequately with the basic policy problems which were at issue, to say *merely* that everything in the economic universe depended upon everything else. This is the methodological principle which lies behind Quesnay's constant insistence in the *Dialogue* that the sterile class cannot be said to be 'productive' simply by virtue of the fact that it demands agricultural produce and thereby helps to maintain its price. The doctrine of the exclusive productivity of agriculture, considered on a purely logical plane, was in essence a reflection of the methodological approach which I have just been describing.[1]

The problem of the reason for Quesnay's selection of the productivity or revenue-creating capacity of agriculture as the key factor in the circular process will be further discussed in the next section. Something should be said at this juncture, however, about the wider significance of this aspect of his methodology. Economics was for Quesnay, as it was later to be for Smith and Marx, an integral part of a more general system of sociology in which the structure and development of human society were conceived to be essentially dependent upon the mode of subsistence. To a much greater extent than is generally realized, the Physiocrats shared with Adam Smith, John Millar, and the other members of the Scottish Historical School,[2] a view of history and society which can be described, not too misleadingly, as a materialist conception.[3] The extracts which I have translated above under the heading 'Philosophy and Sociology',[4] which are by no means isolated examples,[5] seem to me to demonstrate this quite clearly. One of the most significant of the red threads running through Physiocratic writing as a whole is the principle stated by Quesnay in a marginal note to one of Mirabeau's manuscripts: 'With us, for us, everything is physical'.[6] The 'physical',

---

[1] The fact that Quesnay, when he wrote *Hommes*, was still prepared to allow a certain degree of 'productivity' (even if only a very limited one) to merchants and landlords, can perhaps be taken as an indication that the principles of his mature methodological approach had not yet been fully worked out. See above, pp. 97–8.

[2] On the Scottish Historical School, see my article 'The Scottish Contribution to Marxist Sociology', in *Democracy and the Labour Movement*, ed. John Saville.

[3] Cf. Weulersse, II, p. 132: 'The Physiocrats deserve to be regarded as the precursors, if not of historical materialism, at least of what has been called the economic interpretation of history.'

[4] Above, pp. 43 ff.

[5] For others, see Weulersse, II, pp. 129 ff.

[6] Weulersse, *Les Manuscrits Economiques de François Quesnay et du Marquis de Mirabeau aux Archives Nationales*, p. 122. Quesnay's comment proceeds:

so far as the social order was concerned, meant for the Physiocrats simply the economic. To understand why different societies have different forms of government, different ideas about morality, etc., then, one must look first at the different ways in which the societies get their living, for this is the key factor in the process of social development. One who was accustomed to thinking in these terms would quite naturally insist, when he came on to consider the circular flow, on the necessity for isolating some strategic determining factor, and would be greatly tempted to find it—in the circumstances of eighteenth-century France—in the sphere of agricultural production.

IV

Let us now pass from the general methodology of the Physiocrats to the actual content of their theoretical model—their key classifications and definitions, their selection of basic variables, their division of these variables into dependent and independent, etc.—and examine the way in which it was related to the economic facts and problems of contemporary France.

The content of an economist's model is usually related much more directly and less intuitively to the facts and problems of his environment than is the general methodology lying behind his model. The model is constructed not so much for its own sake as for the sake of the light which it is hoped it may be able to throw on the basic policy issues of the time.[1] This consideration implies that the model is normally 'realistic' in the sense that the facts which it selects and organizes are facts of the real world. And it also implies that the particular facts selected, and the manner of their organization, are normally in some significant sense 'relevant' to the basic policy issues. The paramount issue, as Rogin has put it, 'largely dictates the scope and direction of the selective appeal to fact and indicates the permissible degree of violence which may be done the selected facts for the purpose of incorporating them into the premises of the theory'.[2]

In many cases, however, and by no means least in the case of the Physiocrats, the nature of the relation between the theory on the one

'. . . and the whole of the moral derives from it.' The question of the Physiocrats' 'materialist' attitude towards the connection between the 'physical' and the 'moral' is referred to above, pp. 373–4

[1] I believe that this proposition is a useful starting-point for the study not only of the Classical, Marxian, and Keynesian systems, but also of those systems in the neo-Classical tradition which deliberately denied the direct relevance of theory to policy. The very fact of this denial may indicate an extremely positive attitude towards certain basic issues of policy.

[2] Rogin, op. cit., p. 3.

hand and the economic facts and policy issues on the other is obscured by the existence of what may be called 'normative' elements in the model. This is a point which should be dealt with before we proceed further. Most of the great economists of the past have been not only scientists, but also to some extent reformers, prophets, and moralists, and this fact often makes the 'scientific' elements in their theoretical systems difficult to disentangle from the 'normative' elements. To take a simple concrete example of the sort of thing I have in mind, Quesnay's doctrine that the earnings of producers are normally limited to the level of their paid-out costs of production was dependent upon the assumption of free competition. But was free competition actually sufficiently prevalent in France at that time to warrant this assumption? Might Quesnay to some extent have been generalizing, not from the *actual* facts, but from the facts *as they would become* if certain Physiocratic policies were put into effect? In so far as this was the case, Quesnay's model must be interpreted not as a description of the actual economy of his time, but as a description of an 'ideal' economy.

The fact that we also come across the same sort of difficulty when interpreting other theoretical systems—notably that of Adam Smith—does not mean that the problem is any easier to solve. If what the economist believes *ought to be typical* coincides roughly with what *in fact is becoming typical*, of course, the problem is less difficult. It seems reasonable, for example, to interpret Quesnay's assumption of free competition, and Smith's inclusion of profit at the average rate in the equilibrium price of commodities, not so much as generalizations from some sort of ideal economy of the future, as indications of a perceptive recognition of the basic significance of certain economic facts which were then in the process of becoming typical. But in so far as the 'ideal' elements in the model cannot be interpreted in this way, the problem remains. My own feeling, however, is that these purely 'ideal' elements were of less importance in the case of the Physiocrats than is commonly supposed. It is true that the basic *Tableau* can be said to have constituted a picture of an 'ideal' economy, in the sense that it represented a state of affairs which the Physiocrats believed could be brought about by an extension of certain current trends, supported by appropriate policy measures; but in the Physiocrats' theoretical system as such it merely played the role of a sort of conceptual standard with reference to which the effects of various policies on the actual contemporary economy could be judged. The important thing to bear in mind is that the really essential and distinctive element of the Physiocratic model, which largely determined the whole content of the model, was the principle of the exclusive productivity of agriculture; and that this principle, which was employed equally in the analysis of the 'ideal' economy and in that of the actual economy, was in a very important sense a generalization from the latter. Thus we can at least start by interpreting the content of the Physiocratic model in accordance with the approach outlined at the beginning of this section.

There can be little doubt that the doctrine of the exclusive productivity of agriculture was indeed the lynch-pin of the Physiocratic model. Upon it depended the vital distinction which the Physiocrats made between productive and sterile occupations, the nature of their classification of basic social groups according to economic function, and the picture they drew in the *Tableau* of the mechanism underlying the circular flow. The interpretation of the content of the Physiocratic model means, in essence, the interpretation of the doctrine of exclusive productivity. Let us approach the problem of its interpretation by asking three questions about it. First, how far can it be said that the contemporary economic facts warranted the formulation of such a doctrine? Second, what were the main reasons for the great emphasis which the Physiocrats laid on the doctrine? And third, what were the main reasons for the Physiocrats' failure to give proper weight to certain new facts, then in the process of becoming typical, which threw doubt on the validity of the doctrine?

So far as the first question is concerned, I think that the doctrine of the exclusive productivity of agriculture can be said to have 'fitted the facts' with a reasonable degree of accuracy. The doubts which various commentators have felt about this have usually sprung either from vulgar misconceptions concerning the essential meaning which the Physiocrats ascribed to the terms 'productive' and 'sterile', or from a tendency to imagine that the Physiocrats were living in an economy much nearer in character to our own than was in fact the case. It cannot be too strongly emphasized that by 'productive' the Physiocrats did *not* mean simply 'capable of creating utility', or 'capable of adding value', or 'socially useful'. A 'productive' occupation certainly did possess these three characteristics— but so, too, after all, did most 'sterile' occupations. The real essence of a 'productive' occupation, according to the normal Physiocratic use of the term, lay in its inherent capacity to yield a disposable surplus over necessary cost; and the real essence of a 'sterile' occupation lay in its inherent incapacity to yield such a surplus.[1] It cannot be too strongly stressed, also, that the French economy at

---

[1] The question of where the line is to be drawn between 'necessary cost' and 'disposable surplus' is of course a very difficult one. The main problem arises in connection with the reward accruing to labour. If the worker receives a wage higher than the physical subsistence minimum, does he to that extent share in the 'disposable surplus'? Ricardo was quite prepared to admit that he does (see *Works*, I, p. 348, footnote); and both he and Marx emphasized that the 'subsistence minimum' was fixed at any given time not only by physical considerations

the time of the Physiocrats was very different indeed from our own: although certain signs of significant change were even then evident enough to those with eyes to see, it was still by and large a predominantly agricultural and feudal economy, in which capitalism and capitalist methods had been applied with conspicuous success only in the field of agriculture and even there only over a limited area, and in which manufacture was quite largely being carried on by artisans working either on their own account or in very small groups.

The doctrine of the exclusive productivity of agriculture was of course compounded of two separable notions—that agriculture was inherently 'productive' in the sense just described, and that manufacture and commerce were inherently 'sterile'. So far as the first of these notions was concerned, it should be noted that there was nothing peculiarly Physiocratic about the idea that agriculture was inherently capable of yielding a disposable surplus over necessary cost *in physical terms*. The fact that agriculture was capable of producing such a surplus must have been perfectly obvious to everyone almost from the days when agriculture was first invented. The amount of 'corn' which has to be used as seed and fed to the men and animals engaged in agricultural production is normally less than the amount of 'corn' which is gathered in at harvest-time—a fact which is conclusively demonstrated by the continued existence of other social groups besides the cultivators. 'It has been so ordained,' wrote Richard Jones, 'that the earth, in ordinary circumstances, yields to the labors of the cultivator more than is sufficient for his subsistence and that of his family', the 'surplus food' being consumed by 'another description of persons'.[1] In so far as the Physiocratic concept of the

---

but also by habit and history. The latter approach, however, historically speaking did not really solve the problem, but merely succeeded in making its solution for the time being less urgent. It is important to note that so far as the Physiocrats were concerned this problem did not arise in an acute form at all, since the great majority of the population of France at that time were in fact living at the bare physical subsistence minimum.

Another problem arises in connection with the pure profit which normally accrues to entrepreneurs in a developed capitalist economy. This profit constitutes a 'surplus over cost' in the sense that it is roughly what is left over for the entrepreneur after all the paid-out costs of production have been met: it was for this reason that Smith and Ricardo included it along with land rent in the 'net revenue' of society. But it is clear that it is not a surplus in quite the same sense as land rent is, since it is not a surplus *over supply price*. Once again it is important to note that this problem did not really arise for the Physiocrats, since in the conditions of their time it appeared quite reasonable to regard pure profit as an 'abnormal' type of income which could be more or less completely abstracted from in one's basic theoretical model. (See the second essay in the present volume.) Thus for the Physiocrats the distinction between 'necessary cost' and 'disposable surplus' appeared much more clear-cut than it does to us today.

[1] *Literary Remains*, p. 552.

productivity of agriculture was based on this simple and ancient idea, then, it cannot be said to have been specifically related to the environment and problems of eighteenth-century France. But the Physiocrats were of course concerned to emphasize not only the productivity of agriculture in physical terms, but also its productivity *in value terms*. Just as its productivity in physical terms was demonstrated by the existence of non-agricultural classes, so in the view of the Physiocrats its value productivity was demonstrated by the existence of land rent. It is clear that the emergence of this concept of value productivity could hardly have antedated the rise of the system of market exchange which the Physiocrats assumed to be dominant in the economy which they were analysing. It is clear, too, that this concept was developed largely in order to throw light on certain burning practical problems of their day. Agriculture, in their view, was certainly productive in both senses—i.e. it was inherently capable of yielding a physical surplus which in a market economy was inherently capable of being transformed into a value surplus. But in the conditions of eighteenth-century France, certain mistaken policy measures were not only preventing an adequate physical surplus from being yielded, but were also preventing the transformation of the existing physical surplus into an adequate value surplus. Policies to secure a 'proper price' for agricultural produce were therefore necessary if the productivity of agriculture was to be maximized; and the concept of value productivity was evolved in order to bring these policies into relief.

The 'sterility' of manufacture, in contradistinction to the 'productivity' of agriculture, was conceived by the Physiocrats solely in value terms. This had necessarily to be so: whereas it is at least plausible in the case of agriculture (especially when the latter is still being conducted in a fairly primitive way) to conceive both output and input as consisting of 'corn', this sort of physical approach is clearly impossible in the case of manufacture, where output and input consist of qualitatively dissimilar commodities. When the Physiocrats claimed that manufacture was sterile, what they meant was simply that it was inherently incapable of yielding any disposable surplus over necessary cost *in terms of value*. The Physiocrats agreed, of course, that this was true only under conditions of free competition: they were quite prepared to admit that when some form of monopoly existed the price of the commodity might be more than sufficient to cover raw material and subsistence costs. Given free competition, however, manufacture was essentially sterile.

Our natural reaction today, when we are faced with this proposition, is to say that it is simply contrary to experience. But to the Physiocrats, living as they did in an economy where manufacture was still largely organized on a non-capitalist and small-scale basis, it appeared to be fully in accord with experience. In France at this time only a very small proportion of those engaged in manufacture were in fact making anything much more than a mere living out of their activities. Production by artisans working either on their own account or in very small establishments was predominant in the manufacturing field throughout the whole of the century. 'Everywhere in France', writes Henri Sée,

'the tanneries, glass-works, paper-manufactories, apart from a few large establishments, dye-works, and bleaching-works are small-scale enterprises employing only a few workers. In the greater part of the towns, small artisans working alone or employing only a single journeyman are in the majority. In Bordeaux, the number of journeymen is only four times as great as the number of masters. In Paris in 1791, if a few textile factories employ several hundreds of workers, the average is nevertheless only 16 workers per employer. A fortiori, in towns of second or third rank, like Rennes, large-scale industrial establishments are very rare.'[1]

We have, in short, a situation in which even in those enterprises where several workers are employed and a master-journeyman relationship therefore exists, the social gulf between master and journeyman is rarely a very wide one,[2] the standard of life of the master does not differ very profoundly from the standard of life of the journeyman,[3] and both groups are usually at or near the subsistence minimum.[4] Under such conditions, a proposition to the effect that manufacture (apart from exceptional cases) *was not in actual fact* yielding anything more than a subsistence income to those engaged in it would not appear in any way quaint or esoteric. It would simply appear as a more or less reasonable generalization from the economic facts.[5]

The Physiocrats' error lay in arguing from this proposition to another—that manufacture *is naturally and inherently incapable* of yielding a surplus over cost. From the fact that manufacture in their time was not yielding a value-surplus under competitive conditions, the Physiocrats concluded that it was inherently incapable of doing so under such conditions; and in this they were clearly wrong. But the nature of their error should be properly appreciated. They were wrong not so much because they were bad scientists, as because they were bad prophets—not so much, that is, because they failed to give

[1] Henri Sée, *La France Economique et Sociale au XVIIIe Siècle* (Armand Colin edn., 1939), pp. 100–101. Cf. ibid., pp. 138–9.

[2] Ibid., p. 145. [3] Ibid., pp. 145–6. [4] Ibid., pp. 141–2.

[5] Even Forbonnais, one of the most acute of the contemporary critics of Physiocracy, was not prepared to attribute to manufacture anything more than the capacity to yield a *very small* surplus: his main criticism was simply that the Physiocrats were using misleading words to draw attention to this relative 'sterility' of manufacture.

proper weight to the typical economic facts of their time, as because they failed to give proper weight to certain other facts, then barely apparent, which were destined to *become* typical.[1] Their error, if such it be, was very much the same in quality as Adam Smith's 'error' in failing to foresee the full effects of the rise of monopoly, or as Marx's 'error' in failing to foresee the full effects of the growth of militant trade unionism in an expanding economy.

The idea that manufacture and commerce do not 'naturally'—i.e. in the absence of monopoly or state interference—yield a value-surplus was not of course confined to the Physiocrats, any more than was the idea that agriculture does yield such a surplus. Most of the Mercantilist writers, for example, had the doctrine of exclusive productivity been presented to them in the simple terms in which I have just stated it here, would undoubtedly have approved of it.[2] But whereas with the Mercantilists the doctrine was rarely stated in anything like a coherent form and played an essentially subordinate role in their writings, with Quesnay it became the great axis around which almost everything else revolved. This leads us to the second question posed above—what were the main reasons for this great emphasis which the Physiocrats placed on the doctrine?

Basically, the reason was very simple. Whereas the Mercantilists believed that a country could develop economically only by beggaring its neighbours, the Physiocrats believed that it could lift itself by its own bootstraps. Both sought for a 'surplus' or 'disposable revenue' which could be used for developmental purposes; but whereas the Mercantilists sought for it in net gains from foreign trade, the Physiocrats sought for it in net gains from home production.[3] Economic development, the Physiocrats argued in effect, requires above all the accumulation of capital; the main source of new capital for accumulation lies in the disposable surplus over necessary cost yielded by home production; therefore our primary task as economists must be to ascertain in which branches of home production such a surplus is yielded. The result of their attempts to undertake this primary task was the doctrine of the exclusive productivity of agriculture. The only revenue which was truly 'disposable'—i.e. available for accumulation as capital—was the surplus or 'net product' yielded by agriculture.

If this interpretation is correct, it may be asked, why did the Physiocrats persist in identifying the agricultural surplus with the income of the class of proprietors?[4] After all, the Physiocrats did not lay their *main* emphasis on the necessity for agricultural investment

---

[1] Some of the reasons for their failure in this respect are discussed below, pp. 385 ff.

[2] Cf. above, pp. 349–50. [3] Cf. above, pp. 349–50.

[4] The exceptions to this identification are discussed above, pp. 299 ff.

by the proprietors, whose duties in this respect were held to be fulfilled if they made the 'ground advances' required to drain the land, to clear it, to provide adequate transport facilities, etc. Even if we make due allowance for the fact that tactical considerations probably led the Physiocrats to play down the importance which they in fact attached to this type of investment, it remains true that they expected the main body of new agricultural investment—the increased 'original advances' and 'annual advances' which above all were required to revivify agriculture—to be undertaken by a quite distinct social class, that of the agricultural entrepreneurs. And although the *initial* capital required to set up an agricultural enterprise could conceivably come from hoarded wealth of one kind or another,[1] it is clear that on the Physiocratic assumptions regular *accretions* to this capital could be obtained by the entrepreneur only from the annual 'net product' of agriculture. And this 'net product', according to the Physiocrats, accrued in its entirety to the landlords in the form of rent.

The question of the Physiocrats' attitude to the 'profit' of the agricultural entrepreneurs has been dealt with fairly fully above,[2] and only one additional comment seems to be required in connection with the present problem. The Physiocrats, in their anxiety to stimulate agricultural investment, were particularly concerned that the agricultural entrepreneurs and their 'advances' should be freed from the arbitrary and oppressive burden of taxation to which they were then subject. It was this concern—together with a general, if muted, opposition to the seigneurial régime—which lay behind their strenuous advocacy of a single tax on land rent. Now the logic, as distinct from the politics, of the Physiocratic single tax lay in the argument that it was only the 'disposable surplus' which *could* be taxed: any other form of tax would ultimately fall back on the 'disposable surplus', burdened with quite unnecessary costs of collection, etc. Had the Physiocrats admitted that the farmers regularly and normally received a part of the 'disposable surplus' in the form of profit, therefore, they would have been hard put to it to defend their proposal that the farmers should be completely exempted from taxation. Thus the Physiocrats were in something of a cleft stick: on the one hand the profits of the farmers had to be shown as being part of the net product (since otherwise they would not have been available for accumulation); and on the other hand they had to be shown as *not* being part of the net product (since otherwise they would not have been able to claim exemption from taxation). The ways in which the Physiocrats tried to get out of this dilemma—mainly by treating the pure profit of the capitalist farmer as a *temporary* share of the net product which ultimately crystallized out

[1] Cf. above, p. 244.　　　　　　　　　　[2] p. 298 ff.

into rent—have been discussed above. It needs only to be added that what I have just said does not of course imply that the Physiocrats' identification of the net product with land rent was a mere political rationalization. At this time there were undoubtedly very serious *conceptual* difficulties standing in the way of the recognition of profit on agricultural capital as a regular and normal category of income receivable even under competitive conditions. The most that my argument implies is that policy considerations were largely instrumental in preventing the Physiocrats from making greater efforts than they in fact did to overcome these conceptual difficulties.

This leads us to the third question about the doctrine of the exclusive productivity of agriculture—what were the main reasons for the Physiocrats' failure to give proper weight to certain new facts, then in the process of becoming typical, which threw doubt on the validity of the doctrine? The most important of the 'new facts' referred to here was of course the gradual emergence of a situation in which capitalist entrepreneurs in all occupations, even under conditions of free competition, regularly received an income which (a) was proportionate to the amount of capital which the entrepreneur employed rather than to the amount of work he personally performed, and (b) contained an element which was truly 'net', in the sense that it did not constitute a compensation for paid-out costs.[1] The great paradox of Physiocracy lies in the fact that whereas on the one hand the founders of the system laid the very greatest emphasis on the necessity for the accumulation of capital and the introduction of capitalist methods of production, on the other hand they strenuously denied the existence (as a 'normal' or 'natural' phenomenon) of the very type of income which is the *primum mobile* of a capitalist economy.

It is easy enough to point out, in answer to the question, that Quesnay's economic views were probably worked out in the early 1750s, if not before, at a time when the 'new facts' just referred to were much less in evidence than they were to be later in the century. Even Adam Smith, working in a much more advanced economy than Quesnay, seems not to have arrived at the concept of a 'natural' rate of profit on capital until after the 1750s.[2] We should not, it may be argued by way of extenuation, expect our economists to be seers: even those who definitely point the way to a new form of economic organization, as Smith and Quesnay did, cannot be expected to foresee all the details of this new society, and in their analyses of it must necessarily remain to some extent prisoners of traditional concepts which are appropriate only to the analysis of the existing society. If Smith finally arrived at the concept of a 'natural' rate of

[1] Cf. above, p. 307.
[2] Cf. my *Studies in the Labour Theory of Value*, pp. 46 ff.

N

profit and the orthodox adherents of Quesnay and Mirabeau did not, can this not be adequately explained in terms of the fact that Quesnay's followers formed themselves into a 'sect' which, like all such sects, regarded the defence of its master's original doctrines as its prime duty?

This line of argument is very plausible, and no doubt contains a great deal of truth. But when it has been stated, we still have an uneasy feeling that the mystery has not been fully explained. The interesting thing is that at the time of the Physiocrats the 'new facts' were very rapidly becoming apparent precisely in those prosperous agricultural areas in which the Physiocrats expressed themselves to be most interested.[1] Not only were many agricultural entrepreneurs in these areas receiving regular and substantial profits, but rural industry, too, was manifestly becoming subject to the capitalist form of organization. Whereas in less prosperous areas the merchants were usually confining themselves to purely commercial transactions, in these more prosperous areas of the north they were beginning to take over the distribution of raw materials and the actual direction of the work.[2] If the Physiocrats wanted a model of the capitalist economy of the future, it was there in the north of France for them to see.

There were, I think, two main reasons—both of them closely related to current issues of policy—which prevented the Physiocrats from seeing the full significance of these new developments. The first, concerning agriculture, has already been mentioned in another connection above:[3] the Physiocrats were disinclined to include the farmer's profits in the net product because they were anxious, in the interests of agricultural development, to claim exemption from taxation for the farmer. The second, concerning manufacture, is a little more complex. The Physiocrats were aware, even if only dimly and even if the horizon of the founders tended to be limited to agriculture, that the accumulation of capital—the main prerequisite of economic development—could be maximized only under conditions of economic freedom. Given this viewpoint, they were bound to see all manifestations of monopoly in production as 'unnatural' and 'abnormal' and to advocate their abolition. Now it was precisely in those branches of manufacture and commerce where monopoly in one form or another was most apparent that net gains were most conspicuously being received. Whenever competition was artificially restricted—not only, be it noted, in the case of the *Manufactures d'Etat* and the *Manufactures Royales*,[4] but also in the case of the many trades in which guilds had become powerful[5]—something like an

---

[1] These were the areas specified by Quesnay in *Grains*: see I.N.E.D., II, p. 461.
[2] See Henri Sée, op. cit., pp. 132–3.   [3] Pp. 384–5.
[4] See Henri Sée, op. cit., pp. 127–8.   [5] See ibid., pp. 104–5.

industrial 'net product' was usually generated. Under these circumstances, it was only to be expected that the profits yielded in such cases should be regarded by the Physiocrats as an 'unnatural' and 'abnormal' product of the monopolies themselves. From here it was an easy step to the notion that the existence of industrial profits in certain industries and areas did not disprove the doctrine of the sterility of manufacture: it was evidence merely of the presence of some form of monopoly, and not of any innate capacity in manufacture to yield a value-surplus.

So far we have dealt with the factors motivating the Physiocrats in their search for a net product, and the factors which induced them to argue that agriculture alone was inherently capable of yielding a net product. It remains to discuss their views as to the basic reason for this state of affairs. The problem here can be put very simply: if competition causes manufacture to be sterile, why does it leave agriculture productive? Competition, according to the Physiocrats, wipes out all surplus gains in the case of manufactured products. Why, then, does it not also reduce the price of agricultural produce to the level of paid-out costs, thus wiping out rent? The Physiocrats themselves occasionally came near to posing the problem in these terms, but the answers which they gave to it when they did so were vague in the extreme. 'It is the expense of the labour,' Quesnay wrote in the *Dialogue on the Work of Artisans*, 'which determines the price of the artisan's goods, and the competition of the latter sets limits to the expense of their labour. It is not the same, I repeat, with the price of the products of the land, which is determined not only by the expenses of cultivation but also by many other causes which are capable of maintaining the market value of the products, notwithstanding economies in the costs of cultivation'.[1] But what exactly *are* these 'many other causes' which allegedly prevent competition from reducing the price of agricultural produce to the level of the 'costs of cultivation'? Was Quesnay in this passage on the verge of giving an explanation of rent in terms of the possession by the landed proprietors of some sort of class monopoly?[2] Mirabeau certainly toyed on at least one occasion with an explanation in something like these terms;[3] but even if we take full account of the natural reluctance which the Physiocrats must have felt to pursuing this line of thought further, I do not think we can say that an explanation of this type was uppermost in their minds. There is rather more warrant for underlining in this connection such statements as that of Quesnay to the effect that the needs of the purchasers of agricultural produce 'are always greater than the total amount of the reproduction'.[4] The Physiocrats do seem to have assumed the

<hr>

[1] Above, p. 228.   [2] Cf. Weulersse, I , p. 227.
[3] *Philosophie Rurale* (1764 edn.), Vol. III, p. 266.   [4] Above, p. 227.

existence of a kind of permanent excess of demand over supply in the case of agricultural produce. But their main explanation was couched in quite different terms: the net product was simply the gift of nature, or of the 'Author of nature'. This is a familiar line of argument in the early history of economic thought: in agriculture 'nature labours along with man', so that rent may be conceived as 'the produce of those powers of nature, the use of which the landlord lends to the farmer'.[1] The defect of this argument, considered as an answer to the problem with which we are now dealing, is fairly obvious. While it might be conceded to provide a plausible explanation of the emergence of a *physical* surplus in agriculture (at any rate in a society like that of eighteenth-century France, where the powers of nature were not yet being used to any great extent in manufacture),[2] it does not provide an adequate explanation of the emergence of a *value*-surplus in agriculture. To explain the emergence of a value-surplus, a general theory of value, capable of explaining (*inter alia*) what determines the price of the factor land, is clearly required. And with such a theory of value the Physiocrats did not succeed in providing themselves. By and large, it is fair to say that they simply took the existence of rent as such for granted, and did not feel it necessary to enquire at all closely into the *economic* forces which permitted it to emerge and persist in a competitive economy.

This was not a wholly unreasonable attitude for the Physiocrats to take up, given the particular policy issues with which they were confronted. Agriculture, they argued in effect, was inherently capable of producing, and under 'normal' conditions did in actual fact produce, a surplus of corn-output over corn-input, the origin of which could be explained and the extent of which could be measured in purely physical terms, without the intervention of any theory of value. It was this physical surplus of corn, in essence, which accrued to the landlords as rent. In a market economy, however, what they actually received as rent was not the corn-surplus itself but the money obtained when the corn-surplus was sold on the market at current prices. The level of rent thus varied not only with the size of the physical corn-surplus, but also with the price at which it could be sold. Now in the view of the Physiocrats certain mistaken policy measures—notably the restrictions on free trade in corn—were making the price of corn unnecessarily low and unsteady, thereby causing the level of rent—i.e. the aggregate value of the physical corn-surplus—to be lower and more variable than it need be. This meant, in effect, that the revenue available for accumulation as capital was not being maximized. In the interests of economic development, then, the Physiocrats were concerned to advocate the abolition of these mistaken policy measures. Thus it was quite

---

[1] *Wealth of Nations*, Vol. I, pp. 343–4.   [2] Cf. Weulersse, I, p. 276.

natural that their discussion of the factors determining prices should have been oriented only incidentally towards the abstract problem of why the market price of corn normally exceeded its cost of production—i.e. why rent as such persisted in a competitive market economy. The main orientation of their discussion was towards the practical problem of how, *given the fact of rent*, its level could be raised through an appropriate price-policy.

The set of value-concepts normally employed by the Physiocrats, then, was designed not to *explain* the exclusive value-productivity of agriculture, but merely to *express* it in a way which would illuminate this practical problem. The price at which goods sold 'at first hand' on the market constituted what the Physiocrats called their 'market value' (*valeur vénale*); the paid-out costs of producing them constituted their 'fundamental value' (*valeur fondamentale*). In the case of manufactured goods, the 'market value' was normally equal to the 'fundamental value'; in the case of agricultural produce, the 'market value' was higher than the 'fundamental value' by an amount equal (roughly) to rent. The aim of price-policy should be to maximize this surplus by ensuring that a 'proper price' (*bon prix*) was received for agricultural produce—i.e. a price which was both higher than the existing one and less subject to violent fluctuations in years of extreme plenty and scarcity. This 'proper price' could be secured by the adoption of various measures designed to stimulate home demand for agricultural produce, and by the lifting of the existing restrictions on the internal and external corn trade.[1]

Finally, let us note very briefly the way in which the doctrine of the exclusive productivity of agriculture helped to determine the particular classification of social groups which the Physiocrats employed in their model, and the basic relations which they postulated

---

[1] When these restrictions were lifted, the Physiocrats argued, excessive price fluctuations would be eliminated. The interplay of supply and demand could thus be regarded not as a cause of fluctuations but as the basic cause of the relative invariability of prices; and one could therefore speak in terms of a sort of 'absolute price' which existed *prior to* individual exchange transactions in the goods concerned. This approach to the general problem of price-formation was of considerable importance in the Physiocratic system, since it enabled Quesnay to maintain that all exchanges are conducted on the basis of 'value for equal value', and on this foundation to argue that commerce was essentially sterile. It was also of great importance from the point of view of the subsequent history of economic thought, since the British Classical economists tended to adopt a somewhat similar sort of general approach (although they did not, of course, draw from it the same conclusion concerning the sterility of commerce). Weulersse describes this approach as an 'annulment of the psychological element in the consideration of social value and in the study of the circulation of wealth', and calls it 'a fruitful discovery of the Economists' (II, p. 145). This 'annulment of the psychological element' should be carefully borne in mind when we are interpreting the more sophisticated treatment of the value problem given by Le Trosne and Turgot. Cf. above, pp. 371–2.

as existing between these groups. It seemed clear to the Physiocrats that the classification of social groups should be based not on their juridical position (as had until then been usual) but on their economic function;[1] and that their economic function should be defined with reference to their relation to the 'disposable surplus' which was the Physiocrats' main object of attention. Now men were related in several different ways to the disposable surplus. The various groups engaged in agriculture *produced* the surplus; one of these groups, the agricultural entrepreneurs, *increased* the physical magnitude of the surplus by means of capital accumulation; and another group, the landlords, *consumed* the surplus and thereby contributed to the maintenance of its value. Since the *production* of the surplus was in a sense the primary economic function, upon which the others ultimately depended, it seemed apparent to the Physiocrats that the basic distinction which must be made was that between the social groups engaged in agriculture (the 'productive' class), and the social groups engaged in non-agricultural pursuits (the 'sterile' class). Given this basic classification, it was clear that the landlords were in a somewhat anomalous position. It was difficult to group them with the productive class, since, although they contributed (or ought to contribute) to the production of the surplus through their 'ground advances', their predominant role was that of consumers of the surplus. On the other hand, it was difficult to group them with the sterile class, since such a classification, quite apart from the unfortunate political implications which would have been drawn from it, might have led to a serious underestimation of the importance of the economic effects of their close connection with agriculture. The landlords (together with other recipients of the surplus) were therefore distinguished as a 'mixed class'[2] standing as it were in between the two basic classes. The only remaining problem was that of the place to be given to the agricultural entrepreneurs. When it was a question of merely depicting the general 'static' process of the production and circulation of wealth (as for example in the basic *Tableau*), there appeared to be no necessity to distinguish the agricultural entrepreneurs from the other members of the productive class. When it was a question of depicting the general 'dynamic' process whereby wealth was increased, however, it was obviously necessary to make this distinction, in view of the vital role played in this process by the capital accumulation carried on by the entrepreneurs. Thus we find in Physiocratic writing, side by side with static models in which the

---

[1] On the significance of this change in attitude, see the interesting discussion of 'La Notion de Classes Sociales chez Turgot' by Henri Sée, in his work *La Vie Economique et les Classes Sociales en France au XVIIIe Siècle* (Paris, 1924), pp. 209 ff.

[2] Above, p. 205.

existence and activities of the class of agricultural entrepreneurs are in effect abstracted from, other dynamic models (both verbal and tabular)[1] in which this class appears as the primary agent of economic growth.

In all this, for fairly obvious reasons, there is little appreciation of the economic significance of that class relation between wage-earners and property-owners which was later to appear so important to the British Classical economists.[2] While it is true that the leading emphasis of the Physiocrats was laid on the accumulation of capital, and that for this reason if for no other their system can properly be called a 'capitalist' one, it is equally true that the central position which they afforded to the doctrine of the exclusive productivity of agriculture prevented their system from being *fully* 'capitalist'. At best, it was a system of *agricultural* capitalism—'a bourgeois reproduction of the feudal system', as Marx called it.[3] But it is worth noting in conclusion that when the Physiocrats departed, as they sometimes did, from the rigidities which the doctrine of the exclusive productivity of agriculture imposed on their formal system, and described the process of economic development in more abstract and general terms, these 'feudal' limitations were largely overcome. 'A man can acquire wealth,' wrote Quesnay in *Men*, 'only through the wealth which he already possesses, and through the gains which the wealth of others procures for him'.[4] Here Quesnay is using the term 'wealth' in three different senses: the first time as 'revenue' or net income; the second as capital; and the third as the power to consume.[5] The general picture which statements like this conjure up, in spite of the deliberately paradoxical language in which they are often expressed, is one of a society in which everything is produced through the investment of capital, and production is dependent upon demand. 'Great capitals applied to production', writes Weulersse, 'and vast markets opened up for the products—such is in fact the theoretical ideal of the Physiocrats, a simple transcription of their practical

---

[1] The most effective of the tabular models is that translated above, pp. 138 ff.
[2] Turgot, as distinct from the more orthodox Physiocrats (apart from Baudeau), had more than an inkling of the importance of this relationship. 'The whole Class occupied in supplying the different wants of the Society with the vast variety of industrial products', he writes, 'finds itself, so to speak, subdivided into two orders: that of the Undertakers, Manufacturers, Employers, all possessors of large capitals which they make profit from by setting men at work, by means of their advances; and the second order, which is composed of simple Artisans who have no other property but their arms, who advance only their daily labour, and receive no profit but their wages' (*Reflections on the Formation and the Distribution of Riches*, English translation of 1898, ed. Ashley, p. 54). Even with Turgot, however, this class division is definitely subordinate to that between the 'productive' and 'stipendiary' classes.
[3] *Theories of Surplus Value* (London, 1951), p. 50.
[4] I.N.E.D., II, p. 537.   [5] Cf. Weulersse, II, p. 147.

programme; an ideal which can properly be called capitalist, in the sense in which political economy employs this word today. No doubt for them the only true production was in agriculture, and as a result of this their school was indeed one of *agricultural capitalism*; but in the abstract part of their doctrine, where the largeness of the words hides the narrowness of the conceptions, they were led to formulate the scientific principles of capitalism pure and simple, of capitalism in its complete form.'[1]

V

In the above discussion, the problem of the interpretation of the work of the Physiocrats has been approached by relating their general methodology and their 'pure theory' to the environment in which they worked, and in particular to the policy issues which this environment revealed to them as especially significant. It remains in this final section to say a little about the light which the specific attitudes taken up by the Physiocrats towards some of these policy issues can throw on the general character of their system as a whole.

Consider, for example, their advocacy of a single tax on land rent. There are various possible ways of interpreting this particular policy, upon which the Physiocrats, after an initial period of hesitation, always insisted so strongly. One can regard it, for example, as a mere logical corollary of the doctrine of the exclusive productivity of agriculture: since the net product is the only income which *can* in fact be taxed, it is the only income which *should* be taxed. The Physiocrats did indeed lay emphasis on this logical connection between their basic theory and their taxation policy. But there is reason to suspect, as we have already seen,[2] that the connection was not simply a one-way one: at any rate it seems safe to say that their identification of the net product with rent was due at least in part to their desire that the agricultural entrepreneur should escape taxation. And there is also reason to suspect that the policy of the single tax, which would have thrown the whole burden of taxation directly on to the landlords, had in itself certain important political implications.

Norman J. Ware, in an interesting article on the Physiocrats,[3] has argued in this connection that the single tax was essentially

'a device of the commoner landowner, eager for profit, to escape the multiplicity of taxes which fell on land under the *ancien régime* and to substitute one tax upon the agricultural surplus, thus insuring to

---

[1] Weulersse, II, pp. 147–8.   [2] Above, pp. 384–5.
[3] *The Physiocrats: A Study in Economic Rationalization*, in the *American Economic Review*, December 1931, pp. 607 ff.

the landowner, not only his cost of production, but a profit before taxation could be applied.'[1]

At this time, Ware claims, a 'new class of commoner landowners' was emerging from the French bureaucracy, 'aping the nobility they superseded, but retaining their bourgeois ideas of profit-making';[2] and Physiocracy was in essence an 'economic rationalization' of the interests of this new class.

This is a very plausible interpretation, and one in which there is clearly a strong element of truth. In so far as the Physiocrats were concerned with the interests of the landowning classes as such, there is little doubt that they favoured the new owners of the land as against the old hereditary nobility. Their proposals for facilitating the transfer of landed property and for the employment of 'monetary fortunes' in the purchase of land were probably designed, at least in part, to hasten the contemporary trend towards a situation in which the landowner's title to his land would normally consist simply of the money he had invested in buying it.[3] And the Physiocrats also emphasized on occasion that the burden of the single tax, in so far as its imposition resulted in an increase in the charges payable by the landed proprietors, would not fall on new purchasers of property, since the reduced net income would naturally be taken account of in the purchase price.[4] What they did *not* emphasize, significantly enough, was the other side of this argument—that in the assumed case the former owner who was obliged to sell his land would suffer what really amounted to a partial expropriation.[5]

The most one can deduce from this attitude of the Physiocrats, however, is a general bias on their part towards a 'capitalist' form of landownership, in which rent would be regarded not as a hereditary income but rather as a reward for the investment of capital in the purchase of land. One cannot, I think, legitimately deduce from it the thesis that Physiocracy was essentially an 'economic rationalization' of the interests of the new class of 'commoner landowners'. The main virtue of the single tax, the Physiocrats always emphasized, was that it would exempt *the agricultural entrepreneur and his capital* from taxation, thereby stimulating the investment of capital in agricultural production, raising output, and increasing the size of future net products. If we are anxious to see the single tax as a 'rationalization' of somebody's interests, then, should we not see it as a 'rationalization' of the interests of the new class of agricultural entrepreneurs rather than of those of the new class of 'commoner

[1] Ware, *op. cit.*, pp. 607–8.   [2] Ibid., p. 607.
[3] Cf. Weulersse, II, p. 695.
[4] Cf. Mercier de la Rivière, *L'Ordre Naturel*, in Daire, II, p. 451.
[5] Cf. Weulersse, II, p. 695.

landowners'? In so far as these 'commoner landowners' were themselves entrepreneurs, of course, the two sets of interests coincided;
but in actual fact this identification of the two functions was the
exception rather than the rule in France at this time.[1] It is true that
the Physiocrats, in an attempt to forestall the opposition of those
members of the nobility (both hereditary and new) whom the
imposition of a single tax would have divested of the pecuniary
privileges of the seigneurial régime, emphasized that one of the
ultimate results of the single tax would be a large increase in the level
of land rent. But this particular benefit would have been shared by all
landowners, whether the old nobility or the new commoners, and on
this count there is no warrant for saying that the single tax was in
the interests of the new class rather than in those of the old. It could
be argued, of course, that the relatively small section of the 'commoner landowners' which had not succeeded in gaining admission
to the ranks of the new nobility,[2] and which therefore still suffered
to a greater or lesser extent from the existing tax system, would have
received an extra benefit from the imposition of the single tax: not
only would this section have shared in the general increase in the
level of rent which ultimately accrued to all landowners, but it would
also have received an immediate gain from the substitution of a
single, fixed, and foreseeable tax for a host of arbitrary and variable
ones. But the Physiocrats did not lay very much emphasis on this
point. The distinction between the different types of landowners
seemed to them much less important than the distinction between
the landowning class as a whole and the new class of agricultural
entrepreneurs.

The single tax policy, then, cannot properly be described as
merely 'a device of the commoner landowner'. It is nearer to the
truth, as we have just seen, to regard it as a 'rationalization' of the
interests of the new class of agricultural entrepreneurs; but even this
is true only in a very broad sense. The Physiocrats were, indeed,
concerned to break down certain barriers standing in the way of the
development of the capitalist *zeitgeist*, of which the agricultural
entrepreneurs appeared to them as the most important personifica-
tion. But it is essential to remember, first that this concern was
motivated by the interests of increasing national output rather than
by the selfish interests of any particular social group; and second that
it was tempered by a reluctance, by no means wholly tactical, to

---

[1] Cf. J. H. Clapham, *The Economic Development of France and Germany,
1815–1914*, 4th edn., pp. 16–17; and M. H. Dobb, *Studies in the Development of
Capitalism*, pp. 239–40. Ware's reference to the 'cost of production' *of the
landowner* in the passage quoted on pp. 392–3 above would seem to indicate that
he is assuming that the 'commoner landowners' were also entrepreneurs.

[2] Ware, it seems to me, does not sufficiently distinguish between the interests
of the ennobled and non-ennobled landowners.

advocate policies which would result in the complete subversion of the old feudal order. The single tax would certainly have done away with a number of undesirable aspects of this old order (notably the seigneurial régime); it would have stimulated the further growth of the new class of agricultural entrepreneurs; and it would to some extent have encouraged the rise of a new 'capitalist' type of land-ownership. But to the Physiocrats these developments appeared desirable, not because of the material benefits which they would have brought to particular social groups, but rather because of the increase in national output which they would have produced. And the land-owning class as a whole, it is important to note, would by no means have been expropriated as a result of the single tax: on the contrary, its income would ultimately have been increased, and it would have retained substantially the same position of predominance which it enjoyed under the feudal order. The society which the Physiocrats visualized, in short, was indeed a 'capitalist' society in the broad sense, but a capitalist society in which the landowning classes, by accommodating themselves to the new conditions, would be able to retain their old position of predominance.[1]

Consider, again, the Physiocrats' advocacy of complete freedom for manufacture and commerce, which at first sight seems to stand in such startling contrast to their doctrine of the 'sterility' of these occupations. Logical considerations no doubt played some part here: having proclaimed the rights of property and personal liberty as sacred and eternal principles, with 'legal despotism' as their political guardian, the Physiocrats could hardly have refused to extend these rights to manufacture and commerce as well as to agriculture. But much more important than this is the fact that freedom for manu-facture and commerce was an essential precondition for the develop-ment of the 'capitalist' form of society at which they were aiming. Freedom for manufacture and commerce implied, in the minds of the Physiocrats, the abolition of the system of regulation, the guilds, the state monopolies and other 'exclusive privileges', the restrictions on trade, and the crippling system of taxation; and it was precisely these features of economic life which constituted the main obstacles to the further development of capitalism in industry in France at this time. The Physiocrats' attacks on these hindrances were almost as forth-right as those which the economists of the 'school of Gournay' were making at the same time.

Once again it must be emphasized, however, that the 'capitalism'

---

[1] Cf. Weulersse, II, p. 710: 'What they demanded, from the social point of view, was that the new bourgeoisie, which was soon to be the dominant class, should be above all a landed bourgeoisie, into which the old nobility could find its way.' The sort of society which they seem to have had in mind was roughly similar to that which existed in Britain between, say, 1750 and 1850.

which the Physiocrats desired was an *agricultural* capitalism, as distinct from the industrial capitalism which the disciples of Gournay were in effect advocating. The Physiocrats were of course well aware that the removal of the above-mentioned obstacles would lead directly to some increase in the output of the sterile occupations: the system of regulation, for example, was clearly hindering enterprise and innovation in manufacture.[1] But the main tenor of their arguments in favour of freedom of manufacture and commerce was that in the general 'capitalist' atmosphere which the removal of the obstacles would bring about there would be a big increase in *agricultural* output and in the magnitude of the net product. In their discussions on the benefits of freedom of trade, for example, they laid their main emphasis on the way in which freedom of trade *in corn* could help to secure a 'proper price' for that commodity: not only would it raise the price of corn above its present inadequate level, but the very 'equalization' of prices which would result would also in itself procure a considerable benefit to the producer without costing the consumer anything at all. And in their discussions on the benefits of the abolition of the 'exclusive privileges' of manufacture, they usually concentrated on showing the disastrous effects *on agriculture* of a régime based on the 'spirit of monopoly'.[2] When Quesnay urged that a policy of *laisser aller* should be applied to 'sterile expenditure', his main aim was simply to do away with a situation in which manufacture and commerce were deliberately favoured and protected, as they were under the Colbertian system, *at the expense of agriculture.*[3]

Historically speaking, the removal of this type of 'artificial' monopoly was a necessary precondition of the emergence of that 'natural' monopoly of the owners of the means of production as a class upon which a developed capitalist economy is based. The Physiocrats, however, did not visualize their anti-monopoly policy as leading to a fully-fledged capitalist society in which a new class of capitalist entrepreneurs would rival and eventually overshadow the landowners: on the contrary, they visualized it as leading to a modified type of capitalist society in which the landowners would remain predominant and might even become more powerful. Generally speaking, taking the Physiocrats' writing as a whole, it is clear that they regarded the distinction between capitalist entrepreneurs and wage-earners in the sterile occupations as of little economic significance. It was only later writers like Baudeau and Turgot who began to conceive of manufacturing, commercial, and agricultural entrepreneurs as constituting a single social class. In their work, the relationship between this profit-receiving class and the

---

[1] Cf. above, p. 101.   [2] Above, p. 245.
[3] Cf. above, pp. 244 ff.

class of wage-earners begins to appear as one of the basic economic relations in society. But even in the case of these relatively advanced writers, their Physiocratic preconceptions prevented them from visualizing this relation as existing otherwise than within a basically 'feudal' framework.

We see, then, that the 'feudal' or 'agricultural' character of the Physiocrats' capitalism is demonstrated not only by the fact that they did not *foresee* that manufacture would become 'productive', but also by the fact that they did not *want* it to become 'productive'. The economists of the 'school of Gournay' were quite correct in sensing that there was an important difference of outlook between themselves and the Physiocrats, in spite of their apparent unanimity on the question of industrial and commercial freedom. It is to this aspect of Physiocracy that Rogin draws particular attention in his interesting and thoughtful estimate of the validity of their theoretical system:

'When, as with the physiocrats, the practical interest is dictated pre-eminently by the requirements of capitalist entrepreneurs in agriculture and by the fiscal requirements of a moribund state, at a time when nonagricultural capitalists were leading in economic, political, and social reconstruction and on the eve of a time when the dynamics of accumulation and productivity were to be associated primarily with the career of industry, then the value of the doctrine not only is limited for the later demands of effective policy, but is also highly qualified in its own age and in the country which gave it birth.'[1]

'A normative theoretical model', Rogin argues, 'which is not susceptible of being translated into the realm of historical fact is not a scientific theory, but a utopian one. . . . Though physiocratic theory had the great merit of addressing itself to some of the outstanding evils of the *ancien régime*, it provides an interesting illustration to the effect that the significance of an economic theory is contingent on the choice of attainable objectives. Thus a high measure of prescience is called for regarding the dominant social tendencies in the community to which the theory is directed'.[2]

It has to be admitted that there was indeed a 'utopian' element in Physiocracy, which it has been one of the main purposes of this section to elaborate. It must also be admitted—and indeed emphasized—that the question of whether or not a theory is oriented towards 'attainable objectives' is very relevant to the question of its 'validity'. In so far as an economist is limited in his 'prescience' regarding the 'dominant social tendencies', and in so far as this makes his selection of basic variables and his view of the relations between them radically different from what they would have been had his 'prescience' been greater, it is quite proper to view his theory as being in some significant sense 'invalid'. But one should not, I think, in the case of the Physiocrats, apply this principle too mechanically. After all, it would have required an exceptionally high degree of 'prescience'—a much higher degree, I suggest, than we have a right to expect from any economist—for Quesnay, in France in the 1750s, to have foreseen in their entirety even the main outlines of the future capitalist society, let alone the details of its organization. Was it really the case that in France in the 1750s 'nonagricultural capitalists were leading in economic, political, and social reconstruction'? And if this was not in fact the case, should we not grant the Physiocratic system a rather greater degree of 'validity', at any rate for the time and place in which Quesnay first formulated it, than Rogin is prepared to grant it?

But this is not the most important point. In interpreting Physiocracy, the significant fact is surely not so much that the theory was subject to certain 'feudal' limitations, as that the Physiocrats so often and so brilliantly managed to transcend these limitations. It is not sufficient, in other words, to regard their theory as being oriented only towards a particular type of capitalism which later turned out to be unattainable: this specific orientation must be regarded as part of a more general orientation towards the perfectly attainable objective of *capitalism as such*. As we have seen above, a great deal of Physiocratic theory was in fact oriented towards capitalism in this more general sense, and in particular towards the system of market exchange which capitalism was extending over the whole economy. These aspects of the Physiocrats' theory, although they can certainly be said to have been *influenced* by their 'agricultural' preoccupations, can hardly in any useful sense be said to have been *invalidated* by them.

INDEX

A

Abeille, L. P., 30
Abraham, 61
Absenteeism, 23
Academies of Science, 68
Accumulation, 308, 320 ff., 332, 336, 337–8, 351, 362, 388
  Classical emphasis on, 320
  dynamics of, 397
  over-rapid, 322
  source of, 343
  See also Advances, Capital
Accumulation of Capital (J. Robinson), 368
Activity(ies), 64, 275–6
  commercial, 26
  innovatory, 368
  non-agricultural, 20
  productive, 286
Addison, J., 32
Administration, 66, 99, 147, 160, 232, 238, 240, 244, 257, 260–2
Advances, 82, 109, 110, 112, 115, 116, 127 ff., 147, 149, 155, 157, 193, 199, 205, 232, 240–1, 243, 251, 254, 310
  annual, 41, 110, 111, 115, 120, 128 ff., 138 ff., 146–9, 150 ff., 168 ff., 187 ff., 242–3, 274, 276, 279–81, 283, 299, 308, 384
  employment of, 311
  ground, 302, 384, 390
  increase in, 143
  interest on, 121, 127, 129, 131–3, 138 ff., 147–9, 154 ff., 161, 169 ff., 187, 189, 191, 199, 276, 278–9, 281
  original, 41, 120, 131 ff., 138 ff., 147, 149, 154–5, 161, 168 ff., 187, 189, 197, 242, 248, 274, 276, 281, 299, 302, 308–9, 384
  perishable, 155
  ratio between original and annual, 143–4
  refund of, 275
  renewal of, 302
  'repair' of, 175
  replacement of, 152, 191, 299
  restitution of, 276

sterile, 133
stock, 356
— and profits, 311
— of agricultural entrepreneurs, 384
— of cultivation, 170, 189, 201, 238, 242, 308
— of cultivators, 111, 119, 120, 136, 140, 142, 187, 189, 197, 209, 233
— of farmers, 121, 254, 300
— of husbandmen, 132, 239
— of large enterprises, 244
— of productive class, 156 ff., 169 ff., 173, 182, 188–9, 191, 197–9, 274–5, 277–8, 281, 288–9, 290–1
— of productive expenditure, 243
— of sterile class, 173, 189, 191, 199, 274–5, 277, 281, 288, 290–1
  See also Accumulation, Capital, Expenditure, Production
Aggregates, Physiocratic, 295
Agricultural improvements, 324
Agricultural nations, 60, 66–7, 130, 134–6, 153, 162, 164, 166–7, 238, 246–7, 250–1, 256, 259, 260
Agricultural produce, 26, 131, 274, 314, 335, 343, 360–1, 387–9
Agricultural revolution, 369
Agriculture, 16, 20, 24, 25, 33, 57, 62, 66, 69, 76, 79, 87, 89, 96, 103, 106, 110, 113, 116, 120, 123–5, 127, 128, 139, 147, 149–51, 158–61, 163–5, 168, 180, 181, 185, 187, 201, 232, 233, 240 ff., 246–8, 252 ff., 256–8, 298, 299, 304, 305, 307, 309, 311, 314, 317, 332–3, 336–8, 341–2, 343, 347, 348, 353–6, 361–4, 386–7, 395, 397
  capitalist methods of, 346
  capitalization of, 317
  costs of, 105, 115
  decline of, 138
  development of, 24
  exclusive value-productivity of, 389
  French, 23, 25, 273
  gains yielded by, 306
  large-scale, 138, 139, 151, 267, 273, 298
  monopoly in, 163

Printed in the United States
by Baker & Taylor Publisher Services